REAL-TIME SYSTEMS
DESIGN AND ANALYSIS

Also from IEEE PRESS ...

REAL-TIME SYSTEMS DESIGN AND ANALYSIS

An Engineer's Handbook

Second Edition

Phillip A. Laplante
Dean, BCC/NJIT Technology and Engineering Center

IEEE PRESS

IEEE COMPUTER SOCIETY PRESS

The Institute of Electrical and Electronics Engineers, Inc., New York

This book and other books may be purchased at a discount
from the publisher when ordered in bulk quantities. Contact:

> IEEE Press Marketing
> Attn: Special Sales
> 445 Hoes Lane, P.O. Box 1331
> Piscataway, NJ 08855–1331
> Fax: (908) 981–9334

For more information about IEEE PRESS products, visit the
IEEE Home Page: http://www.ieee.org/

Information on special prices and services for IEEE Computer
Society members may be obtained by contacting:

> IEEE Computer Society Marketing
> Attn: Special Sales
> P.O. Box 3014
> Los Alamitos, CA 90720-1314
> Fax: (714) 821-4010
> Phone: 1-800-CS-BOOKS

Printed in the United States of America

10   9   8   7   6   5   4   3   2

IEEE PRESS   **IEEE COMPUTER SOCIETY PRESS**
Order Number: PC5383   **Order Number: BP07732**
ISBN 0-7803-3400-0

Library of Congress Cataloging-in-Publication Data

Laplante, Phillip, A. (1961–)
  Real-time systems design and analysis : an engineer's handbook /
  Phillip A. Laplante. – 2nd ed.
    p.   cm.
  Includes bibliographical references and index.
  ISBN 0–7803–3400–0
  1. Real-time data processing. 2. System design.   I. Title.
QA76.54.L37   1997
  004' .33–dc20   96-29044
                                                     CIP

To my daughter
Charlotte

Contents

Preface

WHY THIS BOOK?

Over the past 14 years I have designed and implemented several significant real-time systems, consulted on many others, and taught and learned from hundreds of engineers who themselves were developing practical real-time systems of all kinds. This book is, in essence, a compendium of information gained from these experiences. My intent is to provide a practical framework for software engineers to design and implement real-time systems. This approach is somewhat different from that of other texts on the subject.

Many good theoretical treatments of real-time systems exist, and where applicable, I note them in the text. However, these books are usually too theoretical for practicing software engineers and students who are often too impatient to wade through the derivations for the resultant payoff. They want results that they can use now in the trenches, and they want to see how they can be used, not just know that they exist. In this text, I try to distill the best of the theoretical results, combined with practical experience to provide a toolkit for the real-time designer.

Because of the pragmatic approach of this book, many of the results and viewpoints presented in this text may be controversial. I adapted many of the formal definitions from their traditional rigid form into words that I think are more compatible with practical design. In many places I have omitted theoretical treatments where they would have obscured applied results. In these cases, I leave the reader with references to additional reading. I hope I have not offended any of the more traditional experts in real-time systems. I am a great believer in research in this area, and in many places I have indicated where I think research needs to be done or is being done.

Real-time software designers must be familiar with computer architecture and organization, operating systems, software engineering, programming languages, and compiler theory. The text provides an overview of these subjects from the perspective of the real-time systems designer. Because this is a staggering task, I necessarily sacrifice depth for breadth. Again, I try to provide suggested additional reading where depth has been sacrificed.

WHO WILL BENEFIT AND HOW TO USE THIS BOOK

This text is an introductory level, hands-on book. A book of this type is intended for junior-senior level and graduate computer science and electrical engineering students, and practicing software engineers. It is especially useful for new real-time systems designers who need to get "up to speed" very quickly. This book can also be used in commercial courses in real-time systems design such as the one that is available from the IEEE Educational Activities Board. It will aid students and practitioners in developing their own real-time systems or understanding those written by others.

Finally, because of the broad survey of computer science topics, this text can be used in introductory computer science courses. For example, the text provides coverage of every recommended topic (except for ethics) in the IEEE ACM first course, and I have used drafts of this text in course, Introduction to Computer Science, with great success.

PREREQUISITES

The reader is assumed to have a background in programming in one of the more popular languages, but other than this, the prerequisites for this text are minimal. Some familiarity with discrete mathematics and mathematical notation is helpful in understanding some of the formalizations, especially Chapter 5, but it is not essential. A background in basic calculus and probability theory will assist in the reading of Chapters 10 and 11. For example, the reader is assumed to know how to integrate and differentiate and have at least an intuitive feel for "sample space," "random variable," and so on, but again, sufficient information within the book is provided for the general reader to get along.

PROGRAMMING LANGUAGES

Although there are certain "preferred" languages for real-time system design such as Ada, Modula-2, and increasingly C++, many real-time systems are still written in FORTRAN, C, assembly language, and the like. It would be unjust to focus this book on one language, say Ada, when the theory should be language independent. Nevertheless, some language whether real or contrived must be selected to illustrate ideas and present sample programs. Because it is in common use and well-suited for algorithm description, pseudo-Pascal will be used to represent algorithms. By "pseudo" I mean that attention will be focused on logic rather than syntactic correctness of the algorithms. Furthermore, the pseudo-code can be easily modified into compilable code if desired.

ORGANIZATION OF THE BOOK

The book is organized into chapters that are essentially self-contained. Thus, the material can be rearranged or omitted depending on the background and interests of the audience or instructor. The chapters are organized in a "bottom-up" fashion; that is, I tried to work from the hardware to the higher levels of abstraction provided by computer programming languages and systems design techniques. Each chapter contains challenging exercises that stimulate the reader to confront actual problems. The exercises, however, cannot serve as a substitute for practical project experience.

The first chapter provides a brief review of basic computer architecture concepts and applies these terms in the definition of a real-time system. Much of the basic vocabulary relating to real-time systems is developed along with a discussion of the challenges facing the real-time system designer. Finally, a brief historical review is conducted. The purpose of this chapter is to foreshadow the rest of the book as well as quickly acquaint the reader with pertinent terminology. Readers who are already familiar with the real-time problem may wish to skip this chapter.

In the second chapter, I present a more detailed review of basic computer architecture concepts from the perspective of the real-time systems designer. Specifically, the impact of different architectural features on real-time response is discussed. To illustrate the discussions and to provide a framework for the rest of the text, an assembly language is developed for a generic machine architecture. The remainder of the chapter discusses, in very generic terms, the impact of different memory technologies, input/output techniques, and peripheral support to the real-time problem. The intent here is to increase the reader's awareness of the impact of the computer architecture on real-time design considerations. Those readers who are very familiar with computer architecture can simply skim this chapter.

Chapter 3 begins with a discussion of language features desirable in good software engineering practice in general and real-time systems design in particular. A review of several of the most widely used languages in real-time systems design, with respect to these features, follows. The intent is to provide a criterion for rating a language's ability to support real-time systems and to alert the user to the possible drawbacks of using each language in real-time applications. Most readers will not want to skip this chapter.

The next chapter is necessarily smaller than it could be, because to do it justice requires a book of its own. In this chapter, we look at some software life-cycle models that we can apply to real-time systems. For brevity, I only review the steps required in each phase of the model and provide references to works that detail their implementation. The point of this chapter is to provide a software engineering framework for subsequent chapters, without having to digress too far into details. Although some readers may be disappointed with the lack of details provided, the referred-to documents are the authorities on this matter and to "rewrite them," in my opinion, would be dangerous. My only intention was to survey their contents from the perspective of the real-time designer. However, the reader is advised not to skip this chapter, for it provides the skeleton for the rest of the text.

Chapter 5 is also shorter than it could be, but I had to sacrifice length in the interest of compactness. In this chapter I survey several commonly used design specification techniques. An emphasis on their applicability to real-time systems is made throughout. I also try to make the point that no one technique is a silver bullet, and the reader is encouraged to adopt his or her own formulation of specification techniques for the given application. Most readers will want to study this chapter carefully. And don't be disappointed that most of the examples provided are short. In an actual design specification, most software modules should not be longer than those given, and so they are quite realistic.

Chapters 6, 7, and 8 provide the meat of the text for those who are building practical real-time systems. In these three chapters I describe the basics of providing the three critical real-time kernel services: scheduling/dispatching, intertask communication, and memory management. Throughout I provide Pascal code pseudo-algorithms to get you started in constructing your own system. I also provide what I hope are valuable insights from my own and others' practical experiences. Please don't skip these chapters.

In Chapter 9, I discuss several techniques for improving the response time of real-time systems through efficient coding techniques and with "tricks." Many of the ideas I discuss in this chapter are well known but unwritten laws of programming. Some are compiler optimization techniques that can be used to improve your code. Others are tricks I've learned from old-timers which have been passed down by word of mouth. This chapter can help you wring out that extra bit of performance from your system that you have been looking for, so don't ignore it.

Chapter 10 contains a brief review of some basic concepts of probability theory and their application in the analysis of the producer/consumer problem. Specifically, the chapter will help you decide process execution rates, hardware requirements, and buffer sizes. In this chapter, I tried to present a sampling of the varied problems that arise in producer/consumer analysis so that you can gain some insight into specific problems. I hope that this chapter is useful to you.

Next, Chapter 11 discusses techniques for measuring and improving the fault-tolerance and reliability of real-time systems. Some of the measurement techniques are theoretical and not widely used, but may be applicable to certain situations. The techniques for improving fault tolerance are well known and have been used in many practical situations. Later in the chapter, I discuss techniques for improving reliability through rigorous testing. These techniques are also widely used and are very practical. This chapter should not be skipped.

Chapter 12 is an introduction to the special problems that arise in multiprocessing real-time systems. Specifically, I look at the Byzantine generals' model for a distributed system, and discuss the real-time implications. I also examine special multiprocessing architectures and discuss their use in the design of real-time image/signal processing systems. Finally, I look at design specification techniques that are suited to these architectures. A couple of topics not discussed are security and networking issues. Both of these topics are usually discussed in a book on distributed systems. The intent of this chapter is to introduce these ideas for the first time and to stimulate research.

Chapter 13 is about systems integration–that is, combining the work of several programmers into a viable system. In real-time systems, some special techniques are needed and these techniques are reviewed here. Please don't skip this chapter.

The final chapter covers a variety of interesting real-time applications and serves to tie everything together.

When I teach this course in a college setting, I typically ask my students to build a real-time multitasking system of their choice. Usually, it is a game on a PC, but some students have built embedded hardware controllers of surprising complexity. My "assignment" to you would be to build the game, using at least the coroutine model (interrupt driven would be better). The application should be useful or at least pleasing, so some sort of a game is a good choice. The project should take no more than 15 hours and cover all phases of the software life-cycle model discussed in the text. Hence, those students who have never built a real-time system will have the benefit of the experience.

TRADEMARKS

- STATEMATE is a trademark of i-Logix.
- UNIX is a trademark of AT&T.
- SPARC is a trademark of Sun Microsystems.
- 80386, 80486 are registered trademarks of Intel Corporation.
- 68000 is a registered trademark of Motorola.
- VAX is a trademark of Digital Equipment Corporation.
- CICS is a trademark of IBM.
- Presentation Manager is a trademark of IBM.
- OS/2 is a trademark of IBM

Acknowledgments

First to all the folks at IEEE for their wonderful support, particularly, John Griffin, Lisa Dayne, Dudley Kay, Debbie Graffox, Denise Gannon, and Savoula Amanatidis. The anonymous reviewers also provided invaluable assistance in improving the book. Additional thanks are owed to Mary DeMaria of the Technology and Engineering Center Library for assistance in some of the background research. Finally, thanks to my wife for her incredible patience while I was occupied with this and other projects.

1

Basic Real-Time Concepts

KEY POINTS OF THE CHAPTER

1. Real-time systems are those in which timeliness is as important as the correctness of the outputs.
2. Real-time systems do not have to be "fast systems."
3. Real-time system design and analysis is a complex holistic engineering science.
4. Performance estimation and reduction are crucial in real-time systems.

Most of us are familiar with systems in which data need to be processed at a regular and timely rate. For example, an aircraft uses a sequence or stream of accelerometer pulses to determine its current position. In addition, other systems require a rapid response to events that are occurring at nonregular rates, such as an over-temperature failure in a nuclear plant. In some sense it is understood that these events require real-time processing.

Now consider a situation in which you approach an airline reservation counter and request Flight 432 from New York to Boston, leaving in 30 minutes. The reservation clerk enters your request in the computer and a few seconds later produces a boarding pass. Is this a real-time system? Indeed, all three systems mentioned here—aircraft, nuclear plant, and airline reservations—are real-time because they must process information within a specified interval or risk system failure. Although these examples provide an intuitive definition of a real-time system, we need to define clearly when a system is real-time and when it is not.

1.1 BASIC COMPUTER ARCHITECTURE

Before formulating definitions, it is appropriate first to review briefly some basic concepts of computer architecture.

You can think of computer systems as having three basic components: a *central processing unit* (CPU); *memory*; and *input/output* (I/O) devices (see Figure 1.1) connected via a collection of transmission paths called a *bus*. There are actually three buses in the system: power, address, and data. The *power bus* is the collection of wires used to distribute power to the various components of the computer system; the *address bus* is the collection of wires needed to access individual memory addresses; the *data bus* is used to carry data between the various components in the system. When we refer to the *system bus*, we mean the address and data buses collectively.

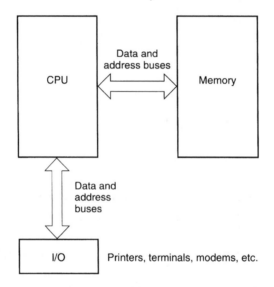

Figure 1.1 A basic computer.

For the most part, this book deals with single-processing systems—those that use one central processing unit and one memory store. Some real-time systems employed today are multiprocessing (i.e., they use more than one CPU and one or more memory stores). In general, many concepts that apply to single-processing real-time systems also apply to multiprocessing ones. Chapter 12 examines certain techniques that are appropriate for multiprocessing real-time systems.

1.1.1 Bus Transfer Mechanisms

To deposit data into memory, the CPU places the target address on the address bus. The CPU then places the data on the data bus. A signal called the *data strobe* (DST) is then set to its TRUE state to indicate that data are on the bus. The DST signal is kept in its TRUE state for a fixed period of time to enable the data to settle in

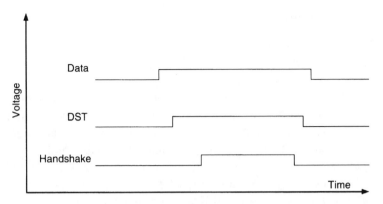

Figure 1.2 Data transfer timing diagram.

memory. The DST signal is then placed in its FALSE state. In many cases a handshake signal is sent from the receiving device to the CPU to indicate that the data were successfully transferred. Figure 1.2 illustrates the timing sequence.

Similarly, to transfer data from memory (read), the CPU places the source address on the address bus and again issues a DST signal. Another line called a *read/write* line is then set to logic 0 during memory write and to logic 1 during memory read.

When the CPU is using the address and data buses, all other devices are placed in a high-impedance state, an electrical condition that effectively disconnects the device from the data and address buses.

The process of retrieving data from memory is similar. Other devices transferring data to or from other devices via the bus use a similar procedure.

1.1.2 Input and Output

You are already familiar with the input/output devices of the computer, for example, printers, terminals, plotters, and card readers. Other devices are controlled through a single logic line called a *discrete signal* or *discrete*, which is of great importance in real-time systems. We are not particularly interested in the design of devices in this text, and therefore we treat these as black boxes only. In Chapter 2, however, we examine the three basic methods for input and output of data to and from the CPU.

1.1.3 Memory

Traditionally, memory is divided into two types: *primary* or *main*—that which is directly addressable by the CPU; and *secondary*—that characterized by long-term storage devices such as tapes, disks, and cards. Secondary memory is a kind of I/O device and will be treated as such. We discuss memory hardware in more detail in the next chapter.

1.1.4 CPU Operation

Because a good understanding of the basic operation of the CPU is essential in real-time system design, we provide a sketch of those ideas here. Further detail is provided in Chapter 2.

The CPU can be thought of as containing several components connected by its own internal bus, which is distinct from the memory and address buses of the system. The CPU contains a *program counter* (PC), an *arithmetic logic unit* (ALU), internal CPU memory—*scratch pad memory* and *micromemory, general registers*, an *instruction register*, and a *control unit* (CU). In addition, a *memory address register* (MAR) holds the address of the memory location to be acted on, and a *memory data register* (MDR) holds the data to be written to or that has been read from the memory location held in the MAR (see Figure 1.3). There are also various internal clocks and other signals used for timing and data transfer, and other hidden internal registers that are typically found inside the CPU but are not shown.

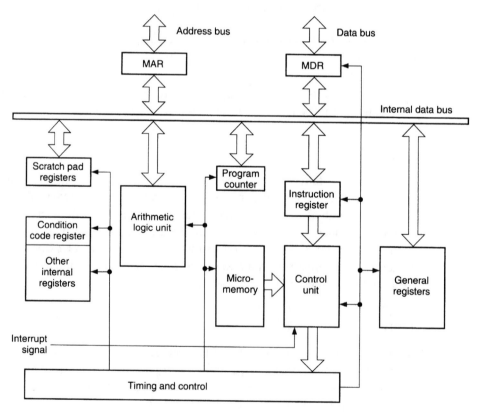

Figure 1.3 Basic CPU structure.

1.1.4.1 The Fetch-Execute Cycle   Programs are a sequence of *macro-instructions* or *macrocode*. These are stored in the main memory of the computer in binary form and await execution. One at a time, macroinstructions are retrieved or *fetched* from the main memory location pointed to by the program counter, and placed in the instruction register. The instruction consists of an operation code or *opcode* field and operand field. The opcode is typically the starting address of a lower-level program stored in micromemory (called a *microprogram*), and the operand represents registers, memory, or data to be acted upon by this program. The control unit *decodes* the instruction. This usually means determining the location of the program in micromemory and then acting on or *executing* this program, using the ALU and scratch-pad memory to perform any necessary arithmetic computations. The various control signals and other internal registers are used to facilitate data transfer, branching, and synchronization.

After executing the instruction, the next macroinstruction is retrieved from main memory, and it too is executed. Certain macroinstructions or external conditions may cause a nonconsecutive macroinstruction to be executed. This case is discussed shortly.

The process of fetching and executing an instruction is called the *fetch-execute cycle*. Even when "idling," the computer is fetching and executing a dummy instruction called a *no-op* (for no-operation). Hence, the CPU is constantly active.

1.1.4.2 Macroinstructions and Microinstructions   Often novice engineers and computer scientists exhibit great confusion about the difference between *macrocode* and *microcode*. Macroinstructions, or macrocode (in its symbolic form, assembly code), are the lowest-level instructions available to the programmer. These instructions differ depending on the computer architecture (see Chapter 2). They usually include operations such as LOAD, STORE, and ADD, each of which is represented by a unique opcode; thus, the programmer must have exact knowledge of the computer's architecture. Each macroinstruction stored in main memory can be thought of as a microprogram consisting of several microinstructions stored in micromemory. The microinstructions needed for constructing microprograms are not generally known to the programmer (although some computers have programmable microcode). Understanding the microinstruction programs requires that the programmer be intimate with the computer's organization. The distinction between microinstructions and macroinstructions becomes important later.

1.1.4.3 Interrupt Handling   Hardware signals, whether generated internally by exceptional conditions such as floating point overflow, or externally by devices, need to be able to signal events to the CPU. Such signals have a special name.

> **Definition** An *interrupt* is a hardware signal that initiates an event.

Upon receipt of the interrupt signal, the processor completes the instruction that is currently being executed. Next, the contents of the program counter are saved to a designated memory location called the *interrupt return location*. The contents of a memory location called the *interrupt handler location* are loaded into the program counter. Execution then proceeds with the special code stored at this location called the *interrupt handler*. This process is outlined in Figure 1.4.

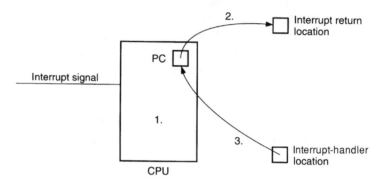

1. Finish current instruction.
2. Save program counter in interrupt return location.
3. Load program counter with contents of Interrupt-handler location.

Figure 1.4 The interrupt-handling process in a single interrupt system.

Modern processors are usually equipped with circuitry that enables them to handle more than one interrupt in a prioritized fashion. This additional hardware includes special registers such as the interrupt vector, status register, and mask register. The *interrupt vector* contains the identity of the highest-priority interrupt request; the *status register* contains the value of the lowest interrupt that will presently be honored; and the *mask register* contains a bit map that either enables or disables specific interrupts. Another specialized register is the *interrupt register*, which contains a bit map of all pending (latched) interrupts. (See Figure 2.17 and the discussion in Chapter 2 for additional detail.)

Upon receipt of interrupt *i*, the circuitry determines whether the interrupt is allowable given the current status and mask register contents. If the interrupt is allowed, the CPU completes the current instruction and then saves the PC in interrupt return location *i*. The PC is then loaded with the contents of interrupt handler location *i*. The code at the address there is used to service the interrupt. The overall scheme is depicted in Figure 1.5.

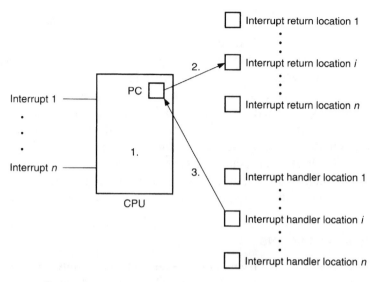

1. Finish current instruction.
2. Save program counter in interrupt return location *i*.
3. Load program counter with contents of Interrupt-handler location *i*.

Figure 1.5 The interrupt-handling process in a multiple interrupt system.

Interrupts can be caused by internal or external events. Internal events, sometimes called *traps*, include divide-by-zero errors, overflow conditions, and non-error conditions like floating point operations. Many machines do not support floating point operations in their macroinstruction set; instead, these are handled by special routines invoked by traps. External interrupts are caused by other devices (e.g., clocks and switches), and in most operating systems such interrupts are required for scheduling.

1.2 SOME TERMINOLOGY

Now that we have discussed some basic hardware concepts, we can begin to construct some important definitions. Definitions—especially nonmathematical ones—appear in many forms and are often contradictory, depending on the author and context in which they are used. The terms we are about to define are used widely throughout industry and academia, and most can be found in the literature (see the Bibliography at the end of this book). They have been refined here to the smallest common subset of agreement to form the vocabulary of this text.

1.2.1 Software Concepts

The hardware of the general-purpose computer can be used to solve problems with collections of macroinstructions or *software*. Software is traditionally divided into two categories: *system programs* and *application programs*. System programs consist of software that interfaces with the underlying computer hardware, such as schedulers, device drivers, dispatchers, and programs that act as tools for the development of application programs. These tools include *compilers*—which translate high-order language programs into assembly code; *assemblers*—which translate the assembly language into a special binary format called *object* or machine code; and *linkers*—which prepare the object code for execution. An *operating system* is a specialized collection of system programs that manage the physical resources of the computer.

Application programs are programs written to solve specific problems, such as payroll preparation, inventory, and navigation. Real-time design considerations play a role in the design of certain systems programs and application software.

1.2.2 System Concepts

Until now we have been using the term *system* loosely, but it is time to define it more precisely because it is a central theme in all software engineering.

> **Definition** A *system* has a set of one or more inputs entering a black box and a set of one or more outputs exiting the black box (see Figure 1.6).

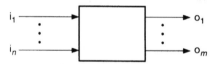

Figure 1.6 A system with n inputs and m outputs.

More formally:

> **Definition** Let $i_1 \in I_1 \ldots i_n \in I_n$ and $o_1 \in O_1 \ldots o_m \in O_m$. Then the system S is a subset of the cross product of $I_1 \ldots I_n$ and $O_1 \ldots O_m$:
>
> $$S \subseteq I_1 \times \cdots \times I_n \times O_1 \times \cdots \times O_m \qquad (1.1)$$
>
> The i_j are called *inputs* and the o_j are called *outputs*. $I_1 \times \cdots \times I_n$ is called the *input space* and $O_1 \times \cdots \times O_m$ is called the *output space*.

The internal process by which the inputs are converted to outputs may be unknown, and you should not be concerned with it. It is not difficult to find examples of systems: every real-world entity—whether synthetic or occurring naturally—can be modeled as a system. In software systems, the inputs represent digital data from hardware devices and other software systems. The outputs are digital data. The digital data can be converted to voltages on wires to control external hardware devices.

In any real-world system there is some delay between presentation of the inputs and appearance of the outputs. We can formalize this notion as follows:

> **Definition** The time between the presentation of a set of inputs to a software system and the appearance of all the associated outputs is called the *response time* of the software system.

How fast the response time needs to be depends on the application of the system. In addition, there is no way to write a general purpose program to determine the response time of a second, arbitrary program. Such an oracle, if it existed, would have to determine when the program under inspection would respond to a set of inputs; that is, it would need to know if and when the program would halt on the inputs. This is considered an unsolvable problem—the Halting Problem (see for example, [81]).

1.2.3 Real-Time Definitions

The three previous definitions allow us finally to state a formal definition of a real-time system.

> **Definition** A *real-time system* is a system that must satisfy explicit (bounded) response-time constraints or risk severe consequences, including failure.

What is considered a "failed" system? In the case of the space shuttle or a nuclear plant it is painfully obvious when a failure has occurred. For other systems, such as an automatic bank teller machine, the notion of failure is less clear. For now, we will define failure as the "inability of the system to perform according to system specification." More formally:

> **Definition** A *failed system* is a system that cannot satisfy one or more of the requirements stipulated in the formal system specification.

Because of this definition of failure, precise specification of the system operating criteria, including timing constraints, is important; this matter is discussed in Chapter 5. Numerous other definitions can be given for real-time, depending on which source you are consulting. Nonetheless, the common theme among all definitions is that the system is time critical. For example:

> **Defintion** A *real-time system* is one whose logical correctness is based on both the correctness of the outputs and their timeliness.

Notice how by obviating the notion of timeliness, every system is a real-time system.

Real-time systems are often reactive or embedded systems. *Reactive* systems are those that have an ongoing interaction with their environment—for example, a fire-control system that constantly reacts to buttons pressed by a pilot. *Embedded* systems are those used to control specialized hardware in which the computer system is installed. For example, the microprocessor system used to control the fuel/air mixture in the carburetor of many automobiles is clearly embedded. Similarly, the software used to control the inertial measurement unit (IMU) of the space shuttle is embedded, because it operates in a highly specialized hardware environment. Incidentally, systems that are not embedded are sometimes called *organic systems* if they are completely independent of the hardware on which they run, and *loosely coupled* or *semi-detached* if they can run on other hardware with the rewrite of certain modules [16]. To summarize:

- *Embedded system* A software system that is completely encapsulated by the hardware that it controls.
- *Organic system* A software system that is not highly dependent on the hardware on which it runs and that includes a generalized user interface.
- *Semi-detached system* A software system that displays characteristics of both embedded and organic systems.

1.2.3.1 Real-Time Systems Of course, the three examples mentioned earlier satisfy the criteria for a real-time system precisely. An aircraft must process accelerometer data within a certain period that depends on the specifications of the aircraft; for example, every 10 milliseconds (10 thousandths of a second). Failure to do so could result in a false position or velocity indication and cause the aircraft to go off-course at best or crash at worst. For a nuclear reactor thermal problem, failure to respond swiftly could result in a meltdown. Finally, an airline reservation system must be able to handle a peak rate of passenger requests within the passenger's perception of a reasonable time (or as fast as the competitor's system).

In short, a system does not have to process data in microseconds (millionths of a second) to be considered real-time; it must simply have response times that are constrained and thus predictable.

1.2.3.2 When is a System Real-Time? All practical systems can be said to be real-time systems. Even a batch-oriented system—the kind many insurance companies now use to process automobile insurance punch cards—is real-time. Although the system may have response times of days or weeks (the time that elapses between mailing your card and receiving your insurance certificate), it must respond within a certain time or your insurance will lapse—a disaster. Even a word-processing program should respond to your commands within a reasonable amount of time (e.g., 1 second) or it will become torture to use. Most of the literature refers to such systems as *soft real-time systems*—that is, systems in which performance is degraded but not destroyed by failure to meet response-time constraints. Furthermore, systems where failure to meet response-time constraints leads to system failure are called *hard real-time systems*. Recently, the term *firm real-time systems* has been defined to include those systems with hard deadlines where some low probability of missing a deadline can be tolerated. As noted, all practical systems minimally represent soft real-time systems. Since we are most interested in the so-called hard real-time systems, we will use the term *real-time system* to mean hard real-time system without loss of generality.

1.2.4 Events and Determinism

In software systems, a change in state results in a change in the flow-of-control of the computer program. What is flow-of-control? Consider the flowchart in Figure 1.7. The decision block represented by the diamond suggests that the stream of program instructions, like water flowing through a pipe into a Y-shaped valved joint, can take one of two paths depending on the response to the question. IF-THEN, GOTO, and CASE statements in any language represent possible changes in flow-of-control. Statements like subroutine calls in FORTRAN and invocation of procedures in C, Pascal, or Ada represent changes in flow-of-control. In general, consider the following definition.

> **Definition** Any occurrence that causes the program counter to change non-sequentiality is considered a change of flow-of-control, and thus an event.

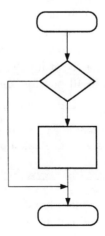

Figure 1.7 A simple program flowchart.

We have already mentioned that interrupt signals can cause a change in flow-of-control and thus are events.

1.2.5 Synchronous and Asynchronous Events

Events can be divided into two categories: *synchronous* and *asynchronous*. Synchronous events are those that occur at predictable times in the flow-of-control—such as at the decision box in the flowchart. You can anticipate this change in flow-of-control (although it may not always happen).

Asynchronous events occur at unpredictable points in the flow-of-control and are usually caused by external sources. A clock that pulses "regularly" at 5 milliseconds is not a synchronous event. Even if the clock were able to tick at a perfect 5 milliseconds without drift (which it cannot for physical reasons), the point where the tick occurs within the flow-of-control is subject to many factors. These factors include the time at which the clock starts relative to the program, and propagation delays in the computer system itself. You can never count on a clock ticking exactly at the rate specified, and so you must design any system with that in mind.

1.2.6 Determinism

In any system, but especially a real-time system, maintaining control is extremely important. For any physical system certain states exist under which the system is considered to be out of control; the software controlling such a system must therefore avoid these states. For example, in certain guidance systems for robots or aircraft, rapid rotation through a 180° pitch angle can cause a physical loss of gyro control. The software must be able to foresee and prepare for this situation or risk losing control of the hardware.

Another characteristic of a controlled software system is the computer's ability to fetch and execute instructions from the program rather than the data area of memory. Fetching from the data area can occur in poorly tested systems and is a catastrophe from which there is almost no hope of recovery.

Software control of any real-time system and associated hardware is maintained by the software's ability to predict the next state of the system given the current state and a set of inputs. In other words, the goal is to predict how a system will behave in all possible circumstances. This leads to a definition:

> **Definition** A system is said to be *deterministic* if, for each possible state and each set of inputs, a unique set of outputs and next state of the system can be determined.

In particular, a certain kind of determinism called *event determinism* means that the next states and outputs of system are known for each set of inputs that trigger events. Thus, a system that is deterministic is event deterministic. Although it would be difficult for a system to be deterministic only for those inputs that trigger events, this is plausible, and so event determinism may not imply determinism. We are, however, only interested in purely deterministic systems.

Finally, if in a deterministic system the response time for each set of outputs is known, then the system also exhibits *temporal determinism*.

NOTE 1.1   Each of these previous definitions of determinism implies that the system must have a finite number of states. It is reasonable to make this assumption in a digital computer system where all inputs are digitized to within a finite range. (Finite state machines are discussed in Chapter 5.)

A side benefit of designing deterministic systems is that you can guarantee that the system is able to respond at any time, and in the case of temporally deterministic systems, when they will respond. This reinforces the association of control with real-time systems.

1.2.7 Time-Loading

One final term needs to be defined because it is often used as a measurement of real-time system performance.

> **Definition** *Time-loading*, or the *utilization factor*, is a measure of the percentage of "useful" processing the computer is doing.

A system is said to be *time-overloaded* if it is 100% or more time-loaded. Time-loading differs from CPU *throughput*, which is a measure of the number of macroinstructions per second that can be processed based on some predetermined instruction mix. This type of measurement is typically used to compare CPU horsepower for a particular application.

Recall that the CPU is constantly busy with the fetch-execute cycle even when idling (executing no-ops). If the computer is never idling, that is, it executes no no-ops, then it is 100% time-loaded. Systems that are too highly time-loaded (e.g., 98%) are undesirable because changes or additions cannot be made to the system without risk of time-overloading. Systems that have low time-loading factors (e.g., 10%), are not necessarily good because this implies that the processor and related hardware are too powerful for the application and that costs can be reduced by procuring a less powerful processor. There is no magic number for time-loading. While 50% is common for new products, 80% is acceptable for systems that do not expect growth. However, 70% as a desired time-loading figure has some grounding in theory. See Chapter 9 for a discussion of this as well as methods for measuring and reducing time-loading.

1.3 REAL-TIME DESIGN ISSUES

Why study real-time systems? The design and implementation of real-time systems requires closer consideration of issues normally addressed in system design. These include:

- The selection of hardware and software, and the appropriate mix needed for a cost-effective solution.
- The decision to take advantage of a commercial real-time operating system or to design a special operating system.
- The selection of an appropriate software language for system development.
- The maximizing of system fault tolerance and reliability through careful design and rigorous testing.
- The design and administration of tests, and the selection of test and development equipment.

In addition, the prediction and measurement of response time, and its reduction, are paramount. Finally, the techniques you learn by building real-time systems enable you to develop non-real-time systems that are faster and use less code.

1.4 EXAMPLE REAL-TIME SYSTEMS

In the introduction to this chapter we briefly alluded to some real-time systems that are used throughout the text to illustrate ideas. The following descriptions provide more details for each system, although they are not intended as formal specifications. The process of specifying systems clearly and concisely is discussed in Chapters 4 and 5.

■ EXAMPLE 1.1

You are working on an aircraft navigation system for a fast military aircraft. From the program specification you know that the software will receive x, y, and z accelerometer pulses at a 5 millisecond rate from special hardware. Analog-to-digital converters provide the software with roll, pitch, and yaw angles from gyros or spinning "tops" inside the inertial measurement unit via DMA; these angles indicate the aircraft's orientation at a 40-millisecond rate. Figure 1.8 illustrates these quantities.

The software will also receive information such as temperature at a 1-second rate. The task of the software is to compute the actual velocity vector based on the orientation, accelerometer readings, and various compensation factors (such as for temperature effects) at a 40-millisecond rate. You are to output this true velocity to a pilot's display every second.   ■

How can you create programs that execute at four different rates in the navigation system, and how can these programs communicate? The accelerometer readings

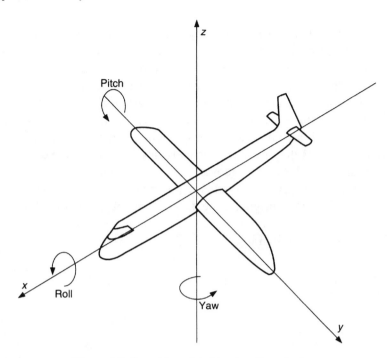

Figure 1.8 Quantities related to aircraft navigation.

and gyro pulses must be time-relative or correlated; that is, you don't want to process an x accelerometer pulse from time t with z and y pulses from time $t + 1$. How is this done?

■ EXAMPLE 1.2
You are writing a monitoring system for a nuclear plant that (for simplicity) will be handling essentially two events signaled by interrupts. The first event is triggered by any of several signals at various security points that will indicate a security breach. The system must respond to this signal within 1 second. The other (and more important) event indicates that the nuclear core has reached an over-temperature. This signal must be dealt with within 1 millisecond.   ■

The nuclear plant system requires a mechanism to ensure that the "meltdown imminent" indicator can interrupt any other processing. How is this accomplished?

■ EXAMPLE 1.3
Consider the airline reservation system mentioned earlier. Management has decided that to prevent long lines and customer dissatisfaction, turnaround time for any transaction must be less than 15 seconds, and no overbooking will be permitted (how lovely this would be). At any time, several agents may try to access the database and perhaps book the same flight simultaneously.   ■

Here record-locking and communications mechanisms are needed to protect against the alteration of the database containing the reservation information by more than one clerk simultaneously. How do you do this?

The challenge presented by these systems is to determine the appropriate design approach with respect to the issues discussed in Section 1.3. We will try to answer these and other questions as we proceed through the text.

This history of real-time systems, as characterized by developments in the United States, illustrates that real-time systems are part of the evolution of the computer. Modern real-time systems, such as those that control nuclear power stations, military aircraft weapons systems, or medical monitoring equipment, are complex, and they exhibit characteristics of systems developed from the 1940s through the 1960s. Moreover, today's real-time systems exist because the computer industry and systems requirements grew. As a result, computing goals far exceeded their original expectations, and thus, the field of real-time computing was born. A summary of some of the milestones in early American real-time systems is given in Table 1.1.

TABLE 1.1 Some Significant Events in Early American Real-time Systems Development

Year	System/Machine	Developer	Type of System	Innovations
1947	Whirlwind	MIT/U.S. Navy	Flight simulator	Ferrite core memory "Real response times"
1957	SAGE	IBM	Air defense	Specifically designed for real-time
1957	Cytac	Various	Navigation	First real-time navigation system
1957	Stretch	IBM	General purpose	All transistor
1958	Scientific 1103A	Univac	General purpose	Hardware interrupt
1959	SABRE	IBM	Airline reservation	Hub-go-ahead policy
1962	Basic Executive	IBM	General purpose	First real-time executive
1963	Basic Executive II	IBM	General purpose	Diverse real-time scheduling Disk resident user/systems programs

1.5 BRIEF HISTORY

The origin of the term *real-time computing* is unclear. It was probably first used either with project Whirlwind, a flight simulator developed by IBM for the U.S. Navy in 1947, or with SAGE, the Semiautomatic Ground Environment air defense system developed for the U.S. Air Force in the early 1950s. Both projects qualify as real-time systems by today's standards. In addition to its real-time contributions, the Whirlwind project included the first use of ferrite core memory and a form of high-order language compiler that predated FORTRAN.

Other early real-time systems were used for airline reservation, such as SABRE (developed for American Airlines in 1959), as well as for process control, but the advent of the national space program provided even greater opportunities for the development of real-time systems for spacecraft control and telemetry. Only in the 1960s did the rapid development of such systems take place, as significant nonmilitary interest in real-time problem solutions became coupled with the availability of equipment well adapted to real-time processing.

1.5.1 Software

Early real-time systems were written directly in microcode, assembly language, and later in higher-level languages. As mentioned previously, Whirlwind used an early form of high-order language called an algebraic compiler to simplify coding. Later systems employed FORTRAN, CMS-2, and JOVIAL, the preferred languages of the U.S. Army, Navy, and Air Force, respectively.

In the 1970s, the need to develop a single language that all branches of the service and the federal government could use—and that provided high-level language constructs for real-time programming—was identified. After a selection and refinement process, the Ada language was selected as the real-time language of the 1980s and 1990s.

Although many real-time systems are currently developed in Ada, a large portion still employ assembly language and FORTRAN. In addition, Pascal, BASIC, Modula-2, and C are widely used in commercial real-time systems. The real-time aspects of these languages are discussed in Chapter 3.

1.5.2 Hardware

Many of the earliest systems were handicapped by weak processors and exceptionally slow and sparse memories. Whirlwind introduced the ferrite core memory (see Chapter 2)—a vast improvement over its predecessor, the vacuum tube.

In the early 1950s the asynchronous interrupt was introduced and incorporated as a standard feature in the Univac Scientific 1103A. The middle 1950s saw a distinct increase in the speed and complexity of large-scale digital computers designed for scientific computation, without an increase in size. These developments made it possible to apply "real-time" computation in the field of control systems. Such improvements were particularly noticeable in IBM's development of SAGE.

In the 1960s and 1970s, advances in integration levels and processing speeds enhanced the spectrum of real-time problems that could be solved. In 1965 alone it was estimated that more than 350 real-time process control systems existed [33].

The 1980s and 1990s have seen a proliferation of theoretical work on improving the predictability and reliability of real-time systems. In addition, multiprocessing systems and other non-von Neumann architectures have expanded the nature and viability of real-time applications. These issues are discussed further in Chapters 11 and 12, respectively.

1.6 EXERCISES

1. Discuss whether or not the following are hard, soft, or firm real-time systems.
   (a) The Library of Congress database system.
   (b) A police database that provides information on stolen automobiles.
   (c) The computer system controlling the Panama Canal locks.
   (d) An automatic teller machine.
   (e) A computer-controlled arcade game.
   (f) The IRS 1040 form processing system.
   (g) The U.S. Postal Service's mail-processing system, which scans a letter as it moves through a conveyor belt and routes it to the appropriate bin depending on ZIP code.
   (h) A university's grade-processing system, which takes grade sheets and generates report cards.
   (i) A computer-controlled routing switch used by a phone company.

2. Consider a real-time weapon control system aboard an aircraft. Discuss which of the following events would be considered synchronous and which would be considered asynchronous to the software.
   (a) A 10-millisecond clock interrupt.
   (b) A divide-by-zero error.
   (c) A built-in-test software failure.
   (d) A signal indicating the pilot has pressed the "fire rocket" button.
   (e) A signal indicating "low on fuel."

3. For the systems mentioned in exercise 1, discuss reasonable response times.

4. For the systems mentioned in exercise 1, discuss which are embedded, loosely coupled, or organic.

5. Can you describe a computer system that is completely non-real-time (that is, in which there are no bounds whatsoever on the response time)?

6. In general terms, suggest a possible scheme that would allow a CPU macroinstruction to be interruptable. What would be the overall effect (if any) on macroinstruction execution time?

2

Computer Hardware

KEY POINTS OF THE CHAPTER

1. Architectural features such as the instruction set and addressing modes can affect real-time performance.
2. The more complex the instruction set, the fewer the instructions needed to achieve a particular function, but the longer each individual instruction will take. RISC architectures rely on short, simple instructions and thus are ideal for real-time.
3. Memory access times have a profound effect on real-time performance and should influence the choice of instruction modes used—both when coding in assembly language and through the careful selection of high-order language constructs.
4. There are three basic modes of input/output to and from a computer; program I/O, memory-mapped I/O, and DMA.
5. Coprocessors improve real-time performance because they extend the instruction set to support faster, specialized instructions.

Understanding the underlying hardware of the real-time system makes the use of both hardware and software resources more efficient. Although the role of current language theory is to isolate the programmer from the underlying hardware, those who have implemented practical real-time systems realize that this role is impossible to achieve—if not at the design stage, certainly at the hardware/ software integration stages. In this chapter we present a basic review of computer architecture ideas that impact real-time system design. For completeness, you should also consult the excellent computer architecture texts listed in the references.

2.1 CPU

Not all real-time systems are based in the microprocessor; some involve mainframe or minicomputers, while others are based in the microcontroller. A *microcontroller* is a computer system that is programmable via microinstructions (see Figure 2.1). Because the complex macroinstruction decoding process is not supported, program execution tends to be very fast.

In Chapter 1 we examined the basic architecture of a computer, which consisted of a CPU, memory, and input and output devices. This computer has binary instructions in memory called *machine language*, which are fetched and executed continuously as part of the fetch-execute cycle. Computers that satisfy this basic description—stored program, serial fetch-execute cycle—are generically called *von Neumann computers* after the Hungarian-American mathematician John von Neumann, who proposed them. Most of the techniques that we will discuss apply to von Neumann-style computers but can be extended for use with other types of computer architectures.

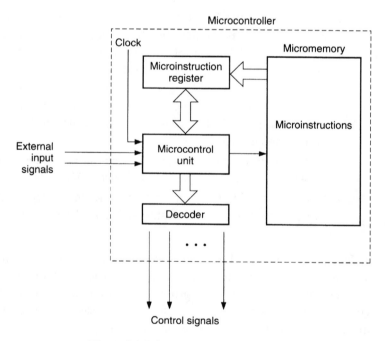

Figure 2.1 Microcontroller block diagram.

Computer architectures that do not use the stored program, serial fetch-execute cycle are called *non–von Neumann* architectures. These include array and vector processors, dataflow processors, systolic processors, wavefront processors and most other advanced architectures. These architectures are discussed briefly in Chapter 12.

Let us now examine the structure of several von Neumann architectures from the perspective of the machine language used to program them. We present some generic machine languages in terms of their symbolic equivalents or *assembly language*, which will be used throughout the text. The macroinstruction sets for these different assembly languages are summarized in Tables 2.2, 2.3, 2.4, and 2.5.

2.1.1 Addressing Modes

The execution time of a macroinstruction is a function of a variety of factors including the instruction decode time, the length of its microprogram, and the number of memory fetches or *bus cycles* required. This number is in turn influenced by the standard word length versus data bus size, and the addressing mode of the instruction.

For simplicity we will classify macroinstructions as having one of six different addressing modes. These addressing modes—implied, immediate, direct, indirect, register direct, and register indirect—enhance instruction set flexibility. The richer the addressing mode selection, however, the longer the instruction decode time will be. In addition, some addressing modes have longer execution times than others because the number of microinstructions per macroinstruction is increased.

All instructions require at least one bus cycle for retrieval from main memory. Memory access times have a profound negative effect on real-time performance and should influence the choice of instruction modes used—both when coding in assembly language and through the careful selection of high-order language constructs. It is always desirable to select or force instruction addressing modes so that the number of memory accesses will be minimized. Similarly, by selecting hardware with faster memory access times, we can also decrease instruction execution times. It will simplify the discussions somewhat if we assume a standard address bus, data bus, and internal word length of 16 bits. We will illustrate our points with symbolic equivalent macroinstructions based on a generic assembly language. Table 2.1 lists instruction types and the number of bus cycles required.

2.1.1.1 Implied Mode   *Implied mode instructions* involve one or more specific registers that are implicitly defined in the operation performed by the instruction. Usually, an anonymous register called an *accumulator* is used. Implied mode instructions require only a single bus cycle to fetch the instruction

TABLE 2.1   Addressing Modes and Their Bus
Cycle Requirements

Mode	No. of Bus Cycles
Implied	1
Register direct	1
Register indirect	2
Immediate	2
Direct	3
Indirect	4
Double indirect	5

and thus are very fast. For example, the COMP instruction in a 1-address
architecture indicates that the two's complement of the accumulator is to be taken
(the two's complement of a signal binary number involves changing all "I"'s to
"O"'s and "O"'s to "I"'s in the original number, then performing binary addition
of I to that number).

2.1.1.2 Immediate Mode   For *immediate mode instructions* the operand is
an integer that is usually contained in the next address after the instruction. This
type of instruction typically requires only two memory fetches and is thus quite
fast (see Figure 2.2). For example, consider the following instruction, which
places the value of 2 into register 1:

```
LOAD R1,2          register 1 ← 2
```

Immediate mode instructions require two bus cycles, one to fetch the
instruction and another to fetch the operand. Certain instruction sets, however,
allow the operand to be embedded in the opcode. Although the allowable range of
the operand is necessarily restricted, this scheme does eliminate one bus cycle,
thus keeping execution time low. A good programmer recognizes this and uses the
appropriate macroinstruction, or forces the compiler to do so.

■ EXAMPLE 2.1

In many instruction sets, an instruction such as LOAD 2 will load an implied register with a 2, yet
requires only a single bus cycle because the operand is embedded in the opcode. This is more
desirable than, say, a LOAD R1,2 instruction which requires two bus cycles, one to fetch the
instruction and the other to fetch the operand.   ■

2.1.1.3 Direct Mode   In the case of *direct mode instructions*, the operand
is the data contained at the address specified in the address field of the instruction
(see Figure 2.3). This type of instruction requires three bus cycles; one for the

Main Memory

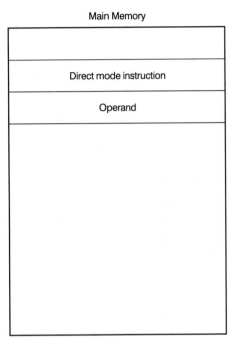

Figure 2.2 Immediate mode addressing.

instruction, one for the operand field, and one for the data (once the operand address is resolved). The following assembly code fragment is an example of this type of addressing.

```
MULT a          accumulator ← accumulator · contents of a
```

Here the contents of the accumulator are multiplied by the contents of memory location "a," and the result is placed in the accumulator.

2.1.1.4 Indirect Mode *Indirect memory instructions* require additional bus cycles (see Figure 2.1). The operand field of the instruction is a memory location containing the effective address of the address of the operand. Four bus cycles are needed: one for the instruction, another to fetch the operand field address, a third to fetch the contents of the operand field, and the last to fetch the data. The following example illustrates such an instruction in symbolic form. The modifier ",I" is used to indicate that the instruction is to be in indirect mode.

```
MULT R1,a,I      register 1 ← register 1 · contents of memory location
                               pointed to by symbolic location a
```

Here the contents of register 1 are multiplied by the contents of the memory location contained in location *a*. The result is then placed in register 1.

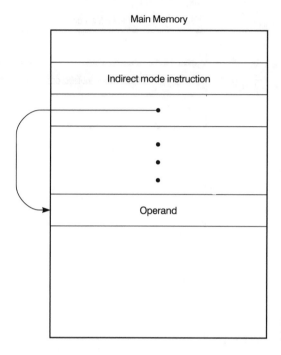

Figure 2.3 Direct mode addressing.

2.1.1.5 Register Direct Mode *Register direct mode instructions* are similar to direct instructions except that the operand field is a register and not an address. This type of instruction requires one bus cycle to fetch the instruction. The operand data are contained in registers, and the target of the instruction is a register so that no further memory accesses are required. For example:

```
MOVE R1,R2          register 2 ← register 1
```

Here the contents of the register 1 are placed in register 2.

2.1.1.6 Register Indirect Mode *Register indirect instructions* are similar to indirect instructions except the operand address is kept in a register rather than in another memory location. This type of instruction requires two bus cycles, one for the instruction and one for the data at the address held in the specified register. To illustrate:

```
STORE R2,R1,I       location in register 1 ← register 2
```

Here the contents of register 2 are stored in the location contained in register 1. Register direct mode is typically faster than register indirect mode.

2.1.1.7 Double Indirect Mode Double, which is similar to an indirect mode with another level of indirection, is frequently used to pass parameters by

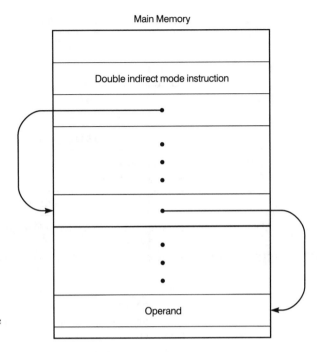

Main Memory

Double indirect mode instruction

Operand

Figure 2.4 Indirect mode addressing.

reference through a stack of activation records. It is also used for indexing into two-dimensional arrays. Additional levels of indirection are also possible.

2.1.1.8 Other Addressing Schemes   There are, of course, other variations on these addressing schemes [63], [108], but we will use only the aforementioned modes in order to illustrate further points.

2.1.2 0-Address Architecture

In 0-address or *stack* architecture, instructions are centered on an internal memory store called a stack and on an accumulator. No other registers are available in the machine. This type of architecture is generally uncommon in "real" systems, although many commercially available programmable calculators are based on it. The instruction set for a generic 0-address machine is given in Table 2.2.

Memory references are allowed only through LOAD and STORE instructions. The LOAD instruction moves data from the specified memory location to the accumulator, while the STORE instruction moves data from the accumulator to the specified memory location. The LOAD and STORE operations can be performed only on the accumulator, and only in immediate, direct, or indirect addressing modes.

TABLE 2.2   Instruction Set for a Generic 0-Address Machine

	Stack Instructions
PUSH	top ← top + 1
	stack(top) ← accumulator
POP	accumulator ← stack(top)
	top ← top − 1

	Data Transfer Instructions
LOAD m	(accumulator) ← m
STORE m	m ← (accumulator)

	Arithmetic Instructions
ADD	stack(top − 1) ← stack(top − 1) + stack(top)
	top ← top − 1
SUB	stack(top − 1) ← stack(top − 1) − stack(top)
	top ← top − 1
MULT	stack(top − 1) ← stack(top − 1) · stack(top)
	top ← top − 1
DIV	stack(top − 1) ← stack(top − 1)/stack(top)
	top ← top − 1
COMP	stack(top) ← − stack(top)
SQRT	stack(top) ← $\sqrt{\text{stack(top)}}$

	Test and Transfer Instructions
TEST	if stack(top − 1) = stack(top) then CCR ← 0
	if stack(top − 1) < stack(top) then CCR ← −1
	if stack(top − 1) > stack(top) then CCR ← 1
JUA m	PC ← m
JNE m	if CCR ≠ 0 then PC ← m
JEQ m	if CCR = 0 then PC ← m
JLT m	if CCR = −1 then PC ← m
JLE m	if CCR < 1 then PC ← m
JGT m	if CCR = 1 then PC ← m
JGE m	if CCR > −1 then PC ← m
BRANCH m	(subroutine return location) ← PC
	PC ← m
RETURN	PC ← (subroutine return location)
⟨interrupt⟩	(interrupt return location) ← PC
	PC ← (interupt vector location)
RI	PC ← (interrupt return location)

	Operand Field
m: n	the constant n
a	contents of symbolic address *a*
a,I	contents of memory location pointed to by symbolic address *a*
@x	address of symbolic location *x*

2.1.2.1 Stack Operations Two special implied mode instructions are available in the 0-address architecture. These instructions, PUSH and POP, are used to transfer data to the accumulator from the stack and vice versa.

The PUSH operation places the contents of the accumulator onto the stack and increments the stack top:

> top ← top + 1
> stack(top) ← accumulator

The POP instruction moves the data at the top of the stack to the accumulator and decrements the top pointer. Hence:

> accumulator ← stack(top)
> top ← top − 1

Notice that the top is really an anonymous internal register, and that appropriate stack overflow and underflow conditions are checked when a PUSH or POP is performed.

2.1.2.2 Arithmetic Operations Arithmetic instructions, which are always in implied mode, use the stack in one of two ways. For binary operations (in the algebraic sense), the top of the stack less one receives the result of the binary operation on the first two data items in the stack. The top of the stack is then decremented by one. That is,

> stack(top − 1) ← stack(top − 1) op stack(top)
> top ← top − 1

where *op* represents a binary operation such as +, −, ·, or /.

■ EXAMPLE 2.2

Suppose the stack is as follows:

Location	Contents	
2	6	← top
1	7	

and a SUB instruction is executed. Then the stack will look like:

Location	Contents	
1		
	1	← top

■

For unary operations such as − or two's complement, the topmost location of the stack is operated on by the unary operation. That is:

stack(top) ← op stack(top)

■ **EXAMPLE 2.3**

Suppose a COMP operation is executed on the following stack:

Location	Contents	
1	25	← top

The result will look like this:

Location	Contents	
1	−25	← top

■

NOTE 2.1   The details involving the arithmetic operations on the stack are actually more complicated. For example, rather than performing the arithmetic operation on stack memory directly, the operands are popped from the stack into hidden registers, the arithmetic logic unit operates on these, and the result of the calculation is pushed back onto the stack. In the case of binary operations, the stack pointer is then decremented. Since these operations are performed in microcode, the programmer need not worry about them.

2.1.2.3 Programming a 0-Address Machine   Programs for stack machines can be constructed by building a binary parse tree, which is then traversed in post-order fashion (called *reverse Polish notation* after the Polish logician Jan Lukasiewicz).

> **Definition** A *binary tree* is defined recursively as a collection of *n* nodes, one of which is a special one called the *root*. The remaining *n*−1 nodes form at most two subtrees. A *leaf* is any node in the tree with no subtrees.

We can represent an arithmetic equation by placing operands at the leaves of the binary tree with the associated operators at the roots of the subtrees. The hierarchy of the post-order traversal is used to enforce the precedence of operations.

The tree is constructed while parsing the equation to be represented and traversed during code generation. Operands at the leaves of the tree generate LOAD and PUSH instructions (in some implementations these are combined into a single instruction). Operands at the root of each subtree generate the corresponding operational instructions.

■ EXAMPLE 2.4

Consider one root of the quadratic equation; namely,

$$\text{root} = \frac{-b + \sqrt{b^2 - 4 \cdot a \cdot c}}{2 \cdot a}$$

We construct the parse tree as in Figure 2.5. (Note that we use the symbol ~ to represent the two's complement operation.) Traversing this tree in post-order fashion yields the following: b, ~, b, b, ·, 4, a, ·, c, ·, −, $\sqrt{}$, +, 2, a, ·, /. Replacing the operands with LOAD and PUSH instructions, and the

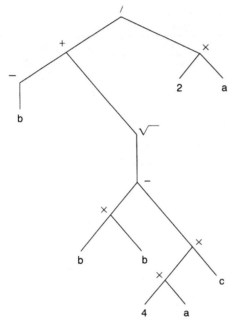

Postorder traversal: b − bb × 4a × c × − √‾ + 2a × /

Figure 2.5 Binary parse tree for one root of quadratic equation.

operators with the appropriate arithmetic instructions, yields the following assembly language equivalent code, with associated stack contents:

Instruction	Location	Stack Contents	
LOAD b			
PUSH	1	b	← top
COMP	1	−b	← top
LOAD b			
PUSH	2	b	← top
	1	−b	

Instruction	Location	Stack Contents	
LOAD b			
PUSH	3	b	← top
	2	b	
	1	−b	
MULT	2	b · b	← top
	1	−b	
LOAD 4			
PUSH	3	4	← top
	2	b · b	
	1	−b	
LOAD a			
PUSH	4	a	← top
	3	4	
	2	b · b	
	1	−b	
MULT	3	4 · a	← top
	2	b · b	
	1	−b	
LOAD c			
PUSH	4	c	← top
	3	4 · a	
	2	b · b	
	1	−b	
MULT	3	4 · a · c	← top
	2	b · b	
	1	−b	
SUB	2	$b \cdot b - 4 \cdot a \cdot c$	← top
	1	−b	
SQRT	2	$\sqrt{b \cdot b - 4 \cdot a \cdot c}$	← top
	1	−b	
ADD	1	$-b + \sqrt{b \cdot b - 4 \cdot a \cdot c}$	← top
LOAD 2			
PUSH	2	2	← top
	1	$-b + \sqrt{b \cdot b - 4 \cdot a \cdot c}$	

Instruction	Location	Stack Contents	
LOAD a			
PUSH	3	a	← top
	2	2	
	1	$-b + \sqrt{b \cdot b - 4 \cdot a \cdot c}$	
MULT	2	$2 \cdot a$	← top
	1	$-b + \sqrt{b \cdot b - 4 \cdot a \cdot c}$	
DIV	1	$(-b + \sqrt{b \cdot b - 4 \cdot a \cdot c})/2 \cdot a$	← top
POP			
STORE root		answer goes in "root"	■

As shown, 0-address machines require many instructions to do even simple computations, and thus may be unsuitable for certain real-time applications. Yet 0-address machines often exhibit characteristics of RISC machines (see Section 2.1.11), where the effect of a bloated instruction count can be moderated because each instruction is faster than in a more complicated architecture.

2.1.3 1-Address Architecture

In this type of architecture an implied accumulator is used, as in the 0-address machine, but all instructions are allowed up to one memory or general register reference. Immediate instructions are also permitted. This type of computer typically has several general-purpose registers that can be part of the operand field of any instruction. Each binary instruction takes the contents of the accumulator operated on by the given register and places the result back into the accumulator. In general, for binary operations we have the following format:

    op Ri   accumulator ← accumulator op Ri

where Ri represents register i and op represents a binary operation.

Unary operations such as LOAD, STORE, and COMP have these effects, respectively: load from memory to the accumulator, store from the accumulator to memory, and negate the accumulator. The instruction set for a generic 1-address machine is given in Table 2.3.

■ EXAMPLE 2.5

We can rewrite the quadratic root solution in 1-address code as follows.

    LOAD   2   accumulator ← 2
    MULT   a   accumulator ← accumulator · a
    STORE R1   register 1 ← accumulator
    LOAD   a   accumulator ← contents of a
    MULT   4   accumulator ← accumulator · 4

TABLE 2.3   Instruction Set for a Generic 1-Address Machine

Data Transfer Instructions

LOAD m	(accumulator) ← m
STORE m	m ← (accumulator)

Arithmetic Instructions

ADD m	(accumulator) ← (accumulator) + m
SUB m	(accumulator) ← (accumulator) – m
MULT m	(accumulator) ← (accumulator) · m
DIV m	(accumulator) ← (accumulator) / m
COMP	(accumulator) ← –(accumulator)
SQRT	(accumulator) ← $\sqrt{\text{(accumulator)}}$

Test and Transfer Instructions

TEST Ri	if (accumulator) = Ri then CCR ← 0
	if (accumulator) < Ri then CCR ← –1
	if (accumulator) > Ri then CCR ← 1
JUA m	PC ← m
JNE m	if CCR ≠ 0 then PC ← m
JEQ m	if CCR = 0 then PC ← m
JLT m	if CCR = –1 then PC ← m
JLE m	if CCR < 1 then PC ← m
JGT m	if CCR = 1 then PC ← m
JGE m	if CCR > –1 then PC ← m
BRANCH m	(subroutine return location) ← PC
	PC ← m
RETURN	PC ← (subroutine return location)
⟨interrupt⟩	(interrupt return location) ← PC
	PC ← (interrupt vector location)
RI	PC ← (interrupt return location)

Operand Field

m: n	the constant n
a	contents of symbolic address *a*
a,I	contents of memory location pointed to by symbolic address *a*
Rn	contents of register n
Rn,I	contents of memory location pointed to by register n
@x	address of symbolic location *x*

MULT	c	accumulator ← accumulator · contents of c
STORE	R2	register 2 ← accumulator
LOAD	b	accumulator ← contents of b
MULT	b	accumulator ← accumulator · contents of b
SUB	R2	accumulator ← accumulator − register 2
SQRT		accumulator ← square root of accumulator
STORE	R2	register 2 ← accumulator
LOAD	b	accumulator ← contents of b
COMP		accumulator ← − accumulator
ADD	R2	accumulator ← accumulator+register 2
DIV	R1	accumulator ← accumulator / register 1
STORE	answer	answer ← accumulator ■

Of course, this program is much simpler than it would be for the 0-address machine (and could be optimized further), but this does not imply that the code is necessarily faster, since the decode times for each instruction may have increased.

2.1.4 2-Address Architecture

In the 2-address architecture, a maximum of two memory or general register references are allowed for each instruction, and no implied accumulator is used. Immediate instructions are allowed. Here, binary instructions have the form:

        OP Ri,Rj   Ri ← Ri OP Rj

and unary instructions have the form:

        OP Ri   Ri ← OP Ri

where Ri and Rj represent memory locations or registers i and j, respectively. The instruction set for a generic 2-address machine is given in Table 2.4.

■ **EXAMPLE 2.6**

Rewriting the program for the quadratic root in 2-address code yields

LOAD	R1,a	R1 ← contents of a
MULT	R1,c	R1 ← a·c
MULT	R1,4	R1 ← a·c·4
LOAD	R2,b	R2 ← contents of b
MULT	R2,R2	R2 ← b·b
SUB	R2,R1	R2 ← b·b − 4·a·c
SQRT	R2	R2 ← sqrt(b·b − 4·a·c)
LOAD	R1,b	R1 ← b

```
COMP   R1              R1 ← –b
ADD    R1,R2           R1 ← –b+sqrt(b·b – 4·a·c)
LOAD   R2,a            R2 ← a
MULT   R2,2            R2 ← 2·a
DIV    R1,R2           R1 ← (–b+sqrt(b·b – 4·a·c))/2·a
STORE  R1,answer       contents of answer ← result                    ■
```

Notice that as the instruction set becomes more complex, the number of instructions required to do the job is reduced.

2.1.5 3-Address Architecture

As you might guess, 3-address computers allow up to three memory or general register references in each instruction. Such instructions have the format:

```
OP R1,R2,R3        R3 ← R1 OP R2
```

where R1, R2, and R3 are general registers or memory locations. Unary and binary instructions are the same as for the 2-address machine. The instruction set for a generic 3-address machine is given in Table 2.5.

■ EXAMPLE 2.7

Rewriting the quadratic root solution in 3-address code, we have

```
LOAD   R2,b            R2 ← contents of b
LOAD   R3,a            R3 ← contents of a
LOAD   R4,c            R4 ← contents of c
MULT   R3,R4,R4        R4 ← a·c
MULT   4,R4,R4         R4 ← 4·a·c
MULT   R2,R2,R5        R5 ← b·b
SUB    R5,R4,R4        R4 ← b·b–4·a·c
SQRT   R4              R4 ← sqrt(b·b–4·a·c)
SUB    R4,R2,R2        R2 ← sqrt(b·b–4·a·c) –b
MULT   R3,2,R4         R4 ← 2·a
DIV    R2,R4,R2        R2 ← (sqrt(b·b – 4·a·c) –b )/2·a
STORE  R2,answer       contents of answer ← result                    ■
```

2.1.6 Compare, Jump, and Subroutine Instructions

In all four previously mentioned architectures, instructions are provided to alter the flow-of-control. These involve conditional and unconditional transfers and subroutine type instructions. The formats of these instructions are generally the same for all four architectures.

TABLE 2.4   Instruction Set for a Generic 2-Address Machine

Data Transfer Instructions	
LOAD Ri,m	Ri ← m
STORE Ri,m	m ← Ri

Arithmetic Instructions	
ADD Ri,m	Ri ← Ri + m
SUB Ri,m	Ri ← Ri − m
MULT Ri,m	Ri ← Ri · m
DIV Ri,m	Ri ← Ri / m
COMP Ri	Ri ← −Ri
SQRT Ri	Ri ← $\sqrt{\text{Ri}}$

Test and Transfer Instructions	
TEST Ri,Rj	if Ri = Rj then CCR ← 0
	if Ri < Rj then CCR ← −1
	if Ri > Rj then CCR ← 1
JUA m	PC ← m
JNE m	if CCR ≠ 0 then PC ← m
JEQ m	if CCR = 0 then PC ← m
JLT m	if CCR = −1 then PC ← m
JLE m	if CCR < 1 then PC ← m
JGT m	if CCR = 1 then PC ← m
JGE m	if CCR > −1 then PC ← m
BRANCH m	(subroutine return location) ← PC
	PC ← m
RETURN	PC ← (subroutine return location)
⟨interrupt⟩	(interrupt return location) ← PC
	PC ← (interrupt vector location)
RI	PC ← (interrupt return location)

Operand Field	
m: n	the constant n (cannot be target operand)
a	contents of symbolic address a
a,I	contents of memory location pointed to by symbolic address a
Rn	contents of register n
Rn,I	contents of memory location pointed to by register n
@x	address of symbolic location x

TABLE 2.5   Instruction Set for a Generic 3-Address Machine

Data Transfer Instructions	
LOAD Ri,m	Ri ← m
STORE Ri,m	m ← Ri

Arithmetic Instructions	
ADD m,n,Ri	Ri ← m + n
SUB m,n,Ri	Ri ← m − n
MULT m,n,Ri	Ri ← m · n
DIV m,n,Ri	Ri ← m / n
COMP Ri	Ri ← −Ri
SQRT Ri	Ri ← $\sqrt{Ri}$

Test and Transfer Instructions	
TEST Ri,Rj	if Ri = Rj then CCR ← 0
	if Ri < Rj then CCR ← −1
	if Ri > Rj then CCR ← 1
JUA m	PC ← m
JNE m	if CCR ≠ 0 then PC ← m
JEQ m	if CCR = 0 then PC ← m
JLT m	if CCR = −1 then PC ← m
JLE m	if CCR < 1 then PC ← m
JGT m	if CCR = 1 then PC ← m
JGE m	if CCR > −1 then PC ← m
BRANCH m	(subroutine return location) ← PC
	PC ← m
RETURN	PC ← (subroutine return location)
⟨interrupt⟩	(interrupt return location) ← PC
	PC ← (interrupt vector location)
RI	PC ← (interrupt return location)

Operand Field	
m,n: n	the constant n (cannot be target operand)
a	contents of symbolic address *a*
a,I	contents of memory location pointed to by symbolic address *a*
Rn	contents of register n
Rn,I	contents of memory location pointed to by register n
@x	address of symbolic location *x*

2.1.6.1 Test Instructions   Certain instructions are needed to provide for *conditional transfer*, that is, change of the program counter based on some condition. For example, suppose you wish to compare the contents of two registers and change the flow-of-control if they are equal, but maintain the flow-of-control if they are not. To accomplish this, most processors are equipped with one or more *condition code registers* (CCRs). These internal CPU registers may be accessible as part of the instruction set, but normally are tested indirectly as part of a jump instruction.

■ **EXAMPLE 2.8**

Consider the following code fragment for a 2-address machine:

```
LOAD R1,a        R1 ← a
LOAD R2,b        R2 ← b
TEST R1,R2       Set CCR
JNE  11          PC ← symbolic location "11" if not equal
```

In this case, the content of register 1 is tested against that of register 2. If the contents are equal, CCR ← 0, if register 1 is less than register 2, CCR ← −1, and if register 1 is greater than register 2 then CCR ← 1. The JNE instruction following the TEST instruction will be discussed shortly.   ■

NOTE 2.2   The instruction immediately following a TEST instruction is typically uninterruptable because of the danger of an interrupting process changing the CCR. If this type of instruction is to be interruptable, then the CCR must be saved.

For 0-address machines, the two comparands are the top of the stack and the second from the top. For a 1-address machine the comparands are the accumulator and a register or memory location. The 3-address machine uses an instruction format similar to that of the 2-address machine.

Certain arithmetic instructions (ADD, SUB, etc.) and logical instructions (AND, OR, etc.) also set bits in the CCR. For example, if the result of adding two registers is 0, then the CCR is set to 0; if the result is negative, the CCR is set to −1; and if the result is positive, the CCR is set to 1.

Logical instructions such as AND, OR, and NOT can also set the CCR. For example, applying the OR instruction to two registers will set those bits in the target register to logic "1" when the corresponding bit is set to "1" in either operand register. The instruction will then set the CCR to 1 if at least one bit in the target register has been set to "1." The CCR is set to "0" otherwise. Similar operations can be described for the logical AND, exclusive OR, and NOT instructions (see chapter exercises).

2.1.6.2 Conditional and Unconditional Jump Instructions   The change of flow-of-control in the computer via jump instructions is straightforward. The *jump unconditional absolute* (JUA) simply loads the program counter with the instruction argument, which is an address in absolute or symbolic form. For example,

```
JUA    1000          load program counter with address 1000
```

Some architectures may support an indirect form of the instruction. In this case the argument of the instruction is the address of a memory location containing the address to be loaded into the program counter.

Conditional forms of the jump instruction, which rely on the result of a previous TEST instruction, are also available. For example, the JLT, JLE, JGT, JGE, JEQ, and JNE instructions will jump to the argument address if the result of the comparison was less than, less than or equal to, greater than, greater than or equal to, equal to, or not equal to, respectively. These instructions also may have indirect forms.

2.1.6.3 Subroutine Instructions Most processors provide special subroutine BRANCH instructions that do more than change the program counter. These instructions also save the current contents of the program counter in some memory location (either internal or external to the CPU), called the *return location*, and may save all or some CPU registers in an area of main memory called the *stack*. The BRANCH instruction takes the address of the subroutine as an argument.

The RETURN instruction is in effect the inverse of the BRANCH instruction. It has no argument, and it serves to restore the contents of the CPU registers from the stack and the old program counter saved by the BRANCH instruction. The RETURN instruction should always be the last instruction executed in a subroutine.

NOTE 2.3 Anything the subroutine pushes onto the stack must be popped off when a RETURN is executed.

A similar instruction, *return from interrupt* (RI), serves the same purpose as the RETURN instruction except that it undoes the effects of vectoring to an interrupt-handling routine. The effect of both instructions on the program counter is the same as the BRANCH instruction except that they are needed when interrupt processing has finished.

2.1.7 Interrupt Enable and Disable

Two other instructions should be mentioned which are needed in all four architectures. The *enable priority interrupt* (EPI) is used to enable interrupts for processing by the CPU. The *disable priority interrupt* (DPI) instruction prevents the CPU from processing interrupts (i.e., being interrupted). Disabling interrupts does not remove the interrupt; rather, the CPU "holds off" the interrupt until an EPI instruction is executed.

Although these systems may have several interrupt signals, assume that the CPU honors only one interrupt signal. This has the advantage of simplifying the instruction set and offloading certain interrupt processing. Such tasks as prioritization and masking of certain individual interrupts are handled by manipulating the interrupt controller via memory-mapped I/O or programmed I/O. This is discussed in Chapter 6.

2.1.8 Floating Point Instructions

All the arithmetic instructions discussed for our generic machines thus far operate on integer quantities only. Most applications require that the computer be able to process data stored in some floating point representation. While integer data can usually be stored in 2 or 4 bytes, floating point quantities typically need 4 or more bytes of memory. This necessarily increases the number of bus cycles for any instruction requiring floating point data.

In addition, the microprograms for floating point instructions are considerably longer. Combined with the increased number of bus cycles, this means floating point instructions always take longer than their integer equivalents. Hence, for execution speed, instructions with integer operands are always preferred over instructions with floating point operands.

Finally, the instruction set must be equipped with instructions to convert integer data to floating point and vice versa. These instructions add overhead while possibly reducing accuracy. Therefore you should try to avoid mixed mode calculations. This point is discussed in Chapter 3 and again in Chapter 9.

Because the format and nature of floating point operations vary widely, no specific examples are given at this time.

2.1.9 Pipelining

Von Neumann computer architectures suffer from at least one serious flaw—the von Neumann bottleneck. The *von Neumann bottleneck* refers to the fact that the serial fetch and execution of the instructions limits overall execution speed. That is, two or more instructions cannot be executed simultaneously. This seriously limits CPU performance. Various schemes have been devised to mitigate this problem within the context of the von Neumann architecture.

One of the first schemes to be implemented takes advantage of the fact that the fetching of the instruction is only one portion of the fetch-execute cycle, and that this can overlap with different parts of the fetch-execute cycle for other instructions. This technique is called *pipelining*.

■ **EXAMPLE 2.9**

Consider a computer that has a three-step fetch and execute process (although they are usually longer). An instruction is fetched into memory during the first tick of the CPU clock. During the second tick, the instruction is decoded; that is, the program register is loaded with the starting address in micromemory of the appropriate procedure. Finally, the microprogram is started. Figure 2.6 shows how the fetch of a second instruction can be overlapped (performed simultaneously) with the decoding

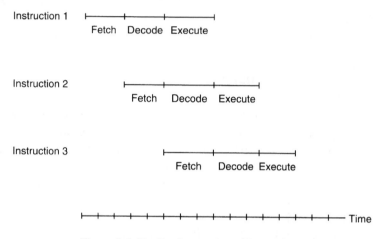

Figure 2.6 Pipelined execution of instructions.

of the first instruction and how the fetch of a third can overlap with the execution of the first and the decoding of the second. This process continues indefinitely. In this way the serial resources of the computer are constantly being used to their fullest, and throughput is increased.   ■

The drawback of the pipelining technique is that if the flow-of-control changes, then the other instructions further back in the pipeline are no longer correct. Hence, these types of computers must empty or *flush* the pipeline when branching due to an event occurs.

For the real-time programmer it must be realized that before an interrupt can be handled, the oldest instruction in the pipeline must be completed and then the others either saved somehow or flushed (the preferred technique). Saving the intermediate steps of the other instructions requires a sophisticated processor and increases system response time.

2.1.10 Coprocessors

Some computer configurations include a second specialized CPU, called a *coprocessor*, to perform certain operations. These devices typically are used to extend the instruction set, and not for multiprocessing. The main processor loads certain registers with data for the coprocessor, issues an instruction starting the coprocessor, and then suspends itself until the coprocessor finishes. Usually, this involves two handshaking signals between the main processor and coprocessor. For example, consider a typical microprocessor and associated coprocessor. Suppose there are two signals between them. When the main processor wishes to use the coprocessor, it loads global variables with the operands and sends a signal to the coprocessor. Then the main processor suspends itself. When the coprocessor finishes the operation, it places the result in another global variable, issues a signal to awaken the main processor, and suspends itself. The main processor then resumes its fetch-execute cycle. Figure 2.7 depicts this relationship.

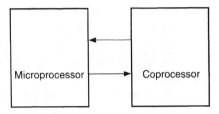

Figure 2.7 A microprocessor/coprocessor pair.

   Despite decreasing latency by reducing the longest instruction time, coprocessors present special problems to real-time systems. For example, should the coprocessor be interruptable? What registers belonging to the coprocessor should be saved as part of the context-switching process? Should a separate stack be kept for the coprocessor? The answers to these questions are highly configuration-dependent, but the rule of thumb is to treat coprocessors as serially reusable resources (i.e., make them uninterruptable). However, if they are interruptable, you must save all applicable registers as part of context. This issue is discussed in Chapter 6.

2.1.11 RISC Machines

As the need for more computer power grows, various plans are being implemented to increase processor speeds. Most approaches involve complicated microcode schemes to reduce the number of high-order language instructions needed to implement a specific function. For example, advanced processors may include a square root or matrix multiply function as part of the macroinstruction set, rather than requiring the programmer to implement these functions in a procedure. Supplying complex functions as part of the processor firmware gives the programmer a variety of powerful software tools. In addition, program memory savings are realized because implementing complex instructions in high-order language requires many words of main memory. Finally, functions written in microcode always execute faster than those coded in the high-order language. In this way, some processors seek to reduce the programmer's coding responsibility, increase execution speeds, and minimize memory usage. Processors of this sort are termed *complex instruction set computers* (CISC) and were the prevailing architecture until the 1980s. For example, Digital Equipment Corporation's VAX architecture has over 290 instructions in 10 addressing modes. In addition, many older microprocessors are CISC, including Intel's 80386 and 80486, and Motorola's 68000 series.

Studies have shown, however, that most compilers generate code that makes heavy use of LOAD, STORE, ADD, SUB, and jump instructions [13], [110]. The remaining part of the instruction set makes up few of the compiler-generated instructions. But in computer architectures with complex instruction sets, the decode and execution times for every instruction increase, to the point where a single instruction may take 10 or 20 CPU clock ticks to decode. The same complex decoding procedure needed for a square root instruction is also needed for a simple LOAD instruction. Thus, execution times for all instructions are being increased only for the benefit of implementing a few, seldom used instructions.

However, proponents of a different type of computer, the *reduced instruction set computer* (RISC) argue that by simplifying the computer instruction set, execution speed can be increased.

In pure RISC architectures, each instruction takes only one machine cycle (defined as the time needed for a 2-address instruction). Classically, RISCs employ little or no microcode. This means the instruction decode procedure can be implemented as a fast combinational circuit, rather than a complicated microprogram scheme. In addition, reducing chip complexity allows for more on-chip storage (i.e., general-purpose registers). Effective use of register direct instructions can decrease unwanted memory fetch time (bus cycles).

Unfortunately, the spirit of RISC has been lost in most newer machines that are portrayed as "RISCs." These lack features that were once required of RISCs.

While a CISC architecture may have over 250 instructions in its macroinstruction set, a RISC has fewer than 100. Incidentally, a single macroinstruction suffices to provide a complete instruction set for a general-purpose computer [93], [94].

The main drawback of RISC is that, in general, the number of macroinstructions needed per high-order language instruction is increased over CISC machines. Stated simply, a RISC relies on the compiler to generate efficient code while a CISC bets that fast hardware can compensate for coding inefficiencies.

RISCs are widely available today. For example, Sun Microsystems' popular SPARC (Special Application of RISC) series and DEC's Alpha processors are based on RISC architectures.

In summary, RISCs have a major real-time advantage in that, in theory, the average instruction execution time is shorter than for CISCs. The reduced instruction execution time leads to shorter interrupt latency and thus shorter response times. Moreover, RISC instruction sets tend to lead to compilers that generate good code. Because the instruction set is limited, the number of special cases that the compiler must consider is reduced, thus permitting a greater number of optimization approaches. On the downside, increasingly RISC processors are associated with caches and elaborate multistage pipelines. Generally, this greatly improves the average case performance of the processor by reducing the memory access times for frequently accessed instructions and data. However, in the worst case, response times are increased because low cache hit ratios and frequent pipeline flushing can degrade performance. But in many real-time systems, worst case performance is typically based on very unusual, even pathological conditions. Thus, greatly improving average case performance at the expense of degraded worst case performance is considered acceptable. The importance of RISC architectures in modern real-time systems cannot be overemphasized. The battle of the CISC advocates versus the RISC advocates that raged in the late 1970s and early 1980s was handily won by the RISC side. Increasingly, economic factors favor the use of vendor-supplied single-board RISC computers or systems on a chip as part of real-time control schemes. Large-scale systems utilize standard RISC workstations deployed on local area networks (LANs). Many embedded systems are designed around single-chip RISC processors. A popularized discussion of the application of RISC to real-time systems can be found in [8], while [154] presents a more theoretical treatment.

2.2 MEMORIES

An understanding of the available memory technologies is important when designing real-time systems because they impact all measures of system performance. Memory can be *volatile* (the contents will be lost if power is removed) or *nonvolatile* (the contents are preserved upon removing power). In addition there is *random-access memory* (RAM), which is both readable and writeable, and *read-only memory* (ROM). Within these two groups are many different classes of memories, and we will discuss the more important ones briefly.

RAM memories may be either *dynamic* or *static*, and are denoted DRAM and SRAM, respectively. DRAMs use a capacitive charge to store logic 1s and 0s, and must be refreshed periodically to restore the charge lost due to capacitive discharge. SRAMs do not suffer from discharge problems and therefore do not need to be refreshed. SRAMs are typically faster and require less power than DRAMs, but are more expensive.

The most important real-time characteristic of memory is *access time*, the interval between when data are requested from the memory cell and when they are actually available. The access time depends on the memory type and technology, the memory layout, and other factors; its method of determination is complicated, and beyond the scope of this book. Other important memory considerations are power requirements, number of bits per unit area (called the *density*), and cost. In the following discussions, however, we are concerned primarily with access times for a number of memory types and technologies.

2.2.1 Core

Ferrite core, a type of nonvolatile static RAM, is a bistable device that replaced memories based on vacuum tubes in the early 1950s. Core memory consists of a doughnut-shaped magnet through which a thin wire called a *drive line* passes. Perhaps as a child you built a simple electromagnet with a 9-volt battery, nail, and wire. The operating principle of core memory is related.

In the core memory, the direction of flow of current through the drive line establishes either a clockwise or counterclockwise magnetic flux through the doughnut corresponding to either a logic 1 or a logic 0. A second wire called the *sense line* is used to "read" the memory (see Figure 2.8). When a current is passed through the drive line, a pulse is generated (or not) in the sense line depending on the orientation of the magnetic flux.

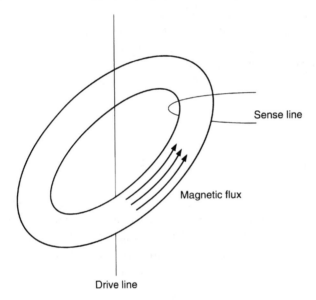

Drive line   **Figure 2.8** Core memory element.

Core memories are slow (10-microsecond access) and bulky, and consume lots of power, but they do have one advantage—they cannot be upset by electrostatic discharge or by a charged particle in space [95]. This consideration is important in the reliability of space-borne and military real-time systems.

2.2.2 Semiconductor Memories

RAM devices can be constructed from semiconductor materials in a variety of ways. The semiconductor material is used to form a bistable logic device called a *flip-flop*. The excitation for an RS type flip-flop is given in Table 2.6. The flip-flop has two inputs: the set line, S, and the reset line, R. The next state of the flip-flop (shown in the table) is determined by the input lines and its current state, Q. The x represents a "don't care" state—that is, it should be unachievable.

TABLE 2.6 RS Flip-Flop Excitation Table

Current	RS Input			
State (Q)	00	01	10	11
0	0	1	0	x
1	1	1	0	x
		Next State		

The flip-flops are so configured as to form a single bit of storage, an example of which is shown in Figure 2.9. The basic one-bit cells are then configured in an array as in Figure 2.10 to form the memory store.

Both static and dynamic RAM can be constructed from several types of semiconductor materials and approaches. Typically, dynamic memories require less power and are denser than static ones; however, they are much slower.

The required refresh of the dynamic RAM is accomplished by accessing each row in memory by setting the RAS (row address strobe) signal without the need to activate the CAS (column address strobe) signals. This is called a RAS

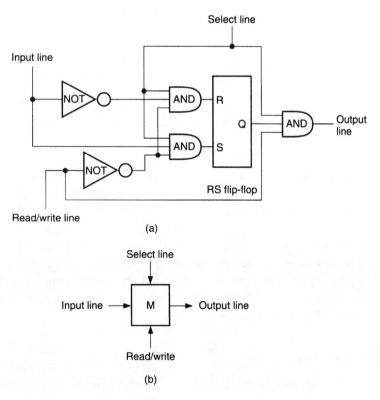

Figure 2.9 Logic diagram for single bit of memory (a) and block diagram representation (b).

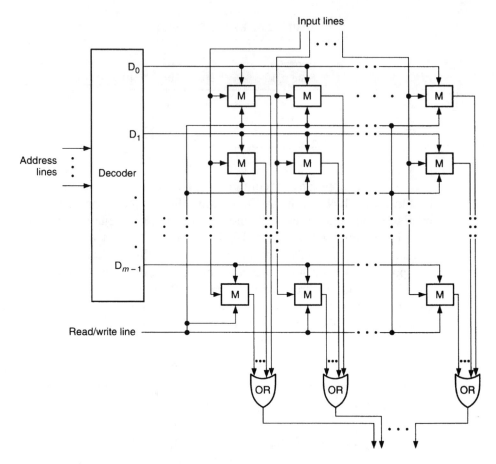

Figure 2.10 The $n \times m$ memory array using single-bit block representation.

only refresh. The RAM refresh can occur at a regular rate (e.g., 4 milliseconds) or in one burst. A significant amount of bus activity can be held off during the dynamic refresh, and this must be taken into account when calculating instruction execution time (and hence system performance). When a memory access must wait for a DRAM refresh to be completed, we call this *cycle stealing*. If burst mode is used to refresh the DRAM, then the timing of critical regions may be adversely affected when the entire memory is refreshed simultaneously. Depending on the materials used and the configuration, access times of 15 nanoseconds (15 billionths of a second) or better can be obtained for static semiconductor RAM.

2.2.3 Fusible Link

Fusible-link ROMs are a type of nonvolatile memory used to store programs. These memories are sometimes generically called *programmable read-only memories* (PROMs), or *programmable logic arrays* (PLAs), and consist of an

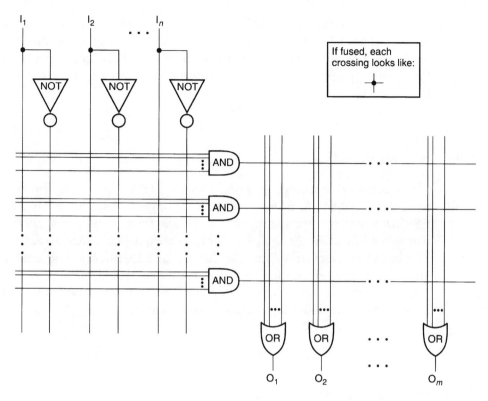

Figure 2.11 The *n*-input *m*- output fusible-link PROM.

array of paths to ground called *fusible links*. During programming these fuses are "blown" to represent either 1s or 0s thus embedding the program into the memory. Since fusible-link memories cannot be reprogrammed, they cannot be accidentally altered. They are very fast and can achieve access times of around 50 nanoseconds. A fusible link PROM is depicted in Figure 2.11.

2.2.4 UVROM

Ultraviolet read-only memory (UVROM) is a type of nonvolatile PROM with the special feature that it can be reprogrammed a limited number of times. For reprogramming, the memory is first erased by exposing the chip to high-intensity ultraviolet light. UVROM is typically used for the storage of program and fixed constants. UVROMs have access times similar to those of fusible-link PROMs.

2.2.5 EEPROM

Electronically erasable programmable read-only memory (EEPROM) is another type of nonvolatile PROM, with the special feature that it can be reprogrammed. EEPROMs are used for long-term storage of variable information. These memories are erased by toggling control signals on the chip, which can be accomplished under program control. For example, the high score information on an arcade-type video game is stored in EEPROM. These memories are slower than other types of PROMs (50–200 ns access times) and have higher power requirements.

2.2.6 Flash Memory

A new memory technology for programmable ROMs has recently emerged. This technology, called *flash memory*, uses a single transistor per bit, whereas EEPROM uses two transistors per bit. Hence, flash is more cost-effective and dense then EEPROM. Access times for flash are quite fast, 20 to 30 nanoseconds. The main disadvantage of flash is that it can be written to and erased about 100,000 times, whereas EEPROM is at 1 million. This technology is finding its way into commerical electronics applications, but it is expected to appear increasingly in embedded applications such as avionics.

2.3 INPUT AND OUTPUT

Input and output of data to a computer system is accomplished through one of three different methods: programmed I/O, memory-mapped I/O, or DMA (direct memory address). Each method has advantages and disadvantages with respect to real-time performance, cost, and ease of implementation.

2.3.1 Programmed I/O

In programmed I/O, special instructions in the CPU instruction set are used to transfer data to and from the CPU. An IN instruction will transfer data from a specified I/O device into a specified CPU register. An OUT instruction will output from a register to some I/O device. Normally, the identity of the operative CPU register is embedded in the instruction code. Both the IN and OUT instructions require the efforts of the CPU and thus cost time that could impact real-time performance.

■ **EXAMPLE 2.10**

A computer system is used to control the speed of a motor. An output port is connected to the motor, and a signed integer is written to the port to set the motor speed. The computer is configured so that when an OUT instruction is executed, the contents of register 1 are placed on the data bus and sent to I/O port at the address contained in register 2. The following code fragment allows the program to set the motor speed.

```
LOAD R1, speed              motor speed into register 1
LOAD R2, motoraddress       address of motor control into register 2
OUT                         output from register 1 to the memory-mapped I/O
                            port address contained in register 2          ■
```

2.3.2 Memory-Mapped I/O

Memory-mapped I/O provides a data transfer mechanism that is convenient because it does not require the use of special CPU I/O instructions, and has the additional advantage that the CPU and other devices can share memory. In memory-mapped I/O certain designated locations of memory appear as virtual input/output ports. (See Figure 2.12.)

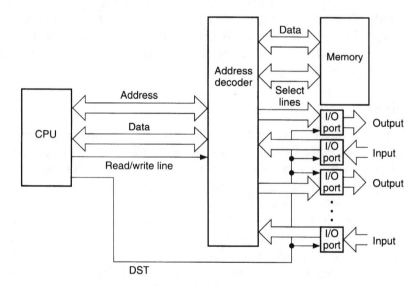

Figure 2.12 Memory-mapped I/O circuitry.

■ **EXAMPLE 2.11**

Consider the motor speed control discussed in Example 2.10. If it were to be implemented via memory-mapped I/O, it might look like the following:

```
LOAD  R1, speed             motor speed into register 1
STORE R1, motoraddress      store to address of motor control
```

Note that a memory location would have to be tied to the motor control via I/O card circuitry.   ■

■ **EXAMPLE 2.12**

In many computer systems, the video display uses memory-mapped I/O. The screen is a 24 row by 80 column array (a total of 1920 characters). Each screen cell is associated with a specific location in memory. To update the screen, characters are stored to the address assigned to that cell on the screen. Although actual memory does not exist at this location, the memory circuitry decodes this address into an existing output port and initiates a DST or data strobe transmit signal to initiate the data transfer to the video display card.   ■

Reading from a memory-mapped location involves executing a LOAD instruction on a pseudomemory location connected to an input device.

It should be noted that the overhead incurred in decoding the memory-mapped read or write instruction and the response time of the device involved must be consistent with the normal response time of actual memory. If the instruction decode and response time is faster than actual memory, then no problem exists. If this time is slower than actual memory, then the overall memory response time must be adjusted to conform through the use of extra clock cycles called *wait states*.

Memory-mapped I/O locations are not usually input and output simultaneously. Thus, if a record of what has been output to or input from a memory-mapped location is needed, a RAM image of it should be kept. This mirror image should be updated to reflect the current "contents" (most recent output or input) of the memory-mapped location.

2.3.3 DMA

In *direct memory access* (DMA), access to the computer's memory is given to other devices in the system without CPU intervention. That is, information is deposited directly into main memory by the external device. Here, the cooperation of a device called a *DMA controller* is required. Because CPU participation is not required, data transfer is fast.

The DMA controller is responsible for assuring that only one device can place data on the bus at any one time, a role called *bus arbitration*. If two or more devices attempt to gain control of the bus simultaneously, *bus contention* is said to occur. When a device already has control of the bus and another obtains access, this undesirable occurrence is called a *collision*.

The DMA controller prevents collisions by requiring each device to issue a DMA request signal (DMARQ) that will be acknowledged with a DMA acknowledge signal (DMACK). Until the DMACK signal is given to the requesting device, its connection to the main bus remains in a *tri-state* condition—that is, a high-impedance state that, in effect, disconnects the device. Any device that is tri-stated cannot affect the data on the memory data lines. Once the DMACK is given to the requesting device, its memory bus lines become active, and data transfer occurs as with the CPU.

The CPU is prevented from performing a data transfer during DMA through the use of a signal called a *bus grant*. Until the bus grant signal is given by the

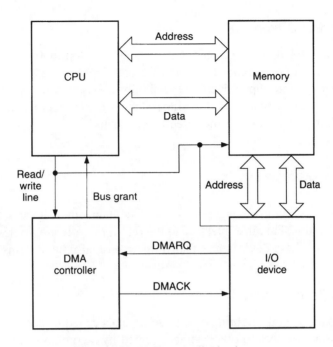

Figure 2.13 DMA controller hardware.

DMA controller, the normal CPU data transfer processes cannot proceed. At this point, the CPU is effectively suspended until it receives the bus grant, or until it gives up (after some predetermined time) and issues a *bus time-out* signal. See Figure 2.13 for a block diagram of typical DMA-controller hardware and Figure 2.14 for the timing sequence.

Because of its speed, DMA is the best method for input and output for real-time systems. Usually a special area of memory is designated for DMA memory.

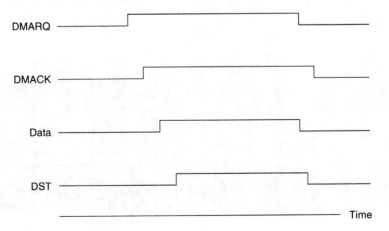

Figure 2.14 DMA transfer timing diagram.

2.3.4 Interrupt Driven I/O

Some persons may comment that there is a fourth type of I/O in addition to program I/O, memory-mapped I/O, and DMA—that is, interrupt driven I/O. However, interrupt driven I/O is simply a variation of one of the other three in which an interrupt is used to signal that an I/O transfer has completed or needs to be initiated via one of the three mechanisms.

2.4 OTHER DEVICES

Real-time computer systems usually contain other devices that depend on the application, but must interface to the real-time software. In this section we discuss some of these devices and their impact on real-time systems.

2.4.1 MUX Transceivers

Transmit/receive hybrid devices, sometimes called *transceivers*, provide communication services to other devices joined by a common bus.

If the bus is serial in nature, or if the number of lines on the bus is less than those internal to the device, then a device called a *multiplexer* or MUX is needed. The MUX card usually interfaces with the CPU through DMA hardware and is responsible for ensuring that all transmitted and received data conform to an appropriate protocol. This process includes parallel to serial conversion and vice versa with shift registers and other circuitry (see Figure 2.15). For example, the well-known *universal asynchronous relay terminal* (UART) is used for parallel-to-serial bus interfaces and is seen in many commercial applications.

Another example of such a bus structure is represented by the Mil-Std-1553B bus standard that specifies (besides hardware guidelines) transmission and receipt protocols. The 1553B standard is arranged so that one module on the bus

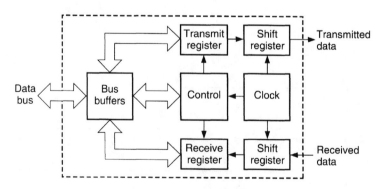

Figure 2.15 A typical transmit/receive hybrid.

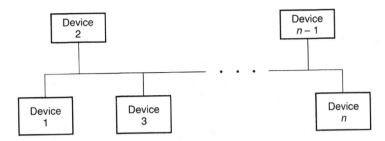

Figure 2.16 Mil-std-1553B bus arrangement.

acts as a bus controller and the others respond to its commands. This type of configuration is common in many commercial networks and computer subsystems, and is illustrated in Figure 2.16. Another example of MUX transceiver commonly in use is the IEEE488 parallel configuration.

2.4.2 A/D Circuitry

Analog-to-digital conversion or A/D circuitry converts continuous (analog) signals into discrete (digital) ones. Circuitry like this can be used to sample temperature, sound, pressure, and so on, and uses a variety of schemes to perform the conversion. The methodology involved is beyond the scope of this book, but interested readers can refer to [138].

The output of A/D circuitry is a discrete version of the signal being monitored, which changes at some rate. This information can be passed on to the real-time computer system using any of the three data transfer methods, but in each case the A/D circuitry makes available an n-bit number that represents a discrete version of the signal. The quantized version of the continuous value is usually handled as a scaled number (see Chapter 10).

The key factor in the service of A/D circuitry is the *sampling rate*. In order to convert an analog signal into a digital form without loss of information, samples of the analog signal must be taken at twice the rate of the highest frequency component of the signal (the Nyquist rate). Thus, a signal at 60 Hz must be sampled at 120 times per second. This implies that software tasks serving A/D circuitry must run at least at the same rate, or risk losing information. This consideration is an inherent part of the design process for the scheduling of tasks.

2.4.3 D/A Circuitry

Digital-to-analog conversion or D/A circuitry performs the inverse function of A/D circuitry; that is, it converts a discrete quantity to a continuous one. D/A devices are used to allow the computer to output analog voltages based on the digital version stored internally. Communication with D/A circuitry uses one of the three methods discussed. With D/A conversion, the issues are related to the scaled numbers discussed in Chapter 10.

2.4.4 Interrupt Controllers

Not all CPUs have the built-in ability to prioritize and handle multiple interrupts. An external interrupt-controller device can be used to enable a CPU with a single-interrupt input to handle interrupts from several sources. These devices provide the ability to prioritize and mask interrupts of different priority levels. The circuitry on board these devices is quite similar to that used by processors which can handle multiple interrupts, including mask circuitry, interrupt registers, and the like (see Figure 2.17).

When configured as in Figure 2.18, a single-interrupt CPU in conjunction with an interrupt controller can handle multiple interrupts.

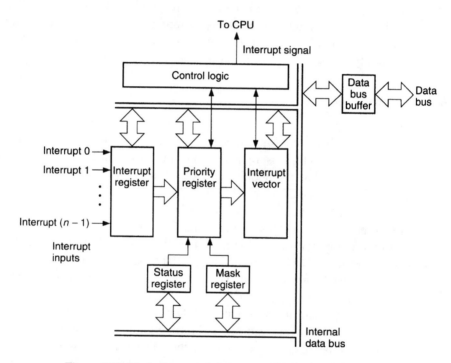

Figure 2.17 Block diagram of a programmable interrupt controller.

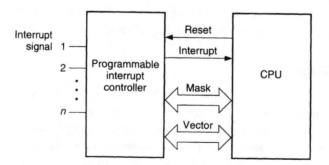

Figure 2.18 Handling multiple interrupts with an interrupt handler.

The following scenario illustrates the complexity of writing interrupt-handler software, and points out a subtle problem that can arise.

■ EXAMPLE 2.13

An interrupt handler executes upon receipt of a certain interrupt signal indicated by a logic 1. The first instruction of the routine is to clear the interrupt by strobing bit 0 of the interrupt clear signal. Here, intclr is a memory-mapped location whose least significant bit is connected with the clear interrupt signal. Successively storing 0, 1, and 0 serves to strobe bit 0.

Although the interrupt controller automatically disables other interrupts upon receipt of an interrupt, we immediately reenable them to detect spurious ones. The following code fragment illustrates this process for a 2-address architecture:

```
LOAD   R1,0
LOAD   R2,1
STORE  R1,intclr          set clear interrupt signal low
STORE  R2,intclr          set clear interrupt signal high
STORE  R1,intclr          set clear interrupt signal low
EPI                       enable interrupt
```

The timing sequence is illustrated in Figure 2.19. Note, however, that a problem could occur if the interrupt is cleared too quickly. Suppose that the clear, LOAD, and STORE instructions take 0.75 microsecond, but the interrupt pulse is 4 microseconds long. If the clear interrupt instruction is executed immediately upon receipt of the interrupt, a total of 3 microseconds will elapse. Since the interrupt signal is still present, when interrupts are enabled, a spurious interrupt will be caused. This problem is insidious because most of the time, software and hardware delays hold off the interrupt handler routine until long after the interrupt signal has latched and gone away. It often manifests itself when the CPU has been replaced by a faster one.

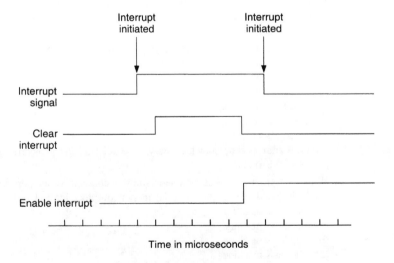

Figure 2.19 Timing sequence for interrupt handling.

■

2.4.5 Watchdog Timer

In many computer systems, the CPU or other devices are equipped with a counting register, which is incremented at some rate but must be cleared before the register overflows. This type of hardware is called a *watchdog timer* or WDT (see Figure 2.20). Watchdog timers are used to ensure that certain devices are serviced at regular intervals and that the CPU continues to function. For example,

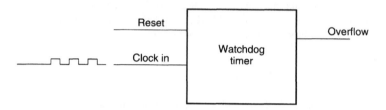

Figure 2.20 Watchdog timer configuration.

if the CPU is required to reset a watchdog timer every second and a WDT overflow occurs, then either the CPU has malfunctioned or the 1-second cycle has time-overloaded. Watchdog timers are useful in detecting deadlocks. Incidentally, resetting the timer is sometimes called "petting the watchdog."

2.5 EXERCISES

1. Discuss why it is unlikely that there exists an "*n*-address" machine where $n > 3$.
2. Update Tables 2.2, 2.3, 2.4, and 2.5 for the logical instructions AND, OR, XOR, and NOT.
3. Change Tables 2.2, 2.3, 2.4, and 2.5 to reflect how the CCR might be updated by the arithmetic instructions already described, and the logical instructions you defined in the previous exercise.
4. Write a program that selects the largest of a list of 10 numbers stored consecutively at symbolic location *list*, and stores the result in symbolic location *max*. Do this using the generic assembly language for a
   (a) 0-address machine
   (b) 1-address machine
   (c) 2-address machine
   (d) 3-address machine
   For the 0-address code draw the binary parse tree, and also show the contents of the stack after each instruction.
5. Write a program that sums the integers in five consecutive memory locations starting at symbolic location *x*. Store the result in symbolic location *y*. Do this using the generic assembly language for a
   (a) 0-address machine
   (b) 1-address machine
   (c) 2-address machine
   (d) 3-address machine
   For the 0-address code draw the binary parse tree, and also show the contents of the stack after each instruction.

6. Write a program that sums the integers in n consecutive memory locations starting at symbolic location x. (n is stored in symbolic location *num*.) Store the result in symbolic location y. Do this using the generic assembly language for a
   (a) 0-address machine
   (b) 1-address machine
   (c) 2-address machine
   (d) 3-address machine
   For the 0-address code draw the binary parse tree, and also show the contents of the stack after each instruction.

7. Write a program that performs the calculation

$$z = \frac{x^2 - xy + y^2}{x^2 + y^2}$$

   x, y, and z are symbolic locations. x and y are real numbers. Do this using the generic assembly language for a
   (a) 0-address machine
   (b) 1-address machine
   (c) 2-address machine
   (d) 3-address machine
   For the 0-address code draw the binary parse tree, and also show the contents of the stack after each instruction.

8. Write a program that performs the calculation

$$z = -\sqrt{4x^2 - y^2 + 8xy}$$

   x, y, and z are symbolic locations. Do this using the generic assembly language for a
   (a) 0-address machine
   (b) 1-address machine
   (c) 2-address machine
   (d) 3-address machine
   For the 0-address code draw the binary parse tree, and also show the contents of the stack after each instruction.

9. Write a program that performs the convolution of two discrete signals. The first signal is stored in 10 consecutive memory locations starting with symbolic location x. The second signal is stored in 10 consecutive memory locations starting with the symbolic location y. The resultant signal is to be stored in consecutive locations starting with the symbolic location z. The convolution sum is given by

$$z(t) = \sum_{i=1}^{10} x(i)\, y(t - i)$$

   Do this using the generic assembly language for a
   (a) 0-address machine
   (b) 1-address machine
   (c) 2-address machine
   (d) 3-address machine
   For the 0-address code draw the binary parse tree, and also show the contents of the stack after each instruction. You may use the program of the previous problem as a subroutine.

10. Write a bubble sort routine in assembly language for a
    (a) 2-address machine
    (b) 3-address machine
    (*Hint:* Assume the instruction EXCH is available. This instruction exchanges the contents of the two operands given.)

11. The instruction set of a certain processor does not have the JLE, JLT, JGE, and JGT instructions. Assume the processor does have all other arithmetic instructions and the JNE and JUA instructions. Implement the missing instructions for the generic assembly language in a

    (a) 0-address machine
    (b) 1-address machine
    (c) 2-address machine
    (d) 3-address machine

    (*Hint:* You will have to load registers or the stack with the two comparands and the conditional transfer locations.)

12. Why is DMA controller access to main memory in most systems given higher priority than CPU access to main memory?

13. Discuss the relative advantages/disadvantages of DMA, program I/O, and memory-mapped data transfers as they pertain to real-time systems.

14. Based on your understanding of computer architecture, rank the assembly language instructions in Table 2.3 from fast (1) to slow (10) for a machine with which you are familiar. Assume all instructions use direct addressing and that the memory access times are fixed. Also assume all instructions starting with a "J" have the same execution time.

15. Describe the relationship between the main processor and coprocessor in a system with which you are familiar. If you are not familiar with any, use the Intel 8086 microprocessor and its associated coprocessor, the 8087.

16. What special problems do pipelined architectures pose for real-time system designers? Are they any different for non-real-time systems?

17. Redraw Figure 2.8 using a ferrite core memory instead of an RS flip-flop.

18. Compare and contrast the different memory technologies discussed in this chapter as they pertain to real-time systems.

19. Should the instruction following the "TEST" instruction be interruptable? If so, what must the implicit BRANCH instruction (interrupt) do?

20. It is common practice for programmers to create continuous test and loop code in order to poll I/O devices or wait for interrupts to occur. Some processors provide an instruction (wait) that allows the processor to hibernate until an interrupt occurs. Why is this second form more efficient and desirable?

3

Language Issues

KEY POINTS OF THE CHAPTER

1. Generally, more abstraction leads to degradation of real-time performance.
2. Certain language features, such as unbounded recursion, while loops, and interrupt handlers, have nondeterministic run-time performance.
3. Certain language features such as pass-by-value parameter passing have desirable real-time performance impact.
4. It is important to understand the compiler in use and how it generates code from a particular usage of the language.

In this chapter we identify language features and their impact on real-time programming. In addition, we address the issues involved in understanding how compilers generate assembly code based on the high-level language input. Finally, we survey some of the languages commonly used for real-time systems on the basis of the criteria previously developed.

We discuss only those languages that are most often used in real-time systems.

When I first wrote this chapter, I included those languages that were being used chiefly to write embedded real-time systems (Ada, Fortran, C, Assembly language). Since then, C++ and Visual Basic have become very hot commercial programming languages, and the new object-oriented Ada 95 has been released. Furthermore, since writing this chapter significant research has occurred in programming languages that are suitable for real-time. Interested readers are referred to [156].

The United States Army's former principal language, FORTRAN, is included in this chapter because it is still taught at universities and is used in many real-time applications. In addition, the U.S. Army, Air Force, and Navy are currently required to procure software written in the Department of Defense's language standard, Ada. Conspicuously absent from the discussion are CMS-2 (a language once favored by the U.S. Navy) and JOVIAL (a language historically used by the U.S. Air Force), because they have been displaced, for the most part, by Ada.

Next, Pascal and C are discussed because they are widely taught and used in many real-time applications. BASIC is included for comparison purposes only. The chapter is rounded out with a look at assembly language and its role in real-time systems.

We do not discuss the use of applicative languages such as LISP in real-time. Although the importance of such languages in the construction, for example, of real-time artificial intelligence or expert systems is undeniable, research in this area has been limited thus far (for example, see [4]). The reader is referred to the Bibliography for additional reading on such real-time languages as occam 2 [21], CSML [25], or ESTEREL [18].

Although there are also several specialized languages for real-time, discussion here of these are deferred. However, it should be stated that real-time languages seek to support expression and analysis of temporal behavior in one of three ways:

- Elimination of constructs that have indeterminate execution times, such as infinite loops (e.g., Real-Time Euclid [157]).
- Extension of existing languages (e.g., real-time C).
- Construction of languages jointly with the operating system (e.g., MARUTI [103]).

3.1 LANGUAGE FEATURES

Several language features are desirable in a real-time language. These include versatile parameter passing mechanisms, strong typing, exception handling, interrupt types, and modularity. Many of these features are desirable for well-written non-real-time programs. We discuss these and other important language features, with emphasis on their impact on real-time performance.

3.1.1 Parameter Passing

Methods of parameter passing include the use of global variables, call-by-value, and call-by-reference. Not every parameter-passing mechanism is supported by all languages, and each has its merits and problems.

3.1.1.1 Call-By-Value   In *call-by-value* parameter passing, the value of the *actual parameter* (the named variable passed to the procedure) is copied into the called procedure's *formal parameter* (the dummy variable used in the definition of the procedure). Since the procedure manipulates the formal parameter, the actual parameter is not altered by execution of the procedure. This type of methodology works well when either a test is being performed on data or the data are to be used as the input to some mathematical function. Languages such as Pascal, C, and Ada support this parameter-passing scheme.

■ EXAMPLE 3.1

In this C code fragment, function "abs" will return the absolute value of any integer value passed to it without changing the value of the integer itself. In this case call-by-value is the preferred method.

```
int abs(int x)
{
  if (x < 0 )
        return(-x);
  else
        return(x);
}                                                                    ■
```

Parameters that are passed using call-by-value are typically copied onto a stack at run-time, at considerable execution time cost.

3.1.1.2 Call-by-Reference   In *call-by-reference* or *call-by-address*, the address of the parameter is passed by the calling routine to the called procedure so that it can be altered there. Execution of a procedure using call-by-reference parameters usually takes longer than when all the parameters are passed using call-by-value, since indirect instructions are needed for any calculations involving the variables passed. Most versions of FORTRAN are strictly call-by-reference, whereas Pascal and Ada provide for this mode in addition to call-by-value. C supports call-by-value, but call-by-reference can be simulated using pointer types.

Call-by-reference can present problems in some languages like FORTRAN.

■ EXAMPLE 3.2

In this FORTRAN code fragment subroutine "AVERAGE" is accidentally being called with the number 4 as the first parameter (something the compiler would not complain about). In order to pass the address of the number 4 to the subroutine, many compilers will create a hidden, anonymous, variable and pass its address to the subroutine. Unfortunately, the contents of this memory location will be altered by the subroutine, causing problems for any other subroutines using the number 4 as a parameter.

```
SUBROUTINE  AVERAGE(AVG,X,Y)
REAL AVG,X,Y
AVG = (X + Y)/2
RETURN
END


PROGRAM TEST
REAL X, Y
X = 4.0
Y = 3.0
CALL AVERAGE(4,X,Y)
END
```

Although this kind of problem seems contrived, it and its variations have historically haunted FORTRAN programmers. Other languages such as Pascal can also be plagued by such a problem [66].   ■

So what's the lesson to be learned from this example? Don't put a literal as an input parameter if the routine called modifies the variable. Also, don't write routines which modify an input variable that is not an output variable when using call-by-address.

3.1.1.3 Call-by-Value versus Call-by-Reference

In call-by-value, a copy of the parameter is placed in the activation record (which resides on the run-time stack maintained by the run-time memory manager), and so indirect mode instructions can be used. The chief drawback of call-by-reference versus call-by-value is that in call-by-reference, the compiler may generate double indirect mode instruction since pointers to variables are passed to procedures and placed on the run-time stack. In this case, some form of double indirect addressing is needed. This is more complex than indirect mode since such instructions use other levels of indirection and hence one more memory access.

It is important to determine the appropriate calling mechanism for different data structures prior to building the application. The relative advantages and disadvantages of call-by-value versus call-by-reference are dependent on many things, including the programming language used, compiler implementation, coding style, target hardware, type of application code, and size of parameters passed. For example, never use call-by-value to pass large (or even modest-sized) data structures; use call-by-reference instead. Call-by-value will require the generation of a very large activation record that could overflow the run-time stack.

Before deciding on a set of rules concerning parameter passing for optimum performance, one should construct a set of test cases that exercise different variations. Because these factors can vary the instruction mix these test cases need to be rerun every time the compiler, hardware, or application changes in order to update the rules.

3.1.1.4 Other Calling Methods Two other calling methodologies, *call-by-name* and *call-by-value-result*, were peculiar to ALGOL-60 and ALGOL-W, respectively. We are not concerned with the particulars of these calling schemes, but mention them only for completeness.

NOTE 3.1 There is a humorous, apocryphal story about Niklaus Wirth, inventor of Pascal, Modula, and Modula-2, among other achievements, who was once asked how he pronounced his name. Wirth is reputed to have responded, "If you call me by name it's *veert*, if you call me by value it's *worth*."

3.1.1.5 Parameter Lists versus Global Variables Global variables are available in many languages such as C, Pascal, and Ada. In languages like FORTRAN they are called COMMON variables, and in BASIC these are called COM variables. In any case, global variables are those within the scope of all modules of the software system. This usually means that references to these variables can be made in direct mode, and thus are faster than references to variables passed via parameter lists. The decision to use one method of parameter passing or the other represents the tradeoffs between accepted software engineering methodology and speed.

Using parameter lists is advantageous because the interfaces between the modules are clearly defined. Furthermore, in Ada and Modula-2, whether the parameters are to be input, output, or both is specified.

Unfortunately, parameter lists can get long, and often interrupts are disabled during parameter passing (which is in effect a series of LOAD and STORE instructions). Thus, interrupt latency may be increased in a place where it is least anticipated and in a way that is hard to spot. Why are interrupts disabled during parameter passing? Because if they were not, the following scenario can occur.

■ **EXAMPLE 3.3**

Consider the Pascal function with interface containing formal input parameters (called by value) a, b, c, and d and output parameter (called by reference), o, which depends on the actual values for a, b, c, and d.

```
procedure function1(a,b,c,d : integer, var o : integer);
```

where the actual parameters x, y, z, and q (which are declared globally) replace formal parameters a, b, c, d when the procedure is called. The values of x, y, z, and q must be pushed onto a stack (using a series of LOAD and STORE instructions). Suppose that when it is called, procedure function 1 pushes x and y onto the stack, but then is interrupted by a higher-priority process before z and q can be pushed onto the stack. The interrupting process may alter the values of x, y, z, and q, and then complete. When function 1 resumes, the new values of z and q are pushed onto the stack along with the old value of x and y—a potentially catastrophic situation if x, y, z, and q need to be correlated (time-relative). Thus, to prevent this occurrence, interrupts are disabled during parameter passing. ■

Global variables, although they introduce no subtle timing problems, can be dangerous in that access to such variables may be made by unauthorized modules, thus introducing bugs that are devilishly hard to find. For example, in FORTRAN, mismatched COMMON overlays are notoriously elusive. For these and other reasons, overuse of global variables is to be avoided (see [165]).

The choice of parameter-passing techniques is difficult, but the rule of thumb is to use parameter lists as long as timing is not affected unacceptably (although this is difficult to predict). Global passing should be used only when timing warrants it, and it should be clearly documented. The final system usually employs all parameter-passing techniques in some combination, reflecting the tradeoffs between good software engineering technique and the realities of timing constraints.

3.1.2 Recursion

Many programming languages provide a mechanism, called *recursion*, whereby a procedure can be self-referential; that is, it can call itself. Because of the Recursion Theorem, all functions on integers can be written as recursive procedures. The following example illustrates a recursive procedure.

■ EXAMPLE 3.4

This Pascal procedure calculates the greatest common divisor of two positive integers using Euclid's algorithm.

```
procedure gcd(x, y : integer);    {recursive procedure}

begin
   if (y = 0) then               {GCD found}
     writeln(x)
   else
     gcd(y,(x mod y))            {recursive step}
end;
```

■

Although recursion is elegant, its adverse impact on real-time perform-ance cannot be overemphasized. Procedure calls require the allocation of storage on one or more stacks for the passing of parameters and for storage of local variables. The execution time needed for the allocation and deallocation, and for the storage of those parameters and local variables, can be ill-afforded. In addition, recursion necessitates the use of a large number of costly memory indirect and register indirect instructions. Moreover, the use of recursion often makes it impossible to determine the size of run-time memory requirements. Finally, re-entrant code often includes critical regions that must be protected by semaphores (see Chapter 11). Thus, iterative techniques such as loops must be used in those languages that do not support recursion, and when real-time performance is crucial.

This is not to suggest that recursion is a detriment to a language; on the contrary, it promotes a top-down and structured style. However, in real-time systems this benefit may be offset by the deleterious impact on performance.

In retrospect, it would be nice if the compiler would allow the programmer to write recursive routines, so that he or she could take advantage of the more elegant representation, and then let the translation process map the code into either recursive or iterative form in order to optimize performance. Some compilers may do this, although the author is unaware of any.

3.1.2.1 Re-entrant Procedures   Languages that allow recursion do so by supporting re-entrant procedures. A *re-entrant procedure* can be used by several concurrently running tasks in a multitasking system.

Languages such as Ada, C, Modula-2, and Pascal provide for re-entrant code and thus recursion, whereas some older versions of FORTRAN compilers and BASIC interpreters do not.

In the absence of re-entrancy, awkward schemes are sometimes needed to allow several processes to share code. For example, many older FORTRAN IV compilers, which did not support re-entrancy, needed several versions of the same SUBROUTINE, with different names, which could only be called by one task. For example, two SUBROUTINES for matrix multiplication called MULT1 and MULT2, identical in all but name, would be needed to allow two different tasks to perform matrix multiplication.

3.1.3 Dynamic Allocation

The ability to dynamically allocate memory is important in the construction and maintenance of stacks needed by the real-time operating system. Although dynamic allocation is time-consuming, it is necessary. Languages that do not allow dynamic allocation of memory require a stack of fixed size. Although it is faster to maintain a fixed size stack, flexibility is sacrificed, and the maximum size of the stack must be known *a priori*.

Linked lists, trees, heaps, and other dynamic data structures used in real-time applications can benefit from the clarity and economy of memory introduced by dynamic allocation—at the expense of speed, of course.

For example, the NEW statement in Pascal and the malloc() procedure found in C are used to dynamically allocate storage. (As a language, C does not really support dynamic allocation.) The malloc() library function call invokes an operating system call that manages memory requests.) There are, of course, corresponding constructs (DISPOSE in Pascal, and free() in C) to de-allocate storage.

Finally, Ada and Modula-2 have dynamic allocation facilities, whereas BASIC and most versions of FORTRAN generally do not.

3.1.4 Typing

The notion of typing was introduced by ALGOL-60 and has been implemented in most modern languages. Typed languages require that each variable and constant be of a specific type (e.g., integer, real, character, etc.) and that it be declared as such before use. Strongly typed languages prohibit the mixing of different types in operations and assignments.

3.1.4.1 Advantages of Strong Typing   Strongly typed languages force the programmer to be precise about the way data are to be handled. In addition, strong typing can prevent unwanted or unnoticed molestation of data through truncation or rounding.

Ada, Pascal, Modula-2, and C all have some level of type checking. While FORTRAN has the notion of a typed variable, it is not strongly typed, which can lead to problems. To illustrate how implicit variable typing in FORTRAN can lead to problems, consider the following:

■ EXAMPLE 3.5

In FORTRAN the following loop construct uses variable I as a loop index to execute the loop body five times. The statement "20 CONTINUE" marks the end of the loop body. There is an error, however, in that there is a period instead of the desired comma between the 1 and the 5

```
        DO 20 I = 1.5

            .

            .

            .

    20  CONTINUE
```

Since FORTRAN generally ignores spaces, and undeclared variables starting with the letter "D" are assumed to be REAL, the replacement of "," by "." causes this statement to be interpreted as

```
    DO20I=1.5
```

where DO20I is a REAL variable. The problem is further compounded in that the matching statement

```
    20  CONTINUE
```

is not seen to be extraneous, a situation that could not happen in C or Pascal.   ■

This scenario caused the loss of a U.S. space satellite in the 1970s.

3.1.4.2 Disadvantages of Weak Typing   Languages such as C which are typed, but do not prohibit mixing of types in operations, can cause rounding and truncation problems. In addition, C generally performs calculation at the type that has the highest storage complexity. That is, it "promotes" variables to the highest type necessary. This can generate "unseen" and time-consuming instructions to perform the promotion.

■ EXAMPLE 3.6

The following C-code fragment illustrates automatic promotion and demotion of variable types. Variable *i* is promoted to type "float" and the multiplication is performed. The result is then demoted to type "int" before assignment to variable *j*.

```
int i,j;
float k,l,m;
   .
   .
j = i=*k=+m;                                                    ■
```

Here the variable *i* will be promoted to a float type (real), and then the multiplication and addition will take place. Afterward, the result will be truncated and stored in *j*.

Explicit type conversion using casting should always be used in C.

■ EXAMPLE 3.7

In Example 3.6, the line

$$j = i * k + m$$

should be replaced with

$$j = (int)((float)i * k + m)$$

This explicitly illustrates what was happening surreptitiously before.   ■

In addition, if constants and variables are not properly declared, unnecessary hidden promotion instructions will be generated. For example, consider the following:

■ EXAMPLE 3.8

This Pascal program fragment has two real variables but a constant of type integer. Some compilers will not convert the constant to real at compile-time, creating the need for conversion from integer to real at run-time.

```
var
    x,y: Real;
     .
     .
x := y+60;
```

The line x := y + 60; should be replaced with

$$x := y + 60.0$$

to prevent an unwanted run-time promotion of the constant.   ■

The same can happen for variables:

■ **EXAMPLE 3.9**

Consider the C-code fragment.

```
float x,y;
int   z;
  .
  .
  .
x = y+z;
```

Variable *z* is promoted to type float. The LOAD and "convert-to-float" instructions generated by the compiler probably take longer than the FLOAD (floating variable LOAD). This kind of waste is discouraged in real-time systems. If *z* cannot be of type float, it should be explicitly cast; that is, use

$$x = y + (\text{float})z$$ ■

Whereas Pascal discourages mixed-type usage more vigorously than C, both Ada and Modula-2 completely prohibit mixed-type calculations.

3.1.5 Exception Handling

Certain languages provide facilities for dealing with errors or other anomaly conditions that arise during program execution. Such situations are called *exceptions* [79]. During run-time, when an exception occurs, a certain code is invoked to handle it. Such code is called an *exception handler.*

Conditions such as divide-by-zero errors, floating point operations in certain CPUs, and the like, are normally considered exceptions but are handled in microcode. The ability to define and handle exceptional conditions at the high-order language level distinguishes true exception handling.

Of all the languages discussed in this chapter, Ada has the most explicit exception-handling facility. ANSI-C provides some exception-handling capability through the use of signals.

Finally, exception handling can often be implemented in languages such as C, Pascal, and Modula-2 as a user-definable library when permitted by the compiler.

3.1.6 Abstract Data Typing

The ability to represent abstract ideas succinctly is as important to computer languages as it is to human ones. Certain languages provide facilities for the abstract representation of entities that cannot be handled by simple numbers. Languages with such a capability tend to make program design easier and clearer to an outside observer.

Abstract data typing includes the ability to represent and manipulate data types that are not a standard type supported by the language—for example, the complex data type defined in Example 3.13 and the stack data type described later in Example 4.3. Language features such as the ability to compile modules separately, and explicit parameter passing (input, output, or both), are particularly useful in developing abstract data types. Hence, Ada and Modula-2 provide the most explicit abstract data typing facilities, although this technique can be employed in most of the other languages except BASIC.

To a lesser extent, *enumerated types* and *type definition* provide methods for implementing data abstraction. Enumerated types are illustrated in Example 3.10, while type definition is illustrated in Example 3.11. Languages such as Ada, Pascal, ANSI-C, and Modula-2 provide enumerated data types to handle such entities.

■ EXAMPLE 3.10
Use of enumeration types in Ada:

```
type DAY is (MON, TUE, WED, THU, FRI, SAT, SUN);
type VOLTAGE is delta 0.01 range 0.0 .. 5.0;
type COLOR is (RED, GREEN, BLUE);
```

The specification of enumerated data types is similar in Pascal and Modula-2. In ANSI-C there is no equivalent for the VOLTAGE type, but the others would be

```
enum DAY {MON, TUE, WED, THU, FRI, SAT, SUN};
enum COLOR {RED, GREEN, BLUE};                                    ■
```

■ EXAMPLE 3.11
Use of type definition in C:

```
/* defines a data type "string" as 16 characters */
typedef char string[16];
```

The specification of type definition is similar in Pascal, Ada, and Modula-2.   ■

One drawback of these enumerated data types is that they only permit the grouping of similar kinds of data. Ada, C, Pascal, and Modula-2, however, all provide a mechanism for organizing a collection of dissimilar data types into a single data type. In Ada, Modula-2, and Pascal these are called record types, whereas in C this data type is called a structure. Records and structures provide a kind of data abstraction that is useful in writing clear programs.

■ EXAMPLE 3.12
In Modula-2 a record type for a personnel record could be

```
Employee = RECORD
           firstName : Array [0..23] of CHAR;
           lastName  : Array [0..23] of CHAR;
           badgeno   : CARDINAL;
       END
```

The specification of such a record is quite similar in Ada and Pascal. In C it would look like

```
struct Employee {
        char            firstname[23];
        char            lastname[23];
        unsigned int badgeno;
        }
```
■

The use of an abstract data type does not improve real-time performance of the system. In fact, it may degrade performance depending on the internal representation format of the data type involved.

3.1.6.1 Object-Oriented Programming

Those languages that provide constructs encouraging a high degree of information hiding and data abstraction are called *object-oriented*. These languages include C++, the interpreted Smalltalk, an object-oriented version of Ada, Ada++ [46], and the real-time language DRAGOON [37].

Object-oriented languages provide many of the features necessary to encourage good software engineering technique. Formally, object-oriented programming languages support

■ Abstraction data types
■ Inheritance
■ Polymorphism.

We have already discussed abstract data types. Object *inheritance* allows the programmer to define new objects in terms of other objects so that the new objects can inherit the others' characteristics. For example, an object of type "dog" would have at least the same characteristics as an object of type "animals." Finally, function *polymorphism* allows the programmer to create a single function that operates on different objects depending on the type of object involved.

Objects are an effective way to manage system complexity, as they provide a natural environment for encapsulation, which is similar to information hiding. In encapsulation, a class of objects and the operations that can be performed on them (called *methods*) are enclosed or encapsulated into packages called *class definitions*. An object can utilize another object's encapsulated data only by sending a message to that object with the name of the method to apply.

For example, consider the problem of sorting objects. We might have a method for sorting an object class of integers in ascending order. For a class of people, we might sort them by height. For a class of objects that have an attribute of color, we might sort them by color according to the rainbow. Because these objects have similarly named methods with different implementations, if another object sends a message to sort one of these objects, the run-time code must resolve which method to apply dynamically—with significant execution time penalty.

For example, in one study, code written in objective-c, another object-oriented variant of C, was 43% slower than code written in conventional C [26]. In addition, programs written in the (interpreted) language Smalltalk, are known to be approximately 5 to 10 times slower than those written in conventional C [73].

The execution time penalty in object-oriented languages may be due, in part, to their relative immaturity. But in compiled object-oriented languages, it seems clear that the requirements for late binding (run-time as opposed to link-time) necessitated by function polymorphism and inheritance are considerable delay factors.

In both interpreted and compiled object-oriented languages, additional delays result from automatic storage management (including garbage collection—see Chapter 8) needed by objects over their lifetime. For example, Ingalls [73] mentions that for programs written in Smalltalk, 10% of the execution time is spent in automatic storage management.

Nevertheless, the promise of object-oriented programming languages in real-time applications lies in clearer design and better maintainability. The shortcomings of object-oriented languages in real-time will be overcome. For example, hybrid languages that reduce the amount of late binding required are already being used [27], and better methods for automatic storage management (as well as faster computers) will make the use of even interpreted object-oriented languages like Smalltalk viable for use in real-time. One thing is certain—we can look forward to the increased use of object-oriented languages in real-time.

3.1.7 Modularity

Parnas [125] presents a set of criteria that can be used in partitioning software systems into modules in a way that both clearly defines intermodule communication and prevents unwanted intermodule interference. From a software engineering perspective, modular software is highly desirable. But there is a price to pay in the resultant overhead associated with procedure calls. This affects real-time performance adversely and should be considered in the system design.

The most important concept in defining modularity is the ability to perform *information hiding*. We will discuss this concept further in Chapter 4. However, note that it is of the utmost importance that code modules be treated as "black boxes," with the inner workings of the module invisible to the user, but with the interface to the module clearly defined. Certain languages have constructs designed to promote such techniques, while others do not. For example, the concept of the MODULE is implicit in the language Modula-2. A MODULE consists of a set of clearly defined input and output parameters, local, invisible variables, and a series of procedures.

In Ada the notion of a *package* exquisitely embodies the concept of Parnas information hiding. The package consists of a package specification and declarations, which include its *public* or visible interface, and its *private* or invisible parts. In addition the package body, which has additional externally invisible components, contains the working code of the package. Packages are separately compilable entities, which further enhances their application as black boxes.

■ **EXAMPLE 3.13**

This Ada package defines a data type called "complex" and a set of operations to be performed on it. Notice that a complete set of binary, unary, and relational operations must be defined.

```
package COMPLEX_NUMBERS is

--
-- define complex data type
--

   type COMPLEX is
     record
        REAL_PART : FLOAT :=0.0;
        IMAG_PART : FLOAT :=0.0;
     end record;

   function EQUAL (X,Y : COMPLEX) return BOOLEAN;
   function "+"   (X,Y : COMPLEX) return COMPLEX;
   function "-"   (X,Y : COMPLEX) return COMPLEX;
   function "*"   (X,Y : COMPLEX) return COMPLEX;
   function "/"   (X,Y : COMPLEX) return COMPLEX;
end;

--
-- define operations on data type
--
package body COMPLEX_NUMBERS is
   function EQUAL(X,Y : COMPLEX) return BOOLEAN is
     begin
       if (X.REAL_PART = Y.REAL_PART) and (X.IMAG_PART =
            Y.IMAG_PART) then
            return TRUE;
       else
            return FALSE;
       end if;
     end EQUAL;

   function "+" (X,Y : COMPLEX) return COMPLEX is
     begin
       return (REAL_PART => X.REAL_PART+Y.REAL_PART,
            IMAG_PART => X.IMAG_PART+Y.IMAG_PART);
     end "+";
```

```
function "-" (X,Y : COMPLEX) return COMPLEX is
  begin
    return (REAL_PART => X.REAL_PART - Y.REAL_PART,
            IMAG_PART => X.IMAG_PART - Y.IMAG_PART);
  end "-";

function "*" (X,Y : COMPLEX) return COMPLEX is
  begin
    return (REAL_PART => (X.REAL_PART * Y.REAL_PART)
    - (X.IMAG_PART * Y.IMAG_PART),
            IMAG_PART => (X.IMAG_PART * Y.REAL_PART)
    + (X.REAL_PART * Y.IMAG_PART));
  end "*";

function "/" (X,Y : COMPLEX) return COMPLEX is
  begin
    return (REAL_PART => ((X.REAL_PART * Y.REAL_PART)
    + (X.IMAG_PART * Y.IMAG_PART))/((Y.REAL_PART *
      Y.REAL_PART) + (Y.IMAG_PART * Y.IMAG_PART)),
            IMAG_PART => ((X.IMAG_PART * Y.REAL_PART)
    - (X.REAL_PART * Y.IMAG_PART))/((Y.REAL_PART *
      Y.REAL_PART) + (Y.IMAG_PART * Y.IMAG_PART));
  end "/";
```

■

Many versions of Pascal support a separately compiled module called a UNIT. Similarly, FORTRAN provides the SUBROUTINE and separate compilation of source files. These language features can be used to achieve modularity and to design abstract data types.

The C language also provides for separately compiled modules and other features that promote a rigorous top-down design approach, leading to a good modular design. Finally, in BASIC no provision is made for any kind of modular construction other than the GOSUB statement, which is a simple change of flow-of-control. There is no way to pass parameters in BASIC.

3.2 SURVEY OF COMMONLY USED PROGRAMMING LANGUAGES

This section summarizes the key features of programming languages that have been widely used in the development of real-time software. In particular, it focuses on those language features just discussed. The highlights of this discussion are summarized in Table 3.1.

TABLE 3.1   Feature Comparison of Various Languages

Language	Call-by-Value	Call-by-Reference	Dynamic Allocation	Strong Typing	Type Interrupt	Exception Handling	Enumerated Type	Modularity	Re-entrant Code
Ada	y	y	y	y	y	y	y	y	y
BASIC	n/a	n/a	n	n	n	n	n	n	n
C	y	y*	y	n	n	y	y	y	y
FORTRAN	n	y	n	n	n	n	n	n	n
Modula-2	y	y	y	y	y	n	y	y	y
Pascal	y	y	y	y	n	n	y	y	y

 * Simulated.

3.2.1 BASIC

The BASIC programming language was introduced at Dartmouth College in the mid-1960s to introduce students to computers via an easy-to-learn, interactive language. BASIC was originally designed as an interpreted language. In interpreted languages, the source code is not compiled; rather, it is a set of directives to another program, the *interpreter*, which is constantly running. Interpreted languages can perform syntax checking as the program is typed in, and thus they tend to help the programmer avoid syntactical errors. Interpreted languages are slow, however—often a thousand times (or more) slower than an equivalent compiled language.

Thus, in its interpreted form, BASIC is wholly unsuited to real-time systems. And although there are compiled versions of BASIC which are much faster, these are also undesirable. BASIC is a weakly typed language, with little or no provisions for modular design, exception handling, or abstract data typing. All variables are global in nature and there is no mechanism for passing parameters. In fact, the language encourages the use of the GOTO statement (which is considered harmful [165]), and there is no support for re-entrant code or construct suitable for building interrupt handlers. Finally, it is unstandardized.

3.2.2 FORTRAN

The FORTRAN language is the oldest high-order language extant (developed circa 1957). Because in its earlier versions it lacked recursion and dynamic allocation facilities, real-time systems written in this language typically included a large portion of assembly language code to handle interrupts, scheduling, and low-level I/O (communication with external devices through the use of memory-mapped I/O, DMA, and I/O instructions). Later versions of the language included such features as re-entrant code, but even today, a FORTRAN solution requires some percentage of assembly language code to accompany it.

NOTE 3.2   FORTRAN was developed in an era when compilers were suspect, and efficient code was essential to wringing performance out of small, slow machines. As a result, the language constructs were selected for efficiency, and early FORTRAN code generators were unusually so.

To its detriment, FORTRAN is weakly typed, but because of the SUBROUTINE construct and the IF-THEN-ELSE construct introduced in later versions, it can be used to design highly structured code. FORTRAN has no built-in exception handling or abstract data types. FORTRAN is still used to write real-time systems in scientific, avionics, and process-control applications. Many versions of the FORTRAN language are available, including FORTRAN IV, FORTRAN 77, and the latest ISO standard FORTRAN 90.

3.2.3 C

The C programming language, invented around 1971, is a good language for "low-level" programming. That is, machine-related objects like characters, bytes, bits, and addresses can be handled directly through the language. These entities must be manipulated to control interrupt controllers, CPU registers, and other hardware needed by a real-time system.

Until recently the language was not standardized, and the text written by Kernighan and Ritchie [80]—the inventors of the language—was the *de facto* standard. ANSI-C has since been defined, however, with resultant benefits.

C provides for global variables and call-by-value. Call-by-reference can be simulated through the use of pointer types. The language is inherently modular and recursive, and provides for dynamic memory allocation through library routines and pointer types.

3.2.3.1 Special Variable Types   C also provides special variable types such as register, volatile, static, and constant, which allow for control of code generation at the high-order language level. For example, declaring a variable as a register type indicates that it will be used frequently. This encourages the compiler to place such a declared variable in a register, which often results in smaller and faster programs.

Variables declared as type volatile are not optimized by the compiler. This is useful in handling memory-mapped I/O and other instances where the code should not be optimized.

■ EXAMPLE 3.14
In the following C-code fragment, the low-order bit of memory-mapped I/O location outport is strobed.

```
outport = 1;
outport = 0;
outport = 1;
```

You can prevent the compiler from optimizing this ostensibly redundant code by declaring outport as type volatile.   ■

Type static variables can be used to provide private communication between modules. The following example demonstrates the use of static variables as well as the construction of an abstract data type in C.

■ EXAMPLE 3.15

The following set of modules, stored in the same source file, can be used to implement the abstract notion of a stack. The use of the static data type limits access to, and hides the implementation of, the stack top and the stack itself within this set of modules. Furthermore, their value upon exiting is preserved upon exiting any one of these routines. Interface to the stack from other routines is only through the PUSH, POP, and init routines.

```
#define MAXSIZE 1000         /* arbitrary maximum stack size */

static int top;
static char stack[MAXSIZE]; /* the stack itself            */

void init()
{
    top=0;                   /* reset to bottom of stack    */
}

int pop(void)
{
  int temp;
  temp=stack[top];           /* remove data from stack      */
  top--;                     /* decrement top pointer       */
  return(temp);
}

void push(int data)
{
  top++;                     /* increment top pointer       */
  stack[top]=data;           /* push data onto stack        */
}                                                                        ■
```

Note that stack underflow and overflow are not treated; they are left as an exercise.

Finally, variables declared as type constant can be forced into the ROM area of memory at link time. This is particularly useful in lining up the logical memory map with the physical hardware memory map.

3.2.3.2 Exception Handling   The C language provides for exception handling through the use of *signals* which are discussed in Chapter 7. In addition, two other mechanisms, *setjmp* and *longjmp*, are provided to allow a procedure to return quickly from a deep level of nesting, a useful feature in procedures requiring an abort. The setjmp procedure call, which is really a macro (but often implemented as a function), saves environment information that can be used by a subsequent longjmp library function call. The longjmp call restores the program to the state at the time of the last setjmp call. Procedure process is called to perform some processing and error checking. If an error is detected, a longjmp is performed which changes the flow of execution directly to the first statement after

---

■ **EXAMPLE 3.16**

Consider the following C program which performs a generic process.

```
#include <signal.h>          /* contains setjmp and longjmp prototypes */

typedef long jmp/buf[16];     /* define environment type */
jmp_buf env;                  /* holds environment */

main()
{
    ...                       /* do some processing */

    if (setjmp(env)== 0)      /* return from longjmp or normal return? */
        process();            /* perform normal processing */
    else
        abort_process();      /* returned via longjmp with error */
}

void process()
{
        int value;            /* return value to setjmp */

        ...                   /* do some processing*      /

        if (no_error)         /* error occurred? *        /

            ...               /* no error -- normal processing =*/
        else
            longjmp(env,value)/; /* error, abort             */

}
```

■

---

the last setjmp—the abort process procedure in main. The processing done in procedure process prior to the abort is lost (unless global variables were changed).

3.2.3.3 Disadvantages of C   To its detriment, C is weakly typed, although the ANSI-C version has somewhat stronger typing. ANSI-C has added the concept of enumeration types, but abstract data types are better handled by C++.

Overall, however, the C language is good for real-time programming because it provides for structure and flexibility without complex language restrictions.

3.2.4 C++

C++ is an object-oriented programming language that was originally implemented as a macro-extension of C. Today, C++ stands by itself as a separately compiled language, although strictly speaking, C++ compilers should accept straight C code.

C++ exhibits all three characteristics of an object-oriented language. It promotes better software engineering practice through encapsulation and better abstraction mechanisms than C. Significantly, more real-time systems are being constructed in C++, and many practitioners are asking, "Should I implement the system in C or C++?" My answer to them is always "it depends." Choosing C in lieu of C++ in real-time embedded applications is, roughly speaking, a tradeoff between a "lean and mean" C program that will be faster and easier to predict but harder to maintain and a C++ program that will be slower and unpredictable but potentially easier to maintain. I say "potentially" because it remains unproven whether many of the advantages of C++ (namely, easier maintainability) are really there.

3.2.5 Pascal

Pascal was designed in 1968 by Niklaus Wirth as a teaching tool—he never intended to implement it as a language for professional or production use. The first functional compiler was introduced around 1971. Pascal is elegant in its simplicity, and there exists a widely accepted (but often violated) ANSI/IEEE standard. Pascal includes such features as strong typing (although not strong enough), recursion, dynamic data structures through pointer types, enumerated types for data abstraction, and an enforced high degree of modularity.

Nevertheless, Kernighan [79] has developed strong arguments against the use of Pascal for writing "real" programs. Since his points are so compelling, we shall quote them directly.

1. Since the size of an array is part of its type, it is not possible to write general-purpose routines—that is, to deal with arrays of different sizes. In particular, string handling is very difficult.

2. The lack of static variables, initialization, and a way to communicate nonhierarchically combine to destroy the "locality" of a program—variables require much more scope than they ought to.

3. The one-pass nature of the language forces procedures and functions to be presented in an unnatural order; the enforced separation of various declarations scatters program components that logically belong together.

4. The lack of separate compilation impedes the development of large programs and makes the use of libraries impossible.

5. The order of logical expression evaluation cannot be controlled, which leads to convoluted code and extraneous variables.

6. The case statement is emasculated because there is no default clause.

7. The standard I/O is defective. There is no sensible provision for dealing with files or program arguments as part of the standard language, and no extension mechanism.

8. The language lacks most of the tools needed for assembling large programs, most notably file inclusion.

9. There is no escape. The language is inadequate but circumscribed, because there is no way to escape its limitations. There are no casts to disable type-checking when necessary. There is no way to replace the defective run-time environment with a sensible one, unless one controls the compiler that defines the "standard procedures." The language is closed.

The author tends to agree with this assessment and would add that Pascal generally does not provide interrupt function types, which complicates the writing of interrupt handling routines. The use of the semicolon as a statement separator rather than a statement terminator leads to confusion and prolongs the coding process. Although various implementations of the language bypass some of these problems, this is not true for all. In general, Pascal is not recommended as a real-time language.

3.2.6 Modula-2

In 1975 Niklaus Wirth developed a language specifically for multiprogramming systems—Modula. In 1977 as part of a research project to develop computer hardware and software specifications simultaneously, Wirth developed Modula-2, a language with features similar to both Pascal and Modula.

Modula-2 includes all aspects of Pascal and extends the language with the concept of a module or program package. A *module* is divided into a definition part and an implementation part, and is crucial to a multitasking system. In addition, Modula-2 has the following language features:

1. The concept of a *process* or thread-of-execution as the key to multitasking facilities.
2. Low-level facilities such as an interrupt procedure type, which makes it possible to interact directly with the underlying hardware.
3. A procedure type that makes it possible to assign variables dynamically.
4. Clearly defined interfaces between modules in terms of the modules' import lists.

In addition, many of the Pascal features listed as detrimental in the previous section have been eliminated.

Because of its multitasking orientation, Modula-2 lends itself well to implementation in real-time systems.

3.2.7 Ada

In the late 1970s, Department of Defense[1] analysts became concerned that large quantities of expensive software were being produced in several different languages, often for the same purpose. In order to reduce costs and to standardize the language in which software was developed, a bidding process was created to select the appropriate language for the 1980s and beyond.

After a rigorous and competitive selection process, the Ada language was born. Designed specifically for real-time embedded applications, it is truly a language of consensus. This language has been mandated as the language of choice for all DoD software. But because of the early lack of good compilers, too few Ada programmers, difficulty of program construction, and the inefficiency of the language, less software has been written in Ada than had been hoped.

The stated foci of the Ada language were [7]

1. Program reliability and maintenance.
2. Programming as a human activity.
3. Program efficiency.

The first of these considerations is addressed through the use of extensive compile-time type checking. This minimizes run-time errors and error checking, which take time (although Ada does include provisions for run-time error checking through, for example, range checks). In addition, the concept of separately compilable modules, packages, or units provides for easy program development and maintenance by large teams of programmers, and an explicit exception handling capability provides for robust error recovery. Finally, strict type checking and enforcement prevents unwanted or undesirable type conversions from occurring.

---

[1] DoD is the largest single purchaser of software in the world.

The human aspect of programming is treated in the form of abstract data types as well as the programming style enforced by the language. This notion led to the decision that program readability would be emphasized over ease of program construction. Although the language was meant to be compact in its syntax, the designers have arguably failed in this intent.

Program efficiency has been one of the most debated aspects of the Ada language. Early compilers for the language were difficult to write and generated poor code (in terms of execution time). Newer compilers have been more readily produced but have also been criticized for their real-time performance. One feature of the Ada language that does portend efficient operation is the Ada multitasking/multiprocessing model which allows modules to be written directly for independent tasks/processors. This greatly reduces development effort and increases efficiency in multiprocessing systems. Of the other languages discussed, only Modula-2 has a similar facility.

As mentioned, Ada is a strongly typed language, provides for dynamic allocation and recursion, has an explicit exception handling capability, abstract data types, low-level programming features, and separate compilation facilities. In addition, it has an explicit interrupt type used in the construction of interrupt handlers. These features seem to make Ada an exceptional choice for a real-time language, which it was intended to be. However, the sheer bulk of the language has rendered it less efficient than it would have to be for use in some applications.

3.2.8 Ada 95

Although the original Ada language (now casually referred to as Ada 83) was intended specifically for embedded real-time systems, as noted it has experienced significant problems. Systems builders have typically found the language to be too bulky and inefficient. Moreover, significant problems were found when trying to implement multitasking using the limited tools supplied by the language, such as the roundly criticized rendezvous mechanism. This construct, intended to provide synchronization, has been likened to "an agreement to meet with a friend but not when nor where." Limited control of priorities leads to priority inversions (discussed later). The uncertainty of these and other mechanisms has made the language not just "slow" but, more importantly, unpredictable.

The programming language community has long been aware of the problems with Ada, and practically since the first delivery of an Ada 83 compiler, has been meeting regularly to discuss a new version of the language. Referred to as Ada 9X during its development, the new version has frozen language changes. The new language, now called Ada 95, is the first internationally standardized object-oriented programming language. It revises and supersedes the 1983 standard.

Some of the new tasking features of the language are

- A pragma `Task_Dispatching_Policy` that controls how tasks are dispatched.
- A pragma `Locking_Policy` that controls the interaction between task scheduling.
- A pragma `Queuing_Policy` that controls the queuing policy of task/resource entry queues. First-In-First-Out and priority queuing policies are available.

These three pragmas were clearly designed to resolve some of the uncertainty in scheduling, resource contention, and synchronization.

Other expansions of the language were intended to make Ada 95 an object-oriented language. These include:

- Tagged types
- Packages
- Protected units.

Proper use of these constructs permits the construction of objects that exhibit the three characteristics of object-oriented languages. Discussion of this aspect of Ada 95, however, is beyond the scope of the text. For more information, see [116].

Working versions of Ada 95 are becoming widely available. For additional information on the use of Ada 95 in real-time systems, see [15]. For up-to-the-minute information and additional details on other features of Ada 95, check the Internet Ada user groups for one of the many free tutorials.

3.2.9 Assembly Languages

In Chapter 2 we discussed the variety of assembly languages that depend on the underlying computer architecture. Assembly language, though lacking most of the features discussed for the high-level languages, does have certain advantages in that it provides more direct control of the computer hardware. Unfortunately, because of its unstructured nature and because it varies widely from machine to machine, coding in assembly language is usually difficult to learn, tedious, and error prone. The resulting code is also unportable.

Until recently, most assembly language programmers could generate code that was more efficient than the code generated by a compiler. But with improvements in optimizing compilers, probably only the very best assembly language programmers can generate code that is faster and more compact than the best compilers. Thus, the need to write assembly code exists only in cases where the compiler does not support certain macroinstructions, or when the timing constraints are so tight that hand-tuning is needed to produce optimal code.

In any case, a system will likely employ a 90/10 solution—that is, 90% of the code will be written in the high-order language, while the rest is written in assembly language.

NOTE 3.3   The 90/10 solution theme, which is also known as the Pareto Principle, has many variations. One states that 90% of a software project takes 50% of the time, whereas the other 10% also takes 50% of the time. Another states that 10% of the code executes 90% of the time.

In cases where complex prologues and epilogues are needed to prepare an assembly language program, often a shell of the program is written in the high-order language and compiled to an assembly file, which is then massaged to obtain the desired effect. Some languages such as Ada and versions of Pascal provide a *pragma* pseudo-op which allows for assembly code to be placed in-line with the high-order language code.

In summary, assembly language programming should be limited to use in very tight timing situations or in controlling hardware features that are not supported by the compiler. In general, it should be discouraged.

3.3 CODE GENERATION

The way in which the compiler will map your code into machine language is as important as the code you write yourself. The output of the compiler can be affected by optimization for speed, memory and register usage, jumps, and so on, which can lead to inefficient code, timing problems, or critical regions. Thus real-time programmers must be masters of their compilers. That is, at all times you must know what assembly language code will be output for a given high-order language statement.

3.3.1 Know Your Compiler

Understanding the mapping between high-order language input and assembly language output for your compiler is essential in generating code that is optimal in either execution time or memory requirements. The easiest and most reliable way to learn about your compiler is to run a series of tests on specific language constructs.

For example, in many C and Pascal compilers the case statement is efficient only if more than three cases are to be compared— otherwise nested if statements should be used. Sometimes the code generated for a case statement can be quite convoluted—for example, a jump table with an offset table. The code then performs an indirect jump through a register, offset by the table value. This can be time-consuming.

We have already mentioned that procedure calls cost time; that is, overhead involved in the passing of parameters via the stack. You should determine whether your compiler passes the parameters by byte or by word.

Good compilers in any language should provide optimization of the assembly language code output. Some of these techniques are discussed in Chapter 9.

■ **EXAMPLE 3.17**

Consider the following two mixed listings consisting of a C-code fragment and the compiler output:

```
int i = 4;
   LOAD  R1,4  load register 1 with 4
   STORE R1,i  store register 1 into symbolic location i

int i = 4;
   STORE 4,i   store 4 into symbolic location i
```

The first listing illustrates a compiler that registerizes the variable for potential reuse. While this method initially generates two instructions, in the long run it may be more effective. If, however, the instruction occurs inside a tight loop or during a critical time period, the second method illustrated may be favorable.   ■

3.4 Schedualability Analysis

This chapter focused on those language features that minimize the final code execution time that lend themselves to performance prediction. The compile-time prediction of execution time performance is known as *schedualability analysis*. In the design of modern real-time languages, the emphasis is on eliminating those constructs that render the language nonanalyzable. For example, the following common language constructs are taboo:

■ Unbounded recursion
■ While loops
■ Interrupts

Most so-called real-time languages must eliminate all of these constructs.

3.5 EXERCISES

1. Why is BASIC a bad language for real-time design?
2. Why is Modula-2 a good language for real-time design?
3. Ada is designed for embedded hard real-time applications and is intended to support static priority scheduling of tasks. The definition of Ada tasking, however, allows a high-priority task to wait for a low-priority task for an unpredictable duration. Discuss potential problems with this scenario.
4. Rewrite Euclid's algorithm shown in Example 3.4 in
   (a) Ada using recursion.
   (b) Modula-2 using recursion.
   (c) C using recursion.
   (d) FORTRAN.

(e) BASIC.

(f) Assembly language for a 2-address machine without recursion.

(g) C++.

5. In one of the languages mentioned in this chapter (except BASIC), write a short program that accepts an integer $5 \geq x \geq 1$ and prints out the English word for that number (e.g., "one"). Is it better to use nested if-then statements or a case statement? To answer this question, you must examine the assembly output from the compiler.

6. Do the same as above but accept a number $x \in \{0,11,101,1001\}$. Is it better to use nested if-then statements or a case statement here? Explain what is happening in the assembly language code that is generated.

7. Rewrite the enumerated type in Example 3.10 in
   (a) Pascal
   (b) Modula-2
   (c) C++

8. Rewrite the complex arithmetic package described in Example 3.13 as
   (a) A Modula-2 module.
   (b) As a series of C procedures.
   (c) As a Pascal UNIT.
   (d) As a set of GOSUB commands in BASIC.
   (e) C++.

9. Examine the assembly language code generated by each of the programs in the previous problem. Which seems to generate the least number of assembly language instructions?

10. Rewrite the stack abstract data type in Example 3.15 to handle stack underflow and overflow.

11. Which of the languages discussed in this chapter provide for some sort of GOTO statement? Does the GOTO statement affect real-time performance? If so, how?

12. Some software engineers (including the author) believe there is an apparent conflict between good software engineering techniques and real-time performance. Consider the relative merits of recursive program design versus iterative techniques, and the use of global variables versus parameter lists. Using these topics and an appropriate programming language for examples, compare and contrast real-time performance versus good software engineering practices as you understand them.

4

The Software
Life Cycle

KEY POINTS OF THE CHAPTER

1. A proper software engineering framework is essential for developing reliability, maintainability, and cost-effective real-time software.

2. Inherent tradeoffs exist between good software engineering practice and real-time performance.

3. Information hiding should be used in the design of reliable, understandable, and maintainable real-time systems.

4. IEEE Std 830 provides a reasonable methodology for software specification.

5. DOD-STD-2167A provides a rigorous (if not strict) framework for the development of software.

6. There are numerous other useful standards for conduct during the software life cycle.

An engineering approach to the specification, design, construction, testing, and maintenance of software is essential for maximizing the reliability and maintainability of the system as well as for reducing life-cycle costs. This chapter looks at one formal model for the software life cycle and discusses some of the activities that occur within it.

Although we discuss several documents that must be prepared during the software life cycle, detailed discussion is prohibited in the interests of brevity. The standard set of guidelines for the development of defense-related software and documentation in a strictly controlled environment is DOD-STD-2167A [38]. The reader would do well to consult this document before preparing any software system.

Nevertheless, for some of the documents mentioned in the chapter, we discuss techniques needed specifically for real-time systems. The approach taken reflects the author's background in the development of military avionics systems; other approaches may, of course, be preferred.

4.1 PHASES OF THE SOFTWARE LIFE CYCLE

The life cycle of a software project has been partitioned in several different waterfall models [1], [23], [68]. The term *waterfall* is used to describe the idealized notion that each stage or phase in the life of a software product occurs in time sequence, with the boundaries between phases clearly defined. We use the idealized waterfall model similar to the one given in [68] throughout the text. Later on we add modifications to take into account the state changes that are not related to time sequencing.

To begin, we consider a software product to be in the following phases, in time order, during its lifetime:

1. Concept phase
2. Requirements phase
3. Design phase
4. Programming phase
5. Test phase
6. Maintenance phase.

This breakdown differs from Howden [68] in the addition of the concept and test phases. Table 4.1 depicts each phase and its main byproducts.

The next sections discuss each phase and their activities in some detail. In particular, we examine some of the activities over the software life cycle suggested by Parnas [124], for they are the most practical. Parnas recognizes that in the real world, the software life cycle and many of the activities that are supposed to occur during it cannot be followed strictly. This is, of course, due to

TABLE 4.1   Phases of the Software Life Cycle, Their Activities, and Their Byproducts

Phase	Activity	Output
Concept	Define project goals	White paper
Requirements	Decide what the product must do	Requirements Document
Design	Show how the product will meet the requirements	Design Document
Code	Build the system	Program code
Test	Check if the system meets the requirements	Test reports
Maintenance	Maintain system	Maintenance reports

the realities of budget, time, shifting customer requirements, and so forth. In short, this model is simply an abstraction. But Parnas suggests that after the project has been completed, tested, and delivered, users can "cover their tracks" by modifying the documentation so that it appears that a formal methodology was followed. The benefit of this modification is that a traceable history is established between each program feature and the customer requirement dictating it. This promotes a maintainable, robust, and reliable product. Hence when the activities suggested in the following sections cannot be followed strictly, they should be "faked" over the life of the project.

4.1.1 Concept Phase

The concept phase includes determination of software project need and overall goals. This phase is often driven by management directive, customer input, technology changes, and marketing decisions. At the onset of the concept phase, no formal requirements are written, generally no decisions about hardware/ software environments are made, and budgets and schedules cannot be set. In other words, only the features of the software product and the feasibility of testing them are discussed. Usually, no documentation other than internal feasibility studies, white papers, or memos are generated.

NOTE 4.1   This is not always true. For example, for larger DoD systems, the user agency develops an "operational concept document."

Other authors have not defined this phase because it was either included in the requirements phase or not thought to be part of the software project at all. Nonetheless, the concept phase is indeed a *bona-fide* stage in any software project.

In short, the purpose of the concept phase is to

■ Identify product need and goals.
■ Produce feasibility studies.

4.1.2 Requirements Phase

The requirements phase is the point at which ideas are committed to paper, usually as a requirements document or software specification. This document is prepared by the customer. (The "customer" could be an actual customer, your boss, the instructor of your class, and so forth.) The requirements document contains specific information about what the software product is to do: timing/throughput (in real-time systems), user interface, accuracy requirements, and so on. Usually, little or no information on how these requirements are to be met is dictated, but schedule and budget are often stipulated. Finally, all interfaces to existing software and hardware are clearly defined.

From a testing perspective, it is at this point that test requirements are determined and committed to a formal test plan. The test plan is used as the blueprint for the creation of test cases used in the testing phase. (Testing is discussed more fully in Chapter 11.)

The requirements phase can and often does occur in parallel with the concept phase, and as mentioned before, most authors simply combine the two. It can be argued that the two are separate because the requirements generated during the concept phase are not binding, whereas those determined in the requirements phase are. This difference is also important from a testing perspective.

4.1.2.1 Functional Requirements The requirements document includes specific information about *functional requirements*—those system features that can be directly tested by executing the program.

■ **EXAMPLE 4.1**

The following text describes a functional requirement for an aircraft navigation system.

"Within 1 millisecond of issuance of the level 1, high-priority interrupt, the navigation subsystem shall make available all compensated acceleration data to the main computer, which will read it via DMA. This data cannot be updated while the main computer is in the process of reading it."   ■

Other specific functional requirements include system response times and throughput requirements.

4.1.2.2 Nonfunctional Requirements *Nonfunctional requirements* are characterized as system features that cannot easily be tested by program execution. Nonfunctional requirements include specification of the type of machine that the system will run on, programming language to use, time- and memory-loading, and version control. Other nonfunctional requirements might cover programming style, test conduct, maintainability, modularity, schedule, and security of the development site.

■ **EXAMPLE 4.2**

The following excerpt from the nuclear power plant system is a nonfunctional requirement.

"The system shall be coded in ANSI-C using accepted practices of software engineering. No 'GOTO' statements are permitted."   ■

See Lamb's software engineering text [88] for a nice breakdown of functional requirements, goals, and implementation constraints (hardware considerations).

The following, then, are the chief goals of this phase:

■ Define all hardware and software interfaces.
■ Write requirements document.
■ Write test plan.
■ Prepare project schedule.

The requirements document should be prepared in accordance with accepted standards; for example, DOD-STD-2167A [38] or IEEE standard 830 [69]. (These can be obtained from the Government Printing Office or IEEE, respectively, and should be part of your engineering library.)

4.1.2.3 Rules for Requirements and Design Documents   When implementing requirements and design documents, the modeling techniques used are not nearly as important as adherence to the following principles.

1. *The document must be complete.* There should be no holes or gaps. This goal of writing requirements and design documents is the most difficult to achieve.
2. *The document should be correct.* No laws of physics or international standards should be violated. The specified system must be consistent with the intent of the final deliverable product.
3. *The document should be consistent.* There should be no internal conflicts or contradictions.
4. *Each requirement or design element should be testable.* Specifying that a system should have "reliable performance" is meaningless because it cannot be objectively tested. Specifying that no faults should be detected before one hour of operation is meaningful.

Other texts list numerous other criteria, but these are the most reasonable.

4.1.3 Design Phase

The design phase is characterized by the conversion of the requirements document to a detailed design specification we call a *detailed design document*. Preparation of the detailed design document cannot begin until the requirements have been fully defined. The design document specifies how the requirements are to be met by partitioning the functional features prescribed in the requirements document into software modules. Techniques for doing this are discussed in Chapter 5. The format of the detailed design document should be in accordance with an accepted standard such as DOD-STD-2167A [38] or IEEE standard 1016 [72]. Adherence to a strict design procedure is, of course, important for all software systems, but particularly for real-time systems.

Concurrent with the preparation of the design document, a set of test cases based on the test plan are developed. That is, the requirements document is to the design document as the test plan is to the test cases. Techniques for developing test cases are discussed in Chapter 11.

Often it is in the design phase that problems in the requirements document are identified. These problems may include conflicts, redundancies, or requirements that cannot be met with current technology. Usually, problems such as these require changes to the requirements document or the granting of exemptions from the requirements in question. Such modifications must be approved by the group that originally generated the requirements document. In any case, the problem resolution shows up as a specific directive in the design document.

Two major steps are involved in partitioning the system: partitioning into hardware and software components, and partitioning the software. Discussion of the first step is beyond the scope of this text, but discussion of the second is of great importance to our purposes.

To summarize the tasks of the design phase:

■ Partition software into modules.

■ Prepare detailed design document.

■ Develop test cases.

4.1.3.1 Parnas Partitioning   Partitioning the software into modules is governed by a set of rules given by David Parnas[125] and in fact are often referred to as *Parnas partitioning*. In this technique, a list of difficult design decisions or things that are likely to change is prepared. Modules are then designated to "hide" the eventual implementation of each design decision or feature from the rest of the system. Thus, only the function of the module is visible to other modules, not the method of implementation. Changes in these modules are therefore not likely to affect the rest of the system.

■ EXAMPLE 4.3

To understand Parnas partitioning, consider writing a module to implement an abstract data type called a *stack* with associated operations PUSH and POP. The implementation of this module should be hidden from all calling modules. A data item should be passed to the PUSH procedure with assurance that it will be placed on the stack. Similarly, the POP procedure should return a data item from the stack and adjust the stack accordingly. Access to the stack in memory via any means other than PUSH and POP (except perhaps for initialization) should be prohibited.   ■

I recently had the pleasure of hearing Parnas speak at a conference. He is still carrying the banner for sanity in software engineering. The following points were made at his talk:

■ Some aspects of a system are fundamental, whereas others are arbitrary and likely to change.

■ It is the unlikely things, the arbitrary things, and things that are likely to change that contain "information."

■ Arbitrary facts are hard to remember and usually require lengthier descriptions. They are the sources of complexity.
   1. Begin by characterizing the likely changes.
   2. Estimate the probabilities of each type of change.

    3. Organize the software to confine likely changes to a small amount of code.
    4. Provide an "abstract interface" that abstracts from the differences.
    5. Implement "objects" that hide changeable data structures.
    These steps reduce the "strength" of intermodule connections.

■ Strength of connection is consistent with an information theoretic view, but numerical calculations are not practical.

    Parnas also indicated that although modular design is easy to describe in textbooks, it is difficult to achieve. He suggested that extensive practice and examples are needed to illustrate the point correctly.

    Another example of Parnas partitioning is shown in Figure 4.1. Here a graphics system is shown in heirarchical form. It consists of graphical objects (trees, houses, cars, and so on) that are composed from circles and boxes. Different objects can also reside in different display windows. The implementation of circles and boxes is based on the composition of line drawing calls. Thus, line drawing is the most basic hardware-dependent function. Whether the hardware is based on pixel, vector, turtle, or other type of graphics does not

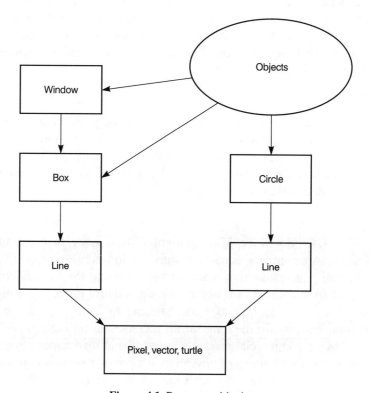

Figure 4.1 Parnas partitioning.

matter; only the line drawing routine needs to be changed. Hence, we have isolated the hardware dependencies to a single module.

4.1.4 Programming Phase

Having proposed the software product in the concept phase, defined the product requirements in the requirements phase, and partitioned the software functions in the design phase, programmers can now write the code in what is termed the programming phase. In theory, this phase should only begin when the design phase has completely ended. In practice, however, there is some overlap—which is desirable since problems in the requirements not detected in the design phase are usually flushed out during programming. In addition, the test team can implement the test cases specified in the design phase in some form using batch files or other techniques. This approach guarantees the efficacy of the tests and facilitates repeat testing.

4.1.4.1 Responsibilities   The responsibility of the software engineer(s) in this phase is to write and debug the software modules to perform as specified in the detailed design specification. Thus, the software engineer now fills in the details omitted in the design phase. Numerous approaches to attacking this problem are available, and a good discussion of these can be found in [20]. This phase is probably the most discussed—though least understood—phase of the software life cycle.

4.1.4.2 Termination   The programming phase ends when the software has been integrated and has successfully passed the integration testing specified by the software designers. This type of testing is usually *ad hoc* testing done by the programmers themselves, but it can be specified in the requirements document or the detailed design specification.

4.1.4.3 Software Management   The management of the programming phase can be greatly enhanced with version control software. *Version control software* is a system that manages the access to the various components of the system from the software library. Version control prevents multiple access to the same source code, provides mechanisms for tracking changes, and preserves version integrity. In the long run, it increases overall system reliability.

Many commercial products are available for various development environments, and many standard environments provide version control facilities. Unix, for example, provides the well-known source code control system (sccs) for management of system code.

■ **EXAMPLE 4.4**

A commercial product called the COHESION environment (available through Digital Equipment Corporation) provides many of the tools necessary for the total management of the software life cycle. COHESION runs on a variety of platforms, supports several programming languages, and can target a number of commercially available microprocessors. COHESION apparently provides a total integrated environment for the development of any type of system, including real-time. It includes:

- Requirements capture, analysis, and development tools
- Code generators
- Expert systems
- Editors
- Debuggers
- System builders
- Documentation support services
- Software configuration.

and many more features. Although I have no direct experience with this product, I believe it merits further investigation.   ■

In summary, the major accomplishments of this phase are

- Write software modules.
- Debug software.
- Develop automated test cases.
- Integrate modules.

Where appropriate, commercial tools should be used to assist in the administration of this phase.

4.1.5 Test Phase

Although ongoing testing is an implicit part of the software development process, an explicit testing phase exists as well. The explicit phase begins when the programming phase has completely ceased. It is during the explicit testing phase that the software is confronted with a formal set of test cases (module and system level) developed in parallel with the software. Acceptance or rejection of the software is based on how well it fares against the test set. Chapter 11 discusses many of the techniques used in formal testing. One technique we have not discussed is that of formal program proving. It was disregarded for two reasons. First, some experts are still skeptical of its viability for a large system, for example, [32], [45], and [96]. Second, formal program proving for real-time systems requires the use of methods including temporal logic or process algebra, both of which are beyond the scope of this text. The interested reader can see [99], [103], or [113] for a discussion of some of these methods.

This phase is rigidly controlled in that only bonded code is used and no changes to the documentation are allowed (except for the software test specification and procedures document for an error in the testing procedure itself). The phase is completed when either the criteria established in the software test requirements document are satisfied, or failure to meet the criteria forces the project to reenter a previous phase (see Section 4.2). Regardless of the outcome, one or more test reports are prepared which summarize the conduct and results of the testing.

This phase, then, takes care of the following items.

- Perform software validation.
- Prepare test reports.

Validation has been defined as "Are we building the right product?", whereas verification has been defined as "Are we building the product right?" This implies that validation is concerned with the correctness of the requirements, whereas verification is concerned with adherence to those requirements. However, many individuals use these terms interchangeably, without any loss of meaning. This text also discusses them interchangeably.

4.1.6 Maintenance Phase

The maintenance phase, which begins when the software has been verified (i.e., has passed its test criteria), consists of product deployment and customer support. It is during this phase that problems in the software will invariably be found and areas for improvement identified. Any changes in the software due to these sources are usually handled by making a software change and then performing regression testing (see Chapter 11). Another approach is to collect a set of changes and then regression test against the set of changes. Later we discuss how these changes are—and should be—incorporated with the existing software, and how this fits into the overall testing strategy (see Chapter 11). The maintenance phase ends when the product is no longer supported.

Thus, in the maintenance phase the following tasks are completed:

- Product deployment.
- Customer support.
- Continuing program error correction.

4.2 NONTEMPORAL TRANSITIONS IN THE SOFTWARE LIFE CYCLE

Although Figure 4.2 implies that the phases in the software life cycle occur in sequence, Parnas states that this is not always to be expected. In fact, transitions can occur from any phase to any other in the software life cycle. Those nontemporal transitions that make more sense than others are discussed here.

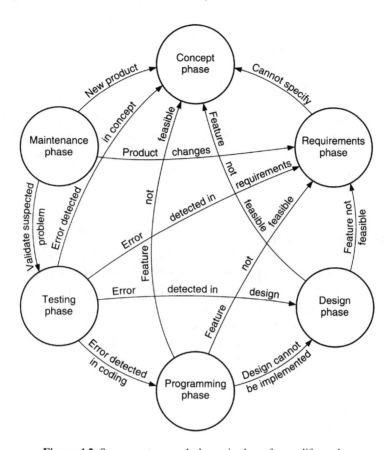

Figure 4.2 Some nontemporal phases in the software life cycle.

Since there are six phases in the software life cycle, there are a total of $6 \cdot 5 = 30$ transitions from one phase to another. Five of these, however, are attributable to temporal transition.

The nine transitions from the other phases back to the concept phase or requirements phase represent a "back to the drawing board" effect. That is, new features, lack of sufficient technology, or other factors force reconsideration of the system purpose or redesign. This leaves us with 16 nontemporal transitions to discuss. Let us discuss some of the transitions depicted in Figure 4.2.

A transition from the programming phase to the design phase represents a feature that cannot be implemented or causes unexpected performance impact. This in turn necessitates redesign, new requirements, or elimination of the feature.

Transition from the testing phase to the programming or design phases is due to an error detected during testing. Depending on the severity of the error, solution may require reprogramming, redesign, modification of requirements, or reconsideration of the system goals.

The three transitions from the maintenance phase to any previous phase other than the concept or requirements phase do not make sense. Errors detected during maintenance should be treated as new customer requirements: enter the concept phase and follow the sequence through the entire software life cycle, adjusting only those requirements specifications and designs having to do with the problem, by running the entire test set.

   Other nontemporal transitions are from the concept phase to other phases. These may represent prototyping or testing proof-of-principle for aspects of the design that represent technical or schedule risks or feasibility. In the final development process, it may be desirable to skip over the steps prescribed in the normal software development process.

4.3 THE SPIRAL MODEL

An alternative life-cycle model, the "spiral model," suggested by Boehm [17], recognizes that the boundaries are not always clearly defined, nor the phases time sequential. The spiral model is shown in Figure 4.3. As the system progresses from the concept and requirements phases, prototyping and risk analysis are used to evaluate the feasibility of potential features. More prototyping is used after a development plan is established, and again after the design and tests have been developed. After that, the model behaves essentially like a waterfall model. The added risk protection benefit from the extensive prototyping can be costly.

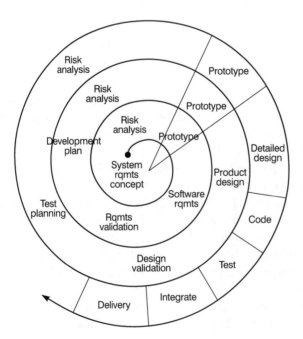

Figure 4.3 The spiral software model.

4.4 STANDARDS

There are many informal standards for the development of software, but most of these are informal or company specific. Three, however, stand out.

4.4.1 DOD-STD-2167A

DOD-STD-2167A (or MIL-STD-2167A) establishes the U.S. Department of Defense's (DoD) uniform requirements for software development throughout the software life cycle. In essence, 2167A, as it is sometimes called, specifies major activities in the software development process, defines a set of deliverables or Data Item Descriptions (DIDs), and prescribes formal audits and reviews.

2167A views the software life cycle in a waterfall model, similar to the one we have adopted for this text. The phases of the 2167A model are as follows.

1. System requirements analysis/design
2. Software requirements analysis
3. Preliminary design
4. Detailed design
5. Coding and Computer Software Unit (CSU) testing
6. Computer Software Component (CSC) integration and testing
7. Computer Software Configuration Item (CSCI) testing
8. System integration and testing.

Table 4.2 shows a rough correspondence between these phases and those that we described in Section 4.4.1. The standard also allows for nine or more audits and reviews at specified way points, and seventeen types of formal reports and documentation. The audits include

TABLE 4.2   Correspondence Between These 2167A Life-Cycle Phases and the Seven-Phase Model of Section 4.4.1

2167A Phase(s)	Section 4.1 Phase(s)
System requirements analysis/design	Concept/requirements
Software requirements analysis	Concept/requirements
Preliminary design	Design
Detailed design	Design
Coding and Computer Software Unit testing	Coding
Computer Software Component integration and testing	Testing
Computer Software Configuration Item testing	Testing
System integration and testing	Testing

- Software Requirements Review (SRR)
- System Design Review (SDR)
- Software Specification Review (SSR)
- Preliminary Design Review (PDR)
- Critical Design Review (CDR)
- Test Readiness Review (TRR)
- Functional Configuration Audit (FCA)
- Physical Configuration Audit (PCA)
- Formal Qualification Review (FQR)

The delivery of these items with respect to the 2167A life cycle is shown in Figure 4.4. The formal reports and documentation, which are largely self-describing, are

- System/Segment Design Document (SSDD)
- Software Development Plan (SDP)
- Software Requirements Specification (SRS)
- Interface Requirements Specification (IRS)
- Interface Design Document (IDD)
- Software Design Document (SDD)
- Software Product Specification (SPS)
- Version Description Document (VDD)
- Software Test Plan (STP)
- Software Test Description (STD)
- Software Test Report (STR)
- Computer System Operator's Manual (CSOM)
- Software Programmer's Manual (SPM)
- Firmware Support Manual (FSM)
- Computer Resources Integrated Support Document (CRISD)
- Engineering Change Proposal (ECP)
- Specification Change Notice (SCN)

The delivery of these items with respect to the 2167A life cyle is shown in Figure 4.5.

Although in the United States many mission-critical applications are developed using 2167A, in its full-blown implementation, 2167A has significant overhead. (Many systems are implemented using a significantly smaller subset of the model.) Few non-DoD enterprises adopt 2167A, and even in DoD the standard is being partially displaced by the IEEE 830 and ISO 9000 standards.

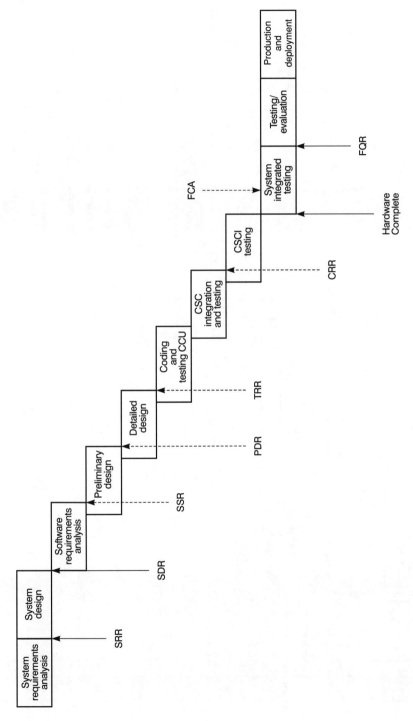

Figure 4.4 The 2167A System development and review process.

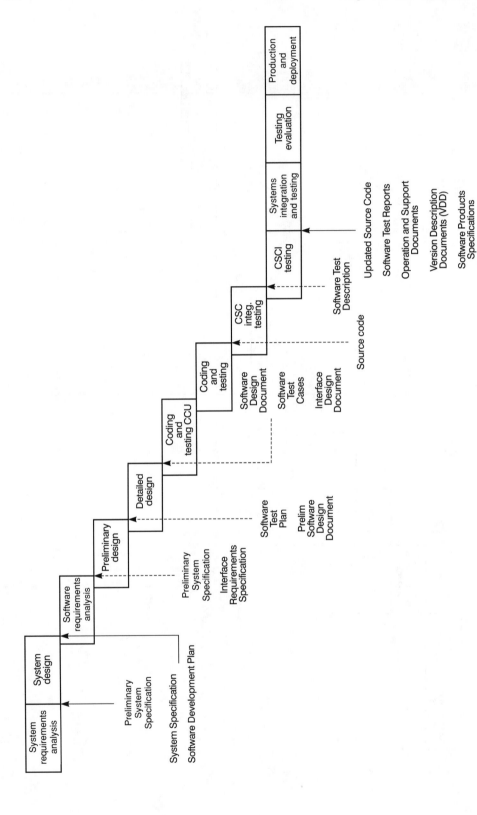

Figure 4.5 Important DIDs and when they are delivered.

4.4.2 ISO 9000

ISO Standard 9000 (International Standards Organization) is a generic, worldwide standard for quality improvement that has taken hold mainly in Europe, but an increasing number of U.S. and Asian companies have also adopted it. The standard, which collectively is described in five standards, ISO 9000 through ISO 9004, was designed to be applied in a wide variety of manufacturing environments. ISO 9001 through ISO 9003 apply to enterprises according to the scope of their activities. ISO 9004 and the ISO 9000-X family are documents that provide guidelines for specific applications domains. For software development, ISO 9000-3 is the document of interest. Many companies that had used DOD-STD-2167A-type development are switching to ISO 9000 because it may be better suited for commercial product development. Even some defense software engineering units are switching to ISO 9000 in its military equivalent, MIL-STD-498.

The ISO standards are process-oriented, "common-sense" practices that help companies create a quality environment. The principal areas of quality focus are

1. Management responsibility
2. Quality system
3. Contract review
4. Design control
5. Document and data control
6. Purchasing/control of customer-supplied product
7. Product identification and traceability
8. Process control
9. Inspection and testing
10. Control of inspection, measuring, and test equipment
11. Inspection and test status
12. Control of nonconforming product
13. Corrective and preventive action
14. Handling, storage, packaging, preservation, and delivery
15. Control of quality records
16. Internal quality audits
17. Training
18. Servicing
19. Statistical techniques.

Focusing on many of these areas, such as inspection and testing (for example, through code walkthroughs), design control, and product traceability (through a "rational design process") indeed increase the quality of a software product. However, in order to achieve certification under the ISO standard, significant paper trails and overhead are required. These need to be weighed against the clear benefits of such a program before it is undertaken.

For further information on ISO 9000, consult [50], [126] or check the Internet for ISO interest groups.

4.4.3 IEEE 830

IEEE Standard 830-1993 contains the recommended practice for Software Design Descriptions (SDDs). The guide is described as a "binding contract among designers, programmers, customers, and testers," and it encompasses different design views or paradigms for system design. The recommended design views include some combination of decomposition, dependency, interface, and detail descriptions. Together with boiler plate front matter, these form a standard template for SDDs as given in Figure 4.6.

Sections 1 and 2 are self-evident; they provide front matter and introductory material for the SDD. The remainder of the SDD is devoted to the four description sections.

The first, Decomposition Description, is used to partition the system into design entities (using Parnas partitioning, for example). Each design entity is described by its identification, type, purpose, function and subordinates. Recommended description techniques include structure charts, Warnier-Orr notation, and natural languages.

The next description section, Dependency, is a description of relationships among entities and system resources. The entity attributes include identification, type, purpose, dependencies, and resources. Example representation techniques include structure charts, dataflow diagrams, petri nets, or statecharts.

The Interface Description section provides a list of everything a designer, programmer, or tester needs to know to use the design entities that make up the system. Each system attribute is recorded along with its identificaiton, function, and interfaces. These interfaces are described using a variety of mechanisms including data dictionaries, parameter lists, or annotated file headers.

Finally, the Detail Description section is used to show the internal details of each system entity whose attributes include identification, processing performed, and data. Any of the representation techniques discussed in this chapter can be used to provide detailed descriptions.

As a software engineering standard, IEEE 830 is incomplete in that it only specifies design (or requirements) description. Additional guidelines are needed for the other phases in the software life cycle. Some of these are discussed next.

4.4.4 Other Standards

Standardizing organizations such as ISO, ACM, IEEE, and others actively promote the development of new standards and the use and improvement of existing standards. A list of standards offered through the IEEE includes

```
1. Introduction
        1.1 Purpose
        1.2 Scope
        1.4 Definitions and Acronyms

2. References

3. Decomposition Description
        3.1 Module Decomposition
                3.1.1 Module 1
                3.1.2 Module 2
        3.2 Concurrent Process Definition
                3.2.1 Process 1 Description
                3.2.2 Process 2 Description
        3.3 Data Decomposition
                3.3.1 Data Entity 1 Description
                3.3.2 Data Entity 2 Description

4. Dependency Description
        4.1 Intermodule Dependencies
        4.2 Interprocess Dependencies
        4.3 Data Dependencies

5. Interface Description
        5.1 Module Interface
                5.1.1 Module 1 Description
                5.1.2 Module 2 Description
        5.2 Process Interface
                5.2.1 Process 1 Description
                5.2.2 Process 2 Description

6. Detailed Design
        6.1 Module Detailed Design
                6.1.1 Module 1 Detail
                6.1.2 Module 2 Detail
        6.2 Data Detailed Design
                6.2.1 Data Entity 1 Detail
                6.2.2 Data Entity 2 Detail
```

Figure 4.6 Table of contents for an SDD.

1. IEEE Std 610.12.1990, Glossary of Software Engineering Terminology
2. IEEE Std 730-1989, Standard for Quality Assurance Plans
3. IEEE Std 828-1990, Standard for Configuration Management Plans
4. IEEE Std 829-1990, Standard for Test Documentation
5. IEEE Std 830-1993, Recommended Practice for Software Requirements Specifications
6. IEEE Std 982.1-1988, Standard Dictionary of Measures to Produce Reliable Software
7. IEEE Std 982.2-1988, Guide for the Use of Standard Dictionary of Measures to Produce Reliable Software
8. IEEE Std 990-1987, Recommended Practice for Ada as a Program Design Language
9. IEEE Std 1002-1987, Standard Taxonomy for Software Engineering Standards
10. IEEE Std 1008-1987, Standard for Software Unit Testing
11. IEEE Std 1012-1987, Standard for Software Verification and Validation Plans
12. IEEE Std 1016-1987, Recommended Practice for Software Design Descriptions
13. IEEE Std 1028-1988, Software Reviews and Audits
14. IEEE Std 1042-1987, Guide to Software Configuration Management
15. IEEE Std 1044-1993, Standard Classification for Software Anomalies
16. IEEE Std 1045-1992, Standard for Software Productivity Metrics
17. IEEE Std 1058.1-1987, Standard for Software Project Management Plans
18. IEEE Std 1059-1993, Guide for Software Verification and Validation Plans
19. IEEE Std 1061-1992, Standard for a Software Quality Metrics Methodology
20. IEEE Std 1062-1993, Recommended Practice for Software Acquisition
21. IEEE Std 1063-1987, Standard for Software User Documentation
22. IEEE Std 1074-1991, Standard for Developing Software Life Cycle Processes
23. IEEE Std 1209-1992, Recommended Practice for the Evaluation and Selection of CASE Tools
24. IEEE Std 1219-1992, Standard for Software Maintenance
25. IEEE Std 1228-1994, Standard for Software Safety Plans
26. IEEE Std 1298-1992, Software Quality Management System IEEE Std stem, Part 1: Requirements

Many of these are joint standards with ISO, ACM, and others. All can be obtained in a single volume [158]. The intent here is not to recommend any of these standards; rather, they provide benchmarks for software life-cycle practices. The decision to adopt or not to adopt is left to the reader.

4.5 EXERCISES

1. Why is it that only "faking" the rational design process is sufficient for the real world?
2. Write the PUSH and POP routines discussed in Example 4.3 in:
   (a) C
   (b) FORTRAN
   (c) Pascal
   (d) Ada
   (e) Modula-2
   Be sure to employ information-hiding techniques.
3. Discuss the importance and purpose of Parnas partitioning in the design phase of the software life cycle. Does Parnas partitioning make sense from a real-time perspective?
4. It has been inferred that a test life cycle similar to the software life cycle occurs in parallel [97]. For each phase in the software life cycle, name the activities that occur in the parallel test life cycle.
5. Redraw Figure 4.2 for the test life cycle phases you listed in the previous problem.
6. Estimate the relative percentage of time spent in each phase of the software life cycle for
   (a) An organic software system.
   (b) A semi-detached software system.
   (c) A nonembedded real-time software system.
   (d) An embedded real-time software system.
   Justify your estimates.
7. Estimate the relative percentage of time spent in each phase for the test life cycle you derived in exercise 4.
8. Discuss the nontemporal transitions for the phases of the test life cycle.
9. A mock-up or *prototype* of a software system is often constructed during the design phase. What are the benefits of using this technique?

5

Real-Time
Specification and
Design Techniques

KEY POINTS OF THE CHAPTER

1. In the absence of a rigorous software engineering model (and sometimes even in its presence), there is a fuzzy line between specification and design.

2. No one specification or design representation technique is a panacea; therefore, a combination of techniques should be used. The nature of the correct combination depends on the system and the designer's intuition, which is developed through experience; hence, practice is essential.

3. The specification of temporal behavior is the most difficult, but most important, aspect of specification/design in a real-time system.

In this chapter we survey the features and flaws of various techniques used in the specification and design of real-time systems. In particular, we examine techniques for generating the software requirements document, which is a byproduct of the requirements phase of the software life cycle, and the design document, which is a byproduct of the design phase.

Recall the difference between specification and design: *specification*, performed by the customer, tells us what the software is to do (and in what environment it will function), and *design*, performed by the system analyst or designer, tells us how the software will do it. However, many customer specifications are so detailed (including, for example, procedure and variable names) as to be practically design documents. In other cases the customer requirements, though clear, tell us nothing about how a requirement is to be accomplished (e.g., see Example 4.1), and thus necessitate the preparation of a separate design document. In still other cases, the requirements are so vague as to preclude system design without further customer input.

With the advent of CASE (*computer-aided software engineering*) tools, a graphical specification, for example, can immediately be converted into code. If properly done, a formal specification can serve as a software design, and this is sometimes done in practice. However, we assume that both are needed, and for the purposes of this chapter, when we say specification, we mean those techniques used in both a good software specification (software requirements document) and a good design (design document). Software design should adhere to the rules of modular decomposition and Parnas partitioning discussed in Chapter 4.

The techniques used in the specification of real-time systems are a rich superset of those used for non-real-time systems. Thus, learning how to specify real-time systems can only enhance the ability to specify other types of systems. Because of the depth of this subject, however, we can only survey some of these methodologies here. For example, Ross's Structured Analysis [135] and Z notation [152] have been omitted, because the author has not used these techniques. A good discussion of the use of techniques like these in the specification of real-time systems can be found in [114]. Throughout the chapter, the interested reader is referred to more detailed discussions on different formal specification techniques.

It is important that we preface the survey with the following observation. Almost without exception, every method available for formal specification is unwieldy for large systems. This is mostly because large systems are inherently complex. But we are typically dealing with large real-time systems. That is why the only recourse is to break the larger system into smaller component systems in some fashion—and the preferred method is to use the Parnas partitioning technique discussed in Chapter 4.

At the Advanced Study Institute on Real-Time Systems sponsored by the North Atlantic Treaty Organisation in 1992, a panel of seven world-renowned experts on software specification and design were asked, "What is the correct technique for specification and design of real-time systems?" Seven different answers were given. These experts' opinions only reinforced the belief that no "silver bullet" exists for specification of real-time systems. Although advances have been made since the use of flowcharts, you should use those techniques that work for you.

5.1 NATURAL LANGUAGES

Natural languages, such as English, are required in the specification of software systems, for it would be impossible to write a requirements document otherwise. But natural languages should be used only to provide redundant descriptions of features that are described by other means.

We have been using the English language throughout this text to describe real-time systems since we have not developed the other tools. For example, in Chapter 1 we talked about the nuclear plant, the avionics system, and the airline reservation system. For later use, let us consider another real-time system.

■ EXAMPLE 5.1

An automobile simulator consists of a steering, braking, display, and acceleration system. Each system executes sporadically except for the display system, which executes every 100 milliseconds.

The steering system is initiated when the driver turns the wheel by an angle, θ, where θ is greater than -30 degrees and less than 30 degrees. The position of the automobile with respect to the x, y plane changes in the x direction by a quantity that is the product of the velocity at time t, the time in which the wheel is turned, and the cosine of the angle in which the wheel is turned.

The position changes in the y direction in a similar manner except the sine of the wheel angle is used.

The velocity of the vehicle at any time t is its acceleration at that instant times the time. The acceleration at any instant is the acceleration due to pressing the accelerator pedal for a fixed time minus the deceleration due to pressing the brake for a fixed time. Both the acceleration and deceleration factors are constant and positive.   ■

The description in Example 5.1 is ambiguous at worst and tedious at best. Clearly, using any natural language alone is insufficient to describe the behavior of complex systems.

In summary, natural languages can be used to describe systems that are extremely simple; to enhance or amplify descriptions provided by other means; or to bring attention to some subtle point in the requirements. But natural languages are inherently ambiguous, and no mechanism exists that produces runnable code from a program specification written entirely in English, for example. Thus, every nontrivial feature of the system needs to be described by some means in addition to natural language.

5.2 MATHEMATICAL SPECIFICATION

The use of mathematics in the specification of software is well understood. Mathematics, when properly used, is precise, unambiguous, and efficient, although some experts still challenge mathematical verification for large systems. Furthermore, methods for optimization of performance can be obtained directly from optimization of the underlying mathematical model using formal methods. Finally, formal proof techniques can be applied to software in the same manner as the underlying mathematics, during the software verification and testing process.

Example 5.2 demonstrates the power of using mathematics in a formal program description by recasting Example 5.1.

■ **EXAMPLE 5.2**

An automobile simulator consists of a steering, braking, display, and acceleration system. Each system can be executed simultaneously and asynchronously except for the display system, which executes every 100 milliseconds.

The steering system is initiated when the driver turns the wheel by an angle $\theta \in [-30, 30]$. The position of the automobile with respect to the x, y plane changes by

$$\Delta x = v(t)T_\theta \cos \theta$$

$$\Delta y = v(t)T_\theta \sin \theta$$

where T_θ is the time in which the wheel is turned.

$v(t)$ is given by

$$v(t) = \alpha(t)t$$

where

$$a(t) = \alpha(t) - \beta(t)$$

and $\alpha(t)$ and $\beta(t)$ are the acceleration and braking functions, respectively, given by

$$\alpha(t) = AT_\alpha(t)$$

$$\beta(t) = BT_\beta(t)$$

A and B are positive constants, and $T_\alpha(t)$ and $T_\beta(t)$ are functions describing when the accelerator and brakes are applied and for how long.   ■

In summary, mathematics is precise and unambiguous. It promotes the application of formal program-proving techniques and rigorous methods for code optimization. It will almost certainly be used in any nontrivial software requirements document. Unfortunately, not all software engineers are appropriately trained in mathematical modeling, and mathematical models can become cryptic. Furthermore, some researchers believe that proofs of mathematics and of code are too error prone, thus leading to a false sense of security in a mathematically based specification.

5.3 FLOWCHARTS

We have all seen examples of *flowcharts* involving anything from toy assembly instructions to VCR operation.

Standard flowcharts are not encouraged for use in the specification of systems because they promote the unwanted GOTO statement. This is no coincidence since the flowchart evolved along with languages such as FORTRAN and assembly language which make extensive use of the GOTO statement.

■ **EXAMPLE 5.3**

Consider the flowchart in Figure 5.1, depicting a BITS (built-in test software) diagnostic feature in an avionics system. The "yes" paths almost beg the programmer to use GOTOs, especially if the program is to be written in an unstructured language such as BASIC or FORTRAN.   ■

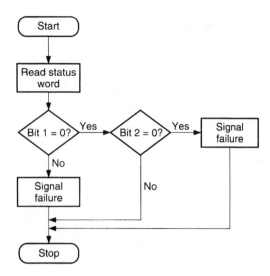

Figure 5.1 Flowchart for BITS feature in avionics system.

Flowcharts are probably the oldest modeling tool for software systems, and are widely understood. For this reason, simple systems can be modeled with flowcharts. According to Parnas, flowcharts are useful for systems on the order of 5,000 to 10,000 instructions, but are not suitable for systems beyond that size [124]. In multitasking systems, flowcharts can be used to describe each task separately, but the interaction between processes is not easily represented, and temporal behavior cannot be described. Finally, the flowchart often encourages the undesirable GOTO statement.

5.4 STRUCTURE CHARTS

Structure charts or *calling trees* are a widely used mechanism for describing the modular decomposition of a system. In structure charts, rectangles are used to represent processes. As you move from left to right in the structure chart, it represents increasing sequence in execution. Moving from top to bottom along any branch of the structure chart indicates increasing detail. There is no formal method for indicating conditional branching in the tree, but this is usually left as "self-evident" or is indicated in some other *ad hoc* manner. A form of structure chart, however, the *Jackson chart*, does depict conditional branching.

Structure charts are found widely in computer science literature and elsewhere in describing systems. For example, many textbooks use structure charts to describe suggested sequences of chapter study. A company's organization chart or your family tree also can be represented by structure charts. And more topically, structure charts can be used for the design of World Wide Web pages.

■ **EXAMPLE 5.4**

Consider a common coffee vending machine that can dispense regular and decaffeinated coffee with or without sugar and milk. We can describe the system using a structure chart as in Figure 5.2. After accepting the customer's coins and remitting any change owed, the machine reads the buttons pressed. Then regular coffee, decaffeinated coffee, or tea is dispensed, depending on the choice. Next, milk and/or sugar is dispensed.   ■

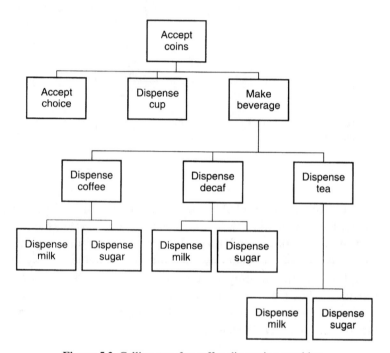

Figure 5.2 Calling tree for coffee dispensing machine.

Notice how the tree enables us to identify common functions such as the modules needed to dispense milk and sugar.

Structure charts have been used as long as flowcharts to describe system functionality, and like flowcharts, they are useful for very simple systems. Structure charts have several advantages: they clearly identify function execution sequence; they help to identify recursion and repeated modules; and they encourage top-down design. However, although structure charts form a part of almost any system specification, they are flat in nature and cannot easily be used to depict conditional branching. Most importantly, structure charts are not useful in the description of concurrent systems.

For example, in a system where several concurrent processes are running, you can represent each process by its own calling tree. There is, however, no way to describe the interaction between processes or to represent temporal behavior in the system. For this reason, modern usage of structure charts is limited to functional specification at the most abstract level.

5.5 PSEUDOCODE AND PROGRAMMING DESIGN LANGUAGES

Program design languages (PDLs) differ slightly from *pseudocode*, but we will treat them in a similar manner. Program design language is a type of high-order language that is very abstract; that is, it is detached from the underlying architecture of the machine on which the system will run. PDLs typically can be input into a compiler and translated into high-order languages. Pseudocode is a programming language with some simple set of semantics for which no compiler is usually built. Both PDLs and pseudocode are used to specify systems in a manner that is close to actually writing the code. For example, Ada has been used as a PDL with some success (see IEEE Std 990-1987, Recommended Practice for Ada as a Program Design Language). In other words, formal requirements have been written in Ada and then translated directly into code. Other Pascal-like languages such as Sparks[67] have been used as either pseudocode or PDL.

■ **EXAMPLE 5.5**

Consider the following pseudocode describing an automatic teller machine. The pseudocode is not a standard one, but its Pascal-like format should render it understandable.

```
begin
  Accept the card
  Display "Please enter your code"
  If  code not correct
   begin
      Display "sorry"
      Exit/Eject card
   end
  else
   begin
      Display "Press Key"
      Accept function key
      If key=query account
       begin
         Display balance
         Exit/Eject card
       end
      else
       begin
        if key=withdraw
         begin
           Display "amount?"
           Accept amount
```

```
            if amount > balance
             begin
                Display "sorry"
                Exit/Eject card
             end
            end
            else
             begin
                Remit cash
                Exit/Eject card
             end
            end
          else
           begin
             if key=deposit
              begin
                Display "amount?"
                Accept deposit
                Exit/Eject card
              end
             else
              begin
                Display "Illegal Function"
                Exit/Eject card
              end
            end
        end
```
■

The chief advantage of pseudocode and PDLs is that they are more abstract than writing specifications directly in high-order languages. Yet they are closer to programming language than any method we have seen thus far. Hence, specifications written in PDLs or pseudocode can often be translated into programs. Languages such as Ada and Modula-2, which have been used as PDLs, can certainly handle concurrent specifications, and this rates as an important advantage. Finally, PDLs and pseudocode adapt themselves to formal program-proving techniques more easily than unstructured techniques such as pictures or English.

On the negative side, it should be clear that a PDL is just another kind of programming language in which the user must be fluent. In addition, the use of higher-level abstractions in no way guarantees that errors cannot be made, and often these errors are more subtle than programming errors. Finally, the additional cost and maintenance of these program design tools are often significant.

5.6 FINITE STATE AUTOMATA

Finite state automata (FSA) or *finite state machines* (FSMs) are a type of mathematical model used in the design of compilers, hard-wired logic, and communication systems, among other places. We have seen a finite state automaton in Figure 4.1.

Intuitively, finite state automata rely on the fact that many systems can be represented by a fixed number of unique states. The system may change state depending on time or the occurrence of specific events—a fact that is reflected in the automaton.

There are three methods for representing finite state automata.

1. Set theoretic method.
2. Diagrammatic method.
3. Matrix representation method.

We present only the second two. The formal mathematical specification can be found in [3], [40], and elsewhere.

There are actually two kinds of FSA, although these are mathematically equivalent [3]. Firstly a *Moore finite state automaton* consists of a nonempty, finite set of states depicted as labeled circles, one of which is the initial state (marked with an arrow) and one or more are terminal states (marked with "halos"). An alphabet of symbols is given, and a transition function—depicted by labeled arcs—shows how given a current state and symbol, a new state is entered.

The Moore machine does not allow for outputs during transition, but output is provided for by the processes represented by states. Outputs during transition are allowed, however, by a variation of the Moore machine called a *Mealy* FSA.

■ EXAMPLE 5.6

Consider a Moore FSA, $\mathcal{M}$, to detect even parity in a stream of bits, where state A corresponds to an even number of 1s, while B corresponds to an odd number of 1s. It is described pictorially in Figure 5.3 and by its matrix representation in Table 5.1.   ■

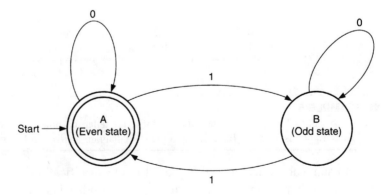

Figure 5.3 Finite state automaton for even parity checker.

TABLE 5.1   Transition Table for Even Parity Checker

	Current State	
Input	A	B
0	A	B
1	B	A

■ EXAMPLE 5.7

Next, consider the Mealy FSA, $\mathcal{M}$, to detect odd parity in a stream of bits. It is described pictorially in Figure 5.4, and by its matrix representation in Table 5.2.   ■

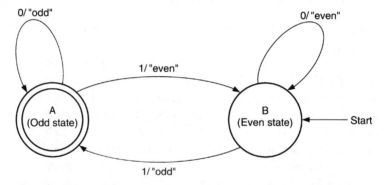

Figure 5.4 Mealy finite state automaton for odd parity checker.

TABLE 5.2   Transition Table for Odd Parity Checker

	Current State	
Input	A	B
0	A/"odd"	B/"even"
1	B/"even"	A/"odd"

■ EXAMPLE 5.8

Finally, consider a Mealy FSA to describe the automatic teller machine in Example 5.5. A partial matrix description is given in Table 5.3, and the state diagram is given in Figure 5.5.   ■

In summary, FSAs are widely used in the specification of systems that are *state driven*. For example, lexical analyzers and other language recognition and translation programs can be easily written using FSAs.

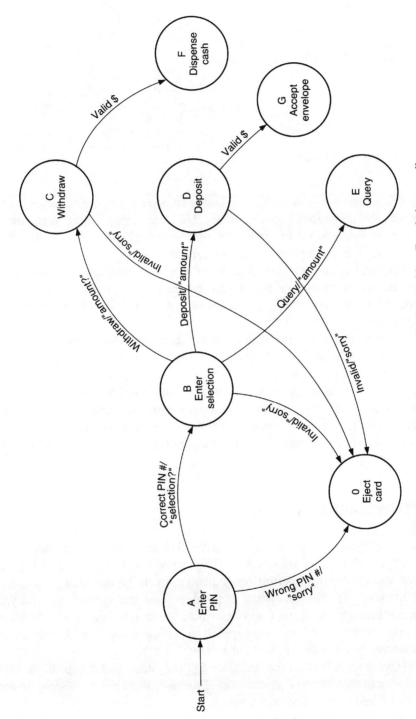

Figure 5.5 Finite state automaton for automated teller machine. For clarity, not all transitions are shown.

TABLE 5.3 Partial Transition Table for Automatic Teller Machine

Input	A	B	C	D
Wrong PIN #	0/"sorry"	NA	NA	NA
Correct Pin #	B/"selection?"	NA	NA	NA
Withdraw	NA	C/"amount?"	NA	NA
Query	NA	E	NA	NA
Deposit	NA	D/"amount?"	NA	NA
Valid $	NA	NA	F	G
Invalid $	NA	NA	0	0

Here NA means not allowed.

FSAs are easy to develop, and code can be easily generated using tables to represent the transitions between states. They are also unambiguous, since they can be represented with a formal mathematical description. In addition, concurrency can be depicted by using multiple FSAs.

Finally, because mathematical techniques for reducing the number of states exist, programs based on FSAs can be formally optimized. A rich theory surrounds FSAs, and this can be exploited in the development of system specifications.

On the other hand, the major disadvantage of FSAs is that "insideness" of modules cannot be depicted. That is, there is no way to indicate how functions can be broken down into subfunctions.

In addition, intertask communication for multiple FSAs is difficult to depict, although, an interesting paper [25] discusses a modification of the FSM model that accounts for intertask communication and synchronization. Finally, depending on the system and alphabet used, the number of states can grow very large.

5.7 DATAFLOW DIAGRAMS

Dataflow diagrams, proposed by DeMarco [31], are used as a structured analysis tool for modeling software systems. Extensions to the original model, given by Hatley and Pribhai [62], permit real-time systems to be modeled.

Starting with the functional requirements of the system, we analyze the dataflow through the system and determine the major functions. The dataflow diagrams are developed and decomposed to sufficient depth to identify the major components of each system and subsystem.

Having identified all the functions in the system, and the dataflow between them, we can then identify concurrency. Processes that feed from separate sources are considered to function concurrently.

Some of the conventions used in the construction of dataflow diagrams are given in Figure 5.6. Circles represent processes or procedures, parallel lines depict

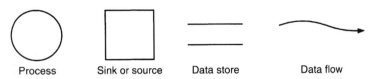

Figure 5.6 Dataflow diagram conventions.

data storage areas, and squares represent producers or consumers of data such as hardware devices. Directed arcs are used to indicate the unidirectional flow of data between the components of the graph.

5.7.1 DeMarco's Rules

DeMarco [30] has given a set of rules for the construction of dataflow diagrams, which are summarized here.

1. Identify all net input and output flows. Draw them in around the outside of your diagram.
2. Work your way from inputs to outputs, backward from outputs to inputs, or from the middle out.
3. Label all the interface dataflows carefully.
4. Label processes in terms of their inputs and outputs.
5. Ignore initialization and termination.
6. Omit details of trivial error paths (initially).
7. Do not show flow-of-control or control information.
8. Be prepared to start over.

Once an overall dataflow diagram has been drawn, further detail within the process blobs is provided. The diagram is then redrawn with the additional detail. This process is called *leveling*.

■ **EXAMPLE 5.9**

Consider an avionics system that collects accelerometer data every 5 milliseconds and gyro data every 40 milliseconds, and compensates both data at 40 milliseconds to obtain position. In addition, the gyros are torqued based on the compensated accelerometer and gyro data every 40 milliseconds, and a display is updated based on position every second. Figure 5.7 describes the system using a dataflow diagram.   ■

■ **EXAMPLE 5.10**

The development of a loadable program from source code is illustrated with a dataflow diagram in Figure 5.8. Looking from the left of the diagram to the right, we see that the source code is input from a file to the language compiler. Errors are logged to the screen or to a file, while the assembly language code is stored in a separate file. This file can be submitted to an assembler, which produces object code and logs any errors to the screen or a file. The object code is then presented to the linker, which generates the loadable program and logs any errors or diagnostics.   ■

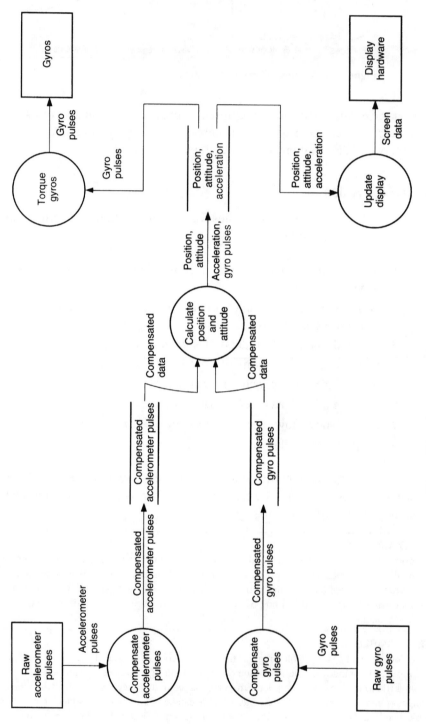

Figure 5.7 Dataflow diagram for navigation system.

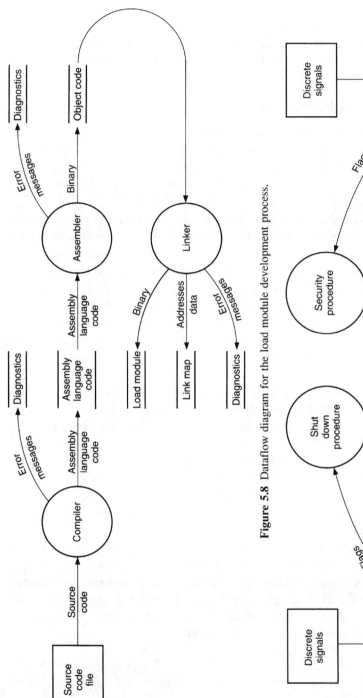

Figure 5.8 Dataflow diagram for the load module development process.

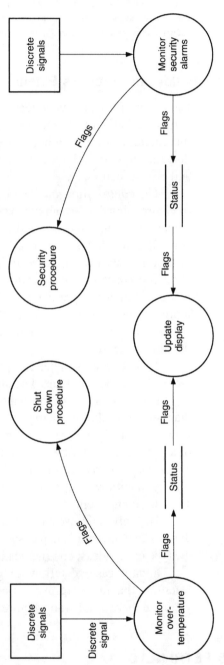

Figure 5.9 Dataflow diagram for nuclear plant.

■ EXAMPLE 5.11

As a final example, consider the dataflow diagram in Figure 5.9, describing the nuclear plant first introduced in Chapter 1. Looking from left to right, we see how discrete signals from the temperature sensor are monitored and displayed, and can trigger a shutdown. In addition, discrete signals from security sensors are monitored and displayed, and can cause the system to alert a police force.   ■

5.7.2 Hatley and Pribhai's Extensions

Hatley and Pribhai have extended the dataflow diagram model in order to render it more suitable to the real-time environment [62]. These extensions include the incorporation of two other types of system representations—the control flow diagram and control specifications—in addition to response time specification and a data dictionary.

The *control flow diagram* is a type of dataflow diagram that shows the flow of control signals through the system. These control signals can represent discrete signal data from switches and sensors, but can also include timing information from discrete clocks. The dataflow diagram and control flow diagram then mesh to describe what is supposed to happen to the data and when it should happen.

The *control specifications* consist of a finite state automaton in diagrammatic and matrix representation. The control signals in the control flow diagram represent the alphabet of this machine, whereas the states represent the state of the system at that particular moment. Each state can be referenced to a different dataflow diagram.

This scheme is rather complicated and, on the whole, may be unsuitable for large and difficult systems. The investigation of this technique is left to the reader.

Let us summarize the features and flaws of dataflow diagrams. Dataflow diagrams have the following features: they emphasize flow of data, deemphasize flow-of-control, and are useful in identifying concurrency. In fact, in the absence of concurrency, dataflow diagrams are finite state automata. In addition, structure charts can be derived from dataflow diagrams to assist in the design process [30]. Finally, dataflow diagrams can be used to partition a system into hardware and software components.

The only major weakness that seems to be inherent in dataflow diagrams is that they make it difficult to depict synchronization in flow. That is, it is difficult to show the type of broadcast communication we will discuss when examining statecharts.

In any case, dataflow diagrams are well understood and widely used. Dataflow diagrams are usually combined with some of the other techniques to yield a coherent software requirements document.

5.8 PETRI NETS

Petri nets are another type of mathematical model used to specify the operations to be performed in a multiprocessing or multitasking environment, but they can also be described graphically. A series of circular blobs called "places" are used to represent data stores or processes. Rectangular boxes are used to represent transitions or operations. The processes and transitions are labeled with a data count and transition function, respectively, and are connected by unidirectional arcs.

The initial graph is labeled with markings given by m_0 which represent the initial data count in the processes. New markings are the result of the firing of transitions. A transition, t, *fires* if it has as many inputs as required for output.

In Petri nets, the graph topology does not change over time; only the "markings" or contents of the places do. The system advances as transitions "fire." To illustrate the notion of "firing," consider the Petri nets given in Figure 5.10 and Figure 5.11, with associated firing table given in Table 5.4.

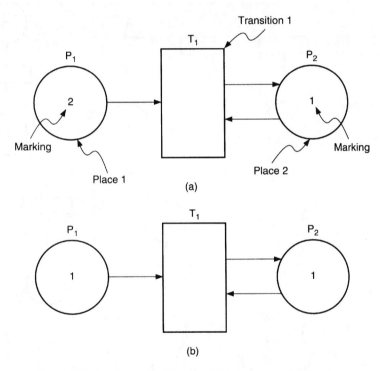

Figure 5.10 (a) Typical Petri net and (b) firing a typical Petri net.

TABLE 5.4   Firing Table for Petri Net

	P_1	P_2	P_3	P_4
m_0	1	1	2	0
m_1	0	0	3	1
m_2	0	0	2	2
m_3	0	0	1	3
m_4	0	0	0	4

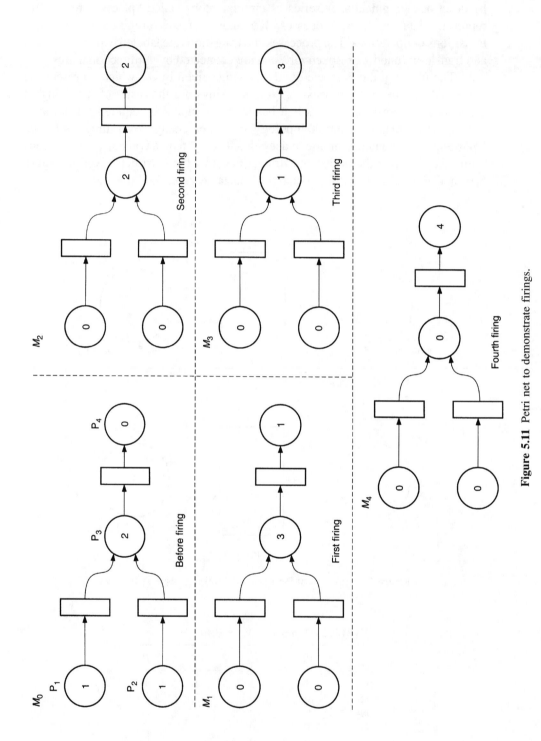

Figure 5.11 Petri net to demonstrate firings.

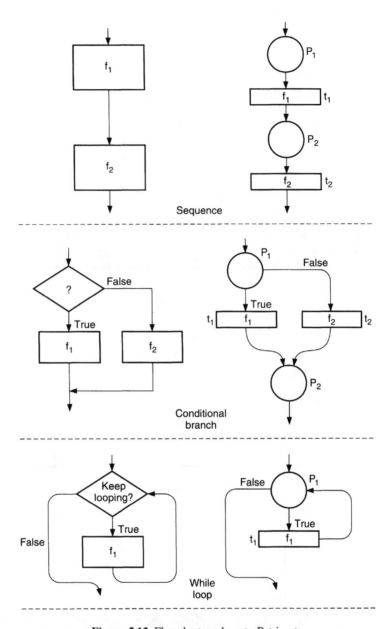

Figure 5.12 Flowchart analogs to Petri nets.

Petri nets can be used to model systems and to analyze timing constraints and race conditions [76], [11]. Certain Petri net subnetworks can model familiar flowchart constructs. Figure 5.12 illustrates these analogies. To further illustrate the use of Petri nets in the specification of systems, consider the following examples.

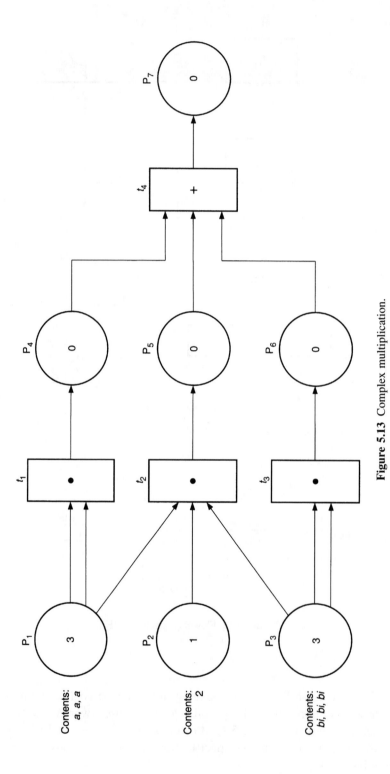

Figure 5.13 Complex multiplication.

■ **EXAMPLE 5.12**

Consider the following identity from complex algebra which is used frequently in many engineering applications.

$$(a + bi)(a + bi) = a^2 - b^2 + 2abi$$

This can be implemented with the Petri net in Figure 5.13, with corresponding firing Table 5.5. ■

TABLE 5.5   Firing Table for Complex Arithmetic Example

	P_1	P_2	P_3	P_4	P_5	P_6	P_7
m_0	3	1	3	0	0	0	0
m_1	0	0	0	1	1	1	0
m_2	0	0	0	0	0	0	1

■ **EXAMPLE 5.13**

Consider a Petri net representation for a hospital's patient monitoring system. Each patient is connected to machines monitoring blood pressure, heart rate, and EKG. These machines issue a Boolean signal indicating a FAIL or NO FAIL condition. The results of each of these machines are ORd together to form a signal called ALARM. The ALARM signals for each of the rooms (one patient per room) are then ORd together and sent to the nurse's station. If any machine on any patient indicates a failure, the emergency alarm is sounded and the nurse is directed to the appropriate patient and machine.

   The diagram for such a system is given in Figure 5.14.   ■

Petri nets are excellent for representing multiprocessing and multiprogramming systems [76], especially where the functions are simple. Because they are mathematical in nature, techniques for optimization and formal program-proving can be employed. But Petri nets can be overkill if the system is too simple. Similarly, if the system is highly complex, timing can become obscured.

5.9 WARNIER-ORR NOTATION

Warnier-Orr notation or Warnier-Orr semantics is a representation methodology that is similar to structure charts, with several improvements [122], [161]. First, it can be used to represent both data structures and processes, whereas structure charts can be used to represent only the processes. Second, it uses a more rigorous set theoretic notation. In this case we use sets with the right curly brace, } omitted to represent processes. We use sets within sets to describe increasing detail of functionality. The ordering of the elements within the set depicts the order of execution. The symbol $\oplus$ represents an "exclusive or," and + represents an "inclusive or."

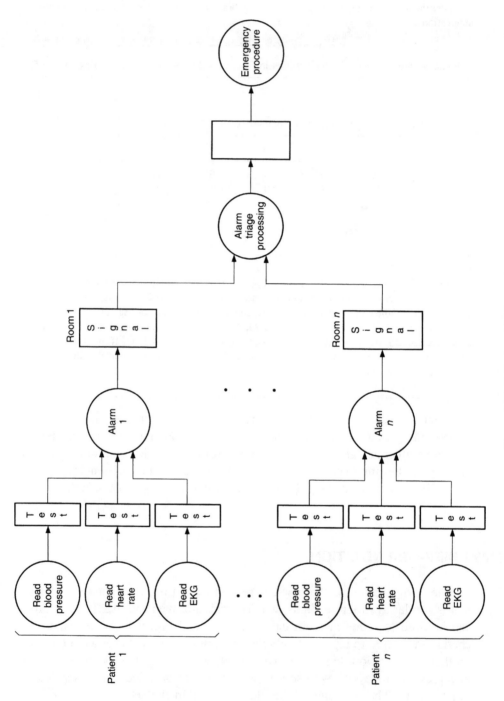

Figure 5.14 Patient monitoring system.

Thus, sequence is depicted from top to bottom, while increasing detail is depicted from left to right. Note that this is just a variation of structure charts (mirror image is rotated 90 degrees). Finally, unlike structure charts, Warnier-Orr notation provides for looping and conditional constructs that can be used to synchronize multiple processes.

■ EXAMPLE 5.14

A process consisting of a series of modules might be described in the following way:

$$
\text{program} \begin{cases} \text{step 1} \begin{cases} \text{step 1.A} \begin{cases} \text{step 1.A.1} \\ \text{step 1.A.2} \end{cases} \\ \text{step 1.B} \\ \text{step 1.C} \end{cases} \\ \text{step 2} \\ \text{step 3} \begin{cases} \text{step 3.A} \\ \text{step 3.B} \\ \text{step 3.C} \end{cases} \end{cases}
$$

The sequence of operations for this system would be step 1, step 1.A, step 1.A.1, step 1.A.2, step 1.B, step 1.C, step 2, step 3, step 3.A, step 3.B, step 3.C.   ■

We can depict modifications in the flow-of-control with the following constructs. In each case, "statement" is considered to be either a single statement or a list of statements, and "condition" is a simple or compound Boolean condition.

The if-then construct is represented as

arbitrary label { condition? {steps

where "condition" is the condition to be tested and "steps" are the actions to be taken if the condition is true.

■ EXAMPLE 5.15

The following tests bit 1 of a memory-mapped location called "BITE." If it is set, an error is indicated.

BITEtest {bit 1 of BITE set? {indicate error

The if-then-else construct can be represented as

$$
\text{arbitrary label} \begin{cases} \text{Condition \{true action} \\ \oplus \\ \text{Complementary condition \{false action} \end{cases}
$$

where if "condition" is true, then the true action or actions are taken; otherwise the false action or actions are taken.   ■

■ EXAMPLE 5.16

In this case, if a particular sensor is detected as "on," then a call is made to the police; otherwise some indication that an intrusion has not been detected is made.

$$\text{intruder detect} \begin{cases} \text{sensor on \{call police} \\ \oplus \\ \text{sensor off \{indicate all clear} \end{cases}$$

A while loop can be indicated as follows.

arbitrary label (condition,W) {statement

The statement or statements are executed until "condition" is not true. It should be noted that unless the condition is actually changed by the statement or an outside event, the loop is infinite.   ■

■ **EXAMPLE 5.17**

Here a polled loop is constructed to check the setting of a particular flag. This technique can be used to indicate that data are available for processing, or it can be used to synchronize two concurrent processes.

polled loop (flag = 0,W) {check flag   ■

A repeat until loop can be indicated.

arbitrary label (condition,U) {statement

Here the statement or statements are executed until the condition is true. As before, unless the condition is changed somehow, the loop is infinite.

■ **EXAMPLE 5.18**

We can simulate the polled loop from the previous example using the repeat until construct as follows:

polled loop (flag = 1,U) {check flag   ■

5.9.1 Indexed Loop

The indexed loop construct can be used to specify that a statement or statements is to be performed n times where $n \geq 0$.

arbitrary label (n) {statement

■ **EXAMPLE 5.19**

The following specifies the addition of a list of 100 numbers, assuming that $n = 0$ and $i = 1$ initially.

$$\text{add 100 numbers} \begin{cases} n = n + n(i) \\ i = i + 1 \end{cases}$$
     ■

■ **EXAMPLE 5.20**

To illustrate the Warnier-Orr semantics on a "larger" system, we can return to our automatic teller machine and describe its function:

$$
\text{Enter PIN \#}
\begin{cases}
\text{correct} \begin{cases} \text{function?} \begin{cases}
\text{``Withdraw''} \quad \{\text{``amount?''}\} \begin{cases} \text{Valid \$?} & \{\text{remit cash} \\ \oplus & \\ \text{invalid} & \{\text{``sorry''} \end{cases} \\
\oplus \\
\text{``Query''} \qquad \{\text{display balance} \\
\oplus \\
\text{``Deposit''} \begin{cases} \text{``amount?''} \\ \text{accept envelope} \end{cases}
\end{cases}
\end{cases} \\
\oplus \\
\text{wrong} \quad \{\text{``sorry''}
\end{cases}
$$

■

■ EXAMPLE 5.21

In an interesting article [78], the authors show how Warnier-Orr notation can be used to specify hypermedia, multimedia, and interactive film systems. The following sequence is a high-level specification for a dubbed foreign movie on digital video and is taken from this article (modified slightly). Here "$\oplus$" is used to indicate parallelism.

$$
\text{foreign movie scene}
\begin{cases}
\text{video stream} \begin{cases} \text{frame-group-a} \\ \text{frame-group-b} \end{cases} \\
\oplus \\
\text{sound-stream} \begin{cases} \text{music} \\ \oplus \\ \text{speech} \end{cases} \\
\oplus \\
\text{text-stream} \quad \{ \text{subtitle}
\end{cases}
$$

Coincidentally, the authors also describe an automatic teller machine using the same technique. ■

The use of Warnier-Orr notation is encouraged as an alternative to structure charts, which we noted were similar but lacked conditional branching. Warnier-Orr notation clearly identifies function execution sequence, is good for a top-down design methodology, and helps to identify recursion and repeated modules. In addition, its conditional branching constructs make it viable for use in multitasking specification. Warnier-Orr notation is a viable alternative to structure charts for describing hierarchical decomposition. As this example shows, it also is an excellent tool for specifying multimedia systems including World Wide Web pages. Finally, both data structures and process specification can be represented with the same mechanisms.

The main disadvantage of Warnier-Orr notation, however, is that the diagrams can grow large and complex, and often cryptic. In addition, the synchronization of concurrent processes using only flags is restrictive. Finally, it is not well-known or widely used.

5.10 STATECHARTS

Harel's statecharts [60], [61] combine FSA with dataflow diagrams and a feature called broadcast communication in a way that can depict synchronous and asynchronous operations. Statecharts can be described succinctly as statecharts = FSA + depth + orthogonality + broadcast communication

Here, FSA is a finite state automaton, depth represents levels of detail, orthogonality represents separate tasks, and broadcast communication is a method for allowing different orthogonal processes to react to the same event. The statechart resembles a finite state automaton, and the various components of the statechart are depicted as follows:

1. The FSA is represented in the usual way, with capital letters or descriptive phrases used to label the states.
2. Depth is represented by the insideness of states.
3. Broadcast communications are represented by labeled arrows, in the same way as FSAs.
4. Orthogonality is represented by dashed lines separating states.
5. Symbols $a, b, \ldots, z$ represent events that trigger transitions, in the same way that transitions are represented in FSAs.
6. Small letters within parentheses represent conditions that must be true for the transitions to occur.

5.10.1 Depth

A main feature of statecharts is its encouragement of top-down design of a module. For example, for any module (represented like a state in a FSA), increasing detail is depicted as states internal to it. In Figure 5.18, the navigation system is composed of six internal states. Each of these in turn can be decomposed into appropriate states that represent program modules. Those states can also be decomposed, and so forth. To the programmer, each state within a state represents a procedure within a procedure. This insideness is similar to the nesting levels depicted in Warnier-Orr notation and encourages the correct application of information-hiding principles.

5.10.2 Orthogonality

Orthogonality depicts concurrency in the system for processes that run in isolation, called AND states. Orthogonality is represented by dividing the orthogonal components by dashed lines. For example, if state Y consists of AND components A and D, Y is called the *orthogonal product* of A and D. If Y is entered from the outside (without any additional information), then the states A and D are entered simultaneously. Communication between the AND states can be achieved through global memory, whereas synchronization can be achieved through a unique feature of statecharts called broadcast communication.

5.10.3 Broadcast Communication

Broadcast communication is depicted by the transition of orthogonal states based on the same event. For example, if a navigation system switches from standby to ready mode, an event indicated by an interrupt can cause a state change in several processes.

Another unique aspect of broadcast communication is the concept of the *chain reaction*; that is, events can trigger other events. The implementation follows from the fact that statecharts can be viewed as an extension of Mealy machines, and output events can be attached to the triggering event. In contrast with Mealy machines, however, the output is not seen by the outside world; instead, it affects the behavior of an orthogonal component.

For example, in Figure 5.15 suppose there exists a transition labeled e/f, and if event e occurs then event f is immediately activated. Event f could in turn trigger a transaction such as f/g. The length of a chain reaction is the number of transitions triggered by the first event. Chain reactions are assumed to occur instantaneously.

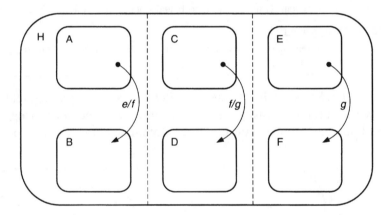

Figure 5.15 Chain reaction illustration.

In this system, a chain reaction of length 2 will occur when the e/f transition occurs.

We now examine two examples of the use of statecharts to illustrate the features that make them unique.

■ **EXAMPLE 5.22**

Consider a simple system consisting of states A through D depicted in Figure 5.16. State D contains states A and B. State D enters state A when event g occurs, or into state B when event p occurs. D can also be entered via a transition from state C when event h occurs. State B is entered from state A when event f occurs. Finally, state C can be entered from state A if event g occurs and condition e is true.   ■

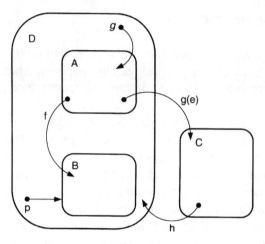

Figure 5.16 Four-state system.

■ **EXAMPLE 5.23**

Next consider the more complex system consisting of states A through J depicted in Figure 5.17. Description of the system in words would be rather complex, but it is important to note that state J is broken up into orthogonal processes containing states A, B, and C. Note also that event h causes a transition from state D to E, state G to F, and state H to I simultaneously.   ■

■ **EXAMPLE 5.24**

Finally, let us return to the navigation subsystem discussed throughout the text, and provide a statechart diagram for it. It is given in Figure 5.18.   ■

Harel's statecharts are excellent for representing real-time systems because they can easily depict concurrency while preserving modularity. In addition, the concept of broadcast communication allows for easy intertask

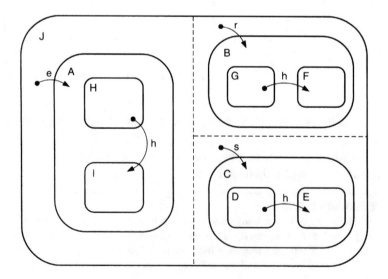

Figure 5.17 Ten-state system.

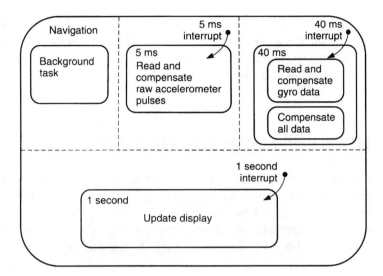

Figure 5.18 Navigation subsystem using statecharts.

communication representation. In short, the statechart combines the best of dataflow diagrams and finite state automata. Finally, commercial products (e.g., STATEMATE by i-Logix) allow an engineer to graphically design a real-time system using statecharts, perform detailed simulation analysis, and generate Ada or C code [61].

TABLE 5.6 A Summary of Modeling Techniques

Technique	Advantages	Disadvantages
Natural language	Widely used; can clarify descriptions	Ambiguous; no code generation
Mathematical specification	Unambiguous; formal methods applicable; code optimization possible	Can be cryptic; hard to use; training not widespread; error-prone
Flowchart	Widely used; good for single tasks	No concurrency; no temporal behavior; encourages GOTOs
Structure chart	Widely used; good for small systems; encourages top-down design	No conditional branching; no concurrency; no temporal behavior
Pseudocode and PDL	Close to programming language; formal methods applicable	Costs can be high; error-prone
Finite state automaton	Widely used; easy to develop; code generation possible; code optimization possible	"insideness" not depictable; no concurrency; number of states grows
Dataflow diagram	Widely used; concurrency; structure charts can be derived; helps in Parnas partitioning	Synchronization hard to show

The major drawback of statecharts is that they are not widely used, although this will change as more designers discover the benefits of statecharts.

Table 5.6 summarizes some of the advantages and disadvantages of the modeling techniques discussed.

5.11 SANITY IN USING GRAPHICAL TECHNIQUES

When using any form of graphical technique, be reasonable in laying out your designs. For example, the depiction in Figure 5.19 is taken from a talk on complex systems design by Parnas. It is essentially a statechart showing the same design and with the boxes redrawn. The effect is astounding. The moral is: use aesthetic reasoning in drawing design diagrams.

The right way

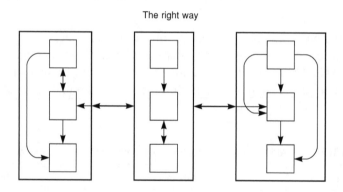

The wrong way

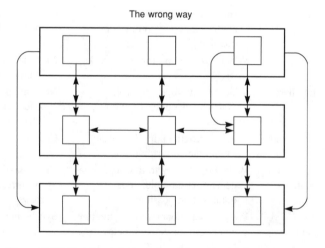

Figure 5.19 Graphical design, the right way and the wrong way.

5.12 EXERCISES

1. Convert the structure chart for the coffee machine in Example 5.4 into Warnier-Orr notation.

2. Use structure charts to describe the automobile simulator in Example 5.1.

3. Use structure charts to describe the patient monitoring system in Figure 5.14.

4. Use flowcharts to describe the automobile simulator in Example 5.1.

5. Use flowcharts to describe the patient monitoring system in Figure 5.14.

6. Build a Moore finite state automaton to accept the words "cab," "cob," "cat," "cot" but no others from the alphabet $L = \{a, b, c, t, o\}$.

7. Build a Moore finite state automaton to accept all words except "cab," "cob," "cat," "cot" from the alphabet $L = \{a, b, c, t, o\}$.

8. Build a Mealy finite state automaton to describe the coffee machine in Example 5.4. The machine should output words such as "adding sugar" when appropriate.

9. Design a Moore finite state automaton for the alphabet, $L = \{0,1\}$ *which accepts the set of all strings with 3 consecutive zeros.*

10. Research the difference between a deterministic and nondeterministic finite state automata. Under what circumstances would a nondeterministic finite state automaton be used to specify system requirements (i.e., what kinds of systems would be amenable to this technique)?

11. In the language of your choice, write a program which implements the finite state automaton described in exercise 6. The program should write "accepted" if the word is recognized and "rejected" if it is not. Input can be either from the keyboard or a file.

12. Use a Moore finite state automaton to describe the BITS process in Figure 5.1.

13. Use Warnier-Orr notation to describe the coffee machine in Example 5.4.

14. Use Warnier-Orr notation to describe the patient monitoring system in Figure 5.1.

15. Use a dataflow diagram to describe the coffee machine in Example 5.4.

16. Use a dataflow diagram to describe the patient monitoring system in Figure 5.14.

17. Use a dataflow diagram to describe the automobile simulator in Example 5.1.

18. Use a Petri net to describe the following:
    (a) The discrete convolution of two real valued functions $f(t)$ and $g(t)$, $t = 0, 1, 2, 3, 4, 5$.

    $$(f * g)(t) = \sum_{i=0}^{5} f(i)g(t - i)$$

    (b) The matrix multiplication of two 4×4 matrices.

19. Draw a Petri net to perform the quadratic equation

    $$\frac{-b \pm \sqrt{b^2 - 4ac}}{2a}$$

    Attempt to maximize parallelism.

20. Use a Petri net to describe the coffee machine in Example 5.4.

21. Use statecharts to describe the automobile simulator in Example 5.1.

22. Use statecharts to describe the patient monitoring system in Figure 5.14.

23. Use statecharts to specify the design of a phone answering machine with which you are familiar.

24. A real-time system is to be designed which models the human body on a single processing system. The simulator consists of the following five subsystems:
    (a) Cardiovascular system
    (b) Digestive system
    (c) Neural system
    (d) Motor system
    (e) Reproductive system
    Model the system using any combination of the techniques discussed in this chapter. This is not a test of physiology; rather, concentrate on clearly modeling the system using the layperson's knowledge of how the subsystems work.

25. Using an appropriate combination of the techniques discussed in this chapter, model the operation of an automobile. Include a description of the following subsystems:
    (a) Steering
    (b) Braking
    (c) Acceleration
    (d) Dashboard display
    Don't worry about the equations underlying these systems; a good intuitive description will do.

26. Use any one of the modeling techniques discussed to model the software life cycle employing the software test cycle as a stimulus.

6

Real-Time Kernels

KEY POINTS OF THE CHAPTER

1. Real-time multitasking can be achieved without interrupts, and when feasible, it is preferred because it leads to systems that are easier to analyze.
2. Foreground/background architectures are the most widely used in embedded applications.
3. The task-control block model is used in commercial real-time executives and in full-featured operating systems where the number of tasks is dynamic or indeterminate.
4. The more features a real-time kernel provides, the more complex it is, the more its performance degrades, and the more difficult it is to analyze.
5. A noninterrupt driven cyclic executive is based on one or several major cycles that describe the order in which minor cycles are executed.

In Chapter 1 we noted that a specialized collection of system programs is called an operating system. Anyone who has used a computer has interacted with the computer's operating system directly or indirectly. Although there are many well-known commercial operating systems, they are often too bulky and too all-purpose to be useful in real-time applications that are embedded and have stringent response-time requirements.

Frequently, the real-time systems designer must design a bare-bones operating system, or use one of the specialized real-time operating systems that are commercially available. (For custom computers such as those used in many embedded applications, there are no commercial operating systems available.) This chapter will help you build your own real-time operating system, or at least identify desirable features if you choose to purchase a real-time operating system or use an existing one.

All operating systems must provide three specific functions: task scheduling, task dispatching, and intertask communication. A *scheduler* determines which task will run next in a multitasking system, while a *dispatcher* performs the necessary bookkeeping to start that task. These functions can be provided either by hardware or by software, as we shall demonstrate. Note also that the terms *task* and *process* are interchangeable.

A *kernel*, *executive*, or *nucleus* is the smallest portion of the operating system that provides for task scheduling, dispatching, and intertask communication. In embedded systems, this essentially represents the entire real-time system, whereas in commercial real-time operating systems this might be all but the device drivers. An onion skin diagram such as that given in Figure 6.1 can be used to depict the role of the kernel in an operating system.

Since the publication of the first edition of this text, new variants of the definition of "kernel" have evolved. They are given here in increasing order of complexity. Of course, as the complexity decreases, so do the code size and response times. The hierarchy is also shown in Figure 6.2.

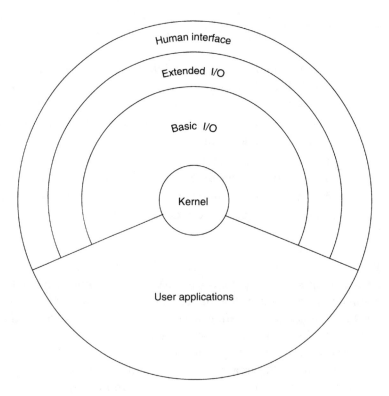

Figure 6.1 The role of the kernel in operating systems.

Users

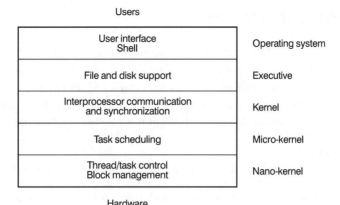

User interface Shell	Operating system
File and disk support	Executive
Interprocessor communication and synchronization	Kernel
Task scheduling	Micro-kernel
Thread/task control Block management	Nano-kernel

Hardware

Figure 6.2 Kernel hierarchy.

- *Nano-kernel*—Simple thread-of-execution (same as "flow-of-control") management. It essentially provides only one of the three services provided by a kernel; that is, it provides for task dispatching.

- *Micro-kernel*—A nano-kernel that provides for task scheduling.

- *Kernel*—A micro-kernel that provides for intertask synchronization and communication via semaphores, mailboxes, and other methods.

- *Executive*—A kernel that includes privatized memory blocks, I/O services, and other complex features. Most commercial real-time kernels are really executives.

- *Operating system*—An executive that provides for a generalized user interface or command processor, security, and a file management system. By this definition, the Unix kernel is indeed an operating system.

UNIX*, a registered trademark of AT&T's UNIX System Laboratories, is the common name for a family of interactive, multiuser operating systems. It is available in one version or another for virtually any computer, ranging from desktop personal computers and workstations to the most powerful super-computers. This capable multitasking system is ideally suited for both stand-alone and distributed processing configurations. It has powerful, yet easy-to-use, hardware interface mechanisms, and it provides an excellent means of organizing and storing files on a variety of media, including magnetic disks, magnetic tapes, and optical disks. Unix systems are available to support individual users, small groups, or entire departments on a wide range of processing platforms.

In this chapter we examine strategies employed in the design of real-time kernels.

*UNIX is not an acronym, and therefore need not be capitalized unless referring to the registered trademark. Generally, the term 'Unix' is used throughout this text.

6.1 POLLED LOOP SYSTEMS

Polled loop systems are the simplest real-time kernel. Polled loops allow for fast response to single devices but can't do much else. In a polled loop system, a single and repetitive test instruction is used to test a flag that indicates whether or not some event has occurred. If the event has not occurred, then the polling continues. No intertask communication or scheduling is needed because only a single task exists.

■ EXAMPLE 6.1

A software system is needed to handle packets of data that arrive at a rate of no more than 1 per second. A flag called "Packet_here" is set by the network, which writes the data into the CPU's memory via DMA. The data are available when Packet_here = 1. Using a Pascal code fragment, we can describe a polled loop to handle such a system:

```
while TRUE do                    { do forever }
 begin
    if Packet_here=TRUE then     { flag set? }
       begin
          process_data;          { this procedure processes the data }
          Packet_here := FALSE   { reset flag}
       end
 end                                                              ■
```

Polled loop schemes work well when a single processor is dedicated to handling the I/O for some fast device and when overlapping of events is not allowed or is kept to a minimum.

■ EXAMPLE 6.2

IBM's OS/2 Presentation Manager reads the application queue using a polled loop.   ■

6.1.1 Polled Loop with Interrupts

A variation on the polled loop uses a fixed clock interrupt to wait a period of time between when the flag is determined to be TRUE and when the flag is reset to FALSE. Such a system is used to treat events that exhibit a phenomenon known as *switch bounce*.

Every electrical engineer knows that it is impossible to build a switch that can change from its OFF condition (e.g., 0 volt) to its ON condition (e.g., 5 volts) instantaneously. A typical response for such a switch is given in Figure 6.3. For example, events triggered by pickle switches, levers, and keyboards all exhibit this phenomenon.

If we wait a sufficient amount of time after the initial triggering of the event, we can avoid interpreting the settling oscillations as events. These are, of course, spurious events that would surely overwhelm our little polled loop handler. A delay

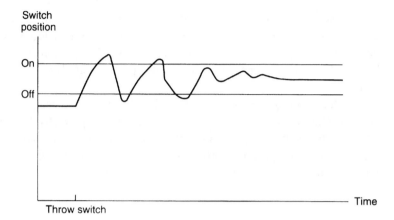

Figure 6.3 Switch bounce.

period can be realized with a programmable timer that issues an interrupt after a countdown period. In the absence of such hardware, a software routine can be written to implement the delay. To illustrate such a technique consider the following.

■ EXAMPLE 6.3

A polled loop system is used to handle an event that occurs randomly but no more than once per second. The event is known to exhibit a switch-bounce effect that disappears after 20 milliseconds. A 10-millisecond fixed-rate interrupt is available for synchronization. The event is signaled by an external device that sets a memory location FLAG to TRUE.

In Pascal a synchronized polled loop would look like:

```
While TRUE do                    { infinite polled loop }
  begin
    if FLAG = TRUE then          { event detected }
      begin
        counter := 0;            { initialize bounce counter }
        while counter < 3;       { wait    }
        FLAG := FALSE            { reset event flag }
        process_event;           { process event }
      end
  end
```

The 10-millisecond interrupt routine might look like:

```
begin
  counter := counter+1
end
```

Interrupts are enabled in an initialization routine. Notice that we wait for three ticks of the interrupt routine in order to ensure that we wait at least 20 milliseconds.   ■

In summary, polled loop systems are simple to write and debug, and the response time is easy to determine. As suggested, polled loops are excellent for handling high-speed data channels, especially when the events occur at widely dispersed intervals and the processor is dedicated to handling the data channel.

Polled loop systems most often fail, however, because bursting of events was not taken into account (this is discussed in Chapter 10). Furthermore, polled loops by themselves are generally not sufficient to handle complicated systems. Finally, polled loops inherently waste CPU time, especially if the event being polled occurs infrequently.

6.2 PHASE/STATE-DRIVEN CODE

Phase-driven or *state-driven* code uses nested if-then statements, case statements, or a finite state automaton to break up the processing of a function into discrete code segments. The separation of processes allows each to be temporarily suspended before completion, without loss of critical data. This, in turn, facilitates multitasking via a scheme such as coroutines, which we will discuss shortly.

Certain types of process lend themselves well to FSA implementation. For example, the compilation process can be regarded as comprising lexical analysis, parsing, code generation, and optimization. A process implementing compilation could be interrupted after each of the phases, but not in between. Communications programs such as network packet handlers are often broken up into phases.

■ **EXAMPLE 6.4**

A simple process consists of three states. At the end of each state a flag is set and the process is terminated. Upon restarting, the process resumes where it left off. The following Pascal code fragment illustrates this.

```
procedure task;

begin
  case flag of
  1:   begin
          perform_part_1;        /* do phase 1 processing */
          flag := 2
       end
  2:   begin
          perform_part_2;        /* do phase 2 processing */
          flag := 3
       end
```

```
3:    begin
         perform_part_3;         /* do phase 3 processing */
         flag := 1
      end
   end
end                                                                    ■
```

This simple nested if-then structure is really just a special case of FSA-driven code.

■ EXAMPLE 6.5

A finite state automaton can be implemented easily in Pascal or another suitable language. First, a two-dimensional array is constructed containing the table representation of the FSA. Let *states* be the variable type depicting the set of states, *alphabet* the variable type representing the input alphabet, and *table* the transition table.

The following code fragment can then be used to read a stream of inputs using procedure *get* (not shown). At the time the current state is determined, an appropriate process is executed. The code determines the final state of the automata after the last input is read.

```
typedef  states:  (state1, ... , staten);      { n is # of states }
         alphabet:(input1, ... , inputn);
         table_row: array [1..n] of states;

procedure move_forward;                { advances the FSA from state to state }

var
         state: states;
         input: alphabet;
         table: array[1..m] of table_row; { m is size of alphabet }

begin
    repeat
      get(input);                       { read one token from input stream }
      state := table[ord(input)][state]; { transition }
      execute_process(state);      { execute relevant process }
    until input = EOF              { last token read }
end;

procedure execute_process(state: states);
begin
    case state of
    state1:  process1;             { execute process 1 }
    state2:  process2;             { execute process 2 }
       .
       .
       .
    staten:  processn;             { execute process n }
end
```
                                                                       ■

To summarize, state-driven systems can be coded in many languages using nested if-then or case statements. For more complex systems, table-driven code is preferable. Such systems can be used in conjunction with polled loops, where the first state tests some flag, and the second state processes the associated data if the flag is set.

Not all processes lend themselves naturally to division into states; some are therefore unsuitable for this technique. In addition, the tables needed to implement the code can become quite large. Finally, the manual translation process from the finite state automaton to tabular form is prone to error.

6.3 COROUTINES

Coroutines or *cooperative multitasking systems* require disciplined programming and an appropriate application. These types of kernels are employed in conjunction with code driven by finite state automata. In this scheme, two or more processes are coded in the state-driven fashion just discussed, and after each phase is complete, a call is made to a central dispatcher. The dispatcher holds the program counter for a list of processes that are executed in round-robin fashion; that is, it selects the next process to execute. This process then executes until the next phase is complete, and the central dispatcher is called again.

Communication between the processes is achieved via global variables. Any data that need to be preserved between dispatches must be deposited in global variables.

Some surprisingly large and complex applications have been implemented using coroutines; for example, IBM's transaction processor, CICS (Customer Information Control System), was originally constructed entirely via coroutines. IBM's OS/2 Presentation Manager uses coroutines to coordinate the activities within the various user windows.

■ **EXAMPLE 6.6**

Consider a system in which two processes are executing "in parallel" and in isolation. After executing phaseA1, process_A returns control to the central dispatcher by executing "exit." The dispatcher initiates process_B, which executes phaseB1 to completion before returning control to the dispatcher. The dispatcher then starts process A, which begins phaseA2 and so on. The Pascal code for such a scheme is depicted below:

```
procedure process_A;          procedure process_B;
  begin                         begin
    while TRUE do                 while TRUE do
      case stateA of                case stateB of
        1:  phaseA1;                  1:  phaseB1;
        2:  phaseA2;                  2:  phaseB2;
        3:  phaseA3;                  3:  phaseB3;
```

```
        4:  phaseA4;                    4:  phaseB4
        5:  phaseA5                  end
    end

                            end

  end
```

where stateA and stateB are state counters that are managed by the dispatcher. Such a scheme can be extended to any number of processes, each broken into any number of phases. ■

If each programmer provides calls to the dispatcher at known intervals, then the response time is easy to determine. We will see how to do this in Chapter 9. Notice that this system is written without hardware interrupts.

A variation of this scheme uses state-driven code and state counters. Another variation is used when a polled loop must wait for a particular event while other processing can continue. This type of system is described below.

■ **EXAMPLE 6.7**

A polled loop routine, Task1, is to monitor an event flag, "event." If the flag is not set, Task1 exits. If the flag is set, then a process routine, process_event, is called. "State" is used to keep track of the state of the polled loop. The Pascal code for this system is

```
procedure Task1;
    begin
     case  state of

     1: if event = TRUE  then  { event detected }
           begin
             state :=2;           { change state flag }
             event :=FALSE        { reset event flag }
           end;                   { call exit }

     2:  begin
             state :=1            { reset state flag }
             process_event;       { process event }
           end                    { call exit }
    end
```

Such a scheme reduces the amount of time wasted polling the event flag, and allows for processing time for other tasks. ■

Note that if there is only one coroutine, then it will be repeated cyclically *ad infinitum*. Such a system is called a *cyclic executive*.

In short, coroutines are the easiest type of "fairness scheduling" that can be implemented. In addition, the processes can be written by independent parties, and the number of processes need not be known beforehand. Finally, certain languages such as Ada and Modula-2 have built-in constructs for implementing coroutines in a way that is superior to the somewhat artificial (but more general) implementation given in Examples 6.6 and 6.7.

On the negative side, this is an error-prone approach that requires strict discipline on the part of the programmers because it assumes that they will relinquish the CPU at regular intervals. It also requires a communication scheme involving global variables, which is undesirable. Finally, processes cannot always be broken easily into uniform size phases, which can adversely affect response time since the minimum size is a function of the longest phase.

6.4 INTERRUPT DRIVEN SYSTEMS

In interrupt driven systems, the main program is a single "jump-to-self" instruction. The various tasks in the system are scheduled via either hardware or software interrupts, whereas dispatching is performed by the interrupt-handling routines.

The interrupts in an interrupt driven system may occur at fixed rates (periodically), aperiodically, or both. Tasks driven by interrupts that occur aperiodically are called *sporadic tasks* [115]. Systems in which interrupts occur only at fixed frequencies are called *fixed-rate systems*, those with interrupts occurring sporadically are known as *sporadic systems*, and those with interrupts occurring both at fixed frequencies and sporadically are called *hybrid systems*.

When hardware scheduling is used, a clock or other external device issues interrupt signals that are directed to an interrupt controller. The interrupt-controller issues interrupt signals depending on the order of arrival and priority of the interrupts involved. If the computer architecture supports multiple interrupts, then the hardware handles dispatching as well. If only a single interrupt level is available, then the interrupt-handling routine will have to read the interrupt vector on the interrupt controller, determine which interrupt occurred, and dispatch the appropriate tasks. Some processors implement this in microcode and so the operating systems designer is relieved of this duty.

In any case, a snapshot of the machine—called the *context*—must be preserved upon switching tasks so that it can be restored upon reinitiating the interrupted process. The context includes the contents of certain registers, the program counter, and other entities that could be altered by another process.

6.4.1 Context Switching

The most important part of the real-time operation of the interrupt driven system is *context switching*. Context switching is the process of saving and restoring sufficient information for a real-time task so that it can be resumed after being interrupted. The context is ordinarily saved to a stack data structure.

6.4.1.1 Context-saving rule Context switching time is a major contributor to response times and is a factor that we strive to minimize. The rule for saving context is simple: save the minimum amount of information necessary to safely restore any process after it has been interrupted.

What information could this be? The following are usually considered part of the context of a process.

1. Contents of registers
2. Contents of the program counter
3. Contents of coprocessor registers
4. Memory page registers (see Chapter 8)
5. Memory-mapped I/O location mirror images (see Section 2.3.2)
6. Special variables.

Normally, within the interrupt handlers, interrupts are disabled during the critical context-switching period. Sometimes, however, after sufficient context has been saved, interrupts may be enabled after a partial context switch in order to handle a burst of interrupts, to detect spurious interrupts, or to handle a time-overloaded condition.

6.4.1.2 Stack Model The stack model for context switching is used mostly in embedded systems where the number of real-time or interrupt-driven tasks is fixed. In this case, context is saved by the interrupt handler. Contrast this scheme with the task-control block model, which is used in more complicated real-time operating systems and is discussed in a later section.

In the stack model, each interrupt handler is associated with a hardware interrupt and is invoked by the CPU, which vectors to the instruction stored at the appropriate interrupt-handler location. The context is then saved to a specially designated memory area that can be static, in the case of a single-interrupt system, or a stack, in the case of a multiple-interrupt system. This type of stack management is discussed in Chapter 8.

■ EXAMPLE 6.8

Consider the following code for a partial real-time system, written in C and consisting of a simple jump-to-self and three interrupt handlers, which saves context using the stack model. The interrupt handlers' starting addresses should be loaded into the appropriate interrupt vector location upon initialization. Alternatively, this can be performed at link time by the link editor or linker control file.

```
void main (void)

{
    init();       /* initialize system, load interrupt handlers */
    while(TRUE);  /* infinite loop */
}
```

```
void int1 (void)
                    /* interrupt handler 1 */


{
    save(context);     /* save context on stack */
    task1();           /* execute task 1 */
    restore(context);  /* restore context from stack */
}


void int2 (void)
                    /* interrupt handler 2 */


{
    save(context);     /* save context on stack */
    task2();           /* execute task 2 */
    restore(context);  /* restore context from stack */
}


void int3 (void)
                    /* interrupt handler 3 */


{
    save(context);     /* save context on stack */
    task3();           /* execute task 3 */
    restore(context);  /* restore context from stack */
{
```

The procedure "save" involves the saving of certain registers to a stack area, whereas "restore" restores those registers from the stack.   ■

6.4.2 Round-Robin Systems

In *round-robin system* several processes are executed sequentially to completion, often in conjunction with a cyclic executive. In round-robin systems with time-slicing, each executable task is assigned a fixed-time quantum called a *time slice* in which to execute. A fixed-rate clock is used to initiate an interrupt at a rate corresponding to the time slice. The task executes until it completes or its execution time expires, as indicated by the clock interrupt. If the task does not execute to completion, its context must be saved. The task is then placed at the end of the executable list. The context of the next executable task in the list is restored, and it resumes execution. Figure 6.4 illustrates the process.

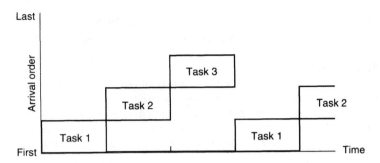

Figure 6.4 Time slicing of three tasks.

6.4.3 Preemptive Priority Systems

A higher-priority task is said to *preempt* a lower-priority task if it interrupts the lower-priority task. That is, the lower-priority task is still running while the higher-priority task is about to begin. Systems that use preemption schemes instead of round-robin or first-come-first-serve scheduling are called *preemptive priority systems*. The priorities assigned to each interrupt are based on the urgency of the task associated with that interrupt (see Figure 6.5).

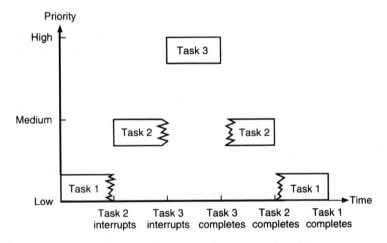

Figure 6.5 Preemptive scheduling of three tasks.

■ **EXAMPLE 6.9**
The nuclear power station monitoring system represents a fixed-priority system. While the handling of intruder events is critical, nothing is more important than processing the core over-temperature alert.   ■

Prioritized interrupts can be either fixed priority or dynamic priority. *Fixed-priority* systems are less flexible in that the task priorities cannot be changed.

Dynamic-priority systems can allow the priorities of tasks to change. This feature is particularly important in certain types of threat-management systems.

■ EXAMPLE 6.10

Dynamic-priority systems can be found in many threat-management systems, such as those related to military aircraft. The aircraft's threat-management computer may be able to track up to six enemy aircraft. Each of these is tracked by a process in a dynamic-priority multitasking computer. At some fixed rate, the relative threat of each enemy aircraft is recomputed based on proximity, posture, and other factors. The priority of each of the tasks managing the individual threats is then readjusted. ■

Preemptive priority schemes can lead to the hogging of resources by higher-priority tasks. This can lead to a lack of available resources for lower-priority tasks. In this case, the lower-priority tasks are said to be facing a problem called *starvation.*

■ EXAMPLE 6.11

Consider the Unix operating system. In Unix, any task that makes a system call cannot be preempted; that is, the set of Unix system services provided has highest priority. This is a problem, since a low-priority task-making system call cannot be preempted. Real-time Unix solutions strive to rectify this problem (see Chapter 14). ■

6.4.3.1 Rate-Monotonic Systems   A special class of fixed-rate preemptive priority interrupt driven systems, called *rate-monotonic* systems, includes those real-time systems where the priorities are assigned so that the higher the execution frequency, the higher the priority. This scheme is common in embedded applications, particularly avionics systems, and has been studied extensively [54], [103], [104], [105], [140], [141].

■ EXAMPLE 6.12

In our aircraft navigation system, the task that gathers accelerometer data every 5 milliseconds has the highest priority. The task that collects gyro data, and compensates these data and the accelerometer data every 40 milliseconds, has the second highest priority. Finally, the task that updates the pilot's display every second has lowest priority. ■

An extremely important paper by Liu and Layland [104] demonstrated that rate-monotonic systems are the optimal fixed-priority scheduling method. This means that if a successful schedule cannot be found for the rate-monotonic system, then no other fixed-priority scheduling system will avail. Rate-monotonic systems are the most highly cited class of real-time system in the literature. Although numerous theoretical results exist, most are based on assumptions that are impractical. For example, in rate-monotic systems, no deadline will be missed if the CPU utilization is <70%. (The number is actually $ln(2)$, which is derived by constructing and then analyzing an event tree.) Even if the CPU utilization is above 70%, a schedule may still be feasible, although no guarantees about missed deadlines can be made. However, these observations (and the basic theory itself) do not take into account practical issues such as context switch time, resource contention, and clock variation. Numerous attempts have been made to address these problems, but to the practicing engineer, most of the solutions are impossible to implement. Despite these drawbacks, many systems have been built using rate-monotonic analysis (RMA) as a sanity check.

However, rate-monotic systems are not a panacea. In particular, *priority inversion* may necessarily occur.

There are actually several kinds of priority inversion. The first occurs in rate-monotonic systems where in order to enforce rate-monotonicity, a low-priority process with a high frequency of execution is assigned a higher priority than a task with higher criticality but lower execution rate. One solution is to exchange execution rates, where possible. Otherwise, the high criticality routine can be placed in the faster cycle, but a counter can be used to control its rate of execution.

Another type of priority inversion occurs when a lower priority routine holds a resource (e.g., using a semaphore) that a higher priority routine needs. One commonly cited, but difficult-to-implement solution to this problem is called the *priority ceiling protocol* (PCP). This protocol states that a task blocking a higher priority task inherits the higher priority for the duration of that task. Apparently, Ada 95 is capable of implementing the PCP utilizing the three new pragmas discussed in Chapter 3.

A third type of priority inversion occurs in object-oriented systems in which attribute inheritance causes a subclass to inherit priorities that are in conflict with its intent. The solution is careful assignment of attributes.

6.4.4 Major and Minor Cycles

Some common terminology applies when tasks are assigned to run at specific frequencies (usually in periodic systems but also in noninterrupt driven cyclic executives). If a time line is drawn showing the scheduling of tasks and if the assignment uses rate-monotonic discipline or is a noninterrupt driven cyclic executive, then the scheduling sequence repeats itself after a certain period of time. This sequence is called a *major cycle*. If within the major cycle, smaller sequences also repeat, they are called *minor cycles*. For example consider the following noninterrupt driven cyclic executive:

```
while(forever) do
begin
   process_a;
   process_b;
   process_a;
   process_c;
   process_a;
```

```
        process_b;
        process_a;
        process_d;
    end
```

Notice how `process_a` runs four times more often than `process_c` or `process_d` and twice as often as `process_b`. Here the major cycle is given by the process sequence `abacabad` with minor cycles `abad`, `abac`, `ab`, `ac`, and `ad`.

6.4.5 Hybrid Systems

Hybrid systems include interrupts that occur at both fixed rates and sporadically. The sporadic interrupts may be used to handle a critical error that requires immediate attention, and thus have highest priority. This type of system is common in embedded applications.

Another type of hybrid system found in commercial operating systems is a combination of round-robin and preemptive systems. In this system, tasks of higher priority can always preempt those of lower priority. However, if two or more tasks of the same priority are ready to run simultaneously, then they run in round-robin fashion.

To summarize, interrupt-only systems are easy to write and typically have fast response times because process scheduling can be done via hardware. Interrupt-only systems are a special case of foreground/background systems, which are widely used in embedded systems.

One weakness of interrupt-only systems, however, is the time wasted in the jump-to-self loop and the difficulty in providing advanced services. These services include device drivers and interfaces to multiple layered networks. Another weakness is vulnerability to malfunctions owing to timing variations, unanticipated race conditions, hardware failures, and so on. Some companies avoid designs based on interrupts for this reason.

6.5 FOREGROUND/BACKGROUND SYSTEMS

Foreground/background systems are an improvement over the interrupt-only systems in that the polled loop (which was really a dummy background process) is replaced by code that performs useful processing. We will discuss the kinds of processes that occur in the foreground and background shortly.

Foreground/background systems are the most common solution for embedded applications. They involve a set of interrupt driven or real-time processes called the *foreground* and a collection of noninterrupt driven processes called the *background*. The foreground tasks run in round-robin, preemptive priority, or combination fashion. The background task is fully preemptable by any foreground task and, in a sense, represents the lowest priority task in the system.

All real-time solutions are just special cases of the foreground/background systems. For example, the polled loop is simply a foreground/background system with no foreground, and a polled loop as a background. Adding interrupts for synchronization yields a full foreground/background system.

Phase-driven code is a foreground/background system with no foreground and phase-driven code for a background. Coroutine systems are just a complicated background process. Finally, interrupt-only systems are foreground/background systems without a background.

It is precisely because all real-time solutions are just variations of foreground/background systems that we study them so extensively. Mastering foreground/background systems allows us to understand all the other real-time kernels.

6.5.1 Background Processing

The question of what processing should be placed in background is an easy one: anything that is not time critical. The background process is the process with the lowest priority. This task will always execute to completion, unless the system is time-overloaded (all processing time is spent in the foreground). But the rate at which the background will be executed can be very low and depends on the time-loading factor. That is, if p represents the time-loading for all the foreground processes (see Chapter 9 to calculate this), and if e is the execution time of the background process, then the background process execution period, t, is

$$t = \frac{e}{1 - p} \tag{6.1}$$

What kind of processes are not time-critical and can be performed in background? It is common, for instance, to increment a counter in the background in order to provide a measure of time-loading or to detect if any foreground process has hung up. For example, you can provide individual counters for each of the foreground processes, which are reset in those processes. If the background process detects that one of the counters is not being reset often enough, you can assume that the corresponding task is not being executed and, that some kind of failure is indicated. This is a form of "software watchdog timer."

Certain types of low-priority self-testing can also be performed in background. For example, in many systems, a complete test of the CPU instruction set is performed. This kind of test could never be performed in foreground, but should be part of a robust system design. The design and coding of these CPU instruction tests require careful planning.

■ **EXAMPLE 6.13**

In the space shuttle inertial measurement unit computer, a process known as *RAM scrubbing* is performed [95]. The memory card of this system is equipped with a Hamming code error correction and detection scheme which, for a 16-bit word, can detect 1-, 2-, and some 3-bit errors, and correct all 1- and some 2-bit errors. The device corrects these errors on the data bus, however, and not in memory. By consecutively reading and then writing back each memory location, the corrected data are restored in RAM. This process helps to reduce errors perpetrated against RAM by charged particles present in space, or in the presence of a nuclear event (such as in our nuclear power station), called *single event upsets* (see Chapter 11). RAM scrubbing is not suggested as a foreground process.   ■

Finally, low-priority display updates, logging to printers, or other interface to slow devices can be performed in background.

6.5.2 Initialization

Initialization of the foreground/background system consists of the following steps:

1. Disable interrupts.
2. Set up interrupt vectors and stacks.
3. Perform self-test.
4. Perform system initialization.
5. Enable interrupts.

Initialization is actually the first part of the background process. Here, we immediately disable interrupts because many systems come up with interrupts enabled, ready, and waiting, and we still need time to set things up. This setup consists of placing the appropriate interrupt vector addresses, setting up stacks if we have a multiple-level interrupt system, and initializing any data, counters, arrays, and so on. In addition, we perform any self-diagnostic tests before enabling any interrupts. Typical diagnostic tests are discussed in Chapter 11. Finally, we begin real-time processing.

6.5.3 Real-Time Operation

The real-time or foreground operation for the foreground/background system is the same as that for the interrupt-only system.

■ EXAMPLE 6.14

Suppose you wish to implement an interrupt handler for a 2-address computer architecture with a single interrupt. The EPI and DPI instructions can be used to enable and disable the interrupt explicitly, and we will assume that upon receiving an interrupt, the CPU will hold off all other interrupts until explicitly re-enabled with an EPI instruction.

For context-switching purposes, we wish to save the eight general registers, R0-R7, on the stack. Note that context switching involves saving the status of the machine as it is used by the background process. The foreground process will run to completion so its context is never saved.

Further assume that the CPU will save the program counter at the time of interruption in memory location 6, and the address of the interrupt-handler routine (the interrupt vector) is stored in memory location 5.

The following code should be used to initialize the foreground/background system:

```
DPI                          disable interrupts
STORE   @handler,5           put interrupt handler address in location 5
EPI                          enable interrupts
```

Of course other initialization, such as initializing flags and other data, should be performed before enabling interrupts.

If symbolic memory locations reg0 through reg7 are used to save the registers, then the interrupt handler, coded in 2-address code, might look as follows:

```
DPI                          redundantly disable interrupts
STORE R0,reg0                save register 0
STORE R1,reg1                save register 1
STORE R2,reg2                save register 2
STORE R3,reg3                save register 3
STORE R4,reg4                save register 4
STORE R5,reg5                save register 5
STORE R6,reg6                save register 6
STORE R7,reg7                save register 7

JU @APP                      execute real-time application program
LOAD R7,reg7                 restore register 7
LOAD R6,reg6                 restore register 6
LOAD R5,reg5                 restore register 5
LOAD R4,reg4                 restore register 4
LOAD R3,reg3                 restore register 3
LOAD R2,reg2                 restore register 2
LOAD R1,reg1                 restore register 1
LOAD R0,reg0                 restore register 0

EPI                          re-enable interrupts
RI                           return from interrupt
```

In many computers, block save and restore instructions are available to save and restore a set of registers to consecutive memory locations.

Also note that our interrupt handler does not permit the interrupt to interrupt itself. If this is to be accomplished, or if more than one interrupt routine existed, a stack rather than just static memory would be needed to save context.

The background program would include the initialization procedure and any processing that was not time-critical and would be written in the high-order language. If the program were to be written in C, it might look like this:

```
void main(void)

/* allocate space for context variable */
    int reg0, reg1, reg2, reg3, reg4, reg5, reg6, reg7;

/* declare other global variables here */
```

```
{
      init();                 /* initialize system */

      while(TRUE)             /* background loop */
          background(); /* non-real-time processing here */
}                                                                    ■
```

Foreground/background systems represent a superset of all the other real-time solutions discussed. They typically have good response times, since they rely on hardware to perform scheduling. They are the solution of choice for embedded real-time systems.

But foreground/background systems have at least one major drawback: interfaces to complicated devices and networks must be written. This procedure can be tedious and prone to error. In addition, these types of systems are best implemented when the number of foreground tasks is fixed and known *a priori*. Although languages that support dynamic allocation of memory could handle a variable number of tasks, this can be tricky. Finally, as with the interrupt-only system, the foreground/background system is vulnerable to timing variations, unanticipated race conditions, hardware failures, and so on. As mentioned before, some companies avoid designs based on interrupts for these reasons.

6.6 FULL-FEATURED REAL-TIME OPERATING SYSTEMS

We can extend the foreground/background solution into an operating system by adding additional functions such as network interfaces, complicated device drivers, and complex debugging tools. These types of systems are readily available as commercial products.

Such systems rely on a complex operating system using round-robin, preemptive priority, or a combination of both schemes to provide scheduling; the operating system represents the highest priority task, kernel, or supervisor. Commercial real-time operating systems are most often of this type. The task-control block model is most often used in these types of systems because the number of real-time tasks is indeterminate and dynamic.

■ **EXAMPLE 6.15**

Real-time Unix represents an example of such a full-featured operating system. There are several commercial versions of this well-known operating system with specific enhancements for real-time operation, most notably, *kernel preemption*.

In standard Unix, a process that makes system calls is not preemptable. Even if the calling process is of low priority, it continues executing until it is stopped or completed. In real-time Unix, preemption points have been built into the kernel so that system calls can be preempted without running to completion. This radically reduces response times.

Real-time Unix includes all the standard Unix device drivers and network interfaces, and usually includes other features—such as memory locking and contiguous file allocation—to improve real-time performance (see Chapter 8). For an excellent study of the real-time Unix, the reader is referred to [58]. ■

Other applications for full-featured commercial operating systems include simulators, in which certain processes are to be run in a round-robin fashion, and data acquisition and transaction processing, in which the operating system host is used to interface the data acquisition or telecommunications unit.

6.6.1 Task-Control Block Model

The task-control block model is the most popular method for implementing commercial, full-featured, real-time operating systems because the number of real-time tasks can be variable. This is useful in interactive on-line systems where tasks (users) come and go. This technique can be used in round-robin, preemptive priority, or combination systems, although it is generally associated with round-robin systems in which a single fixed interrupt or clock tick is used. In preemptive systems, however, it can be used to facilitate dynamic task prioritization. The main drawback of the task-control block model is that when a large number of tasks are created, the overhead of the scheduler can become significant. What follows is only a sketch of the technique. To fully implement it, you need to consult a text that is devoted to the technique, such as [134].

6.6.1.1 The Model In this technique, we associate with each task a context (e.g., program counter and register contents); an identification string or number; a status; and a priority if applicable. These items are stored in a structure called a *task-control block* (or TCB), and the collection is stored in one or more data structures, such as a linked list. Figure 6.6 depicts a sample TCB.

6.6.1.2 Task States The operating system manages the task-control blocks by keeping track of the status or state of each task. A task can typically be in any one of the following states:

1. Executing
2. Ready
3. Suspended
4. Dormant

Figure 6.7 summarizes the relationship of the different states.

Program counter
Task status
Task ID #
Contents of register *0*
Pointer to next TCB
• • •
Contents of register *n*
Other context

Figure 6.6 A typical task-control block.

The *executing* task is the one that is actually running, and in a single-processing system there can be only one executing task. A task can enter the executing state when it is created (if no other tasks are ready), or from the ready state (if it is eligible to run based on its priority or its position in the round-robin ready list). When a task is completed, it returns to the suspended state.

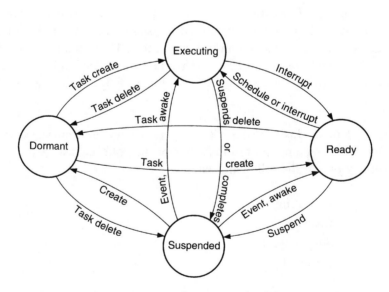

Figure 6.7 State transitions in the task-control block model system.

Tasks in the *ready* state are those that are ready to run but are not running. A task enters the ready state if it was executing and its time slice runs out, or if it was preempted. If it was in the suspended state, then it can enter the ready state if an event that initiates it occurs. If the task was in the dormant state, then it enters the ready state upon creation (if another task is executing).

Tasks that are waiting on a particular resource, and thus are not ready, are said to be in the *suspended* or *blocked* state.

The *dormant* state is used only in systems where the number of task-control blocks is fixed. (This allows for determining memory requirements beforehand, but limits available system memory.) This state is best described as a task that exists but is unavailable to the operating system. Once a task has been created, it can become dormant by deleting it.

6.6.1.3 Task Management   The operating system is in essence the highest priority task. Every hardware interrupt and every system level call (such as a request on a resource) invokes the real-time operating system. The operating system is responsible for maintaining a linked list containing the TCBs of all the ready tasks, and a second linked list of those in the suspended state. It also keeps a table of resources and a table of resource requests. In Chapter 7, we discuss how these tables are managed and how they can be used to facilitate intertask synchronization and communication.

When it is invoked, the operating system checks the ready list to see if the next task is eligible for execution. If it is eligible, then the TCB of the currently executing task is moved to the end of the ready list, and the eligible task is removed from the ready list and made the executing state.

In addition to rescheduling, the operating system checks the status of all resources in the suspended list. If a task is suspended on a resource, then that task can enter the ready state. The list structure is used to arbitrate two tasks that are pending on the same resource. If a resource becomes available to a pending task, then the resource tables are updated and the eligible task is moved from the suspended list to the ready list.

Commercially available real-time operating systems are wide-ranging in features and performance, and can support many standard devices and network protocols. Often these systems come equipped with useful development and debugging tools, and they can run on a variety of hardware and environments. In short, commercial real-time systems are best used when they can satisfy response requirements at a reasonable price, and if the system must run on a variety of platforms.

On the negative side, however, writing these types of real-time operating systems is a large undertaking. Using commercially available operating systems is an advantage, but these may have undesirable features and response times. Finally, these systems are often too large for embedded applications and are overkill for simple systems.

6.7 BUILD OR BUY?

One of the most commonly asked questions is "Should a commercial real-time kernel be used, or should one be built from scratch?" While the answer depends on the situation, the following key points should be remembered. Commercial kernels are the choice in most nonembedded environments because they generally

- Provide robust services.
- Are easy to use.
- Are portable.

Remember, however, that commercial solutions are often slower than necessary because tremendous overhead is incurred in implementing the task-control block model. Furthermore, commercial solutions tend to suffer from "featuritis." That is, in an attempt to make the largest pool of potential customers happy, a large number of features are included in the system that are of no interest to the general user. The run-time and storage costs associated with these features may be excessive. Finally, users should beware of manufacturers' misleading claims about response times, which are given as best or average case—the worst case response times can generally not be known!

In embedded systems, when the per-unit charge for commercial products is too high, or when desired features are unavailable, you will have to write your own kernel. Doing so is often difficult and costly, and the system will not be portable. However, code access and a "lean and mean" system may be dominant considerations.

For a good review of some currently available commercial real-time operating systems and more on the associated pitfalls, see [150].

6.8 POSIX

Much has been made of the POSIX standard (IEEE Portable Operating System Interface for Computer Environments, IEEE 1003.1-1990). The standard provides for standard compliance criteria for operating system services and is designed to allow applications programs to write applications that can easily port across operating systems. At this writing, systems can be certified as compliant with the 1003.1 standard.

However, 1003.1 (sometimes called POSIX.1) does not specifically support real-time applications (although real-time operating systems can run non-real-time applications in compliance). A new standard. POSIX 1003.4 has been proposed to remedy the lack of real-time support. Standard 1003.4 includes five sections that are, at this writing, in various stages of approval. These sections are

- POSIX.4
- POSIX.4a
- POSIX.4b
- POSIX.13
- POSIX.4c

Many of the features they propose to provide are discussed in later chapters of the text. However, for completeness, let us summarize them here.

POSIX.4 provides the base real-time extensions to POSIX.1 such as

- Synchronous and Asynchronous I/O
- Semaphores
- Memory locking
- Shared memory
- Execution scheduling (priority, round-robin)
- Clocks and timers
- Message passing.

POSIX.4a provides further enhancements to POSIX.1 and POSIX.4 such as

- Thread management
- Signals
- Process scheduling
- Condition variables
- Thread scheduling
- Thread-safe reentrant functions.

POSIX.4b provides still more enhancements such as

- Process spawn
- Time-outs on blocking functions
- Execution time monitoring
- Sporadic server scheduling
- Device control
- Interrupt control.

Finally, POSIX.13 proposes to provide four profiles of systems corresponding to various levels of real-time functionality from embedded to full-functioned operating systems. Currently, several commercial implementations that conform to this standard are available.

6.9 EXERCISES

1. For the real-time systems below, described in Chapter 1, discuss which real-time architecture is most appropriate.
   (a) Navigation system
   (b) Airline reservation system
   (c) Nuclear power station

2. Explain which type of real-time kernel would be most appropriate for the following systems, and why:
   (a) An air traffic control system
   (b) A batch update system
   (c) A video arcade game

3. Using whatever assumptions you feel necessary, discuss the differences and similarities in performing a context switch in 0-, 1-, 2-, and 3-address machines.

4. Rewrite the polled loop code in Example 6.1 in
   (a) C or C++
   (b) Ada or Ada 95
   (c) Modula-2

5. Using pseudocode, describe the coffee machine in Example 5.4. Imagine now that a super coffee machine is built which can serve two cups of coffee simultaneously. Describe such a machine using coroutines and phase-driven code. Use the fact that there is a fixed time to brew coffee/tea, to pour milk and sugar. Also assume there is only one brewer and one pourer for sugar and milk.

6. Rewrite the synchronized polled loop code in Example 6.3 in
   (a) C or C++
   (b) Ada or Ada 95
   (c) Modula-2

7. Rewrite the state-driven code in Example 6.4 in
   (a) C or C++
   (b) Ada or Ada 95
   (c) Modula-2

8. Rewrite the table-driven finite state automaton in Example 6.5 in C, using pointers to functions.

9. Rewrite the coroutine system Example 6.6 in
   (a) C or C++
   (b) Ada or Ada 95
   (c) Modula-2

10. Rewrite the coroutine system in Example 6.7 in
    (a) C or C++
    (b) Ada or Ada 95
    (c) Modula-2

11. A polled loop system polls a discrete signal every 50 microseconds. Testing the signal and vectoring to the interrupt-processing routine takes 40 microseconds. If it takes 6.2 milliseconds to process the interrupt, what is the minimum response time for this interrupt? What is the maximum response time?

12. Rewrite the foreground/background system in Example 6.8 in
    (a) Pascal
    (b) Ada or Ada 95
    (c) Modula-2

13. Consider a preemptive priority system. The tasks in the system, time needed to complete, and priority (1 being the highest) are given below.

Task	Time Needed (ms)	Priority
Task 1	40	3
Task 2	20	1
Task 3	30	2

If the tasks arrive in the order 1, 2, 3, what is the time needed to complete task 2?

14. Should a routine be allowed to interrupt itself? If it does, what does this mean?

15. What criteria are needed to determine the size of the run-time stack in a multiple-interrupt system? What safety precautions are necessary?

16. What is the worst case response time for the background process in a foreground/background system in which the background task requires 100 milliseconds to complete, the foreground task executes every 50 milliseconds and requires 25 milliseconds to complete, and context switching requires no more than 100 microseconds. (Recall that the background task can be preempted.)

7

Intertask Communication and Synchronization

KEY POINTS OF THE CHAPTER

1. Double buffering is an effective technique for producer/consumer scenarios where data need to be passed in a time-correlated fashion.
2. Critical regions are sections of code accessing serially reusable resources. Critical sections must be given special consideration.
3. Semaphores are an effective mechanism for protecting critical regions.
4. Mailboxes can be used to implement efficient semaphores.
5. Other mechanisms such as ring buffers and queues can be used to handle more complicated data passing in real-time.
6. Deadlock is a serious problem often introduced by synchronization attempts and must be dealt with in some way.

In this chapter we investigate an important problem in any multitasking system: the communication of data between processes and the synchronization of tasks. Related to these issues is the problem of sharing certain resources that can only be used by one task at a time. These techniques need to be applied in all of the solutions discussed in the previous chapter. With coroutines, synchronization and communication are built into the code, but protection of shared resources is still needed.

7.1 BUFFERING DATA

Several mechanisms can be employed to pass data between tasks in a multitasking system. The simplest and fastest among these is the use of global variables. Global variables, though considered contrary to good software engineering practice [165], are often used in high-speed operations. One of the problems related to using global variables is that tasks of higher priority can preempt lower-priority routines at inopportune times, corrupting the global data. This issue was discussed in Chapter 3.

For example, one task may produce data at a constant 100 units per second, whereas another may consume these data at irregular intervals, but in 9600-unit chunks. In order to provide these data to the consuming task, the producer must fill a storage area called a *buffer* with such data. The buffer can be a stack or other data structure, including an unorganized mass of variables. Of course, if the consumer task consumes this information faster than it can be produced, or if the consumer cannot keep up with the producer, problems occur. Selection of the appropriate size buffer is critical in reducing or eliminating these problems. (Buffer size calculation is discussed in Chapter 10.)

7.1.1 Time-Relative Buffering

A common use of global variables is in *double buffering* or *ping-pong buffering*. This technique is used when *time-relative* (also called *synchronous* or *correlated*) data need to be transferred between cycles of different rates, or when a full set of data is needed by one process but can only be supplied slowly by another process. Many telemetry systems, which transmit blocks of data from one device to another, use double-buffering schemes with a hardware or software switch to alternate the buffers. This strategy is also used in disk controllers, graphical interfaces, navigation equipment, robot controls, and many other places.

■ EXAMPLE 7.1

In certain graphics processes, lines are drawn one by one until the image is completed. In an animated system, we do not want to see this drawing process. If, however, we draw on one screen image while displaying the other and then flip the screens when the new drawing is complete, the

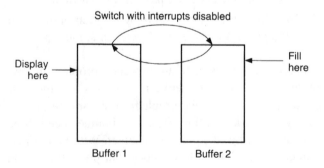

Figure 7.1 Double buffering.

individual line drawing commands will not be seen. If the screens can be updated at about 30 screens per second, the image will appear fully animated. See Figure 7.1.   ■

As an example of time-relative buffering, consider the following.

■ **EXAMPLE 7.2**

A navigation system reads x, y, and z accelerometer pulses in a 5-millisecond cycle. These data are to be processed in a 10-millisecond cycle which has lower priority than the 5-millisecond cycle (i.e., it can be preempted). The accelerometer data processed in the 10-millisecond cycle must be time-relative; that is, we do not wish to process x and y accelerometer pulses from time t along with z accelerometer pulses from time $t + 1$. This could occur if the 10-millisecond cycle has completed processing the x and y data, but gets interrupted by the 5-millisecond cycle. To avoid this problem, we use buffered variables xb, yb, and zb in the 10-millisecond cycle and buffer them, with interrupts disabled. The 10-millisecond routine might look like this in C:

```
introf();             /* disable interrupts */
    xb = x;           /* buffer data         */
    yb = y;
    zb = z;
intron();             /* enable interrupts */
process(xb,yb,zb);                                          ■
```

In practice, the first procedure in any cycle would be a buffering routine to buffer all data from tasks of higher priority into the current task ("buffer in" routine). The last procedure in the cycle is a routine to buffer out data to any tasks of lower priority ("buffer out" routine).

7.1.2 Ring Buffers

A special data structure called a *circular queue* or *ring buffer* is used in the same way as a first-in/first-out list. Ring buffers, however, are easier to manage.

In the ring buffer, simultaneous input and output to the list are achieved by keeping head and tail pointers. Data are loaded at the tail and read from the head. Figure 7.2 illustrates this. An implementation of the "read(data,S)" and "write(data,S)" operations, which read from and write to ring buffer S, respectively, are given below in Pascal code. It is assumed that the buffer has a size of N and that head and tail have been initialized to 0.

```
procedure read(var data : integer, S  : array[0..N-1] of integer);
     begin
        if head=tail then
             data := null            { underflow }
        else
          begin
             data := S[head];        { retrieve data from buffer }
             head := (head+1) mod N  { decrement head pointer }
          end
     end
```

```
procedure write(var data : integer, S : array[0..N-1] of integer)
    begin
       if (tail+1)mod N = head then
            error;                       { overflow, invoke error handler }
       else
          begin
             S[tail] := data;
             tail := (tail+1) mod N   { take care of wrap-around }
          end
    end
```

Additional code is needed to test for the overflow condition in the ring buffer. An overflow occurs when an attempt is made to write data to a full queue. Implementation of this is left as an exercise.

Ring buffers can be used in conjunction with a counting or binary semaphore (see next section) to control multiple requests for a single resource such as memory blocks, modems, and printers. Requests for the resource are placed at the tail of the list, while a special process called a *server* services the requests by reading the list from the head.

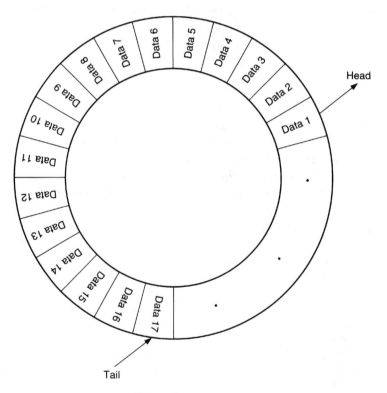

Figure 7.2 Ring buffer.

7.2 MAILBOXES

Mailboxes or *message exchanges* are an intertask communication device available in many commercial, full-featured operating systems. They can also be used like semaphores (next section) but with important advantages.

A *mailbox* is a mutually agreed upon memory location that two or more tasks can use to pass data. The tasks rely on the central scheduler to allow them to write to the location via a *post* operation or to read from it via a *pend* operation. The difference between the pend operation and simply polling the mailbox is that the pending task is suspended while waiting for data to appear. Thus, no time is wasted continually checking the mailbox; that is, the *busy waiting* condition is eliminated. The data that are passed can be a flag used to protect a critical resource (called *key*), they can be a single piece of data, or they can be a pointer to a larger data structure such as a list or an array. In most implementations, when the key is taken from the mailbox, the mailbox is emptied. Thus, although several tasks can pend on the same mailbox, only one task can receive the key. Since the key represents access to a critical resource, simultaneous access is precluded.

We can describe the mailbox operations, *pend(data,S)* and *post(data,S)*, as follows:

```
procedure pend(var data, S : integer)
{ data gets contents of mailbox S if any, suspend task otherwise. }


procedure post(var data, S : integer)    { mailbox S gets data }
```

7.2.1 Mailbox Implementation

Mailboxes are best implemented in systems based on the task-control block model with a supervisor task. A table containing a list of tasks and needed resources (e.g., mailboxes, printers, etc.) is kept along with a second table containing a list of resources and their states. In Tables 7.1 and 7.2, for example, three resources currently exist, a printer and two mailboxes. The printer is being used by task 100, while mailbox 1 is being used (currently being read from or written to) by task 102. Task 104 is pending on mailbox 1 and is suspended because it is not available. Mailbox 2 is currently not being used or pended on by any task.

When the supervisor is invoked by a system call or hardware interrupt, it checks the tables to see if some task is pending on a mailbox. If the key is

TABLE 7.1 Task Resource Request Table

Task id #	Resource	Status
100	Printer	Has it
102	Mailbox 1	Has it
104	Mailbox 1	Pending

TABLE 7.2   Resource Table Used in Conjunction with Task Resource Request Table

Resource	Status	Owner
Printer 1	Busy	100
Mailbox 1	Busy	102
Mailbox 2	Empty	None

available (key status is"full"), then that task must be restarted. Similarly, if a task posts to a mailbox, then the operating system must ensure that the key is placed in the mailbox and its status updated to "full."

7.2.2 Other Operations on Mailboxes

There are often other operations on the mailbox. For example, in some implementations, an accept operation is permitted. *Accept* allows tasks to read the key if it is available, or immediately return an error code if the key is not available. In other implementations, the *pend* operation is equipped with a time-out, to prevent deadlocks (which are discussed in Chapter 11).

7.2.3 Queues

Some operating systems support a type of mailbox that can stack multiple pend requests. These systems provide *qpost*, *qpend*, and *qaccept* operations to post,

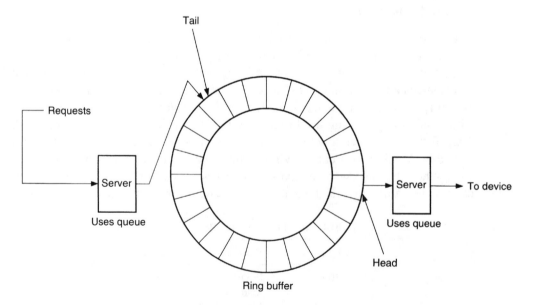

Figure 7.3 Ring buffer and queues used to control a pool of devices.

pend, and accept data to/from the queue. In this case, the queue can be regarded as an array of mailboxes, and its implementation is facilitated through the same resource tables already discussed.

Queues should not be used to pass arrays of data; pointers should be used instead. Queues are useful in implementing device servers where a pool of devices are involved. Here the ring buffer holds requests for a device, and queues can be used at both the head and the tail to control access to the ring buffer (see Figure 7.3). Such a scheme is useful in the construction of device-controlling software such as SPOOL (simultaneous peripheral operation on-line) programs, daemons, or in modem pools. (A *daemon* is a device server that does not run explicitly but rather lies dormant, waiting for some condition(s) to occur.)

NOTE 7.1   Queues can be implemented with mailboxes—use the mailbox to create a counting semaphore (see next section) which restricts access to an array containing keys.

7.3 CRITICAL REGIONS

In multitasking/multiprocessing systems, we are concerned with resource sharing. In most cases, these resources can only be used by one task at a time, and use of the resource cannot be interrupted. Such resources are said to be *serially reusable* and they include certain peripherals, shared memory, and the CPU. While the CPU protects itself against simultaneous use, the code that interacts with the other serially reusable resources cannot. Such a code is called a *critical region*. If two tasks enter the same critical region simultaneously, a catastrophic error can occur.

■ **EXAMPLE 7.3**

Two tasks, Task_A and Task_B are running in a round-robin system. Task_B will write the message "I am task_B" and Task_A will write the message "I am Task_A." In the midst of printing, Task_B is interrupted by Task_A which begins printing. The result is:

```
I am I am Task_A Task_B
```

More serious complications could arise if both tasks were accessing more important devices.   ■

Simultaneous use of a serial reusable resource is called a *collision*. Our concern, then, is to provide a mechanism for preventing collisions.

7.4 SEMAPHORES

A methodology for protecting critical regions was suggested by Dijkstra [34] and involves a special variable called a *semaphore*, and two operations on that variable called *semaphore primitives*. Semaphores appear to be simple, yet they are subtly complex. A thorough understanding of their nuances is essential to avoid implanting logic errors that lead to insidious problems. A semaphore *S* is a memory location that acts as a lock to protect critical regions. Two operations, the *wait* and *signal* operations, are used either to set or to reset the semaphore. Traditionally, one denotes the wait operation as P(S) and the signal operation as V(S). (P and V are the first letters of the Dutch "to test"—*proberen* and "to increment"—*verhogen*.) The primitive operations are defined by the following Pascal code:

```
procedure P(var S : boolean);
   begin
      while S = TRUE do;
      S := TRUE
   end

procedure V(var S : boolean);
   begin
      S := FALSE
   end
```

The wait operation suspends any program calling until the semaphore S is FALSE, whereas the signal operation sets the semaphore S to FALSE. Code that enters a critical region is bracketed by calls to wait and signal. This prevents more than one process from entering the critical region and is illustrated by Example 7.4.

■ EXAMPLE 7.4

Consider two concurrent processes in a multitasking system. Both processes can access the same critical region, so we use semaphores to protect the critical region. Note that the semaphore S should be initialized to FALSE before either process is started.

```
procedure Process1;               procedure Process2;
   .                                  .
   .                                  .
   .                                  .
P(S)                                  .
critical region                    P(S)
V(S)                               critical region
   .                               V(S)
   .                                  .
   .                                  .
                                      .                              ■
```

■ EXAMPLE 7.5

For Task_A and Task_B as before, we can solve the problem as follows

```
procedure Task_A;              procedure Task_B;
begin                          begin
  P(S);                          P(S);
  write("I am Task_A");          write("I am Task_B");
  V(S)                           V(S)
end                            end
```

Note that S is initialized to FALSE.   ■

A process will spend much of its time in *wait* semaphore operation (busy-wait) if a large amount of contention for the resource is protected by it. Because the wait operation involves a repeated test of a while loop condition, semaphore protection is sometimes called a *spin lock*. Furthermore, in many books the semaphore variable of choice is *mutex*, emphasizing the fact that mutual exclusion is enforced.

7.4.1 Mailboxes and Semaphores

Mailboxes can be used to implement semaphores if semaphore primitives are not provided by the operating system.

In this case, there is the added advantage that the pend instruction suspends the waiting process rather than actually waiting on the semaphore.

■ **EXAMPLE 7.6**
Use mailboxes to implement semaphores.

```
procedure P(var T : boolean);

var
   temp : boolean;
   begin
        pend(temp,T);
   end

procedure V(var T : boolean);
   begin
        post(KEY,T)            { place key in mailbox }
   end
```
■

NOTE 7.2 The CPU can be viewed as a critical region protected by a mailbox. The disable or DPI instruction takes the "key" from the mailbox, whereas the enable or EPI instruction puts the "key" back.

7.4.2 Counting Semaphores

The P and V semaphores we have introduced are called *binary semaphores* because they can take on one of two values. A second kind of semaphore called a *counting semaphore* or *general semaphore* can be used to protect pools of resources, or to keep track of the number of free resources. The semaphore must be initialized to the total number of free resources before real-time processing can commence.

The new wait and signal semaphore primitives, MP and MV, are designed to prevent access to a semaphore-protected region when the semaphore is less than or equal to zero. The semaphore is released or signaled by adding 1 to it.

```
procedure MP(var S : integer);        { multiple wait }
    begin
      S := S-1;
      while S <  0 do   { wait }
    end

procedure MV(var S : integer);        { multiple signal }
    begin
      S := S+1
    end
```

Some real-time kernels provide only binary semaphores, but you can simulate the counting semaphore with binary semaphores in the following way. Suppose S and T are binary semaphores and P(S) and V(S) are the wait and signal operations, respectively, on binary semaphores. We can create counting semaphore operations MP(R) and MV(R) on multiple semaphore R using binary semaphores S and T and integer R as follows:

```
procedure MP(R: integer);  { multiple wait }
  begin
      P(S);                  { lock counter }
      R := R-1;              { request a resource }
      if R < 0  then         { none available? }
        begin
          V(S);              { release counter }
          P(T)               { wait for free resource}
        end;
      V(S)                   { release counter }
      end
```

```
procedure MV(R: integer);    { multiple signal }
   begin
       P(S);                  { lock counter }
       R := R+1;              { free resource }
       if R <= 0 then         { any task waiting for free resource? }
           V(T)               { give that task the go ahead }
       else
           V(S)               { release counter }
   end
```

The integer R keeps track of the number of free resources. Binary semaphore S protects R, and binary semaphore T is used to protect the pool of resources. Set the initial values of S to FALSE, T to TRUE, and R to the number of available resources.

The operation of the code is subtly intricate. In the multiple wait routine, we lock the counting variable and decrement it by 1 to indicate a resource request. If enough resources are available ($R > = 0$), then we simply release the counting variable and proceed. If no resources are free, then we must release the counting variable and wait until there is a free resource using the P(T) call. When we return from the P(T) call, we also free the counting variable.

In the multiple signal routine, we lock the counting variable and increment the count on the resource pool. If any process was pending on the resource pool ($R < = 0$), then we signal that process to go ahead using the V(T) call. If no process was waiting, then we simply release the counter. Note that when we give the waiting process the go ahead, it releases the counting variable with the final V(S) call in procedure MP.

Finally, it is easy to see that a binary semaphore can be simulated with a counting semaphore simply by initializing the counting semaphore to 1. You should study this code thoroughly by working out examples for different initial values of R and different resource request scenarios.

7.4.3 Problems with Semaphores

Certain problems arise if the operation of testing and subsequently setting a semaphore is not atomic—that is, uninterruptible. To illustrate the problem, consider the following example.

■ EXAMPLE 7.7

Suppose two tasks in a round-robin system with time-slicing are using a resource protected by a binary semaphore S. The wait instruction discussed in the previous section,

```
procedure P(var S: boolean);
   begin
       while S = TRUE do;
       S := TRUE
   end
```

would generate assembly instructions, in 2-address code, similar to:

```
@1    LOAD  R1,S
      TEST  R1,1
      JEQ   @1        S = TRUE?
      STORE S,1        S := TRUE
```

where "1" is TRUE and "0" is FALSE. Suppose the process using this semaphore primitive were interrupted between the "TEST" and "STORE" instructions. The interrupting routine, which might use the same resource, finds S to be available and begins using it. If this task then suspends (because, say, its time slice ran out) and the interrupted task resumes, it will still see the device as free because the old contents of S are still in R1. Thus, two tasks attempt to use the same resource and a collision occurs. This problem may occur infrequently, and so it may be difficult to test and detect.   ■

7.4.4 The Test-and-Set Instruction

To solve the problem of atomic operation between testing a memory location and storing a specific value in it, some instruction sets provide a *test-and-set* macroinstruction. The instruction fetches a word from memory and tests the high-order (or other) bit. If the bit is 0, it is set to 1 and stored again, and a condition code of 0 is returned. If the bit is 1, a condition code of 1 is returned and no store is performed. The fetch, test, and store are indivisible.

You can implement the wait and signal operations easily with a test-and-set instruction.

```
procedure P(var S : integer);
   begin
     while test_and_set(S)=TRUE do    { wait }
   end

procedure V(var S : integer);
   begin
     S:=FALSE
   end
```

Procedure P would generate assembly language code that may look like:

```
loop:    TANDS S
         JNE loop
```

where TANDS is a test-and-set instruction.

Some machines do not support the TANDS instruction (e.g., a RISC machine). Finally, a semaphore implementation that does not rely on a test-and-set instruction was given by Dijkstra in 1968 [34], namely,

```
procedure P(var S: Boolean); { improved wait, no test_and_set needed }
var
  temp: Boolean

  begin
    repeat
      disable;                   /* disable interrupts */
      temp := S;
      S := TRUE;
      enable                     /* enable interrupts */
    until temp = FALSE
  end
```

Of course, disable and enable must be uninterruptible procedures or in-line assembly code.

7.5 EVENT FLAGS AND SIGNALS

Certain languages provide for synchronization mechanisms called *event flags*. These constructs allow for the specification of an event that causes the setting of some flag. A second process is designed to react to this flag. Event flags in essence represent simulated interrupts, created by the programmer. Raising the event flag transfers flow-of-control to the operating system, which can then invoke the appropriate handler. Tasks that are waiting for the occurrence of an event are said to be *blocked*.

For example, in ANSI-C, the raise and signal facilities are provided. A signal is a type of software interrupt handler that is used to react to an exception indicated by the *raise* operation. Both are provided as function calls, which are typically implemented as macros.

The following prototype can be used as the front end for an exception handler to react to signal S.

```
void (*signal(int S, void(*func)(int)))(int);
```

When signal S is set, function "func" is invoked. This function represents the interrupt handler. The prototype:

```
int raise (int S);
```

Raise is used to invoke the process that reacts to signal S.

■ EXAMPLE 7.8
ANSI-C includes a number of predefined signals needed to handle anomalous conditions such as overflow, memory access violations and illegal instruction, but these signals can be replaced with

user-defined ones. The following C code portrays a generic exception handler that reacts to a certain error condition.

```c
#include <signal.h>

main()
{

  void handler(int sig);
    . . .
      signal(SIGINT,handler);    /* set up to handle signal SIGINT */

      . . .                      /* do some processing   =*/
      if (error) raise(SIGINT);  /* anomaly detected      */
      . . .                      /* continue processing   */
  }

}
void handler(int sig)
{

    Handled error here

}                                                                     ■
```

In C, the signal library function call is used to construct interrupt handlers to react to signals from external hardware, and to handle certain traps—such as floating point overflow—by replacing the standard C library handlers with your own.

Exception handling in Ada looks somewhat different.

■ EXAMPLE 7.9

Consider an Ada exception handler to determine whether a matrix is singular (its determinant is 0). Assume that a matrix type has been defined, and it can be determined that the matrix is singular.

```ada
    begin
      --
      --  calculate determinant
      -- .
      -- .
      --
    exception
       when SINGULAR | NUMERIC/ERROR =>
          PUT(" MATRIX IS SINGULAR  ");
       when others =>
          PUT(" FATAL Error  ");
          raise ERROR;
    end;                                                             ■
```

Modula-2 also provides a type of event flag that can be used for exception or interrupt handlers.

7.6 DEADLOCK

When tasks are competing for the same set of two or more serially reusable resources, then a *deadlock* situation or *deadly embrace* may ensue. The notion of deadlock is best illustrated by example.

■ **EXAMPLE 7.10**

TASK_A requires resources 1 and 2, as does Task_B. Task_A is in possession of resource 1 but is waiting on resource 2. Task_B is in possession of resource 2 but is waiting on resource 1. Neither Task_A nor Task_B will relinquish the resource until its other request is satisfied. The situation is illustrated as follows where two semaphores, S and R, are used to protect resource 1 and resource 2, respectively.

```
Procedure Task_A;                        Procedure Task_B;
begin                                    begin
       .                                        .
       .                                        .
  P(S):                                         .
    Use_resource_1;                       P(R);
       .                                    Use_resource_2;
       .                                        .
       .                                        .
  P(R):              <——Task A is              .
    Use_resource_2;    stuck here        P(S);              <——Task B is
  V(R);                                    Use_resource_1     stuck here
  V(S);                                  V(S);
end                                      V(R)
                                         end                              ■
```

Deadlock is a serious problem because it cannot always be detected through testing. In addition, it may occur very infrequently, making the pursuit of a known deadlock problem difficult. Finally, the solution of the deadlock problem is by no means straightforward and is not without consequences, including significant impact on real-time performance.

Starvation differs from deadlock in that at least one process is satisfying its requirements but one or more are not. In deadlock, no processes can satisfy their requirements because all are blocked. Starvation is sometimes called *livelock*.

Four conditions are necessary for deadlock:

1. Mutual exclusion
2. Circular wait

3. Hold and wait

4. No preemption

Countering any one of the four necessary conditions is needed to prevent deadlock.

Mutual exclusion applies to those resources that can't be shared (e.g. printers, disk devices, output channels). Mutual exclusion can be removed by making such resources shareable, for example, through the use of SPOOLers, which allow these resources to appear to be shareable to an application task.

The circular wait condition occurs when a circular chain of processes exist that hold resources needed by other processes further down the chain (such as in cyclic processing). One way to eliminate circular wait is to impose an ordering on the resources and to force all processes to request resources in increasing order of enumeration. For example, consider the following list of resources and their (increasing) order number.

Device	Number
Disk	1
Printer	2
Motor control	3
Monitor	4

Now if a process wishes to use both the printer and the monitor, it must request first the printer and then the monitor. It can be proved that such a scheme eliminates the possibility of deadlock.

The hold and wait condition occurs when processes request resources and then lock that resource until subsequent resource requests are filled. One solution to this problem is to allocate to a process all potentially required resources at the same time. This can, however, lead to starvation to other processes. Another solution is never to allow a process that locks more than one resource at a time. For example, when writing one semaphore-protected disk file to another, lock one file and copy a record, unlock that file, lock the other file, write the record, and so on. This, of course, can lead to poor resource utilization as well as windows of opportunity for other processes to interrupt and interfere with resource utilization.

Finally, no preemption can lead to deadlock. Namely, if a low-priority task holds a resource protected by semaphore S, and if a higher priority task interrupts and then waits on semaphore S, the priority inversion will cause the high-priority task to wait forever, since the low-priority task can never run to release the resource and signal the semaphore. If we allow the higher priority task to preempt the lower one, then the deadlock can be eliminated. However, this can lead to starvation in the low-priority process as well as to nasty interference problems.

(For example, what if the low-priority task had locked the printer for output, and now the high-priority task starts printing?)

Two other ways of combating deadlock are to avoid it through avoidance algorithms like the Banker's algorithm, or to detect it and recover from it. Detection of deadlock is not always easy, although in embedded systems watchdog timers can be used and in organic systems monitors are appropriate.

7.6.1 Avoidance

Several techniques for avoiding deadlock are available. (A more thorough discussion of the topic can be found in [146].) For example, if the semaphores protecting critical resources are implemented by mailboxes with time-outs, then deadlocking cannot occur. But starvation of one or more tasks is possible. *Starvation* occurs when a task does not receive sufficient resources to complete processing in its allocated time.

A second method for preventing deadlock is to allow preemption. That is, tasks of higher priority which need resources should be allowed to grab them from lower priority tasks. Unfortunately, this can cause problems like starvation or incomplete I/O operations.

The fact that each task acquires a resource and then does not relinquish it until it can acquire another resource is called a *wait and hold* condition. If we eliminate this condition, then deadlock can be avoided.

■ EXAMPLE 7.11

A task needs to read from file 1 and write to file 2. It might open file 1, read a record, close file 1. Then it opens file 2, writes the record and closes file 2. The process is repeated for each record until the file is transferred ■

This technique, however, can slow down response times greatly.

Finally, a technique known as the *banker's algorithm* can sometimes be used to prevent deadlock situations. The technique suggested by Dijkstra [36] uses the analogy of a small-town bank. The banker's algorithm works on like resources, for example, pools of memory or printers. The algorithm ensures that the number of resources attached to all processes can never exceed the number of resources for the system. In addition, we can never make a "dangerous allocation"—that is, allocate resources in such a way that we do not have enough left to satisfy the requirements of any process.

■ EXAMPLE 7.12

Consider a system with three processes, A, B, and C, and a pool of 10 resources of a certain type (e.g., memory blocks). It is known that process A will never need more than 6 blocks at any one time. For processes B and C the totals are 5 and 7, respectively. A table such as the one below is constructed to keep track of the resource needs and availability.

Process	Max Requirement	Used	Possibly Needed
A	6	0	6
B	5	0	5
C	7	0	7
		Total Available	10

When resources are requested, the operating system updates the table, ensuring that a possible deadlock state is not reached. An example of a "safe state" is

Process	Max Requirement	Used	Possibly Needed
A	6	2	4
B	5	3	2
C	7	1	6
		Total Available	4

Here, the requirements of process A or B can be satisfied, so the state is safe. An example of an "unsafe state" is

Process	Max Requirement	Used	Possibly Needed
A	6	4	2
B	5	3	2
C	7	2	5
		Total Available	1

In this case, the total requirements of no task can be met with the total available resources, so deadlock could ensue.   ■

The banker's algorithm is often too slow for real-time systems. Although Habermann [56] has implemented the algorithm for mixed resources, it is not always practical. Finally, resource needs for each task may not be known *a priori*.

7.6.2 Detect and Recover

Assuming that a deadlock situation can be detected (for example, by using a watchdog timer), what can be done? One technique, known as the *ostrich algorithm*, advises that the problem be ignored. If the deadlock situation is known to occur infrequently, for example, once per year, and the system is not a critical one, this approach may be acceptable. For example, if in a video game this problem is known to occur infrequently, the effort needed to detect and correct the problem may not be justified given the cost and function of the system (tell this to the child who just lost his quarter). If the system is a manned one or in control of say, an assembly line, then the ostrich algorithm is unacceptable.

Another method for handling the deadlock is to reset the system completely. Again, this may be unacceptable for certain critical systems.

Finally, if a deadlock is detected, some form of rollback to a pre-deadlock state can be performed, although this may lead to a recurrent deadlock, and operations such as writing to certain files or devices cannot be rolled back easily.

7.7 EXERCISES

1. What effect would size N of a ring buffer have on its performance? How would you determine the optimal size?

2. For a machine you are familiar with, discuss whether the counting semaphore implementation given in this chapter has any critical region problems. That is, can the semaphore itself be interrupted in a harmful way?

3. Why is it not wise to disable interrupts before the while statement in the binary semaphore, P?

4. Rewrite the ring buffer read-and-write procedures in
   (a) C or C++
   (b) Ada or Ada 95
   (c) Modula-2

5. Modify the write procedure for the ring buffer to handle the overflow condition.

6. Write a set of pseudocode routines to access (read from and write to) a 20-item ring buffer. The routines should use semaphores to allow more than one user to access the buffer.

7. Consider a binary semaphore, counting semaphore, queues, and mailboxes. Any three can be implemented with the fourth. We have shown how binary semaphores can be used to implement counting semaphores and vice versa, how mailboxes can be used to implement binary semaphores, and how mailboxes can be used to implement queues. For each pair, show how one can be used to implement the other:
   (a) Binary semaphores for implementing mailboxes.
   (b) Binary semaphores for implementing queues.
   (c) Queues for implementing binary semaphores.
   (d) Queues for implementing mailboxes.
   (e) Queues for implementing counting semaphores.
   (f) Counting semaphores for implementing mailboxes.
   (g) Counting semaphores for implementing queues.
   (h) Mailboxes for implementing counting semaphores.

8. Discuss the problems that can arise if the test and set in the P(S) operation are not atomic. What could happen if the simple assignment statement in the V(S) operation were not atomic?

9. Rewrite the binary semaphore implementation of the counting semaphore in
   (a) C or C++
   (b) Ada or Ada 95
   (c) Modula-2

10. Using the ANSI-C raise and signal facilities, implement the *pend(data,S)* and *post(data,S)* operations for arbitrary mailbox S.

11. Rewrite the test_and_set procedure in:
  (a) C or C++
  (b) Ada or Ada 95
  (c) Modula-2

12. The TANDS instruction can be used in a multiprocessing system to prevent simultaneous access to a global semaphore by two processors. The instruction is made indivisible by the CPU refusing to issue a DMA acknowledge (DMACK) signal in response to a DMA request (DMARQ) signal during execution of the instruction. The other processors sharing the bus are locked out of accessing memory. What are the real-time implications for a processor trying to access memory when another processor is executing a process that is looping for a semaphore using the following code?

```
Process 2:


getlock:    TANDS  semaphore
            JNE    getlock
```

If this busy wait must be used, is there a better way to test the semaphore in process 2 so that the bus is not tied up?

13. Rewrite the exception handler in Example 7.8 in
  (a) Ada or Ada 95
  (b) Modula-2
  (c) C++

14. Write a function to compute x factorial, $x!$, where x is some nonnegative integer. (Recall that $x! = x \cdot (x-1) \cdots 1$ and $0! \equiv 1$.) Write an associated exception handler that handles errors related to trying to take $x!$ for $x < 0$ and to handle overflow conditions. The factorial function should invoke the exception handler if either error type occurs. Do this in
  (a) C
  (b) Ada or Ada 95
  (c) C++

15. Investigate the use of signal handlers in the implementation of a Unix process intertask communication mechanism called a *pipeline*. Pipelines allow the outputs of certain processes to be used as inputs to other processes. Your investigation can be done by examining the source code to any Unix operating system, if available, or by consulting one of the many texts on the Unix operating system.

8

Real-Time Memory Management

KEY POINTS OF THE CHAPTER

1. Dynamic memory management of any kind in real-time, though usually necessary, is detrimental to real-time performance and schedualability analysis.
2. Stacks are typically used in foreground/background systems and the task-control block used in commercial, generic executives.
3. Techniques for managing stacks and task-control blocks are given in the chapter.

An often neglected discussion, dynamic memory allocation, is important in terms of both the use of on-demand memory by applications tasks and the requirements of the operating system. Applications tasks use memory explicitly, for example, through requests for heap memory, and implicitly through the maintenance of the run-time memory needed to support sophisticated high-order languages. The operating system (or kernel) needs to perform extensive memory management in order to keep the tasks isolated.

Dangerous allocation of memory is any allocation that can preclude system determinism. Dangerous allocation can destroy event determinism, for example, by overflowing the stack, or it can destroy temporal determinism by entering a deadlock situation (Chapter 11). It is important to avoid dangerous allocation of memory while at the same time reducing the overhead incurred by memory allocation. This overhead is a standard component of the context switch time and must be minimized. Static memory allocation schemes—that is, the partitioning of memory at system generation time—are discussed in Chapter 9.

Although some of the memory management schemes discussed in Section 8.2 may seem archaic (for example, MFT dates back to the early 1960s), these schemes have recently become relevant again. For example, cache memories are generally very small relative to main memory (just as main memory was small relative to secondary storage devices in early computers). In the case of cache, some of the replacement rules such as LRU and working sets are used to manage the contents of the cache.

8.1 PROCESS STACK MANAGEMENT

In a multitasking system, context for each task needs to be saved and restored in order to switch processes. This can be done by using one or more run-time stacks or the task-control block model. Run-time stacks work best for interrupt-only systems and foreground/background systems, whereas the task-control block model works best with full-featured real-time operating systems. Substantial formalization of this statement can be found in [10].

8.1.1 Task-Control Block Model

If the task-control block model is used, then a list of task-control blocks is kept. This list can be either fixed or dynamic.

In the fixed case, n task-control blocks are allocated at system generation time, all in the dormant state. As tasks are created, the task-control block enters the ready state. Prioritization or time slicing will then move the task to the execute state. If a task is to be deleted, its task-control block is simply placed in the dormant state. In the case of a fixed number of task-control blocks, no real-time memory management is necessary.

In the dynamic case, task-control blocks are added to a linked list or some other dynamic data structure as tasks are created. Again, the tasks are in the suspended state upon creation and enter the ready state via an operating system call or event. The tasks enter the execute state owing to priority or time-slicing. When a task is deleted, its task-control block is removed from the linked list, and its heap memory allocation is returned to the unoccupied or available status.

In this scheme, real-time memory management consists of managing the heap needed to supply the task-control blocks; however, other data structures such as a list or queue can be used. (A heap is a special kind of data structure based on a binary tree. For a discussion of these structures, consult any text on data structures, for example, [83].)

8.1.2 Managing the Stack

If a run-time stack is to be used, certain considerations are required. In order to handle the run-time saving and restoring of context, two simple routines—"save" and "restore"—are necessary. The save routine is called by an interrupt handler to save the current context of the machine into a stack area. This call should be made immediately after interrupts have been disabled to prevent disaster. The restore routine should be called just before interrupts are enabled and before returning from the interrupt handler.

■ EXAMPLE 8.1

Consider the implementation of the save routine. Assume that global variable "stack" is to point to the top of the stack and that eight general registers (R0–R7) are to be saved on a stack. The memory location "PC" corresponds to the interrupt return vector location, and so it contains the PC value at the time of interruption. We need to save this on the stack to allow stacking of interrupts. The code for a 2-address architecture resembles the following:

```
save(context):                  context is a pseudo-argument
                                disable interrupts
      STORE  R0,stack,I         save contents of register 0 onto stack
      LOAD   R0,stack           load index register with address of stack
      ADD    R0,1
      STORE  R1,R0,I            save register 1
      ADD    R0,1
      STORE  R2,R0,I            save register 2
      ADD    R0,1
      STORE  R3,R0,I            save register 3
      ADD    R0,1
      STORE  R4,R0,I            save register 4
      ADD    R0,1
      STORE  R5,R0,I            save register 5
      ADD    R0,1
      STORE  R6,R0,I            save register 6
      ADD    R0,1
      STORE  R7,R0,I            save register 7
      ADD    R0,1
      STORE  PC,R0,I            save return location
      ADD    R0,1
      STORE  R0,stack           save new stack pointer
                                enable interrupts
```

The save operation is illustrated in Figure 8.1.

Next consider the restore routine, written in 2-address code.

```
restore(context):               context is a pseudo-argument
                                disable interrupts
      LOAD   R0,stack
      SUB    R0,1
      LOAD   PC,R0,I            restore return location
      SUB    R0,1
```

```
LOAD   R7,R0,I                  restore register 7
SUB    R0,1
LOAD   R6,R0,I                  restore register 6
SUB    R0,1
LOAD   R5,R0,I                  restore register 5
SUB    R0,1
LOAD   R4,R0,I                  restore register 4
SUB    R0,1
LOAD   R3,R0,I                  restore register 3
SUB    R0,1
LOAD   R2,R0,I                  restore register 2
SUB    R0,1
LOAD   R1,R0,I                  restore register 1
STORE  R0,stack                 reset stack pointer
SUB    R0,1
LOAD   R0,R0,I                  restore register 0
                                enable interrupts
```

The restore operation is illustrated in Figure 8.2.   ■

Certain machine architectures allow block save and block restore instructions to store and load n general registers in n consecutive memory locations. These instructions greatly simplify the implementation of the save and restore routines. Be aware that such macroinstructions may be designed to be interruptable (to reduce context switch time), so that if interrupts have not already been disabled, they should be.

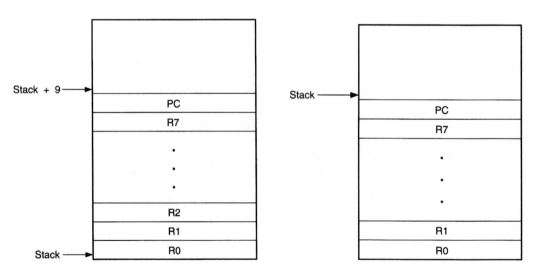

Figure 8.1 The save operation.   **Figure 8.2** The restore operation.

8.1.3 Run-Time Ring Buffer

A run-time stack cannot be used in a round-robin system because of the first-in/first-out nature of the scheduling. In this case a ring buffer or circular queue can be used to save context. The context is saved to the tail of the list and restored from the head. The save and restore routines can be easily modified to accomplish this operation.

8.1.4 Maximum Stack Size

The maximum amount of space needed for the run-time stack needs to be known *a priori*. In general, stack size can be determined if recursion is not used and heap data structures are avoided. If maximum stack memory requirements are not known, then a catastrophic memory allocation can occur, and the system will fail to satisfy event determinism. Ideally, provision for at least one more task than anticipated should be allocated to the stack to allow for spurious interrupts and time overloading. We will discuss this matter further in Chapter 11; also see [95].

8.1.5 Multiple Stack Arrangements

Often a single run-time stack is inadequate to manage several processes in, say, a foreground/background system. Of course, in a multiprocessing system, each process will manage its own stack, but this is not the kind of multiple stack scheme we are talking about.

A multiple stack scheme uses a single run-time stack and several application stacks. Using multiple stacks in embedded real-time systems has several advantages.

1. It permits tasks to interrupt themselves, thus allowing for handling transient overload conditions or for detecting spurious interrupts.
2. The system may be written in a language that supports re-entrancy and recursion, such as C or Pascal. Individual run-time stacks can be kept for each process which contains the appropriate activation records with dynamic links needed to support recursion. Or two stacks for each process can be kept, one for the activation records and the other for the display (a stack of pointers used to keep track of variable and procedure scope). In either case, a pointer to these stacks needs to be saved in the context or task-control block associated with that task.
3. Only non-re-entrant languages such as older versions of FORTRAN or assembly language can be supported with a single-stack model.

We can rewrite the save and restore routines to use the context argument as a pointer to the stack. That is,

```
save(context)
DPI                              disable interrupts
STORE  R0,context               save contents of register 0 onto stack
LOAD   R0,context,I             load index register
ADD    R0,1
STORE  R1,R0,I                  save register 1
ADD    R0,1
STORE  R2,R0,I                  save register 2
ADD    R0,1
STORE  R3,R0,I                  save register 3
ADD    R0,1
STORE  R4,R0,I                  save register 4
ADD    R0,1
STORE  R5,R0,I                  save register 5
ADD    R0,1
STORE  R6,R0,I                  save register 6
ADD    R0,1
STORE  R7,R0,I                  save register 7
ADD    R0,1
STORE  PC,R0,I                  save return location
ADD    context,9                increment stack pointer
EPI                             enable interrupts
```

This is the new restore procedure.

```
restore(context)
DPI                              disable interrupts
LOAD   R0, context,1
SUB    R0,1
LOAD   PC,R0,1                   restore return location
SUB    R0,1
LOAD   R7,R0,I                   restore register 7
SUB    R0,1
LOAD   R6,R0,1                   restore register 6
SUB    R0,1
LOAD   R5,R0,1                   restore register 5
SUB    R0,1
LOAD   R4,R0,1                   restore register 4
SUB    R0,1
LOAD   R3,R0,1                   restore register 3
SUB    R0,1
LOAD   R2,R0,1                   restore register 2
SUB    R0,1
```

```
LOAD   R1,R0,1              restore register 1
SUB    R0,1
LOAD   R0,R0,I              restore register 0
SUB    context,9            decrement stack pointer
EPI                         enable interupts
```

The individual interrupt-handler routines to save to a main stack, written in Pascal, follow.

```
procedure int;

  begin
  save(mainstack);
    case interrupt of
    1: int1;
    2: int2;
    3: int3;
  end
  restore(mainstack)
  end

procedure int1;
                    /*interrupt handler 1 */
  begin
    save(stack1);   /* save context on stack */
    task1;          /* execute task 1 */
    restore(stack1) /* restore context from stack */
  end

procedure int2;
                    /* interrupt handler 2 */
  begin
    save(stack2);   /* save context on stack */
    task2;          /* execute task 2 */
    restore(stack2) /* restore context from stack */
  end

procedure int3;
                    /* interrupt handler 3 */
  begin
    save(stack3);   /* save context on stack */
    task3;          /* execute task 3 */
    restore(stack3) /* restore context from stack */
  end
```

■ **EXAMPLE 8.2**

Suppose three processes are running in an interrupt-only system where a single interrupt based on three prioritized interrupts is generated. Let task1, task2, and task3 be as follows:

```
procedure task1;
       begin
            applic1;
            applic2
       end

procedure task2;
       begin
            applic2;
            applic3
       end

procedure task3;
       begin
            applic3;
            applic4
       end
```

Suppose task1 is running when it is interrupted by task2 during applic2. Later, task2 is interrupted by task3 during applic3. The main and run-time stacks will then look like Figure 8.3. ■

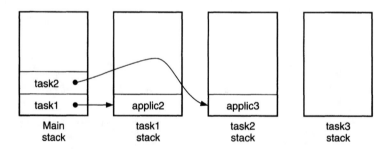

Figure 8.3 Main and run-time stacks for Example 8.2.

8.1.6 Task-Control Block Model

When implementing the task-control block (TCB) model of real-time multitasking, the chief memory management issue is the maintenance of the linked lists for the ready and suspended tasks. As shown in Figure 8.4, when the currently executing task completes, is preempted, or is suspended while waiting for a resource, the next highest priority task in the ready list is removed and is made the executing one. If

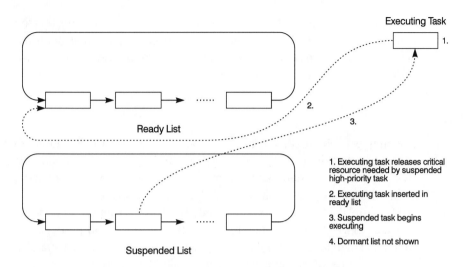

Figure 8.4 Memory management in the task-control block model.

the executing task needs to be added to the suspended list, that is done. (If the executing task has completed, then its TCB is no longer needed.)

Hence, by properly managing the linked lists, updating the status word in the TCBs, and adhering to the appropriate scheduling policy by checking the priority word in the TCBs, round-robin, preemptive priority, or both kinds of scheduling can be induced. Other memory management can include the maintenance of reserved blocks of memory that are allocated to individual task applications as requested.

8.2 DYNAMIC ALLOCATION

Dynamic allocation used to satisfy individual task requirements for memory is accomplished by using a data structure such as a list or heap. For example, memory allocation calls to the procedure "malloc" in C are implemented through library calls to the operating system. In Pascal, the NEW function can be used to generate a new record type in a dynamic memory scheme. Ada and Modula-2 provide similar constructs. How these languages implement the allocation and deallocation of memory is compiler dependent. And, as we discussed before, languages such as FORTRAN and BASIC do not have dynamic allocation constructs. A good book on data structures (e.g., [83]) can be consulted in order to implement these dynamic memory allocation schemes.

In this section, however, we are interested in dynamic memory allocation for process code in main memory, and certain aspects of this need to be considered as they relate to real-time systems. In particular, we are interested in schemes where two or more programs can co-reside in main memory. Several schemes allow this capability, and we will review some of them briefly with respect to their real-time implications. Interested readers can consult a good text on operating systems such as [129] for a more detailed coverage. In general, the types of dynamic allocation that we are about to discuss are not recommended in embedded real-time systems.

8.2.1 Swapping

The simplest scheme that allows the operating system to allocate memory to two processes "simultaneously" is *swapping*. In this case, the operating system is always memory resident, and one process can co-reside in the memory space not required by the operating system, called the *user space*. When a second process needs to run, the first process is suspended and then swapped, along with its context, to a secondary storage device, usually a disk. The second process, along with its context, is then loaded into the user space and initiated by the dispatcher.

This type of scheme can be used along with round-robin or preemptive priority systems, but we would like the execution time of each process to be long relative to the swap time. The access time to the secondary store is the principal contributor to the context switch overhead and real-time response delays.

8.2.2 Overlays

A technique that allows a single program to be larger than the allowable user space is called *overlaying*. In this case the program is broken up into dependent code and data sections called *overlays*, which can fit into available memory. Special program code must be included that permits new overlays to be swapped into memory as needed (over the existing overlays), and care must be exercised in the design of such systems.

This technique has negative real-time implications because the overlays must be swapped from secondary storage devices. Nevertheless, overlaying can be used in conjunction with any of the techniques mentioned later in this chapter to extend the available address space. Many commercial tools are available that facilitate overlaid linking and loading in conjunction with commonly used programming languages and machines.

Note that in both swapping and overlaying a portion of memory is never swapped to disk or overlaid. This memory contains the swap or overlay manager (and in the case of overlaying any code that is common to all overlays is called the *root*).

8.2.3 MFT

A more elegant scheme than simple swapping allows more than one process to be memory-resident at any one time by dividing the user space into a number of fixed-size partitions. This scheme is called *MFT* (multiprogramming with a fixed number of tasks) and is useful in systems where the number of tasks to be executed is known and fixed, as in many embedded applications. Partition swapping to disk can occur when a task is preempted. Tasks, however, must reside in contiguous partitions, and the dynamic allocation and deallocation of memory cause problems.

In some cases main memory can become checkered with unused but available partitions, as in Figure 8.5. In this case the memory space is said to be *externally fragmented*. This type of fragmentation causes problems when memory requests cannot be satisfied because a contiguous block of the size requested does not exist, even though the actual memory is available.

■ EXAMPLE 8.3

In Figure 8.5, even though 40 megabytes of memory are available, they are in noncontiguous blocks, so the request cannot be honored.   ■

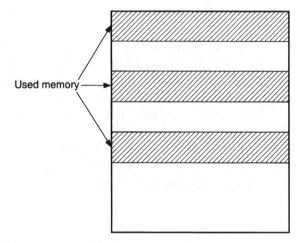

Used memory

Figure 8.5 Fragmented memory.

Another problem, *internal fragmentation*, occurs in fixed partition schemes when, for example, a process requires 1 megabyte of memory when only 2-megabyte partitions are available. The amount of wasted memory or internal fragmentation can be reduced by creating fixed partitions of several sizes and then allocating the smallest partition greater than the required amount.

Both internal and external fragmentation hamper efficient memory usage and ultimately degrade real-time performance because of the overhead associated with their correction.

MFT is not particularly desirable in the real-time operating system because it uses memory inefficiently as a result of the overhead associated with fitting a process to available memory and disk swapping. However, in some implementations, particularly in commercial real-time executives, memory can be divided into regions in which each region contains a collection of different-sized, fixed-sized partitions. For example, one region of memory might consist of 10 blocks of size 16Mb, while another region might contain 5 blocks of 32Mb and so on.

The operating system then tries to satisfy a memory request (either directly from the program via a system call or through the operating system in the assignment of that process to memory), so that the smallest available partitions are used. This approach tends to reduce internal fragmentation.

8.2.4 MVT

In *MVT* (or multiprogramming with a variable number of tasks), memory is allocated in amounts that are not fixed, but rather are determined by the requirements of the process to be loaded into memory. This technique is more appropriate when the number of real-time tasks is unknown or varies. In addition, memory utilization is better for this technique than for MFT because little or no internal fragmentation can occur, as the memory is allocated in the amount needed for each process. External fragmentation can still occur because of the dynamic nature of memory allocation and deallocation, and because memory must still be allocated to a process contiguously.

In MVT, however, external fragmentation can be mitigated by a process of compressing fragmented memory so that it is no longer fragmented. This technique is called *compaction* (see Figure 8.6). Compaction is a CPU-intensive process and is not encouraged in hard real-time systems. If compaction must be performed, it should be done in the background, and it is imperative that interrupts be disabled while memory is being shuffled.

The bottom line is that MVT is useful when the number of real-time tasks is unknown or can vary. Unfortunately, its context-switching overhead is much higher than in simpler schemes such as MFT, and thus it is not always appropriate

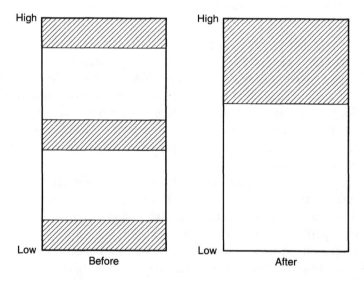

Figure 8.6 Fragmented memory before and after compaction.

for embedded real-time systems. It is more likely to be found in a commercial real-time operating system.

8.2.5 Demand Paging

In *demand page* systems, program segments are permitted to be loaded in noncontiguous memory as they are requested in fixed-size chunks called *pages* or *page frames*. This scheme helps to eliminate external fragmentation. Program code that is not held in main memory is "swapped" to secondary storage, usually a disk. When a memory reference is made to a location within a page not loaded in main memory, a *page fault* exception is raised. The interrupt handler for this exception checks for a free page slot in memory. If none is found, a page frame must be selected and swapped to disk (if it has been altered)—a process called *page stealing*. Paging, which is provided by most commercial operating systems, is advantageous because it allows nonconsecutive references to pages via a *page table*. In addition, paging can be used in conjunction with bank switching hardware to extend the virtual address space. In either case, pointers are used to access the desired page (see Figure 8.7). These pointers may represent memory-mapped locations to map into the desired hard-wired memory bank; may be implemented through associative memory; or may be simple offsets into memory, in which case the actual address in main memory needs to be calculated with each memory reference.

Paging can lead to problems including very high paging activity called *thrashing*, internal fragmentation, and the more serious deadlock (see Chapter 7). But it is unlikely that you would use so complex a scheme as paging in an embedded real-time system where the overhead would be too great and the associated hardware support is not usually available.

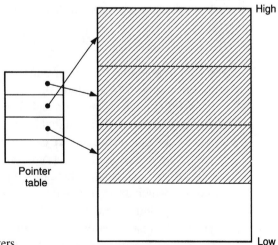

Figure 8.7 Paged memory using pointers.

8.2.5.1 Replacement Algorithms—Least Recently Used Rule Several methods can be used to decide which page should be swapped out of memory to disk, such as first-in/first-out (FIFO). This method is the easiest to implement, and its overhead is only the recording of the loading sequence of the pages. Although other algorithms exist, the best nonpredictive algorithm is the *least recently used* (LRU) rule.

The LRU method simply states that the least recently used page will be swapped out if a page fault occurs. To illustrate the method, consider the following.

■ EXAMPLE 8.4

A paged memory system is divided into sixteen 256-megabyte pages of which any 4 can be loaded at the same time. Each page is tagged (1, 2, etc.). The operating system keeps track of the usage of each page. For example, the page reference string

$$2 \quad 3 \quad 4 \quad 5$$

indicates that pages 2, 3, 4, and 5 have been used in that order. If a request is made for page 7, then page 2 will be swapped out in order to make room for page 7, because it was the least recently used. The loaded pages would then be 3, 4, 5, and 7 with reference string

$$2 \quad 3 \quad 4 \quad 5 \quad 7$$

Please note that references to pages already loaded in memory cause no page fault. For instance, if a reference is now made to page 3, no pages need to be swapped because page 3 is loaded in memory. If this reference is followed by one to page 6, page 4 would have to be swapped out because it had the least recent reference. The loaded pages would then be 3, 5, 7, and 6 with reference string

$$2 \quad 3 \quad 4 \quad 5 \quad 7 \quad 3 \quad 6$$

Note that in a paging memory scheme, the worst possible scenario involves page stealing for each request of memory. This occurs, for example, in a four-page system when five pages are requested cyclically as in the page reference string

$$2 \quad 4 \quad 6 \quad 8 \quad 9 \quad 2 \quad 4 \quad 6 \quad 8 \quad 9 \cdots \qquad ■$$

You should note that the performance of LRU is the same in this case as FIFO (in terms of number of page faults).

In FIFO page replacement schemes (whether or not used in conjunction with working sets), we might think that by increasing the number of pages in memory (or windows in the working set) we can reduce the number of page faults. Often this is the case, but occasionally an anomalous condition occurs whereby increasing the number of pages actually increases the number of page faults. This is **Belady's Anomaly**, which as it turns out, does not occur in LRU replacement schemes.

To conclude, the overhead for the LRU scheme rests in recording the access sequence to all pages, which can be quite substantial. Therefore, the benefits of using LRU need to be weighed against the effort in implementing it *vis-à-vis* FIFO.

8.2.5.2 Memory Locking   In addition to thrashing, the chief disadvantage of page swapping in real-time systems is the lack of predictable execution times. In a real-time system, it is often desirable to lock all or certain parts of a process into memory in order to reduce the overhead involved in paging and to make the execution times more predictable. Certain commercial real-time kernels provide this feature, called *memory locking*. These kernels typically allow code or data segments, or both, for a particular process, as well as the run-time stack segment, to be locked into main memory. Any process with one or more locked pages is then prevented from being swapped out to disk. Memory locking decreases execution times for the locked modules and, more importantly, can be used to guarantee execution times. At the same time, it makes fewer pages available for the application, encouraging contention.

8.2.5.3 Other Points About Paging   In summary,

1. Paging is most efficient when supported by the appropriate hardware.
2. Paging allows multitasking and extension of the address space.
3. When a page is referenced that is not in main memory, a page fault occurs, which usually causes an interrupt.
4. The hardware registers that are used to do page frame address translation are part of a task's context and add additional overhead when doing a context switch.
5. If hardware page mapping is not used, then additional overhead is incurred in the physical address calculations.
6. The least recently used rule is the best nonpredictive page-swapping algorithm.
7. In time-critical real-time systems, we cannot afford the overhead associated with disk swapping in simple swapping, overlays, MFT, MVT, or paging schemes.

8.2.6 Working Sets

Working sets are based on the model of *locality-of-reference*. The idea is if you examine a list of recently executed program instructions on a logic analyzer, you will note that most of the instructions are localized to within a small number of instructions in most cases. (For example, in the absence of interrupts and branching, the program is executed sequentially. Or the body of a loop may be executed a large number of times.) However, when interrupts, procedure calls, or branching occurs, the locality-of-reference is altered. The idea in working sets is that a set of local code windows is maintained in the cache and that upon accessing a memory location not contained in one of the working sets, one of the windows in the working set is replaced (using a replacement rule such as FIFO or

LRU). The performance of the scheme is based entirely on the size of the working set window, the number of windows in the working set, and the locality-of-reference of the code being executed.

8.2.7 Real-Time Garbage Collection

In a memory-management context, *garbage* is memory that has been allocated but is no longer being used by a task (that is, the task has abandoned it). Garbage can accumulate when tasks terminate abnormally without releasing memory resources [144]. It can also occur in object-oriented systems and as a normal byproduct of nonprocedural languages [4], [162].

In C, for example, if memory is allocated using the malloc procedure and the pointer for that memory block is lost, then that block cannot be used or properly freed. The same situation can occur in Pascal when records created with the new statement are not properly disposed of.

Garbage collection algorithms generally have unpredictable performance (although average performance may be known). Garbage can be reclaimed using the following procedure. Tag all memory from the heap which is pointed to by a variable (including those variables in procedure activation frames—a non-deterministic data structure). Then reclaim all nontagged memory for the heap. The loss of determinism results from the unknown amount of garbage, the tagging time of the nondeterministic data structures, and the fact that many incremental garbage collectors require that every memory allocation or deallocation from the heap be willing to service a page-fault trap handler.

Another technique is to build a heap or table of memory blocks along with an associated process ID for the owner of the memory block. This data structure is then periodically checked to determine whether memory has been allocated to a process that no longer exists. If this is the case, the memory can be released. Because of the overhead involved, this method should not be implemented in high-frequency cycles, and ideally garbage collection should be performed as a background activity or not performed at all [4]. Nevertheless, research in real-time garbage collection is still open.

8.2.8 Contiguous File Systems

Disk I/O is a problem in many real-time systems that can be exacerbated by *file fragmentation*. File fragmentation is analogous to memory fragmentation and has the same associated problems, only worse. In addition to the logical overhead incurred in finding the next allocation unit in the file, the physical overhead of the disk mechanism is a factor. For example, physical overhead involved in moving the disk's read/write head to the desired sector can be significant.

To reduce or eliminate this problem altogether, many commercial real-time systems, such as real-time UNIX, force all allocated sectors to follow one another on the disk. This technique is called *contiguous file allocation*.

8.3 STATIC SCHEMES

Static memory issues revolve around the partitioning of memory into the appropriate amount of RAM, ROM, memory-mapped I/O space, and so on. This problem of resource allocation is discussed in Chapter 9.

8.4 EXERCISES

1. Rewrite the save and restore routines assuming that eight general registers (R0–R7) and the program counter are to be saved on a stack. Do this for
   (a) 0-address machine
   (b) 1-address machine
   (c) 3-address machine

2. Rewrite the save and restore routines in 2-address code, assuming block move (BMOVE) and restore (BRESTORE) instructions are available. Make the necessary assumptions about the format of these instructions.

3. Rewrite the save and restore routines so that they save and restore to the head and tail of a ring buffer, respectively.

4. Rewrite the save and restore routines in Pascal so that they employ push and pop procedures.

5. Write a pseudocode algorithm that allocates pages of memory on request. Assume that 100 pages of size 1 megabyte, 2 megabytes, and 4 megabytes are available. The algorithm should take size of the page requested as an argument, and return a pointer to the desired page. The smallest available page should be used, but if the smallest size is unavailable, the next smallest should be used.

6. Write a pseudocode algorithm compacting 64 megabytes of memory that is divided into 1-megabyte pages. Use a pointer scheme.

7. For a four-page memory system with memory reference string, for example,

$$2 \quad 4 \quad 6 \quad 8 \quad 9 \quad 2 \quad 4 \quad 6 \quad 8 \quad 9 \cdots$$

   show that the number or page faults for FIFO replacement is the same as for the LRU replacement scheme.

8. A paged memory system is divided into sixteen 256-megabyte pages of which any four can be loaded at the same time. Each page is tagged (1, 2, etc.). Write a pseudocode algorithm to implement the least recently used rule.

9. Write a heap manager to handle arbitrary-sized data blocks in a link list (analogous to the C malloc() routine). Remember that the run-time stack can collide with the heap. Do this in
   (a) C
   (b) Ada
   (c) Pascal
   (d) Modula-2
   (e) C++

10. Modify the heap manager in the previous exercise so that a table consisting of the memory block number and process ID is stored. Write a garbage collection routine to accompany the heap manager which consults a second table consisting of a list of all existing process IDs and frees all memory blocks belonging to extinct processes.

9

System Performance Analysis and Optimization

KEY POINTS OF THE CHAPTER

1. Noninterrupt driven systems can be easily analyzed for real-time behavior in most cases.
2. It is generally impossible to predict worst case performance in interrupt driven systems.
3. Improving average case performance generally degrades worst case performance and vice versa.
4. Although most compilers perform good optimization, they should be studied first to assess their behavior.
5. There is an inherent tradeoff in time and memory requirements in most systems.

In this chapter we examine issues related to system performance based on response time, time-loading, and memory-loading. Recall that *response time* is the time between receipt of an interrupt and completion of all associated processing. *Time-loading* is the percentage of time the CPU is doing "useful" processing. Finally, *memory-loading* is the percentage of usable memory that is being used. This chapter, more than any other in the present volume, is a codification of experience, folklore, and tricks. Analysis of real-time performance is difficult at best and usually impossible for interrupt driven systems.

9.1 RESPONSE-TIME CALCULATION

The estimation of system response time—the time between when the event signaling the task occurs and when the task completes processing—differs depending on the type of system involved. Throughout the text we have been looking at these calculations, but it is necessary to complete those findings here. We can then discuss the various sources of response-time delay, and how they can be reduced.

9.1.1 Polled Loops

The response-time delay for a polled loop system consists of three components: the hardware delays involved in setting the software flag by some external device; the time for the polled loop to test the flag; and the time needed to process the event associated with the flag. (see Figure 9.1). The first delay is in nanoseconds and can be ignored. The time to check the flag and jump to the handler routine can be several microseconds. The time to process the event related to the flag depends, of course, on the process involved. Hence, calculation of response time for polled loops is quite easy.

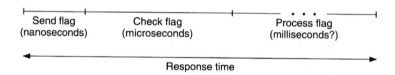

Figure 9.1 Factors affecting polled loop response time.

The preceding case assumes that sufficient processing time is afforded between events. However, if events begin to pile up, that is, if a new event is initiated while a previous event is still being processed, then the response is worse. In general, if f is the time needed to check the flag and P is the time to process the event, including resetting the flag (and ignoring the time needed by the external device to set the flag), then the response time for the nth overlapping event is bounded by

$$n f P \tag{9.1}$$

Typically, some limit is placed on n; that is, the number of events that can overlap, and two overlapping events are often not allowed at all.

9.1.2 Coroutines/Phase-Driven Code

The absence of interrupts in a coroutine system makes the determination of response time rather easy. In this case response time is simply found by tracing the worst case path through each of the tasks (see Figure 9.2). In this example, the

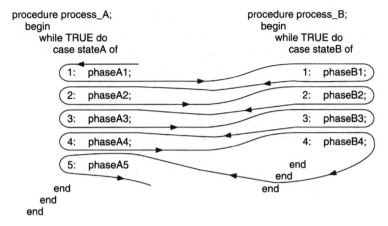

Figure 9.2 Tracing the execution path in a two-task coroutine system.

execution time of each phase must be known. Computation of these execution times is discussed shortly.

9.1.3 Interrupt Systems

The calculation of response times for interrupt systems is dependent on a variety of factors, including interrupt latency, context-switch time, and schedule/dispatch times (see Figure 9.3). The next few sections address the issues involved in calculating interrupt latency and the schedule times. The context switch times are calculated by treating the context switch code as ordinary application code and then following the rules discussed in the next sections.

For preemptive systems with fixed-task rates, the model given in Figure 9.3 represents the factors affecting the response time. In general, the response time for task i, denoted R_i, is

$$R_i = L_i + C_s + S_i + A_i \tag{9.2}$$

where L_i is the interrupt latency, C_s is the context save time, S_i is the schedule time, and A_i is the actual process time (see Figure 9.3).

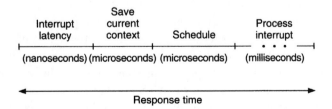

Figure 9.3 Factors affecting interrupt driven system response time.

Calculation of context save/restore times is the same as timing any application code. The schedule time, S_i, is negligible when the CPU is equipped with an interrupt controller with multiple interrupts. When a single interrupt is supported in conjunction with an interrupt controller, S_i can be timed using instruction counting.

First, consider the determination of L_i. There are two cases. The first occurs when process i is of the highest priority; that is, it is uninterruptable. The second case occurs when process i can itself be interrupted.

Case 1: When the highest-priority task interrupts one of lower priority, the total interrupt latency can be computed as

$$L_i = L_P + \max\{L_I, L_D\} \qquad (9.3)$$

where L_P is the interrupt latency due to propagation delay of the interrupt signal, L_I is the longest completion time for an instruction in the interrupted process, and L_D is the maximum time the interrupts are deliberately disabled by the lower-priority routine during, for example, context switching or buffer passing. Since the interrupt will occur either while the interrupts are explicitly disabled during an instruction or when they are not, the latency is dependent on the greater of the two. Determination of macroinstruction execution times is discussed shortly.

Case 2: When a lower-priority routine attempts to interrupt one of higher priority, it cannot be processed until all higher-priority routines have been fully processed. In this case we can represent the interrupt latency as

$$L_i = L_H \qquad (9.4)$$

where L_H is the time needed to complete higher-priority routines.

Since process i might be interrupted, the calculation of L_H is difficult or impossible for most systems; in any case it is too involved for us here. For some examples of bounded response times for preemptive priority and round-robin systems, see [12], [103], or [148].

9.2 INTERRUPT LATENCY

There is an inherent delay between when an interrupt occurs and when the CPU begins reacting to it; this delay is called the *interrupt latency*. It can be caused by several factors that can be both hardware and software related, and both deliberate and incidental. The effect of latency is most pronounced—but easier to find—when lower-priority interrupts are initiated during the execution of a higher-priority task. For the reverse, or in round-robin systems, the effect is generally lessened but more subtle to determine. The following paragraphs describe these latency sources in further detail.

9.2.1 Propagation Delay

The contribution to interrupt latency resulting from the limitation in the switching speeds of the digital devices and the transit time of electrons across wires are called *propagation delays*. These delays can produce built-in latencies of nanoseconds or even microseconds. For example, the amount of time between when an external device initiates an interrupt signal and when it actually latches into the interrupt controller may be several nanoseconds or more, depending on the length of the wire and the switching speed of the interrupt-controller chip. Propagation delay times are available from the manufacturer, or may be measured with an oscilloscope or logic analyzer, but may generally be ignored.

9.2.2 Macroinstruction Execution Times

As we described before, in most computers each macroinstruction is a micro-instruction program (or microprogram) that is, with few exceptions, uninterrupt-able. This is necessary because certain intermediate results, condition code registers, and other data needed to complete execution of the macroinstruction (microprogram) could be destroyed if interrupted. Thus, we need to find the execution time of each macroinstruction by calculation, measurement (see Section 13.2.3), or manufacturer's data sheets. The instruction with the longest execution time in your code—you must check the compiler output to decide this—will cause the maximum interrupt latency if it has just begun executing when the interrupt signal is received.

■ EXAMPLE 9.1

In a certain microprocessor, it is known that all fixed point instructions take 10 microseconds, floating point instructions take 50 microseconds, and other instructions such as built-in sine and cosine functions take 250 microseconds. Your program is known to generate only one such cosine instruction when compiled. The interrupt latency, then, may be as high as 250 microseconds. ■

The latency caused by instruction completion is often overlooked, resulting in serious problems. In certain language implementations, such as versions of FORTRAN, passing parameters via parameter lists are protected by disabled interrupts to ensure that the parameters are correlated. Passing parameters via such lists typically entails multiple indirect loads which—if the list is long—can result in considerable periods during which the interrupts are disabled.

9.2.3 Interrupts Disabled

Deliberate disabling of the interrupts by the software can create substantial interrupt latency, and this must be included in the overall latency calculation. Interrupts are disabled for a number of reasons, including protection of critical regions, buffering routines, and context switching.

9.2.4 Preemption

When a higher-priority task interrupts a lower-priority one, the total interrupt latency can be computed as

$$L_{max} = L_P + \max\{L_I, L_D\} \qquad (9.5)$$

where L_{max} is the maximum interrupt latency, L_P is the interrupt latency due to propagation delay of the interrupt signal, L_I is the longest completion time of an instruction, and L_D is the maximum time the interrupts are deliberately disabled by the lower-priority routine. Since the interrupt will occur either while the interrupts are explicitly disabled during an instruction or when they are not, the latency is dependent on the greater of the two.

■ EXAMPLE 9.2

In a certain round-robin real-time system, it is known that the longest instruction used takes 120 microseconds, interrupts are never disabled for more than 100 microseconds, and propagation delays are 100 nanoseconds for all signals. The total interrupt latency then is $0.1 + \max\{120,100\} = 120.1$ microseconds.   ■

9.2.5 Low Priority Interrupts High

When a low-priority routine interrupts one of higher priority, the greatest concern in the calculation of interrupt latency is the effect of higher-priority tasks running at the time of the interrupt. Since the hardware usually latches the interrupt in the interrupt controller but does not signal the CPU until the higher-priority interrupt has been cleared, the effective latency is determined as the time needed to complete the high-priority task—so the other effects do not apply. Determination of the time to complete the high-priority routine is discussed in subsequent sections. Thus, we can represent the latency as

$$L_{max} = L_H \qquad (9.6)$$

where L_{max} is the interrupt latency and L_H is the time needed to complete higher-priority routines.

9.3 TIME-LOADING AND ITS MEASUREMENT

The need to know the execution time of various modules and the overall system time-loading before implementation is important from both a management and an engineering perspective. Not only are time-loading requirements stated as specific design goals, but also knowing them *a priori* is important in selecting hardware and the system design approach.

During the coding and testing phases, careful tracking of time-loading is needed to focus on those modules that are slow or whose response times are inadequate. Several methods can be used to predict or measure module execution time and system time-loading.

9.3.1 Using a Logic Analyzer

The best method for measuring the execution time of each module and the overall CPU utilization is to use a logic analyzer. One advantage of the logic analyzer is that it takes into account hardware latencies and other delays that are not due simply to instruction execution times. Its drawback is that the software must be completely (or partially) coded, and the target hardware must be available. Thus, the logic analyzer is usually employed only in the late stages of the coding phase, the testing phase, and especially during system integration. For this reason, use of a logic analyzer for timing purposes is discussed in Chapter 13.

9.3.2 Instruction Counting

When it is too early for the logic analyzer, or if one is not available, instruction counting is the best method of determining time-loading due to code execution time. This technique requires that the code already be written, that an approximation of the final code exist, or that similar systems be available for inspection. The approach simply involves tracing the longest path through the code, counting the instruction types along the way, and adding their execution times.

For any periodic system, the total task execution time divided by the cycle time for that module is the time-loading for that task. In sporadic or mixed systems, the maximum task execution rates should be used, if known. Adding these percentages over all the tasks in the system yields the total time-loading. If T is time-loading, T_i is the cycle time (or minimum time between occurrences) for cycle T_i, and A_i is the actual execution time, then for n tasks we have

$$T = \sum_{i=1}^{n} \frac{A_i}{T_i} \tag{9.7}$$

Of course, the actual instruction times are required beforehand. They can be obtained from manufacturer's data sheets, by timing the instructions using a logic analyzer or simulators, or by educated guessing. If manufacturer's data sheets are used, memory access times and the number of wait states for each instruction are needed as well. Example 9.3 illustrates the calculations.

■ EXAMPLE 9.3

Consider, in the navigation system described in Figure 5.7, one of the modules needed to process the raw accelerometer pulses (Δv's which are sent to us via DMA from an A/D converter card) in the 5 ms cycle. This module converts raw pulses into the actual accelerations that are later compensated for airframe orientation, temperature, and other effects. The module is to decide if the aircraft is still on the ground (takeoff has not commenced) in which case only a small acceleration reading by the accelerometer is allowed.   ■

Let's do a time-loading analysis for the corresponding code.

```
#define SCALE   .01  /* .01 delta ft/sec/pulse is scale factor */
#define PRE_TAKE .1   /* .1 ft/sec/5ms max. allowable */

void accelerometer(unsigned x, unsigned y, unsigned z,
   float *ax, float *ay, float *az,
   unsigned on_ground, unsigned *signal)

{
  *ax = (float) x * SCALE;   /* convert pulses to accelerations */
  *ay = (float) y * SCALE;
  *az = (float) z * SCALE;
  if(on_ground)
     if(*ax > PRE_TAKE || *ay > PRE_TAKE || *az > PRE_TAKE)
       *signal = *signal | 0x0001; /* set bit in signal */
}
```

A *mixed listing* combines the high-order language instruction with the equivalent assembly language instructions below it for easy tracing. Following shortly is a mixed listing for this code in a generic assembly language for a 2-address machine. The assembler and compiler directives have been omitted (along with some data allocation pseudo-ops) for clarity and because they do not impact the time-loading.

The instructions beginning in "F" are floating point instructions that we will assume take 50 microseconds. We will assume all other instructions are integer and take 6 microseconds.

```
void accelerometer(unsigned x, unsigned y, unsigned z,
   float *ax, float *ay, float *az,
   unsigned on/ground, unsigned *signal)

{
*ax = (float) x * SCALE; /* convert pulses to accelerations */
        LOAD    R1,x
        FLOAT   R1
        FMULT   R1,_SCALE
        FSTORE  R1,ax,I

  *ay = (float) y * SCALE;

        LOAD    R1,y
        FLOAT   R1
        FMULT   R1,_SCALE
        FSTORE  R1,ay,I
```

```
*az = (float)  z * SCALE;

        LOAD    R1,z
        FLOAT   R1
        FMULT   R1,_SCALE
        FSTORE  R1,az,I

if(on_ground)

        LOAD    R1,on_ground
        CMP     R1,0
        JE      _2

 if(*ax > PRE_TAKE | | *ay > PRE_TAKE | | *az > PRE_TAKE)

        FLOAD   R1,ax,I
        FCMP    R1,_PRE_TAKE
        JLE     _1
        FLOAD   R1,ay,I
        FCMP    R1,_PRE_TAKE
        JLE     _1
        FLOAD   R1,ay,I
        FCMP    R1,_PRE_TAKE
        JLE     _1

_4:
        *signal = *signal | 0x0001; /* set bit in signal */

         LOAD R1,signal,I
         OR   R1,1
         STORER1,signal,I
_3:
_2:
_1:
```

Tracing the worst path and counting the instructions, we see that there are 12 integer and 15 floating point instructions for a total execution time of 0.822 millisecond. Since this program runs in a 5-millisecond cycle, the time-loading is $^{0.822}/_5 = 16.5\%$. If the other cycles were analyzed to have a time-loading as follows—1-second cycle 1%, 10-millisecond cycle 30%, and 40-millisecond cycle 13%—then the overall time-loading for this foreground/background system would be 60.5%. Could the time-loading be reduced for this module?

In this example, the comparisons could have been made in fixed point to save time. This, however, restricts the range of the variable PRE_TAKE. That is,

PRE_TAKE could only be integer multiples of SCALE. If this were acceptable, then this module need only check for the pre-takeoff condition and read the DMAd values into the variables *ax*, *ay*, and *az*. The compensation routines would perform all calculations in fixed point and would convert the results to floating point at the last possible moment.

As a final note, the process of instruction counting can be automated if a parser is written for the target assembly language that can resolve branching.

9.3.3 Pictorial Representation

A pictorial representation of time-loading for periodic systems can be obtained if we use different shading or color patterns (or elevation levels) in a bar chart figure. The width of the boxes corresponds to the actual execution time for the module, whereas the shading patterns are used to differentiate the cycles. The height of the ordinate axis is used to depict priority level.

To do this, draw a time line with time ticks corresponding to the fastest cycle in the system. Starting with the highest-priority module and working from the left, shade the portion of the time line needed to complete the task. Then begin with the next highest task, remembering that it must be interrupted at the appropriate time. Continue with the rest of the tasks in the system, finishing with the lowest-priority one.

■ **EXAMPLE 9.4**

Consider the navigation system discussed previously. If we ignore the 1-second cycle for simplicity, then the timing chart would resemble Figure 9.4.   ■

If the chart cannot be completed, then the system is time-overloaded. The chart gives us a "feel" for the system time-loading and the relative effect of each task

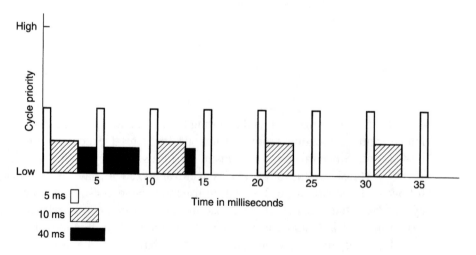

Figure 9.4 Timing chart for navigation system.

on that total. It can also be used to compute the worst case response time for a task in periodic systems. This is discussed in a subsequent section.

This type of representation also works well with round-robin and non-rate-monotonic systems if the maximum interrupt frequencies are known.

9.3.4 Instruction Execution Time Simulators

The calculation of instruction times requires more than just the information supplied in the CPU manufacturer's data books. It is also dependent on memory access times and wait states that are determined by the overall system design. Some companies that frequently design real-time systems on a variety of platforms use simulation programs to predict instruction execution time and CPU throughput. Then engineers can input the CPU type, memory speeds, and an instruction mix, and calculate total instruction times and throughput. Such simulators may be commercially available but are generally difficult to write because most machines today have wide-varying execution times. The worst examples are pipelined machines and RISC architectures for which the sequence of instructions influences instruction timing.

Short sections of code can be timed by reading the system clock before and after the execution of the code. The time difference can then be measured to determine the actual time of execution. Of course, if the code normally takes only a few microseconds, it is better to execute several thousand times and then divide the total execution time by the time spent. This will help to remove any inaccuracy introduced by the granularity of the clock. If you use this technique, be sure to calculate the actual time spent in the open loop, and subtract it from the total. This is analogous to subtracting the weight of the plastic cup used to weigh a specimen.

■ EXAMPLE 9.5

The following Pascal code can be rewritten in a suitable language to time a single high-level language instruction or series of instructions. The number of iterations needed could be 1 or more depending on how short the code to be timed is. The shorter the code, the more iterations should be used. "Current clock time" indicates that a call to the operating system is required to read the current time (or read directly from a register). "Function to be timed" is where the actual code to be timed is placed.

```
procedure timer;
  begin
    time0 = current_clock_time;          { read time now }
    for j=1 to iteration do;             { run empty loop }
    time1 = current_clock_time;
    loop_time := time1-time0;            { open loop time }
    time2 := current_clock_time;         { read time now }
    for j=1 to iteration do
```

```
        begin
            function_to_be_timed
        end;
    time3 := current_clock_time;        { read time now }
    { calculate instruction(s) time }
        total := (time3-time2-loop_time)/iteration
end
```

Appropriate conversion by the clock resolution should be performed. For example, if 2000 iterations of the function take 1.1 seconds with a clock granularity of 18.2 microseconds, the measurement is accurate to

$$\frac{\pm 18.2}{1.1 \times 10^6} \approx \pm 0.0017\%$$

■

9.3.5 Deterministic Performance

Cache, pipelines, and DMA (all designed to improve average real-time performance) destroy determinism and thus make prediction of real-time performance essentially impossible. In the case of cache, for example, is the instruction in the cache? Where it is being fetched from has a significant effect on the execution time of that instruction. So, to do a worst case performance, you must assume that every instruction is not fetched from cache but from main memory. However, to bring that instruction into the cache, one of the cache replacement algorithms discussed in Chapter 8 must be used. This has a very deleterious effect on the predicted performance. Similarly, in the case of pipelines, one must always assume that at every possible opportunity, the pipeline needs to be flushed. Finally, when DMA is present in the system, we have to assume that cycle stealing is occurring at every opportunity, thus inflating instruction fetch times.

Does this mean that these widely used architectural techniques render a system effectively nonanalyzable for performance? Essentially, yes. However, by making some reasonable assumptions about the real impact of these effects, some rational approximation of performance is possible.

9.4 SCHEDULING IS NP-COMPLETE

You may have asked yourself, "Why isn't there a formula or recipe for predicting performance in most real-time systems?" The answer is that most scheduling problems involving real systems are NP-complete problems. An *NP-complete problem* is a seemingly intractable decision problem for which the only known solutions are exponential functions of the problem size. Such solutions are for all practical purposes, intrinsically unsolvable, even on supercomputers. Finding a polynomial time solution to the class of NP-complete problems would represent a major scientific paradigm shift and have fantastic economic ramifications. Most scientists, however, believe that NP-complete problems have only hard solutions (but that we will never be able to show that).

For example, in an excellent exposé on this point [153], a number of classic theorems for real-time scheduling research are given that either contain excessive practical constraints or conclude that the problem concerned is NP-complete or *NP-hard*. (An NP-hard problem is similar to an NP-complete problem except that for the NP-hard problem not even an exponential time solution can be found.) Here is a sampling.

1. When there are mutual exclusion constraints, it is impossible to find a totally on-line optimal run-time scheduler.
2. The problem of deciding whether it is possible to schedule a set of periodic processes that use semaphores only to enforce mutual exclusion is NP-hard.
3. The multiprocessor scheduling problem with two processors, no resources, arbitrary partial order relations, and every task having unit computation time is polynomial. A partial order relation indicates that any process can call itself (reflexivity); if process A calls Process B, then the reverse is not possible (antisymmetry); and if process A calls process B and process B calls process C, then process A can call process C (transitivity).
4. The multiprocessor scheduling problem with two processors, no resources, independent tasks, and arbitrary computation times is NP-complete.
5. The multiprocessor scheduling problem with two processors, no resources, independent tasks, arbitrary partial order, and task computation times of either one or two units of time is NP-complete.
6. The multiprocessor scheduling problem with two processors, one resource, a forest partial order (partial order on each processor), and each computation time of every task equal to 1 unit is NP-complete.
7. The multiprocessor scheduling problem with three or more processors, one resource, all independent tasks, and each computation time of every task equal to 1 unit is NP-complete.

Does anyone want to invest money in such systems?

9.5 REDUCING RESPONSE TIMES AND TIME-LOADING

Identifying wasteful computation is a preliminary step in reducing time-loading. Many approaches employed in compiler optimization can be used [2], but other methods have evolved that are specifically oriented toward real-time systems.

9.5.1 Compute at Slowest Cycle

All processing should be done at the slowest rate that can be tolerated. Checking a temperature discrete for a large room at faster than 1 second may be wasteful, for temperature typically cannot change quickly owing to thermal inertia. In our nuclear plant example, a dedicated sensor is used to monitor the temperature, which then issues a high-level priority if an over-temperature is detected.

9.5.2 Scaled Arithmetic

As we saw in Chapter 2 integer operations were typically faster than floating point operations for most computers. We can take advantage of this fact in certain systems by multiplying integers by a *scale factor* to simulate floating point operations. This solution was one of the first methods for implementing real-number operations in early computer systems. Here a two's complement number is used, the LSB (least significant bit) of which is assigned a scale factor, which is sometimes called the *granularity* of the number (see Figure 9.5). If the number is an *n*-bit two's

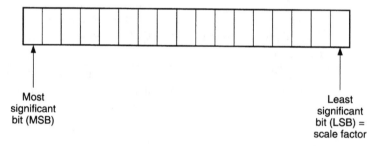

Figure 9.5 A 16-bit two's complement scaled number.

complement integer, then the MSB (most significant bit) of the number acts like a sign bit. The largest number that can be represented this way is $(2^{n-1} - 1) \cdot$ LSB and the smallest number that can be represented is $-2^{n-1} \cdot$ LSB.

■ EXAMPLE 9.6

Consider the aircraft navigation system example again, and recall that the x, y, and z accelerometer pulses are converted into actual accelerations by applying a scale factor of 0.01. The 16-bit number 0000 0000 0001 0011 then represents a delta velocity of $19 \cdot 0.01 = 0.19$ feet per second. The largest and smallest delta velocities that can be represented in this scheme are 327.67 and –327.68 feet per second, respectively.   ■

Scaled numbers can be added and subtracted together, and multiplied and divided by a constant (but not another scaled number), as signed integers. Thus, computations involving such numbers can be performed in integer form and then converted to floating point only at the last step—a process that can save considerable time.

Since there is an inverse relation between accuracy and range of the scaled number, a natural question arises: "How does one decide the appropriate granularity?" Suppose the n-bit number must range between x and $-x$ where x is a positive real number. Then

$$LSB = 2^{-(n-1)} \cdot x \qquad (9.8)$$

will represent any number in this interval to within one LSB. For numbers with nonsymmetric ranges, select the interval similarly, but use the larger of the two range values for x. For example, for numbers with range between 300 and -311, use equation 9.8 but set $x = 311$, yielding an LSB of 0.00949 for a 16-bit number.

9.5.3 Binary Angular Measurement

A variation on the scaled number idea uses the fact that adding 180° to any angle is like taking its two's complement. That is, if $360° < x \le 0°$ is an angle, then $x + 180° = x - 180° = -x$. This technique, called *binary angular measurement* or BAM, works as follows. Consider the most significant bit of an n-bit word to be assigned a value of 180 degrees. Then the least significant bit has an assigned value of

$$2^{-(n-1)} \cdot 180 \text{ degrees}$$

This is the least significant bit or LSB (see Figure 9.6).

Each n-bit BAM word will have minimum value of 0; that is,

$$2^{(n-1)} \cdot \frac{180}{2^{(n-1)}} - 180° = -360° = 0$$

Each n-bit word has a maximum value of

$$2^n - 2^{-(n-1)} \cdot 180° = 360° - LSB$$

with granularity

$$2^{-(n-1)} \cdot 180° = LSB$$

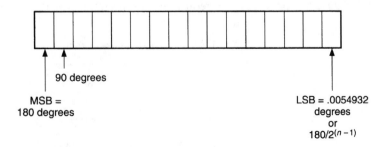

Figure 9.6 A 16-bit binary angular measurement word.

■ **EXAMPLE 9.7**

Consider the 16-bit BAM word:

$$0000\ 0000\ 1010\ 0110$$

Its binary angular measurement is $166 \cdot 180° \cdot 2^{-15} = 0.9118°$ ■

BAM can be added and subtracted together and multiplied and divided by constants as if they were unsigned integers, and converted at the last stage to produce floating point results. For more accuracy, BAM can be extended to two or more words. You should satisfy yourself that the overflow condition for BAM numbers presents no problem as the angle simply wraps around to 0.

9.5.4 Look-Up Tables

A variation on the scaled number concept allows us to compute relatively complicated functions using mostly fixed point arithmetic. *Look-up tables* rely on the mathematical definition of the derivative of a continuous real-valued function.

$$f : \mathcal{R} \to \mathcal{R}$$

That is, suppose that the following limit exists:

$$f'(x) = \lim_{\Delta x \longrightarrow 0} \frac{f(x + \Delta x) - f(x)}{\Delta x} \tag{9.9}$$

Then $f'(x)$ is called the *derivative* of f at x. This derivative at x represents the slope of the function at that point, and we can use this information to interpolate a function at an unknown point x' between the known points of the function at x and $x + \Delta x$.

The first step in applying this technique is to build a table of scaled integers for the function using an array that contains the sample function points at each Δx and possibly $f'(x)$ at that point. The values for x_0, $x_0 + \Delta x$, and so on, do not need to be stored in the table if they are built into the look-up function. If the look-up function is generic (i.e., it can operate on more than one table), then these values must be stored as well.

The choice of Δx represents a tradeoff between the size of the table and the desired resolution of the function. A generic look-up table is given in Table 9.1, and Figure 9.7 provides the geometric interpretation for the technique.

TABLE 9.1   Generic Look-up Table

x_0	$f(x_0)$
$x_0 + \Delta x$	$f(x_0 + \Delta x)$
$\vdots$	$\vdots$
$x_0 + (n - 1)\Delta x$	$f(x_0 + (n - 1)\Delta x)$

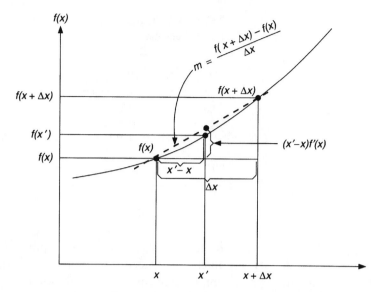

Figure 9.7 Geometric interpretation of interpolation.

As Figure 9.7 shows, the table can be used for the interpolation of $f(x')$ for $x < x' < x + \Delta x$ by the formula:

$$f(x') = f(x) + (x' - x) \frac{f(x + \Delta x) - f(x)}{\Delta x} \tag{9.10}$$

If $f'(x)$ is also stored in the table, then the look-up formula becomes:

$$f(x') = f(x) + (x' - x) f'(x) \tag{9.11}$$

Again this represents a tradeoff between time- and memory-loading.

As a bonus, the look-up table also provides for fast function computation if the desired value happens to be one of the stored values, and any computer implementation of this technique should check for these first.

■ EXAMPLE 9.8

Consider the function $\sin(x)$ for the interval [0,90]. Computing the sine for the rest of the circle can be done by appropriate sign changes, depending on which quadrant the angle is in. For example, $\sin(135)$ is $\sin(45)$, and $\sin(270)$ is $-\sin(90)$.

If we use a Δx of 0.5 degrees for simplicity, we have Table 9.2.   ■

9.5.5 Basic Optimization Theory

It is important to experiment with your compiler and to know how it will react to certain high-order language constructs such as case statements versus nested if-then statements, integer versus character variables, and so on. A set of extensive test cases should be prepared for the high-order language in question to expose the intricacies of the compiler.

TABLE 9.2   Look-up Table
for Sin Function

x_0	$sin(x_0)$
0.0	0.0
0.5	0.0087
1.0	0.0174
⋮	⋮
90.0	1.0

Moreover, many of the techniques used in code optimization underscore the fact that in any arithmetic expression there is no substitute for good algebra. And it is important to reformulate any algorithm or expression to eliminate time-consuming function calls such as those that compute exponentials, square roots, and transcendental functions where possible to enhance real-time performance.

Finally, most of the code optimization techniques used by compilers can be exploited to improve real-time performance. Often these strategies will be employed invisibly by the compiler, or can be turned on or off with compiler directives or switches, but you should know which ones are available. If a particular strategy is not being used, you may want to implement it yourself at the high-order or assembly language level.

Let us briefly, then, examine some commonly used optimization techniques and their impact on real-time performance. Compiler optimization techniques include

- Use of arithmetic identities
- Reduction in strength
- Common subexpression elimination
- Use of intrinsic functions
- Constant folding
- Loop invariant removal
- Loop induction elimination
- Use of registers and caches
- Dead code removal
- Flow-of-control optimization
- Constant propagation
- Dead-store elimination
- Dead-variable elimination

- Short-circuit Boolean code
- Loop unrolling
- Loop jamming
- Cross jump elimination

Many of these techniques are facilitated through the use of *peephole optimization*. In peephole optimization a small window or peephole of assembly language code is compared against known patterns that yield optimization opportunities. These types of optimizers are easy to implement and allow for multiple optimization passes to be performed.

9.5.5.1 Use of Arithmetic Identities   Good compilers should use arithmetic identities to eliminate useless code. For example, multiplication by the constant "1" or addition by the constant "0" should be eliminated from executable code. Although this may seem trivial and would normally be avoided by the programmer, the use of symbolic constants can obscure these calculations from the human programmer.

9.5.5.2 Reduction in Strength   *Reduction in strength* refers to the use of the fastest macroinstruction possible to accomplish a given calculation. For example, many compilers will replace multiplication of an integer by another integer that is a power of 2, by a series of shift instructions. Shift instructions are typically faster than integer multiplication.

In some compilers, character variables are rarely loaded in registers, whereas integer variables are. This may be because it is assumed that calculations will take place involving the integers, whereas those involving characters are unlikely. Care should therefore be taken in deciding whether a variable should be a character or an integer.

Furthermore, it is well known that divide instructions typically take longer to execute than multiply instructions. Hence, it may be better to multiply by the reciprocal of a number than to divide by that number. For example, $x * 0.5$ will be faster than $x/2.0$. Many compilers will not do this automatically.

9.5.5.3 Common Subexpression Elimination   Repeated calculations of the same subexpression in two different equations should be avoided.

■ **EXAMPLE 9.9**

The following Pascal program fragment

```
x := y + a * b;
y := a * b = z;
```

could be replaced with:

```
t := a * b;
x := y + t;
y := t + z;
```

thus eliminating the additional multiplication. This can result in significant savings if *a* and *b* are floating point numbers and the code occurs in a tight loop.   ■

9.5.5.4 Intrinsic Functions   When possible, use intrinsic functions rather than ordinary functions. *Intrinsic functions* are simply macros where the actual function call is replaced by in-line code during compilation. This improves real-time performance because the need to pass parameters, create space for local variables, and release that space is eliminated.

9.5.5.5 Constant Folding   Most compilers perform constant folding, but this should not be assumed. As an example, the statement:

```
x := 2.0 * x * 4.0;
```

would be optimized by folding 2.0 * 4.0 into 8.0.

Performing this operation manually leads to code that is easier to debug, because the programmer performs the optimization explicitly. And although the original statement may be more descriptive, a comment can be provided to explain the optimized statement.

For example, if you will be using $\pi/2$ in your program, it should be precomputed during the initialization portion of your code (the non-real-time part) and stored as a constant called, for example, pi_div_2. This will typically save one floating point load and one floating point divide instruction—potentially tens of microseconds. In a 5-millisecond real-time cycle, this can lead to time-loading savings of 0.1% time-loading. Incidentally, using this strategy again illustrates the inverse relationship between time- and memory-loading—you have just reduced time-loading but have used extra memory to store the precomputed constant.

9.5.5.6 Loop Invariant Optimization   Most compilers will move computations outside loops that do not need to be performed within the loop, a process called *loop invariant optimization*.

■ EXAMPLE 9.10

Consider the following code fragment in Pascal:

```
x := 100;
while (x > 0) do
    x := x - y+z;
```

It can be replaced by

```
x := 100;
t := y+z;
while (x > 0) do
    x := x - t;
```

This moves an instruction outside the loop but requires additional memory.   ■

9.5.5.7 Loop Induction Elimination

A variable i is called an *induction variable* of a loop if every time i changes its value, it is incremented or decremented by some constant. A common situation is one in which the induction variable is i and another variable, j, which is a linear function of i, is used to offset into some array. Often i is used only for a test of loop termination. We can get rid of i by replacing its test for one on j.

■ EXAMPLE 9.11
Consider the following Pascal program fragment.

```
for i := 1 to 10 do
    a[i+1] := 1;
```

An improved version is

```
for j := 2 to 11 do
    a[j] := 1;
```

eliminating the extra addition within the loop.   ■

9.5.5.8 Use of Registers and Caches

When programming in assembly language, or when using languages that support register-type variables, such as C, it is usually advantageous to perform calculations using registers. Typically, register-to-register operations are faster than register-to-memory ones. Thus, if variables are used frequently within a module, and if enough registers are available, you should try to force the compiler to generate register-direct instructions, or do this explicitly when programming in assembly language.

If the processor architecture supports memory caching, then it may be possible to force frequently used variables into the cache at the high-order language or assembly language level. Although most optimizing compilers will cache variables where possible, the nature of the source-level code affects the compiler's abilities.

9.5.5.9 Removal of Dead or Unreachable Code

One of the easiest methods for decreasing memory loading is to remove *dead* or *unreachable* code—that is, code that can never be reached in the normal flow-of-control. Such code might be debug statements that are executed only if a debug flag is set, or redundant initialization instructions. For example, consider the following C program fragment:

```
if(debug)
      {
        .
        .
        .
      }
```

The test of the variable "debug" will take several microseconds—time that is consumed regardless of whether or not you are in debug mode. Debug code should be implemented using the conditional compile facilities available with most language compilers. Thus, we should replace the previous fragment with

```
#ifdef DEBUG
      {
        .
        .
        .
      }
#endif
```

Here, #ifdef is a compiler directive that will include the code between it and the first #endif only if the symbolic constant DEBUG is defined.

Dead code removal also increases program reliability (see, for example, [19]).

9.5.5.10 Flow-of-Control Optimization   In flow-of-control optimization, unnecessary jump-to-jump statements are replaced by a single-jump statement. The following pseudocode illustrates the situation.

```
        goto label1:
label0: y=1;
label1: goto label2;
```

can be replaced by

```
        goto label2:
label0: y=1;
label1: goto label2;
```

Such code is not normally generated by programmers, but might result from some automatic generation or translation process and escape unnoticed.

9.5.5.11 Constant Propagation Certain variable assignment statements can be changed to constant assignments, thereby permitting registerization opportunities or the use of immediate modes.

■ **EXAMPLE 9.12**

In Pascal, one might see the following code as the result of an automated translation process:

```
x := 100;
y := x;
```

The corresponding 2-address assembly language code generated by a nonoptimizing compiler might look like:

```
LOAD  R1,100
STORE R1,x
LOAD  R1,x
STORE R1,y
```

This could be replaced by

```
x := 100;
y := 100;
```

With associated 2-address assembly output:

```
LOAD  R1,100
STORE R1,x
STORE R1,y
```

Again, this type of code often appears during mechanical translation from one language to another.   ■

9.5.5.12 Dead-Store Elimination Variables that contain the same value in a short piece of code can be combined into a single temporary variable.

■ **EXAMPLE 9.13**

The following Pascal code illustrates dead-store.

```
t := y+z;
x := func(t);
```

Although many compilers might generate an implicit temporary location for $y + z$, this cannot always be relied on. This could then be replaced by

```
x := func(y+z);
```
■

9.5.5.13 Dead-Variable Elimination   A variable is *live* at a point in a program if its value can be used subsequently; otherwise it is *dead* and subject to removal.

■ EXAMPLE 9.14

The following Pascal code illustrates that z is a dead variable.

```
x := y+z;
x := y;
```

after removal of z we are left with

```
x := y;
```
■

While this example appears to be trivial, again it could arise as the result of poor coding or an automated code generation or translation process.

9.5.5.14 Short-Circuiting Boolean Code   We can optimize the testing of compound Boolean expressions by testing each subexpression separately.

■ EXAMPLE 9.15

In Pascal, we have

```
if (x > 0) AND (y > 0) then
    z := 1;
```

which could be replaced by

```
if (x > 0) then
   if (y > 0) then
      z := 1;
```

In many compilers, the code generated by the second fragment will be superior to the first.   ■

NOTE 9.1   ANSI-C executes "if(expression)" constructs sequentially inside the "()" and drops out the first FALSE condition. That is, it will automatically short-circuit Boolean code.

9.5.5.15 Loop Unrolling   Loop unrolling duplicates statements executed in a loop in order to reduce the number of loop iterations and hence the loop overhead incurred. In the exaggerated case, the loop is completely replaced by in-line code. For example,

```
for i=1 to 6 do
  a[i] := a[i]*8;
```

is replaced by

```
a[1] := a[1]*8;
a[2] := a[2]*8;
a[3] := a[3]*8;
a[4] := a[4]*8;
a[5] := a[5]*8;
a[6] := a[6]*8;
```

a less drastic version reduces the loop overhead by a factor of three

```
for i= 1 to 6 step 3 do
begin
  a[i] := a[i]*8;
  a[i+1] := a[i+1]*8;
  a[i+2] := a[i+2]*8
end
```

9.5.5.16 Loop Jamming   Loop jamming or loop fusion is a technique for combining two similar loops into one, thus reducing loop overhead by a factor of two. For example, the following Pascal code

```
for i= 1 to 100 do
    x[i] := y[i]*8;

for i= 1 to 100 do
    z[i] := x[i] * y[i];
```

can be replaced by

```
for i= 1 to 100 do
  begin
    x[i] := y[i]*8;
    z[i] := x[i] * y[i]
  end;
```

9.5.5.17 Cross Jump Elimination   If the same code appears in more than one case in a case or switch statement, then it is better to combine the cases into one. This eliminates an additional jump or cross jump. For example, the following code

```
case x of
   0: x:=x+1;
   1: x:=x*2;
   2: x:=x+1;
   3: x:=2
end;
```

can be replaced by

```
case x of
   0,2: x:=x+1;
   1: x:=x*2;
   3: x:=2
end;
```

9.5.6 Other Optimization Techniques

A sampling of other optimization considerations follows.

1. Optimize the common case. The most frequently used path should also be the most efficient.
2. Arrange a series of IF statements so that the most likely value is tested first.
3. Arrange a series of AND conditions so that the condition most likely to fail is tested first. (Arrange OR conditions so that the most likely to succeed is tested first. This technique is called Boolean short-circuiting.)
4. Arrange entries in a table so that the most frequently sought values are the first to be compared. (This technique is just a variation of 3, above).
5. Replace threshold tests on monotone (continuously nondecreasing or nonincreasing) functions by tests on their parameters, thereby avoiding evaluation of the function. (For example, why use the code.

$$\text{if } (e^x < e^y) \text{ then} \dots$$

when

$$\text{if } (x < y) \text{ then} \dots$$

will do?)
6. Link the most frequently used procedures together to maximize the locality of reference. (This only applies in paging or cached systems.)
7. Store data elements that are used concurrently together (to increase the locality of reference; again, this only applies in paging or cached systems).

8. Store procedures in sequence so that calling and called procedures will be loaded together (to increase the locality of reference; again, this only applies in paging or cached systems).

Note that in most cases these techniques will optimize the average case, not the worst case.

9.5.7 Combination Effects

Although many of the optimization techniques given in this text can be automated, many compilers perform only one optimization pass, overlooking opportunities that are not revealed until after at least one pass. Hence, hand optimization can provide additional execution time savings. To see the effects of multiple-pass optimization, consider the following example. The code fragment

```
for (j = 1 to 3) do
  begin
    a[j] = 0
    a[j] = a[j] + 2 * x
  end

for (k = 1 to 3) do
  b[k] = b[k] + a[k] + 2 * k * k
```

is improved by loop jamming, loop invariant removal, and removal of extraneous code (in this case the initialization of a[j]). The resultant code is

```
t = 2 * x
for (j = 1 to 3) do
  begin
    a[j] = t
    b[j] = b[j] + a[j] + 2 * j * j
  end
```

Next, looping unrolling yields

```
t = 2 * x
a[1] = t
b[1] = b[1] + a[1] + 2 * 1 * 1
a[2] = t
b[2] = b[2] + a[2] + 2 * 2 * 2
a[3] = t
b[3] = b[3] + a[3] + 2 * 3 * 3
```

Finally, after constant folding, the improved code is

```
t = 2 * x
a[1]= t
b[1]= b[1] + a[1] + 2
a[2]= t
b[2]= b[2] + a[2] + 8
a[3]= t
b[3]= b[3] + a[3] + 18
```

The original code involved nine additions and nine multiplications, numerous data movement instructions, and loop overheads. The improved code requires only six additions, one multiply, less data movement, and no loop overhead. It is very unlikely that a compiler, even with peephole optimization, would have been able to make such an improvement.

9.5.8 Speculative Execution

Another relatively new compiler optimization technique, *speculative execution*, is showing promise in multiprocessing software systems. Speculative execution optimization is similar to that used in pipeline computer architecture. (Recall the prefetch of the next sequential instructions from memory.) In the case of compiled code, speculative execution involves an idle processor optimistically and predictively executing code in a parallel process block, as long as there is no dependency in that process block on code that could be running on other processors.

This scheme allows idle time and response times to be reduced on individual processors and for the overall system. However, there is a net penalty on average case performance if the optimistic code execution is nullified by some activity on another processor—a time penalty is incurred in order to roll back (as in pipeline flushing).

9.6 ANALYSIS OF MEMORY REQUIREMENTS

With memory becoming denser and cheaper, memory-loading analysis has become less of a concern. Still, its efficient use is important in many airborne and space systems where savings in space, power consumption, and cost are desirable. Thus, we discuss this notion with respect to a highly embedded application, although the arguments are applicable to all real-time systems.

In any real-time system, we can usually divide memory into three distinct areas: stack or system area, program memory, and RAM area. Other areas of memory may be reserved for memory-mapped I/O or DMA locations. Figure 9.8 illustrates a typical memory map.

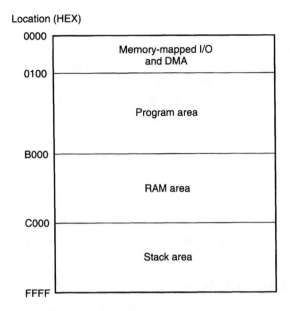

Figure 9.8 A typical memory map.

The total memory-loading is typically the sum of the individual memory-loading for the program, stack, and RAM areas. That is,

$$M_T = M_P \cdot P_P + M_R \cdot P_R + M_S \cdot P_S \qquad (9.12)$$

where M_T is the total memory-loading, M_P, M_R, and M_S are the memory-loading for the program, RAM, and stack areas, respectively, and P_P, P_R, and P_S are percentages of total memory allocated for the program, RAM, and stack areas, respectively. Remember throughout, however, that even if $M_T < 100\%$, if M_P, M_R, or M_S are greater than 100%, then the system cannot operate properly.

■ EXAMPLE 9.16

A computer system has 64 megabytes of program memory that is loaded at 75%, 24 megabytes of RAM area that is loaded at 25%, and 12 megabytes of stack area that is loaded at 50%. The total memory-loading is

$$M_T = 0.75 \cdot \frac{64}{100} + 0.25 \cdot \frac{24}{100} + 0.50 \cdot \frac{12}{100} = 60\% \qquad ■$$

You will see how to calculate M_P, M_S, and M_R shortly.

9.6.1 Memory-Mapped I/O and DMA Memory

We do not include memory-mapped I/O and DMA memory in the memory-loading equation 9.12, since they are fixed in hardware. However, we should allocate the minimum number of memory locations for these purposes needed to get the job done with some room for growth. This frees memory addresses for the more dynamic memory areas.

9.6.2 Program Area

The program area of memory is generally ROM which contains the executable code of the real-time program, including the operating system and applications software. In addition, fixed constants can be stored in this area. Here memory-loading is calculated simply by dividing the number of used locations in the program area by the allowable locations.

$$M_p = \frac{U_p}{T_p} \tag{9.13}$$

where M_p is the memory-loading for the program area, U_p is the number of locations used in the program area, and T_p is the total available locations in the program area. These numbers are available as output from the linker.

9.6.3 RAM Area

Although the program instructions may be stored in RAM instead of ROM for increased fetching speed and modifiability, all global variables should be stored in RAM. Although the size of this area is determined at system design time, the loading factor for this area is not determined until the application programs have been completed. In any case, the memory-loading factor can be computed as

$$M_R = \frac{U_R}{T_R} \tag{9.14}$$

Where M_r is the memory-loading for the RAM area, U_r is the number of locations used in the RAM area, and T_r is the total available locations in the RAM area. Again, these numbers are available as output from the linker.

9.6.4 Stack Area

The real-time operating system uses the stack area for context saving and automatic variables. Although more than one stack can be kept within this area, it is convenient to view it as containing only one. The size of the stack at any time is dependent on the system's state and the size of the context saved for any one task. Suppose the context for any task requires at most c_s locations for registers, program counter, automatic variables, and so on, and t_{max} is the maximum number of tasks that can be on the stack at any time. (You make this determination—if your system is not event-deterministic, then it cannot be known or guaranteed.) Then the maximum stack size is

$$U_S = c_S \cdot t_{max} \tag{9.15}$$

Hence, the memory-loading factor can be computed as

$$M_S = \frac{U_S}{T_S} \qquad\qquad (9.16)$$

where M_S is the memory-loading for the stack area, U_S is the number of locations used in the stack area, and T_S is the total available locations in the stack area.

9.6.5 Memory Management Schemes

The discussions in the preceding section also should be considered within the context of the memory management schemes discussed in Chapter 8. For example, in a bank-switching scheme where four identical banks are used, the analysis is applied to each separate memory bank.

9.7 REDUCING MEMORY-LOADING

As mentioned previously, memory-loading is less of a problem than it has been in the past, but occasionally a system needs to be designed in which the available main memory is small in relation to the program size. Most of the approaches developed to reduce memory-loading date from a time when memory was at a premium and might violate the principles of software engineering. Thus, they should be used with caution.

9.7.1 Variable Selection

Memory-loading in one area can be reduced at the expense of another. For example, all automatic variables (variables that are local to procedures) increase the loading in the stack area of memory, whereas global variables appear in the RAM area. By forcing variables to be either local or global, relief can be purchased in one area of memory at the expense of the other, thus balancing the memory load.

In addition, intermediate result calculations that are computed explicitly require a variable either in the stack or the RAM area, depending on whether it is local or global. The intermediate value can be forced into a register instead by omitting the intermediate calculation. To illustrate, consider the following Pascal code fragment.

■ **EXAMPLE 9.17**

This Pascal code fragment calculates one root of a quadratic:

```
discriminant :=d b * b - 4 * a * c;
root := (-b + sqrt(discriminant)) * .5 / a;
```

this code could be replaced by

```
root := (-b + sqrt(b * b - 4 * a * c) * .5 / a;
```

which saves one floating point variable and thus at least 4 bytes of memory. In addition, this eliminates at least one STORE macroinstruction, hence reducing time-loading as well.   ■

9.7.2 Reuse Variables

Global variables that are used only once—say during initialization—can be reused later for other purposes. Unfortunately, the variable names must be either misleading or generic since they will be playing a dual role. An example of this method is the use of named COMMON overlays in FORTRAN. You can also use this method for loop counters that are generic in nature, but be careful to prevent a process from destroying the contents of a variable when that variable is also being used by another.

9.7.3 Memory Fragmentation

Memory fragmentation (discussed in Chapter 8) does not impact memory-loading, but it can produce effects resembling memory-overloading. In this case, although sufficient memory is available, it is not contiguous.

Although we discussed compaction schemes in Chapter 8 and pointed out that they were not desirable in real-time systems, they may be necessary in serious cases of virtual memory-loading.

9.7.4 Self-Modifying Code

One method that can be used to save space in the code area of memory—albeit an extremely dangerous and tricky one—is the *self-modifying code*. This method takes advantage of the fact that the opcodes of certain instructions may differ by only one bit. For example, by flipping a bit in a JUMP instruction, an ADD instruction is created. Although this type of programming usually arises from coincidence, legends exist about programmers who could write such code effortlessly. The most important disadvantage of such coding is that it destroys the program's determinism. This type of programming is almost never done today and should be avoided.

NOTE 9.2 Many modern processors include on-chip caches that can obviate self-modifying code (the cache does not update the code and executes the unmodified code) or the effect of modifying code within the cache causes performance degradation.

9.8 I/O PERFORMANCE

One performance area that we cannot cover in great depth (owing to device dependencies) is the bottleneck presented by disk and device I/O access. In many cases, disk I/O is the single greatest contributor to performance degradation. Moreover, when analyzing a system's performance through instruction counting, it is very difficult to account for disk device access times. In most cases the best approach is to assume worst case access times for device I/O and include them in your performance predictions.

In other cases, where a real-time system participates in some form of a network, say a local area network (LAN), loading the network can seriously degrade real-time performance and make measurement of that performance impossible. In most cases, we need to assess the performance of the system assuming that the network is in the best possible state (i.e. has no other users). Then measurements of performance can be taken under varying conditions of loading, and a performance curve can be generated.

9.9 EXERCISES

1. What characteristics of RISC architectures tend to reduce the total interrupt latency time as compared to CISC?

2. Consider a foreground/background system that has three cycles: 10 millisecond, 40 millisecond, and 1 second. If the cycle completion times have been estimated at 4 milliseconds, 12 milliseconds, and 98 milliseconds, respectively, what is the total time-loading of the system?

3. A preemptive foreground/background system has three interrupt-driven cycles, described by Table 9.3 (with context switch time ignored):
   (a) Draw an execution time line for this system.
   (b) What is the system time-loading (CPU utilization) factor?
   (c) If we now consider context switch time to be 1 millisecond, redraw the execution time line for this system.
   (d) What is the system time-loading (CPU utilization) factor with the context switch time included?

4. Suppose x is a 16-bit BAM word representing the angle 225° and y is a 16-bit BAM word representing 157.5°. Show using two's complement addition that $x + y = 22.5°$.

TABLE 9.3   Table for Time-Loading Exercise

Task Cycle	Actual Execution Time	Priority (1 is highest, 10 is lowest)
10 ms	4 ms	1
20 ms	5 ms	3
40 ms	10 ms	2
Background	5 ms	—

5. What is the range of an unsigned scaled 16-bit number with least significant bit = 0.00043?

6. What is the range of a signed scaled 16-bit number with least significant bit = 0.00043?

7. Recode Example 9.3 in 2-address assembly language using scaled fixed point arithmetic where possible. If fixed point instructions take 6 microseconds and floating point instructions take 60 microseconds, what are the savings (if any) of using the fixed point approach?

8. A computer has instructions that require two bus cycles, one to fetch the instruction and one to fetch the data. Each bus cycle takes 250 nanoseconds, and each instruction takes 500 nanoseconds (i.e., the internal processing time is negligible). The computer also has a disk with 16,512 byte sectors per track. Disk rotation time is 8.092 milliseconds. To what percentage of its normal speed is the computer reduced during DMA transfer if each DMA takes one bus cycle? Consider two cases: 8-bit bus transfer and 16-bit bus transfer.

9. Code the look-up table $sin(x)$ function described in Example 9.8 using table increments of $\Delta x = 0.5°$. Compare the accuracy and speed of your table function with the macroinstruction to perform $sin(x)$. Do this in
   (a) Pascal
   (b) FORTRAN
   (c) Ada
   (d) C++

10. Write a program in the language of your choice which takes an arbitrary function and table increment and writes a look-up table function. The arbitrary function will have to be hard-coded into the program, but the table size or table increment can be input interactively. Creation of such a program will increase the accuracy of your table look-up functions and reduce the time needed to write them.

11. Use optimization methods to optimize the following C code:

```
#define UNIT 1
#define FULL 1

main()
{
  int a,b;

  a = FULL;
  b = a;

  if(( a == FULL) && (b == FULL))
  {
    if(debug)
            printf("a=%d b=%d",a,b);
    a = (b * UNIT) /2;
    a = 2.0 * a * 4;
    b =d sqrt(a);
  }
}
```

12. Can the number of instructions executed serve as a timer mechanism in a real-time operating system? How?

10

Queuing Models

KEY POINTS OF THE CHAPTER

1. Producer/consumer analysis should be used to determine the appropriate buffer sizes for buffered data when production can exceed consumption for short bursts.
2. Because of their inherent digital nature, discrete probability models are best used when modeling real-time systems.
3. An M/M/1 queue can be used to model a simple interrupt driven real-time system.

This chapter provides a brief introduction to queuing theory and its application in the analysis of real-time systems, and discusses application in the prediction of buffer sizes and in performance measurement. The reader is assumed to be familiar with the concepts of experiment, event, sample space, and probability of occurrence. Interested readers who wish to pursue the study of queuing theory in greater detail should consult the treatments given in [28] and [82].

10.1 PROBABILITY FUNCTIONS

The most important concept in the mathematical modeling of a system is the random variable. A *random variable* is a function that maps elements of the *sample space*, the set of outcomes to some experiment, into the real line. If the sample space is discrete, then the random variable is said to be a *discrete random variable*. If the sample space is continuous, then the random variable is said to be a *continuous random variable*. We will use the appropriate discrete or continuous random variables and associated probability distributions to describe processes depending on the nature of the underlying sample space. For example, the arrival time of an interrupt can be modeled by a continuous random variable, whereas the number of packets received by a certain process is modeled by a discrete random variable.

10.1.1 Continuous

The continuous real-valued function f is called a *probability density function* or *probability distribution* for the continuous random variable X if the following conditions hold:

1. $f(x) \geq 0$ for all $x \, \varepsilon \, \Re$

2. $\int_{-\infty}^{\infty} f(x)\,dx = 1$

3. The probability that the random variable X takes on a value between a and b, denoted $p(a < X < b)$ is given by

$$p(a < X < b) = \int_{a}^{b} f(x)\,dx$$

Note that for a continuous probability distribution and constant c, the value $p(x = c) = 0$. Moreover, recall that the "average value," or *mean* of the density function f, is denoted μ while its *variance*, a measure of how widely scattered the values of x are from the mean, is denoted σ^2.

Some common continuous probability distributions include exponential, Weibull, and Gaussian.

■ **EXAMPLE 10.1**

The Gaussian or normal distribution for a random variable X is given by

$$n(x) = \frac{1}{\sigma\sqrt{2\pi}} e^{-\frac{(x-\mu)^2}{2\sigma^2}} \tag{10.1}$$

with mean μ and variance σ^2. An example of such a density function with $\mu = 0$ and $\sigma^2 = 1$ is given in Figure 10.1.   ■

■ **EXAMPLE 10.2**

The exponential distribution for a random variable T is given by

$$f(t) = \lambda e^{-\lambda t} \tag{10.2}$$

The "average" value for this distribution can be shown to be $\frac{1}{\lambda}$ [82]. The graph of the exponential distribution is shown in Figure 10.2.   ■

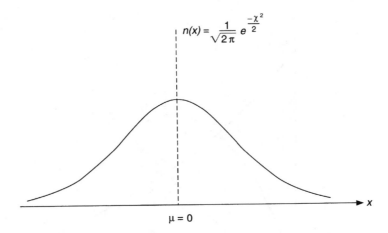

$$n(x) = \frac{1}{\sqrt{2\pi}} \, e^{\frac{-\chi^2}{2}}$$

$$\mu = 0$$

Figure 10.1 The Gaussian probability function with $\mu = 0$ and $\delta^2 = 1$.

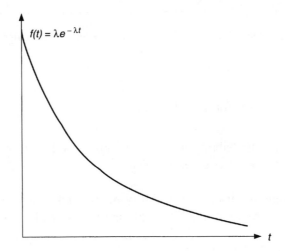

$$f(t) = \lambda e^{-\lambda t}$$

Figure 10.2 The exponential distribution.

■ **EXAMPLE 10.3**

The Weibull distribution for a random variable T is given by

$$f(t) = \alpha \beta \, t^{\beta - 1} \, e^{-\alpha t^{\beta}} \quad t > 0 \qquad (10.3)$$
$$= 0 \qquad\qquad\quad \text{elsewhere}$$

where $\alpha > 0$ and $\beta > 0$. The graphs of the Weibull probability density function for various values of the parameters α and β are given in Figure 10.3. ■

10.2 DISCRETE

The real-valued discrete function f is a called a *probability distribution function* or *probability distribution* for the discrete random variable X if the following three conditions hold:

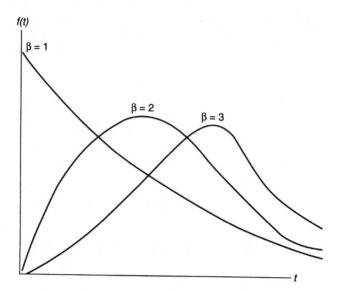

Figure 10.3 The Weibull probability function for different β and $\alpha = 1$.

1. $f(x) \geq 0$ for all values $x \; \varepsilon \; X$.
2. $\Sigma_x f(x) = 1$, where x ranges over values of X.
3. The probability that the random variable X takes on a value x, denoted $p(X = x)$, is given by $f(x)$.

Some common discrete probability distributions include a discrete form of the uniform distribution, the binomial distribution, and the Poisson distribution.

■ **EXAMPLE 10.4**

A frequently used discrete probability distribution, the Poisson distribution is used to describe phenomena in which the occurrence of individual events is independent of any previous events. Formally, it is defined as

$$P_k(t) = \frac{(\lambda \, t)^k \, e^{-\lambda t}}{k!} \tag{10.4}$$

with $k, t \geq 0$. $P_k(t)$ denotes the probability of k occurrences in time t, and λ is the number of occurrences per unit time. Note that the probability distribution of the interarrival time (the time between two consecutive events) in a Poisson process is given by the exponential probability distribution with mean $\frac{1}{\lambda}$. ■

The Poisson process is a good model for many naturally occurring random phenomena. In a Poisson process, the probability distribution for the number of occurrences in time t is Poisson, and the probability distribution of the time between occurrences is exponential. We will be using these two probability distributions exclusively.

10.3 BASIC BUFFER SIZE CALCULATION

Recall that a buffer is a set of memory locations that provide temporary storage for data that are being passed from one process to another, when the receiving process is consuming the data slower than they are being sent for some bounded period of time. Thus, assume that the data are being sent for some finite time called a *burst period*.

To visualize this scenario, imagine an oil funnel placed over the crankcase opening in a car engine. Oil is poured into the funnel at a rate that is clearly faster than it can drip into the crankcase—but only for some fixed interval T (dictated by the size of the oil can; see Figure 10.4). More precisely, if the data are produced at a rate of $P(t)$ and can be consumed at a rate of $C(t)$ (where $C(t) < P(t)$) for a burst period T, what is the size of the buffer needed to prevent data from being lost? The next sections seek to examine this problem.

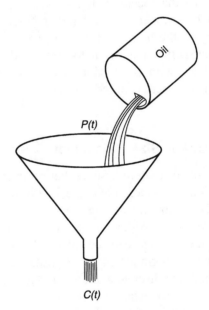

Figure 10.4 Buffering system.

10.3.1 Handling Bursts of Data

If both $P(t)$ and $C(t)$ are constant, denoted P and C, respectively, and if the consumption rate C is greater than or equal to P, then no buffer is needed since the system can always consume data faster than they can be produced. If $C < P$, however, then an overflow will occur. To calculate the buffer size needed to handle the overflow for a burst of period T, note that the total data produced is PT, while the total data consumed in that time is CT. Thus, there is an excess of

$$(P - C)T \tag{10.5}$$

This is how much data must be stored in the buffer. Thus, the buffer size is

$$B = (P - C)T \tag{10.6}$$

where C is the consumption rate, P is the production rate, and T is the burst time.

■ EXAMPLE 10.5

A device is providing data to a real-time computer via DMA at 9600 bytes/second in bursts of one-second duration every 20 seconds. The computer is capable of processing the data at 800 bytes/second. Assuming there is sufficient time to empty the buffer before another burst occurs, what should the minimum buffer size be? Using equation 10.6 yields

$$B = (9600 - 800)\ 1 = 8800 \text{ bytes} \qquad\qquad ■$$

Handling data that occur in bursts with equation 10.6 is possible only if the buffer can be emptied before another burst occurs. For example, in Example 10.5, emptying the buffer will take 11 seconds—sufficient time before the next expected burst. If bursts occur too frequently, then no size buffer will avail. In this case the system is unstable, and either upgrading the processor or downgrading the production process is necessary to solve the problem.

10.3.2 Variable Buffer Size Calculation

It is often not accurate to assume that production and consumption rates as well as production times are fixed; they will frequently be variable.

In this section we examine a case in which production and consumption rates are variable. Although we will perform the analysis for continuous variables, the results can be adapted for discrete variables by replacing summation for integration in the formulas. In addition, they can be generalized to handle both the discrete and continuous cases by employing Riemann-Stieljes integration (see, for example, [163]).

Suppose we have a producer process that produces data at a rate given by the function $p(t)$. Also suppose that another task consumes or uses the data produced by the first task at a rate determined by the function $c(t)$. The data are produced during a burst period $T = t_2 - t_1$, where t_1 and t_2 represent the start and finish times of the burst. Then the buffer size needed at time $\hat{T} > t_1$ can be expressed as

$$B(\hat{T}) = \int_{t_1}^{T} [p(t) - c(t)]\ dt \tag{10.7}$$

Thus, we need to know when $B(\hat{T})$ is a maximum to determine the required buffer size. Note that when $p(t)$ and $c(t)$ are constant, then equation 10.7 becomes equation 10.6 (see Exercises).

■ **EXAMPLE 10.6**

A task produces data at a rate (in bytes per second) that is determined by the function

$$p(t) = \begin{cases} 10000\,t & 0 \le t \le 1 \\ 10000(2 - t) & 1 < t \le 2 \\ 0 & \text{elsewhere} \end{cases}$$

with t representing the burst period. The data are consumed by a task at a rate determined by the function

$$c(t) = \begin{cases} 10000(1/4)t & 0 \le t \le 2 \\ 10000(1 - 1/4t) & 2 < t \le 4 \\ 0 & \text{elsewhere} \end{cases}$$

The graphs for $p(t)$ and $c(t)$ are depicted in Figure 10.5. The question then is: If the burst period is known to be 1.5 seconds, what is the necessary buffer size? In this case it can be seen by inspecting

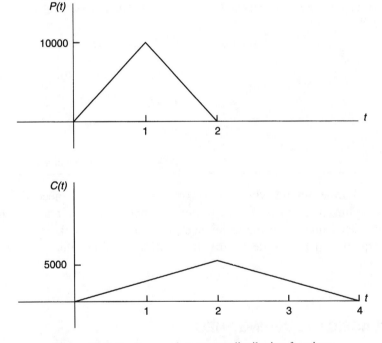

Figure 10.5 Producer and consumer distribution functions.

the areas under the curves for $p(t)$ and $c(t)$ that $B_{\max}(\hat{T})$ occurs when $\hat{T} = 1$. Plugging this into equation 10.7,

$$B(1) = \int_0^1 [p(t) - c(t)]\, dt$$

$$= 10000 \int_0^1 [(t - 1/4t)]\, dt$$

$$= 10000(3/4) \int_0^1 t\, dt$$

$$= 10000(3/8) \; t^2 \Big|_0^1$$

$$= 10000(3/8)$$

$$= 3750 \text{ bytes} \qquad\qquad\qquad ■$$

If the burst period is also variably determined by function $u(t)$, then for a burst occurring at time t_1,

$$B = \int_{t1}^{u(t1)} [p(t) - c(t)] \, dt \qquad (10.8)$$

■ **EXAMPLE 10.7**

In the previous example, if the burst starts at a time determined by the Gaussian distribution

$$u(t) = \frac{1}{\sqrt{2\pi}} e^{-\frac{(t-2)^2}{2}}$$

then $u(0) = 0.053991$. Inspecting the production and consumption curves again shows that the maximum buffer size is needed when $\hat{T} = 0.053991$. Recalculation of the buffer size now yields

$$B(.053991) = \int_0^{0.053991} [p(t) - c(t)] \, dt$$

$$= 10000 \int_0^{0.053991} [(t - 1/4t)] \, dt$$

$$= 10000(3/4) \int_0^{0.053991} t \, dt$$

$$= 10000(3/8) \; t^2 \Big|_0^{0.053991}$$

$$= 10000(3/8)[0.002915] \approx 11 \text{bytes} \qquad ■$$

Determining when the maximum buffer size is needed is easily done by graphing the consumer and producer function curves, and then inspecting them to determine when the difference in the areas under the curves is greatest. Use equation 10.7 to determine this difference and thus the maximum buffer size.

10.4 CLASSICAL QUEUING THEORY

The classical queuing problem involves one or more producer processes called *servers* and one or more consumer processes called *customers*. A standard notation for a queuing system is a three-tuple. The first component describes the probability distribution for the time between arrival of customers, the second is the probability distribution of time needed to service each customer, and the third is the number of servers (see Figure 10.6). In a real-time system, the first component might be the arrival time probability distribution for a certain interrupt request, the second would be the time needed to service that interrupt request, and the third component would be "1" for a single-processing system, more for

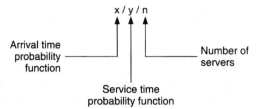

Figure 10.6 Components of a queuing system.

multiprocessing systems. We can use known properties of this model to predict service times for tasks in a real-time system.

10.4.1 The M/M/1 Queue

The simplest basic queuing model is called the M/M/1 queue, which represents a single server system with Poisson arrival model (exponential interarrival times for the customers or interrupt requests with mean $\frac{1}{\lambda}$), and exponential service or processing time with mean $\frac{1}{\mu}$ and $\lambda < \mu$. As suggested before, this model can be used effectively to model certain aspects of real-time systems; it is also useful because it is well known, and several important results are immediately available.

We will present these results without derivation. Further study of the theoretical aspects can be found in [28] or [82]. For example, let N be the number of customers in the queue. Letting $\rho = \lambda/\mu$ then the average number of customers in the queue in such a system is

$$\overline{N} = \frac{\rho}{1 - \rho} \tag{10.9}$$

with variance

$$\sigma^2{}_N = \frac{\rho}{(1 - \rho)^2} \tag{10.10}$$

The average time a customer spends in the system is

$$T = \frac{1/\mu}{1 - \rho} \tag{10.11}$$

The random variable Y for the time spent in the system has probability distribution

$$s(y) = \mu(1 - \rho)e^{-\mu(1 - \rho)y} \tag{10.12}$$

with $y \geq 0$.

Finally, it can be shown [82] that the probability that at least k customers are in the queue is

$$P[\geq k \text{ in system}] = \rho^k \tag{10.13}$$

In the M/M/1 model, the probability of exceeding a certain number of customers in the system decreases geometrically. If interrupt requests are considered customers in a certain system, then two such requests in the system at the same time (a time-overloaded condition) have a far greater probability of occurrence than three or more such requests. Thus, building systems that can tolerate a single time-overload will contribute significantly to system reliability, while worrying about multiple time-overload conditions is probably not worth the bother. Let us now show how the M/M/1 queue can be used in real-time systems.

10.4.2 Service and Production Rates

Consider an M/M/1 system in which the customer represents an interrupt request of a certain type and the server represents the processing required for that request. In this single-processor model, waiters in the queue represent a time-overloaded condition. Because of the nature of the arrival and processing times, this condition could theoretically occur. Suppose, however, that you could vary either the arrival or the processing times. Varying the arrival time, which is represented by the parameter λ could be accomplished by changing hardware or altering the process causing the interrupt. Changing the processing time, represented by the parameter μ could be accomplished by one of the techniques discussed in Chapter 9. In any case, fixing one of these two parameters, and selecting the second parameter in such a way as to reduce the probability that more than one interrupt will be in the system simultaneously, will ensure that time-overloading cannot occur within a specific confidence interval.

■ EXAMPLE 10.8

Suppose $\frac{1}{\lambda}$, the mean interarrival time between interrupt requests, is fixed to be 10 milliseconds. Let us find the mean processing time, $\frac{1}{\mu}$, necessary to guarantee that the probability of time-overloading (more than one interrupt request in the system) is less than 1%. We can use equation 10.13 as follows:

$$P[\geq 2 \text{ in system}] = \left(\frac{\lambda}{\mu}\right)^2 \leq 0.01$$

or

$$\frac{1}{\mu} \leq \sqrt{\frac{0.01}{\lambda^2}} = \sqrt{(0.01)(10 \times 10^{-3})^2}$$

then

$$\Rightarrow \frac{1}{\mu} \le 0.001 \text{ second}$$

Thus, the mean processing time, $\frac{1}{\mu}$, should be no more than 1 millisecond to guarantee that time-overloading cannot occur with 99% confidence.   ■

■ **EXAMPLE 10.9**

Suppose we fix $\frac{1}{\mu}$, the mean service time, to be 5 milliseconds, and seek to find the average arrival time, $\frac{1}{\lambda}$, necessary to guarantee that the probability of time-overloading is less than 1%. We can use equation 10.13 as follows

$$\left(\frac{\lambda}{\mu}\right)^2 \le 0.01$$

or

$$\Rightarrow \frac{\mu}{\lambda} \ge 10$$

then

$$\Rightarrow \frac{1}{\lambda} \ge 0.050 \text{ second}$$

Hence, the average interarrival time between two interrupt requests should be at least 50 milliseconds to guarantee only a 1% risk of time-overloading.   ■

10.4.3 More Buffer Calculations

A second model using the M/M/1 queue portrays the "customers" as data being placed in a buffer. The "service" time is the time needed to pick up the data by some consumer task. Here our knowledge of M/M/1 queues is used to calculate the average buffer size needed to hold the data using equation 10.9, and the average time a datum spends in the system (its age) using equation 10.11.

■ **EXAMPLE 10.10**

A process produces data with interarrival times given by the exponential distribution $4e^{-4t}$, and is consumed by a process at a rate given by the exponential distribution $5e^{-5t}$. To calculate the average number of data items in the buffer, use equation 10.9:

$$\overline{N} = \frac{\rho}{1-\rho} = \frac{4/5}{1-4/5} = 4$$

The average "age" of a data item can be calculated with equation 10.11:

$$T = \frac{1/\mu}{1-\rho} = \frac{1/5}{1-4/5} = 1 \text{ second}$$

■

A probability distribution for the random variable determining the age of the datum can be found by using equation 10.12.

10.4.4 Response-Time Modeling

The "average" response time for a process handling an interrupt request in the absence of other competing processes can also be computed if an M/M/1 model is assumed. In this case use equation 10.11 to measure the average time spent in the system by an interrupt request (the response time).

■ **EXAMPLE 10.11**

A process is based on a sporadic interrupt that occurs with an interarrival rate given by the exponential function with mean $\frac{1}{\lambda} = 5$ milliseconds. A process handles the data in an amount of time determined by the exponential function with mean $\frac{1}{\mu} = 3$ milliseconds. The mean response time for this interrupt request is seen from equation 10.11 to be

$$\frac{3}{1 - \dfrac{\frac{1}{5}}{\frac{1}{3}}} = 7.5 \text{ milliseconds}$$

■

A probability distribution for the random variable determining the mean response time can be found by using equation 10.12. Omitting context switching gives

$$s(t) = \frac{1}{3}\left(1 - \frac{3}{5}\right) e^{-\frac{1}{3}\left(1 - \frac{3}{5}\right)t}$$

or

$$s(t) = \frac{2}{5} e^{-\frac{2}{15}t}$$

Note that the response time will be deleteriously affected if the interrupt rate is less than the mean service rate.

10.4.5 Other Queuing Models

The M/M/1 queue can be used in a variety of other ways to model real-time systems. The only requirements are that the producer be modeled as a Poisson process and that the consumption time be exponential. Although the model assumes an infinite-length queue, confidence intervals can be fixed for modeling realistic finite-sized queues.

Systems that can be modeled to match other queuing system models can benefit from the well-known results there. For example, the M/G/1 queue with Poisson arrival (exponential interarrival) and general service time probability distributions can be used. Other results cover the general arrival and service densities. Relationships involving balking customers, those that leave the queue, can be used to represent rejected spurious interrupts or time-overloads.

10.5 LITTLE'S LAW

An important result in queuing theory, *Little's law*, has some application in real-time system performance prediction. Little's law (which appeared in 1961) states that the average number of customers in a queuing system, N_{av}, is equal to the average arrival rate of the customers to that system, r_{av}, times the average time spent in that system, t_{av}.

$$N_{av} = r_{av}t_{av} \qquad (10.14)$$

If n servers are present, then

$$N_{av} = \sum_{i=1}^{n} r_{i,av}t_{i,av} \qquad (10.15)$$

where $r_{i,av}$ is the average arrival rate for customers to server i and $t_{i,av}$ is the average service time for server i.

Viewing each process as a server and interrupt arrivals as customers, Little's law can be used as a rough estimate for CPU utilization in sporadic, periodic, or mixed interrupt systems.

For example, a system is known to have periodic interrupts occurring at 10, 20 and 100 milliseconds and a sporadic interrupt that is known to occur on average every 1 second. The average processing time for these interrupts is 3, 8, 25, and 30 milliseconds. Then by Little's law the average number of customers in the queue is

$$N_{av} = (1/10)3 + (1/20)8 + (1/100)25 + (1/1000)30 = 0.98$$

This result is the same one we obtained by using equation 9.7 in Chapter 9 of the text. Remember that although this is an estimate of average CPU utilization, transient overloads might still be present, as we will see in the following section.

10.6 ERLANG'S FORMULA

Another useful result of queuing theory is *Erlang's Loss Formula*. Suppose we have m servers (or processes) and arriving customers (interrupts). Each newly arriving interrupt is serviced by a process, unless all servers are busy (a potential time-overloaded condition). In this case the customer (interrupt) is lost. If we assume that the average service (process) time is μ and the average arrival time (interrupt rate) is λ, then the fraction of time that all servers are busy (a time-overloaded condition) is given by

$$p = \frac{(\lambda/\mu)^m/m!}{\sum_{k=0}^{m}(\lambda/\mu)^k/k!} \qquad (10.16)$$

This result dates back to 1917!

Applying Erlang's Formula to the previous example gives $m = 4$, $\lambda = 380$, $\mu = 16.5$:

$$p = \frac{(380/16.5)^4/4!}{1 + (380/16.5) + (390/16.5)^2/2 + (380/16.5)^3/3! + (380/16.5)^4/4!} = 0.834$$

This means there is a potential for time-overloading 83.4% of the time. Based on the average time-loading figure of 98% and what we learned from rate-monotonic analysis (70% or less time-loading is needed to guarantee no overloads in a perfect world), this seems reasonable.

10.7 EXERCISES

1. In Example 10.5 what would be the required buffer size for a given time t if the bursts were at 2400 baud, 2 seconds long, and occurred every 5 seconds?

2. A producer generates data at 1 byte per 200 nanoseconds in bursts of 64 kilobytes. A consumer can read the data in 32-bit words but only at a rate of one word every 2 microseconds. Calculate the minimum-size buffer required to avoid spillover, assuming there is enough time between bursts to empty the buffer.

3. Show that when the producer and consumer tasks have constant consumption rates, then equation 10.7 becomes equation 10.6.

4. A producer process is known to be able to process data at a rate that is exponentially distributed with average service time of 3 milliseconds per datum. What is the maximum allowable average data rate if the probability of collision is to be 0.1%? Assume that the data arrive at intervals that are exponentially distributed.

5. Discuss possible interpretations of equation 10.10 if N is the expected number of data items in some buffer.

11

Reliability, Testing, and Fault Tolerance

KEY POINTS OF THE CHAPTER

1. Reliability is a subjective measure.
2. In the absence of "real" metrics, use the weight of the printout, code size, McCabe's metric, Halstead's metrics—anything that is better than guessing.
3. Reliability, by most definitions, can be increased through fault-tolerant design and rigorous testing.
4. Testing should be performed throughout the Software Life Cycle by using a mixed bag of techniques.

Reliable software is a direct result of a solid design process, good software engineering practice, and rigorous system testing [43]. In this chapter we discuss reliability—and methods for increasing it—through system testing and fault tolerance. For a complete discussion of this topic see, for example [119] or [120].

11.1 FAULTS, FAILURES, BUGS, AND DEFECTS

Software engineers know there is a world of difference in the following terms; fault, failure, bug, and defect. The term *bug* is considered taboo since it somehow implies that an error crept into the program through no one's action. The preferred term for an error in requirement, design, or code is *defect*. The appearance of this defect during the operation of the software system is called a *fault*. A fault that causes the software system to fail to meet one of its requirements is a *failure*. In this text, however, we use these terms somewhat cavalierly because their colloquial interchangeability is implied.

11.2 RELIABILITY

A reliable software system in general can be defined informally in a number of ways. For example, one definition might be "a system which a user can depend on" [50]. Other loose characterizations of reliable software systems include the following:

- It "stands the test of time."
- Downtime is below a certain threshold.
- There is an absence of known *catastrophic* errors—that is, errors that render the system useless.
- *Results* are predictable (i.e., it is a deterministic system).
- It offers *robustness*—the ability to recover "gracefully" from errors.

For real-time systems, other informal characterizations of reliability are

- Event determinism
- Temporal determinism
- "Reasonable" time-loading
- "Reasonable" memory-loading

These characteristics are desirable in a reliable real-time software system, but because some characteristics are difficult to measure, we need a more rigorous definition.

11.2.1 Formal Definition

Rather than define the loose concept of "reliable software," we define the more precise measure of *software reliability*. Let S be a software system, and let T be the time of system failure. Then the reliability of S at time t, denoted $r(t)$, is the probability that T is greater than t; that is,

$$r(t) = P(T > t) \tag{11.1}$$

In words, this is the probability that a software system will operate without failure for a specified period of time.

Thus, a system with reliability function $r(t) = 1$ will never fail. For example, NASA has suggested that computers used in civilian fly-by-wire aircraft have a failure probability of no more than 10^{-9} per hour [85], which represents a reliability function of $r(t) = (0.99999999)^t$ with t in hours (still as $t \to \infty$, $r(t) \to 0$). We will suggest two models for software reliability based on the system *failure function*—that is, the probability that the system fails at time t.

The first and more standard failure function uses an exponential distribution where the abscissa is time and the ordinate represents the failure intensity at that time. Here the failure intensity is initially high, as would be expected in a new piece of software, and decreases with time, presumably as errors are uncovered and repaired.

The second, less standard model (and the one to which the author subscribes) is the general *bathtub curve* given in Figure 11.1. Brooks [19] notes that this curve is often used to describe the failure function of hardware components, and has been used to describe the number of errors found in a certain release of a software product. If we suppose that the probability of system failure is linearly related to the number of errors detected in the system, then we have the failure function defined by Figure 11.1. The interpretation of this failure function is easy for hardware—a certain number of pieces of a particular component will fail early due to manufacturing defects, and a large number will fail late in life due to aging.

The applicability of the bathtub curve to software failure requires a further stretch. Although a large number of errors will be found in a particular software product early (during testing and development), it is unclear why a large number of errors appear later in the life of the software product. These later errors might be due to the effects of patching or to the increased stress on the software by expert users [19].

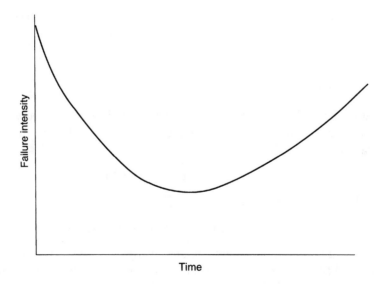

Figure 11.1 A typical failure function.

11.2.2 Calculating System Reliability

Several simple techniques for approximating system reliability have been developed, including the process block model, McCabe's metric, and Halstead's metrics.

11.2.2.1 Process Block Model   Overall system reliability for a system comprised of a series of subsystems, called *process blocks*, connected in parallel and series, can be calculated using simple rules of probability. It is assumed that the failure function of each process block is independent of the others; that is, if one fails, it does not necessarily imply that any other must fail. This might indeed be an oversimplification, if, for example, two software modules are sharing data.

Suppose two subsystems have reliability functions $r_1(t)$ and $r_2(t)$, respectively. If they are connected in parallel as in Figure 11.2, then the composite

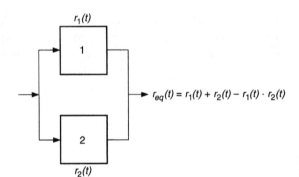

Figure 11.2 Parallel subsystems and their equivalent reliability.

subsystem will fail only if both blocks fail. That is, the failure function of the equivalent system $(1 - r_{eq})(t)$ is the product of the failure functions of the two parallel process blocks. Thus

$$1 - r_{eq}(t) = (1 - r_1(t))(1 - r_2(t))$$

Solving for $r_{eq}(t)$ yields

$$r_{eq}(t) = r_1(t) + r_2(t) - r_1(t)r_2(t) \tag{11.2}$$

Since the reliability functions are always between 0 and 1, the equivalent reliability for parallel process blocks is always greater than or equal to either of the individual reliabilities.

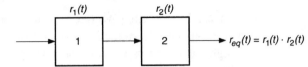

Figure 11.3 Series subsystems and their equivalent reliability.

For series connection, as depicted in Figure 11.3, the equivalent system fails if one or both of the process blocks fails. That is

$$p_{eq}(t) = p_1(t) + p_2(t) - p_1(t)p_2(t)$$

or

$$(1 - r_{eq}(t)) = (1 - r_1(t)) + (1 - r_2(t)) - (1 - r_1(t))(1 - r_2(t))$$

Solving for $r_{eq}(t)$ yields

$$r_{eq}(t) = r_1(t)r_2(t) \qquad (11.3)$$

Again noting that the reliability function is between 0 and 1, we see that connecting systems in series will decrease the reliability of the equivalent overall system.

To further illustrate the point, we examine a more complicated system.

■ EXAMPLE 11.1

A software system can be broken up into subsystems that interact as shown in Figure 11.4. The reliability function for the series subsystems 1 and 2 is, from equation 11.3

$$r_1(t)r_2(t)$$

The composite subsystem is in parallel with subsystem 3, which, from equation 11.2, yields a reliability function of

$$r_1(t)r_2(t) + r_3(t) - r_1(t)r_2(t)r_3(t)$$

The new composite subsystem in series with subsystem 4 yields, from equation 11.3, an overall reliability function of

$$r_{eq}(t) = (r_1(t)r_2(t) + r_3(t) - r_1(t)r_2(t)r_3(t))r_4(t) \qquad ■$$

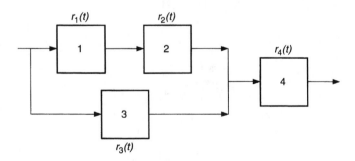

Figure 11.4 System broken into subsystems with associated reliabilities.

11.2.2.2 McCabe's Metric   Some experts believe that the reliability of the software can be determined *a priori* from characteristics of the source code. Although such metrics are far from mainstream, it is interesting to discuss them and their possible application to real-time systems here.

One such metric, developed by McCabe [112], is based on the complexity of the flow-of-control in the system. Suppose we could depict a software system as a directed graph (or graphs), where each block of sequential code represents a node and each synchronous change in flow-of-control is depicted as a directed arc or edge. No provision is made for asynchronous flow-of-control.

In a multitasking or multiprocessing system, each separate task would be represented by a separate flow graph. Interestingly, these graphs could be determined directly from the flow charts, dataflow diagrams, Petri nets, or finite state automata used to model the system.

In any case, the number of edges, e, and nodes, n, are counted. The number of separate flow graphs or tasks, p, also enter into the relationship. We then form the *cyclomatic complexity, C*, as follows:

$$C = e - n + 2p \tag{11.4}$$

McCabe asserts that the complexity of the control flow graph, C, reflects the difficulty in understanding, testing, and maintaining the software. He further contends that well-structured modules have a cyclomatic complexity in the range of $3 \leq C \leq 7$. As judged by empirical evidence, $C = 10$ is an upper limit for the reliability of a single module.

■ EXAMPLE 11.2

Consider the code in Example 6.4. It would have a flow graph as seen in Figure 11.5. Here $p = 1$ since there is only 1 task, and the graph has four nodes and three edges. Thus

$$C = 3 - 4 + 2 \cdot 1 = 1$$

According to McCabe, we can therefore expect the reliability of this code to be high.   ■

Although the McCabe metric provides some nonabstract measure of system reliability, it cannot depict asynchronous changes in flow-of-control, and thus, it has limited utility in a real-time system. Readers interested in forming their own opinions are referred to [111], [127].

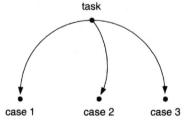

case 1   case 2   case 3   **Figure 11.5** Flow graph for Example 6.4.

11.2.2.3 Halstead's Metrics A drawback of both McCabe's metric and the process block model is that they seem to work well only with synchronous flow-of-control, which is not exactly representative of most real-time systems. A set of metrics proposed by Halstead [58], however, relies not on flow-of-control but on the information content of the program. This information content is based on the following source code characteristics, which have been simplified for clarity:

1. η_1 : the number of distinct begin–end pairs and GOTO statements (or their analogies in other languages) known as "operators."
2. η_2 : the number of distinct lines terminated by semicolons in C or statements in Pascal (or their analogies in other languages) known as "operands."
3. N_1 : the total number of occurrences of operators in the program.
4. N_2 : the total number of occurrences of operands in the program.

■ **EXAMPLE 11.3**

Although the determination of the Halstead numbers is largely intuitive, in Example 6.4, since there are four distinct begin–end pairs and six unique statements, the following numbers seem appropriate: $\eta_1 = 4$, $\eta_2 = 6$, $N_1 = 4$, $N_2 = 6$. (Individuals will obtain different numbers depending on how they count statements.) ■

Halstead has defined a number of concrete measures related to these characteristics, which can be used to determine system reliability.

Definition The program vocabulary, η, is defined as

$$\eta = \eta_1 + \eta_2 \tag{11.5}$$

Definition The program length, N, is defined as

$$N = N_1 + N_2 \tag{11.6}$$

Definition The program volume, V, is defined as

$$V = N \log_2 \eta \tag{11.7}$$

Definition The potential volume, V^*, is defined as

$$V^* = (2 + \eta_2) \cdot \log_2 (2 + \eta_2) \tag{11.8}$$

Definition The program level, L, is defined as

$$L = V^* / V \tag{11.9}$$

L is an attempt to measure the level of abstraction of the program. It is believed that increasing this number will increase system reliability.

Another Halstead metric attempts to measure the amount of mental effort required in the development of the code.

Definition The effort, E, is defined as

$$E = V / L \tag{11.10}$$

Again, decreasing the effort level is believed to increase reliability as well as ease of implementation.

Halstead applied his metrics to a number of programs written in several languages and, for intuitive comparison, to the English used in the novel *Moby Dick* [58].

Language	Level (L)	Effort (E)
English	2.16	1.00
PL/I	1.53	2.00
Algol-58	1.21	3.19
FORTRAN	1.14	3.59
Assembler	0.88	6.02

Note the relative advantage of FORTRAN over assembler and PL/I over FORTRAN. (PL/I is considered a more expressive language.)

Although Halstead's metrics are compatible with asynchronous flow-of-control, the fuzzy nature of the measurable parameters and their interpretation casts doubt on the utility of the technique. This might suggest, however, the application of fuzzy logic techniques in this area to obtain more usable results.

In any case, readers interested in learning more about Halstead's metrics are referred to [51], [58], or [128].

While it may sound facetious, there are no viable metrics for measuring real-time reliability. However, many organizations swear by them. NASA uses McCabe's metric for much of its software and it is now possible to buy commerical tools to determine McCabe's and Halstead's metrics. However, in truth, any metric is better than nothing. For example, do you believe that a million lines of code (any code, not including comments) is more or less reliable than 100? Since a printout of a million lines of code weighs more than that for 100, why not use "weight of printout" as a reliability metric?

Of course, a million lines of PRINT statements will be more reliable than 100 lines of assembly language code, so what now? Of course, metrics like McCabe's and Halstead's take this into account.

11.2.2.4 Function Points *Function points* are a widely used metric set in nomembedded environments, and they form the basis of many commercial software analysis packages. Function points measure the number of interfaces between modules and subsystems in programs or systems. These interfaces are defined by measuring the following five software characteristics for each module, subsystem or system:

- number of inputs (I)
- number of outputs (O)
- number of queries (Q)
- number of files used (F)

A weighted sum is then computed, giving the function point (FP) metric, for example:

$$FP = 4I + 4O + 5Q + 10F$$

The weights can be adjusted to compensate for factors such as application domain and software developer experience. Intuitively, the higher FP, the more difficult to implement. And a great advantage of the function point metric is that it can be computed before any coding occurs.

From the definition, it is easy to see why the function point metric is highly suited for business processing, but not necessarily appropriate for embedded systems. However, there is increasing interest in the use of function points in real-time embedded systems, especially in large-scale real-time databases, multimedia, and Internet support. These systems are data driven and often behave like the large-scale transaction-based systems for which function points were developed.

11.2.2.5 Other Metrics Many other metrics are used in the measurement of software quality and reliability. For a neat review of many of these metrics, along with some new ones, and their application, see [128].

11.3 TESTING

Although testing will flush out errors, this is not the goal of testing. Long ago, software testing was thought of in this way; however, testing can only detect the presence of errors, not the absence of them. This is insufficient, particularly in real-time systems. Instead, the goal of testing is "to ensure that the software meets its requirements." This places emphasis on solid design techniques and a well-developed requirements document. A formal test plan must be developed that provides criteria used in deciding whether the system has satisfied the requirements document.

The test plan should follow the requirements document item by item, providing criteria that are used to judge whether the required item has been met. A set of test cases are then written which are used to measure the criteria set out in the test plan. (This can be extremely difficult when a user interface is part of the requirements.)

The test plan includes criteria for testing the software on a module-by-module or unit level, and on a system or subsystem level; both should be incorporated in a good testing scheme. The system-level testing provides criteria for the hardware/software integration process (see Chapter 13). We follow with a discussion of a variety of test techniques. A more thorough treatment can be found in [65].

11.3.1 Unit Level Testing

Several methods can be used to test individual modules or *units*. These techniques can be used by the unit author and by the independent test team to exercise each unit in the system. These techniques can also be applied to subsystems (collections of modules related to the same function). The techniques to be discussed include black box and white box testing.

11.3.1.1 Black Box Testing   In *black box* testing, only the inputs and outputs of the unit are considered; how the outputs are generated based on a particular set of inputs is ignored. Such a technique, being independent of the implementation of the module, can be applied to any number of modules with the same functionality. But this technique does not provide insight into the programmer's skill in implementing the module. In addition, dead or unreachable code cannot be detected.

For each module a number of test cases needs to be generated. This number depends on the functionality of the module, the number of inputs, and so on. If a module fails to pass a single-module level test, then the error must be repaired, and all previous module-level test cases are rerun and passed, to prevent the repair from causing other errors.

For black box testing, how do you obtain the test cases? There are a number of techniques.

1. Exhaustion (brute force)—All possible combinations of module inputs are tried. For a digital computer this is always a finite, though potentially large, number of test cases.
2. Corner cases—For example, minimum, maximum, or average values given for each input to the module are tested.
3. Pathological cases—These are unusual combinations of input values that may lead to errors. Such combinations are often difficult to identify.

4. Statistically based testing—Random test cases or inputs are based on underlying probability distribution functions. The shortcomings of this technique are discussed shortly.

When choosing the technique to be used for black box testing, brute force testing should be used if feasible for small modules. For larger modules, some combination of the above methods is needed. For example, in manned or critical systems exhaustive testing is still desirable but might not be feasible. An acceptable substitute might be corner case testing followed by pathological case testing. For user interfaces, statistically based testing appears to be reasonable. The point is that the test mix depends on the application and resources available to do the testing.

■ **EXAMPLE 11.4**

A software module used for a built-in test is passed a 16-bit status word, STATUS. If any of the first three (least significant) bits are set, then an error is indicated by returning the Boolean flag ERROR as TRUE. If, however, all three bits are set, then it is assumed that the hardware diagnostic device is in error, and ERROR is set as FALSE. The other 13 bits are to be ignored. It is decided that the input patterns given in Table 11.1 (in hexadecimal) and corresponding expected outputs will be used to test the module. This test case seems sufficient to test the module. Exhaustive test would have required 2^{16} test cases.   ■

TABLE 11.1 Black Box Test Cases for BITS Code

Status	Error
0001	True
0002	True
0004	True
0007	False

An important aspect of using black box testing techniques is that clearly defined interfaces to the modules are required. This places additional emphasis on the application of Parnas partitioning principles to module design.

11.3.1.2 White Box Testing   As we just mentioned, one disadvantage of black box testing is that it can often bypass unreachable or dead code. In addition, it may not test all of the flow-of-control paths through the module. This can lead to latent errors. A technique called *white box* or *clear box* testing can be used to solve this problem.

White box tests are designed to exercise all paths in the module and thus are logic driven. (Black box tests are data driven.) The goal is to try to test every line of code.

■ **EXAMPLE 11.5**

Consider the previous example. The set of test cases we generated tested the "corner cases" for the module—that is, one or all error bits set. A white box test set would seek to exercise the path in the module where only two error bits might be set. In addition it would exercise any paths where the "don't care" bits are inadvertently tested. It is therefore decided that the white box input patterns (in hexadecimal) and corresponding expected outputs given in Table 11.2 will be used to test the module. This test scheme is more robust than the "corner case" test picked in Example 11.4.   ■

TABLE 11.2   White Box Test Cases
for BITS Code

Status	Error
0001	True
0002	True
0003	True
0004	False
0005	True
0006	True
FFF8	False

11.3.1.3 Group Walkthroughs   *Group walkthroughs* or *code inspections* are a kind of white box testing in which a number of persons inspect the code, line-by-line, with the unit author. The author presents each line of code to a review group, thus rethinking the logic and often finding errors in the process. The persons in the review group include users of the modules under review, specification writers, testers, and peer programmers. This technique provides excellent control of the coding techniques used and permits a good check on any logical errors that may have been introduced. In addition, any unreachable code can be detected, and more elegant or faster code is sometimes suggested. Group walkthroughs are recommended for use in any testing strategy. An excellent discussion of code inspection techniques can be found in [41]. IEEE Std 1028–1988, Software Reviews and Audits, provides a step-by-step recipe for code inspections.

11.3.1.4 Formal Program Proving   Formal program proving is a kind of white box testing that treats the specification and code as a formal theorem to be proved. We will not discuss this test here for three reasons. First, some experts are skeptical of its viability in large systems [32], [45], [96]. Second, formal program proving for real-time systems requires the use of methods including temporal logic or process algebra, both of which are beyond the scope of this text. Finally, few commercial tools are available to facilitate this kind of testing. The interested reader can see [98], [102], or [112] for a discussion of some of these instruments.

11.3.2 System-Level Testing

Once individual modules have been tested, then subsystems or the entire system needs to be tested. In larger systems, the process can be broken down into a series of subsystem tests and then a test of the overall system.

System testing views the entire system as a black box so that one or more of the black box testing techniques can be applied. System-level testing always occurs after all modules pass their module-level test. At this point the coding team hands the software over to the test team for validation.

If an error occurs during system-level testing, the error must be repaired. Ideally, every test case involving the changed module must be rerun, and all previous system level tests must be passed in succession. The collection of system test cases is often called a *system test suite*.

Burn-in testing is a type of system-level testing done in the factory, which seeks to flush out those failures appearing early in the life of the system, and thus to improve the reliability of the delivered product.

System-level testing is usually followed by *alpha testing*, which is a type of validation consisting of internal distribution and exercise of the software. This testing is followed by *beta testing*, where preliminary versions of validated software are distributed to friendly customers who test the software under actual use. Later in the life cycle of the software, if corrections or enhancements are added, then *regression testing* is performed. Regression testing (which can also be performed at the module level) is used to validate the updated software against the old set of test cases that have already been passed. Any new test cases needed for the enhancements are then added to the test suite, and the software is validated as if it were a new product.

11.3.3 Statistically Based Testing

A technique useful for both unit and system-level tests is *statistically based testing*. This kind of testing uses an underlying probability distribution function for each system input to generate random test cases. This simulates execution of the software under realistic conditions. The statistics are usually collected by expert users of similar systems or, if none exist, by educated guessing. The theory is that system reliability will be enhanced if prolonged usage of the system can be simulated in a controlled environment.

The major drawback of such a technique is that the underlying probability distribution functions for the input variables may be unavailable or incorrect. In addition, randomly generated test cases are likely to miss conditions with low probability of occurrence. Precisely this kind of condition is usually overlooked in the design of the module. Failing to test these scenarios is an invitation to disaster.

11.3.4 Cleanroom Testing

Some current research [139] focuses on a "cleanroom" software development technique to eliminate software errors and reduce system testing. In this approach, the development team is not allowed to test code as it is being developed. Rather, syntax checkers, code walkthroughs, group inspections, and formal verifications are used to ensure product integrity. Statistically based testing is then applied at various stages of product development by a separate test team. This technique reportedly produces documentation and code that are more reliable and maintainable and easier to test than other development methods.

The principal tenet of cleanroom software development is that, given sufficient time and with care, error-free software can be written. Cleanroom software development relies heavily on group walkthroughs, code inspections, code reading by stepwise abstraction, and formal program validation. It is taken for granted that software specifications exist that are sufficient to completely describe the system.

The program is developed by slowly "growing" features into the code, starting with some baseline of functionality. At this first and subsequent milestones, an independent test team checks the code against a set of randomly generated test cases based on a set of statistics describing the frequency of use for each feature specified in the requirements. This group tests the code incrementally at predetermined milestones, and either accepts or returns it to the development team for correction. Once a functional milestone has been reached, the development team adds to the "clean" code, using the same techniques as before. Thus, like an onion skin, new layers of functionality are added to the software system until it has completely satisfied the requirements.

The programmers are not allowed to test any of their code on a computer other than to do syntax checking. Certain aspects of this technique have been used successfully, and several projects have been developed in this way, in both academic and industrial environments [139].

This approach is experimental, and it does have several problems [96]. The main problem is the lack of studies indicating the amount of overhead required for the cleanroom approach. It is surmised that personnel requirements must be increased and schedules attenuated to accommodate this technique.

11.3.5 Stress Testing

In another type of testing, *stress testing*, the system is subjected to a large disturbance in the inputs (for example, a large burst of interrupts), followed by smaller disturbances spread out over a longer period of time.

11.4 FAULT TOLERANCE

Fault tolerance is the ability of the system to continue to function in the presence of hardware or software failures [51]. In real-time systems, fault tolerance includes design choices that transform hard real-time deadlines into soft ones. These are often encountered in interrupt driven systems, which can provide for detecting and reacting to a missed deadline.

Fault tolerance designed to increase reliability in real-time systems can be classified in two varieties, spatial and temporal [85]. *Spatial* fault tolerance includes methods involving redundant hardware or software, whereas *temporal* fault tolerance involves techniques that allow for tolerating missed deadlines. Of the two, temporal fault tolerance is the more difficult to achieve because it requires careful algorithms design. We discuss variations of both techniques in the next several sections.

11.4.1 General Problem Handling

The reliability of most hardware can be increased using spatial fault tolerance— three or more redundant devices connected via a majority rule voting scheme. Another popular scheme uses two or more pairs of redundant hardware devices. Each pair compares its output to its companion. If the results are unequal, the pair declares itself in error and the outputs are ignored. In either case, the penalty is increased cost, space, and power requirements.

Voting schemes can also be used in software to increase algorithm robustness. Often information is processed from more than one source and reduced to some sort of best estimate of the actual value. For example, an aircraft's position can be determined via information from satellite positioning systems, inertial navigation data, and ground information. A composite of these readings is made using a mathematical construct called a *Kalman filter*. Design and analysis of Kalman filters is complex and beyond the scope of this text.

11.4.1.1 Checkpoints At fixed locations in code, intermediate results can be written to files, printers, or memory for diagnostic purposes. These locations, called *checkpoints*, can be used during system operation and during system verification (see Figure 11.6). If the checkpoints are used only during testing, then this code is known as a *test probe*. Test probes can introduce subtle timing errors

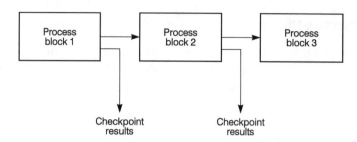

Figure 11.6 Checkpoint implementation.

in the code which are difficult to diagnose (see the discussion on the software Heisenberg uncertainty principle in Chapter 13).

11.4.1.2 Recovery Block Approach Fault tolerance can be further increased by using checkpoints in conjunction with predetermined reset points in software. These reset points mark *recovery blocks* in the software. At the end of each recovery block, the checkpoints are tested for "reasonableness." If the results are reasonable, then flow-of-control passes to the next recovery block. If the results are not reasonable, then processing resumes at the beginning of that recovery block (or some other previous one) (see Figure 11.7). The point, of course, is that some hardware device (or another process that is independent of the one in question) has provided faulty inputs to the block. By repeating the processing in the block, with presumably valid data, the error will not be repeated.

In the process block model, each recovery block represents a redundant parallel process to the block being tested. Equation 11.2 demonstrates why this method increases reliability. Unfortunately, although this strategy increases system reliability it can have a severe impact on real-time performance because of the overhead added by the checkpoint and repetition of the processing in a block.

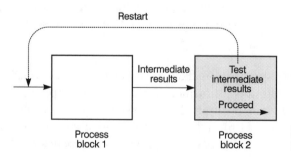

Figure 11.7 Recovery block implementation.

11.4.2 N-Version Programming

In any system, a state can be entered where the system is rendered ineffective or *locks up*. This is usually due to some untested flow-of-control in the software for which there is no escape. In systems terminology we would say that event determinism has been violated.

In order to reduce the likelihood of this sort of catastrophic error, redundant processors are added to the system. These processors are coded to the same specifications but by different programming teams. It is therefore highly unlikely that more than one of the systems can lock up under the same circumstances. Since each of the systems usually resets a watchdog timer, it quickly becomes obvious when one of them is locked up, because it fails to reset its timer. The other processors in the system can then ignore this processor, and the overall system continues to function. This technique is called *N-version programming*, and it has been used successfully in a number of projects including the space shuttle general purpose computer (GPC).

The redundant processors can use a voting scheme to decide on outputs, or, more likely, there are two processors—master and slave. The *master* processor is on-line and produces the actual outputs to the system under control, whereas the *slave* processor shadows the master off-line. If the slave detects that the master has become hung up, then the slave goes on-line.

11.4.3 Built-In-Test Software

Built-in-test software, or BITS (also called built-in-software test or BIST), can enhance fault tolerance by providing ongoing diagnostics of the underlying hardware for processing by the software. BITS is especially important in embedded systems. For example, if an I/O channel is functioning incorrectly as determined by its on-board circuitry, the software may be able to shut off the channel and redirect the I/O.

Although BITS is an important part of embedded systems, it adds significantly to the worst case time-loading analysis. This must be considered when selecting BITS and when interpreting the time-loading numbers that result from the additional software. In the next subsections we discuss built-in testing for a variety of hardware components.

11.4.4 CPU Testing

It is probably more important that the health of the CPU be checked than any other component of the system. A set of carefully constructed tests can be performed to test the efficacy of its instruction set in all addressing modes. Such a test suite will be time consuming and thus should be relegated to background processing. Interrupts should also be disabled during each sub-test to protect the data being used.

There is a catch-22 involved in using the CPU to test itself. If, for example, the CPU detects an error in its instruction set, can it be believed? If the CPU does not detect an error that is actually present, then this, too, is a paradox. These problems should not be cause for omitting the CPU instruction set test.

11.4.5 Memory Testing

All types of memory, including nonvolatile memories, can be corrupted via electrostatic discharge, power surging, vibration, or other means. This damage can manifest itself either as a permutation of data stored in memory cells or as permanent damage to the cell itself. Corruption of both RAM and ROM by randomly encountered charged particles is a particular problem in space. These single-event upsets do not usually happen on earth because either the earth's magnetosphere deflects the offending particle or the mean free path of the particle is not sufficient to bring it to the surface. A discussion of this problem, and how to deal with it via software, can be found in [84]. Many of these concepts are discussed here.

Damage to the contents of memory is called a *soft error*, whereas damage to the cell itself is called a *hard error*. In Chapter 2 we discussed some of the characteristics of memory devices, and referred to their tolerance to upset. We are particularly interested in techniques that can detect an upset to a memory cell and then correct it.

11.4.5.1 ROM The contents of ROM memory are often checked by comparing a known *checksum* with a current checksum. The known checksum, which is usually a simple binary addition of all program-code memory locations, is computed at link time and stored in a specific location in ROM. The new checksum can be recomputed in a slow cycle or background processing, and compared against the original checksum. Any deviation can be reported as a memory error. Checksums are not a very desirable form of error checking because errors to an even number of locations can result in error cancellation. For example, an error to bit 12 of two different memory locations may cancel out in the overall checksum, resulting in no error being detected. In addition, although an error may be reported, the location of the error in memory is unknown.

A reliable method for checking ROM memory uses a *cyclic redundancy code* (CRC). The CRC treats the contents of memory as a stream of bits and each of these bits as the binary coefficient of a *message polynomial* (an extremely long one) (see Figure 11.8). A second binary polynomial of much lower order (for example, 16 for the CCITT or CRC-16 standards) called the *generator polynomial* is divided (modulo-2) into the message, producing a quotient and a remainder. Before dividing, the message polynomial is appended with a 0 bit for every term

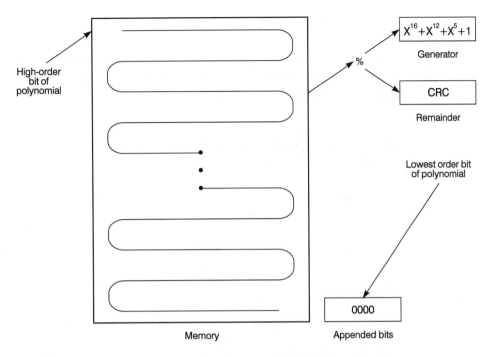

High-order
bit of
polynomial

$X^{16}+X^{12}+X^5+1$

Generator

%

CRC

Remainder

Lowest order bit
of polynomial

0000

Memory   Appended bits

Figure 11.8 Cyclic Reduncancy Code implementation.

in the generator. The remainder from the modulo-2 division of the padded message is the CRC check value. The quotient is discarded.

NOTE 11.1   The CCITT generator polynomial is

$$X^{16} + X^{12} + X^5 + 1 \qquad (11.11)$$

whereas the CRC-16 generator polynomial is

$$X^{16} + X^{15} + X^2 + 1 \qquad (11.12)$$

A CRC can detect all 1-bit errors and virtually all multiple-bit errors. The source of the error, however, cannot be pinpointed.

■ **EXAMPLE 11.6**

ROM consists of 64 kilobytes of 16-bit memory. CRC-16 is to be employed to check the validity of the memory contents. The memory contents represent a polynomial of at most order $65536 \cdot 16 = 1,048,576$. (Whether the polynomial starts from high or low memory does not matter as long as you are consistent.) After appending the polynomial with sixteen 0s, the polynomial is at most of order 1,048,592. This so-called message polynomial is then divided by the generator polynomial $X^{16} + X^{15} + X^2 + 1$, producing a quotient, which is discarded, and the remainder, which is the desired CRC check value.   ■

In addition to checking memory, the CRC can be employed to perform nonvisual validation of screens by comparing a CRC of the actual output with the

CRC of the desired output. The CRC of the screen memory is called a *screen signature*.

The CRC calculation is CPU-intensive, and should only be performed in background or at extremely slow rates. An excellent set of programs in C for computing CRCs can be found in [21].

11.4.5.2 RAM   Because of the dynamic nature of RAM, checksums and CRCs are not viable. One way of protecting against errors to memory is to equip it with extra bits used to implement a *Hamming code*. Depending on the number of extra bits, known as the *syndrome*, errors to one or more bits can be detected and corrected. A good discussion of the Hamming code from a theoretical prospective can be found in [107], and a more practical discussion is given in [117]. Such coding schemes can be used to protect ROM memory as well.

Chips that implement Hamming code error detection and correction (EDC chip) are available commercially. Their operation is of some interest. During a normal fetch or store, the data must pass through the chip before going into or out of memory. The chip compares the data against the check bits and makes correction if necessary (see Figure 11.9). The chip also sets a readable flag, which indicates that either a single or multiple bit error was found. Realize, however, that the error is not corrected in memory during a read cycle, so if the same erroneous data are fetched again, they must be corrected again. When data are stored in memory, however, the correct check bits for the data are computed and stored along with the word, fixing any errors, a process called *RAM scrubbing*.

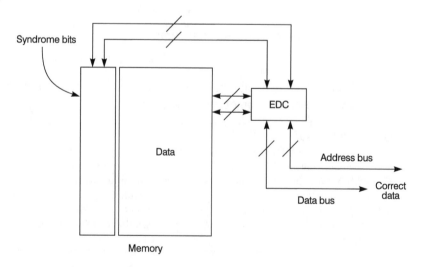

Figure 11.9 Implementation of Hamming code error detection and correction.

In RAM scrubbing, the contents of a RAM location are simply read and written back. The error detection and correction occurs on the bus, and the corrected data are loaded into a register. Upon writing the data back to the memory location, the correct data and syndrome are stored. Thus, the error is corrected in memory as well as on the bus. RAM scrubbing is used in the space shuttle inertial measurement unit (IMU) computer [90].

This device significantly reduces the number of soft errors, which will be removed upon rewriting to the cell, and hard errors, which are caused by stuck bits or permanent physical damage to the memory. The disadvantages of error detection and correction are as follows.

- Additional memory is needed for the scheme (6 bits for every 16 bits—a 37% increase).
- Additional power is required.
- Acreage requirements are imposed.
- An access time penalty of about 50 nanoseconds per access is incurred if an error correction is made.
- Multiple bit errors cannot be corrected.

In the absence of error detecting and correcting hardware, basic techniques can be used to test the integrity of RAM memory. These tests are usually run upon initialization, but they can also be implemented in slow cycles if interrupts are appropriately disabled.

■ EXAMPLE 11.7

Suppose a computer system has 8-bit, data, and address buses to write to 8-bit memory locations. We wish to exercise the address and data buses as well as the memory cells. This is accomplished by writing and then reading back certain bit patterns to every memory location. Traditionally, the following hexadecimal bit patterns are used:

AA	00
55	FF

The bit patterns are selected so that any cross-talk between wires can be detected. Bus wires are not always laid out consecutively, however, so that other cross-talk situations can arise. For instance, the above bit patterns do not check for coupling between odd-numbered wires. The following test set does:

AA	00
55	FF
0F	33

This test set, however, does not isolate the problem to the offending wire (bit). For complete coverage of 8 bits we need,

$$7 + 6 + 5 + 4 + 3 + 2 + 1 = 28$$

combinations of 2 bits at a time. Since we have 8-bit words, we can test four of these combinations per test. Thus, we need

$$\frac{28}{4} = 7$$

8-bit patterns. These are given in the following table:

AA	00
55	F0
0F	33
CC	

In general, for n-bit data and address buses writing to n-bit memory, where n is a power of 2, a total of $\frac{n(n-1)}{2}$ patterns of 2 are needed, which can be implemented in $n - 1$ patterns of n bits each.

11.4.5.3 Other Devices

Devices such as A/D converters, D/A converters, MUXs, I/O cards, and the like need to be tested continually. Many of these devices have built-in watchdog timer circuitry to indicate that the device is still on-line. The software can check for watchdog timer overflows and either reset the device or indicate failure.

In addition, the BITS can rely on the individual built-in tests of the devices in the system. Typically, these devices will send a status word via DMA to indicate their health. The software should check this status word and indicate failures as required.

11.4.6 Spurious and Missed Interrupts

Extraneous and unwanted interrupts not due to time-loading are called *spurious interrupts*. Spurious interrupts can destroy algorithmic integrity and cause run-time stack overflows or system crashes. Spurious interrupts can be caused by noisy hardware, power surges, electrostatic discharges, or single-event upsets. Missed interrupts can be caused in a similar way. In either case, hard real-time deadlines can be compromised, leading to system failure. It is the goal, then, to transform these hard errors into some kind of tolerable soft error.

11.4.6.1 Handling Spurious Interrupts

Spurious interrupts can be tolerated by using redundant interrupt hardware in conjunction with a voting scheme. Similarly, the device issuing the interrupt can issue a redundant check, such as using DMA to send a confirming flag. Upon receiving the interrupt, the handler routine checks the redundant flag. If the flag is set, the interrupt is legitimate. The handler should then clear the flag. If the flag is not set, then the interrupt is bogus and the handler routine should exit quickly and in an orderly fashion. The additional overhead of checking the redundant flag is minimal relative to the benefit derived. Of course, extra stack space should be allocated to allow for at least one spurious interrupt per cycle to avoid stack overflow. Stack overflow caused by repeated spurious interrupts is called a *death spiral*.

Missed interrupts are more difficult to deal with. Software watchdog timers can be constructed that must be set or reset by the routine in question. Routines running at higher priority or at a faster rate can check these memory locations to ensure that they are being accessed properly. If not, the dead task can be restarted or an error indicated. The surest method for sustaining integrity in the face of missed interrupts is through the design of robust algorithms.

11.4.7 Dealing with Bit Failures

Unwanted flipped bits in memory, device registers, the CPU, and so forth can be the source of many types of system problems ranging from performance degradation to total system failure. These failures are due to a variety of sources including hardware failures, charged particle collisions, and radiation effects. A thorough discussion of dealing with these types of problems can be found in [90]. However, the main findings of this work and the relative costs of the remedies are summarized in Tables 11.3 and 11.4.

At the time of this writing, actual data on the relative efficiency of these techniques were unavailable, but it will be interesting to note which technique fares best.

TABLE 11.3   SEU Protection Mechanisms

Adverse Effect	Remedy
Corruption of RAM data	EDC chip, RAM scrubbing
Corruption of ROM data	EDC chip
Corruption of PC	None
CPU latch-up	Watchdog timer
I/O circuitry	None
Spurious interrupts	Confirmation flags
Missed interrupts	Watchdog timer, counters
Mis-prioritized interrupts	Double check status register

TABLE 11.4 Costs of SEU Protection Mechanisms

Remedy	Cost
RAM scrubbing	None
EDC chip	Increased memory access times
Watchdog timer	Increased power, space, weight
Confirmation flags	Increased interrupt response times
Double check status register	Increased interrupt response times

11.5 EXERCISES

1. Draw the subsystem configuration for a system with four subsystems and an overall reliability function given by

$$r_1(t)r_2(t) + r_3(t)r_4(t) - r_1(t)r_2(t)r_3(t)r_4(t)$$

2. For the system depicted in Figure 11.10, calculate the overall system reliability function.

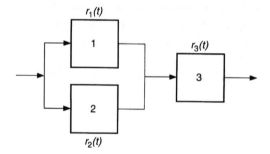

Figure 11.10 System divided into subsystems with associated reliabilities.

3. For the system depicted in Figure 11.10, calculate the overall system failure function.
4. For the Pascal code depicted in Example 6.3, draw the flow graph and calculate McCabe's metric for this code.
5. Derive $r_{eq}(t)$ in equation 11.2.
6. Derive $r_{eq}(t)$ in equation 11.3.
7. For the Pascal code depicted in Example 6.5, draw the flow graph if the number of states is 5 and the alphabet size is 6. Calculate McCabe's metric for this code. What happens to McCabe's metric as the number of states increases? What happens as the alphabet size increases? Can you draw any conclusions about the reliability of table-driven code?
8. Calculate the cyclomatic complexity for all the Pascal code fragments in Chapters 7 and 8.
9. Calculate the Halstead metrics for Example 6.4 using the numbers calculated in Example 11.3.

10. Calculate the Halstead metric for all the Pascal code fragments in Chapters 7 and 8. How do the values for the level of abstraction, L, compare to the cyclomatic complexity, C, of the McCabe metric?

11. A software module is to take as inputs four signed 16-bit integers and produce two outputs, the sum and average. How many test cases would be needed for a brute-force testing scheme? How many would be needed if the minimum, maximum, and average values for each input were to be used?

12. A real-time system has a fixed number of resources of types A, B, and C. There are five tasks in the system, and the maximum amount of resources A, B, and C needed for each task is known. Implement a banker's algorithm scheme in the language of your choice.

13. Describe the effect of the following BITS and reliability schemes without appropriately disabling interrupts. How should interrupts be disabled?
    (a) RAM scrubbing
    (b) CRC calculation
    (c) RAM pattern tests
    (d) CPU instruction set test

14. Suppose a computer system has 16-bit data and address buses. What test patterns are necessary and sufficient to test the address and data lines and the memory cells?

15. Write a module in the language of your choice that generates a CRC checkword for a range of 16-bit memory. The module should take as input the starting and ending addresses of the range, and output the 16-bit check word. Use either CCITT or CRC-16 as generator polynomials.

16. In N-version programming, the different programming teams code from the same set of specifications. Discuss the disadvantages of this (if any).

12

Multiprocessing Systems

KEY POINTS OF THE CHAPTER

1. Building real-time multiprocessing systems is hard because building uniprocessing real-time systems is already difficult enough.
2. Reliability in multiprocessing systems can be increased through redundancy and multiplicity. However, security, processing, and reliability costs are associated with the communication links between processors.
3. Describing the functional behavior and design of multiprocessing systems is difficult and requires nontraditional tools.
4. It is crucial to understand the underlying hardware architecture of the multiprocessing system being used.

In this chapter we look at issues related to real-time systems when more than one processor is used. We characterize real-time multiprocessing systems into two types: those that use several autonomous processors, and those that use a large number of interdependent, highly integrated microprocessors.

Although many of the problems encountered in multiprocessing real-time systems are the same as those in the single-processing world, these problems become more troublesome. For example, system specification is more difficult. Intertask communication and synchronization becomes interprocessor communication and synchronization. Integration and testing is more challenging, and reliability more difficult to manage. Combine these complications with the fact that the individual processors themselves can be multitasking, and you can see the level of complexity.

In a single chapter we can only give a brief introduction to those issues that need to be addressed in the design of real-time multiprocessing systems.

12.1 CLASSIFICATION OF ARCHITECTURES

Computer architectures can be classified in terms of single or multiple instructions streams and single or multiple data streams as shown in Table 12.1. By providing a taxonomy, it is easier to match a computer to an application and to remember the basic capabilities of a processor. In standard von Neumann architectures, the serial fetch and execute process, coupled with a single combined data/instruction store, forces serial instruction and data streams. This is also the case in RISC (reduced instruction set computer) architectures. Although many RISC architectures include pipelining, and hence become multiple instruction stream, pipelining is not a requisite characteristic of RISC.

TABLE 12.1   Classification for Computer Architectures

	Single Data Stream	Multiple Data Stream
Single Instruction Stream	von Neumann architecture/uniprocessors	Systolic processors
	RISC	Wavefront processors
Multiple Instruction Stream	Pipelined architectures	Dataflow processors
	Very long instruction word processors	Transputers

In both systolic and wavefront processors, each processing element is executing the same (and only) instruction but on different data. Hence these architectures are SIMD.

In pipelines architectures, effectively more than one instruction can be processed simultaneously (one for each level of pipeline). However, since only one instruction can use data at any one time, it is MISD. Similarly, very long instruction word computers tend to be implemented with microinstructions that have very long bit-lengths (and hence more capability). Hence, rather than breaking down macroinstructions into numerous microinstructions, several (nonconflicting) macroinstructions can be combined into several microinstructions. For example, if object code was generated that called for a load one register followed by an increment of another register, these two instructions could be executed simultaneously by the processor (or at least appear so at the macroinstruction level) with a series of long microinstruction. Since only nonconflicting instructions can be combined, any two accessing the data bus conflict. Thus, only one instruction can access the data bus, and so the very long instruction word computer is MISD.

Finally, in dataflow processors and transputers (see the following discussion), each processing element is capable of executing numerous different instruction and on different data; hence it is MIMD. Distributed architectures are also classified in this way.

12.2 DISTRIBUTED SYSTEMS

We characterize *distributed real-time systems* as a collection of interconnected self-contained processors. We differentiate this type of system from the type discussed in the next section in that each of the processors in the distributed system can perform significant processing without the cooperation of the other processors.

Many of the techniques developed in the context of multitasking systems can be applied to multiprocessing systems. For example, by treating each of the processors in a distributed system as a task, the synchronization and communication techniques previously discussed can be used. But this is not always enough, because often each of the processors in a multiprocessing system are themselves multitasking. In any case, this type of distributed-processing system represents the best solution to the real-time problem when such resources are available.

12.2.1 Embedded

Embedded distributed systems are those in which the individual processors are assigned fixed, specific tasks. This type of system is widely used in the areas of avionics, astronautics, and robotics.

■ EXAMPLE 12.1

In an avionics system for a military aircraft, separate processors are usually assigned for navigation, weapons control, and communications. While these systems certainly share information (see Figure 12.1), we can prevent failure of the overall system in the event of a single processor failure. To achieve this safeguard, we designate one of the three processors or a fourth to coordinate the activities of the others. If this computer is damaged, or shuts itself off due to a BITS fail, another can assume its role. ■

12.2.2 Organic

Another type of distributed processing system consists of a central scheduler processor and a collection of general processors with nonspecific functions (see Figure 12.2). These systems may be connected in a number of topologies (including ring, hypercube, array, and common bus) and may be used to solve general problems. In organic distributed systems, the challenge is to program the scheduler processor in such a way as to maximize the utilization of the serving processors.

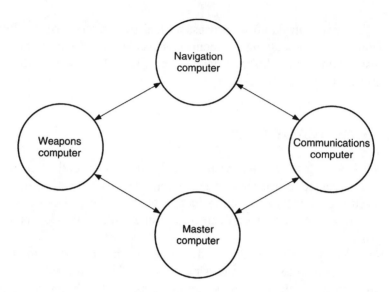

Figure 12.1 A distributed computer system for a military aircraft.

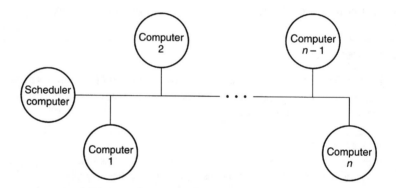

Figure 12.2 Organic distributed computer in common bus configuration.

12.2.3 System Specification

The specification of software for distributed systems is challenging because, as we have seen, the specification of software for even a single-processing system is difficult.

One technique that we have discussed, statecharts, lends itself nicely to the specification of distributed systems because orthogonal processes can be assigned to individual processors. If each processor is multitasking, these orthogonal states can be further subdivided into orthogonal states representing the individual tasks for each processor.

■ **EXAMPLE 12.2**

Consider the specification of the avionics system for the military aircraft. We have discussed the function of the navigation computer throughout this text. The statechart for this function is given in Figure 5.18. The functions for the weapons control and communication systems are depicted in Figure 12.3 and Figure 12.4, respectively. In the interests of space, only this pictorial description of each subsystem will be given.   ■

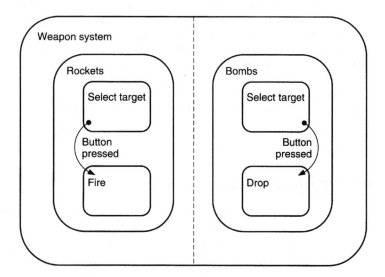

Figure 12.3 Weapons control system for a military aircraft.

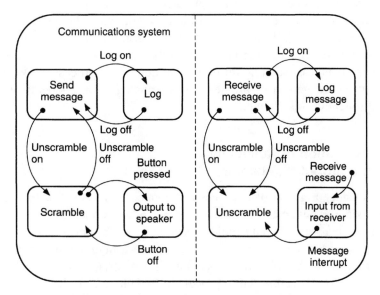

Figure 12.4 Communications system for military aircraft.

A second technique that can be used is the dataflow diagram. Here the process symbols can represent processors, whereas the directed arcs represent communications paths between the processors. The sinks and sources can be either devices that produce and consume data or processes that produce or consume raw data.

■ **EXAMPLE 12.3**

Recall the dataflow diagram for the aircraft navigation system given in Figure 5.7. The sources representing the raw accelerometer and gyro pulses are hardware devices that use DMA to send their data to two separate computers. Two computers concurrently compensate the accelerometer and gyro data, respectively, and send their data to two memory buffers. A third computer reads this shared memory and combines the information to form the current position and orientation. This result is then placed in another memory store that is read by two other computers. The first uses this information to calculate graphics commands that update the pilot's display. The other computer uses this position information to send adjustment pulses (torquing pulses) to the gyro system of the aircraft.   ■

12.2.4 Reliability in Distributed Systems

The characterization of reliability in a distributed system (real-time or otherwise) has been stated in a well-known paper [89], "The Byzantine Generals' Problem." The processors in a distributed system can be considered "generals" and the interconnections between them "messengers." The generals and messengers can be both loyal (operating properly) or traitors (faulty). The task is for the generals, who can only communicate via the messengers, to formulate a strategy for capturing a city (see Figure 12.5). The problem is to find an algorithm that allows the loyal generals to reach an agreement. It turns out that the problem is unsolvable for a totally asynchronous system, but solvable if the generals can vote in rounds [153]. This provision, however, imposes additional timing constraints on the system. Furthermore, the problem can be solved only if the number of traitors is less than one-third the total number of processors. We will be using the Byzantine generals' problem as an analogy for cooperative multiprocessing throughout this chapter.

12.2.5 Calculation of Reliability in Distributed Systems

Consider a group of n processors connected in any flat topology. It would be desirable, but costly, to have every processor connected to every other processor in such a way that data could be shared between processors. This, however, is not usually possible. In any case, we can use a matrix representation to denote the connections between the processors. The matrix, R, is constructed as follows: if processor i is connected to processor j we place a "1" in the ith row, j^{th} column of R. If they are not connected, a "0" is placed there. We consider every processor

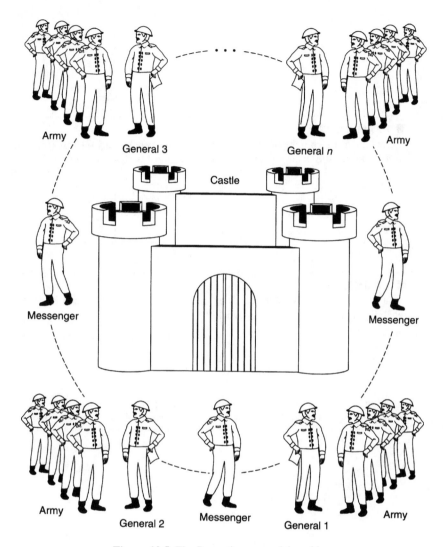

Figure 12.5 The Byzantine generals' problem.

to be connected to itself, and so we place a "1" at each diagonal entry. Matrix R is called an *incidence matrix* or a *reliability matrix* if the entries can take on any value in $[0,1]$. Using the Byzantine generals' problem as an analogy, we see that the diagonal entries of the matrix represent generals, while the off-diagonal entries represent messengers.

■ EXAMPLE 12.4

A topology in which each of n processors is connected to every other would have an n by n reliability matrix with all 1s; that is,

$$R = \begin{pmatrix} 1 & 1 & \ldots & 1 \\ 1 & 1 & \ldots & 1 \\ & & \cdots & \\ & & \cdots & \\ & & \cdots & \\ 1 & 1 & \ldots & 1 \end{pmatrix}$$

■

■ EXAMPLE 12.5

A topology in which none of the n processors is connected to any other (except itself) would have an n by n reliability matrix with all 1s on the diagonal but 0s elsewhere; that is,

$$R = \begin{pmatrix} 1 & 0 & \ldots & 0 \\ 0 & 1 & \ldots & 0 \\ & & \cdot & \\ & & \cdot & \\ & & \cdot & \\ 0 & 0 & \ldots & 1 \end{pmatrix}$$

■

■ EXAMPLE 12.6

As a more practical example, consider the four processors connected as in Figure 12.6. The reliability matrix for this topology would be

$$R = \begin{pmatrix} 1 & 1 & 1 & 0 \\ 1 & 1 & 0 & 1 \\ 1 & 0 & 1 & 1 \\ 0 & 1 & 1 & 1 \end{pmatrix}$$

Since processors 2 and 3 are disconnected, as are processors 1 and 4, 0s are placed in row 2 column 3, row 3 column 2, row 1 column 4, and row 4 column 1 in the reliability matrix.   ■

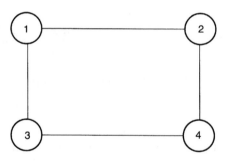

Figure 12.6 Four-processor distributed system.

The ideal world has all processors and interconnections uniformly reliable, but this is not always the case. We can assign a number between 0 and 1 for each entry to represent its reliability. For example, an entry of 1 represents a perfect messenger or general. If the entries are less than 1, then this represents a traitorous general or messenger. (A very traitorous general or messenger gets a 0; a "small-time" traitor may get a "0.9" entry.) Disconnections still receive a 0.

■ **EXAMPLE 12.7**

Suppose the distributed system described in Figure 12.6 actually had interconnections with the reliabilities marked as in Figure 12.7. The new reliability matrix would be

$$R = \begin{pmatrix} 1 & .4 & .7 & 0 \\ .4 & 1 & 0 & 1 \\ .7 & 0 & 1 & .9 \\ 0 & 1 & .9 & 1 \end{pmatrix}$$

■

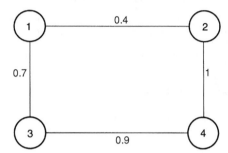

Figure 12.7 Four-processor distributed system with reliabilities.

Notice that if we assume that the communications links have reciprocal reliability (the reliability is the same regardless of which direction the message is traveling in), then the matrix is symmetric with respect to the diagonal. This, along with the assumption that the diagonal elements are always 1 (not necessarily true), can greatly simplify calculations.

12.2.6 Increasing Reliability in Distributed Systems

In Figure 12.7, the fact that processors 1 and 4 do not have direct communications links does not mean that the two processors cannot communicate. Processor 1 can send a message to processor 4 via processor 2 or 3. It turns out that the overall reliability of the system may be increased by using this technique.

Without formalization, the overall reliability of the system can be calculated by performing a series of special matrix multiplications. If R and S are reliability matrices for a system of n processors each, then we define the *composition* of these matrices, denoted $R \diamond S$, to be

$$(R \diamond S)(i,j) = \bigvee_{i=1}^{n} R(i,k)S(k,j) \tag{12.1}$$

where $(R \diamond S)(i, j)$ is the entry in the ith row and j^{th} column of the resultant matrix and $\bigvee$ represents taking the maximum of the reliabilities. If $R = S$, then we denote $R \diamond R = R^2$, called the *second-order reliability matrix*.

■ **EXAMPLE 12.8**

Consider the system in Figure 12.7. Computing R^2 for this yields

$$R^2 = \begin{pmatrix} 1 & .4 & .7 & .63 \\ .4 & 1 & .9 & 1 \\ .7 & .9 & 1 & .9 \\ .63 & 1 & .9 & 1 \end{pmatrix}$$

■

12.2.6.1 Higher-Order Reliability Matrices   Higher-order reliabilities can be found using the same technique as for the second order. Recursively, we can define the nth *order reliability matrix* as

$$R^n = R^{n-1} \diamond R \qquad (12.2)$$

■ **EXAMPLE 12.9**

The utility of the higher-order reliability can be seen in Figure 12.8, where processors 1 and 4 are two connections apart. Here, the reliability matrix is

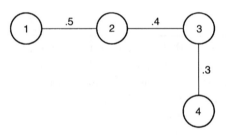

Figure 12.8 Four-processor distributed system with reliabilities.

$$R^2 = \begin{pmatrix} 1 & .5 & 0 & 0 \\ .5 & 1 & .4 & 0 \\ 0 & .4 & 1 & .3 \\ 0 & 0 & .3 & 1 \end{pmatrix}$$

The second-order reliability is

$$R^2 = \begin{pmatrix} 1 & .5 & .2 & 0 \\ .5 & 1 & .3 & .12 \\ .2 & .3 & 1 & .3 \\ 0 & .12 & .3 & 1 \end{pmatrix}$$

Calculating the third-order reliability matrix gives

$$R^2 = \begin{pmatrix} 1 & .5 & .2 & .06 \\ .5 & 1 & .3 & .12 \\ .2 & .3 & 1 & .3 \\ .06 & .12 & .3 & 1 \end{pmatrix}$$

■

The higher reliability matrix allows us to draw an equivalent topology for the distributed system. One obvious conclusion that can be drawn from looking at the higher-order reliability matrices, and one that is intuitively pleasing, is that we can increase the reliability of message passing in distributed systems by providing redundant second-, third-, and so on. Order paths between processors.

■ EXAMPLE 12.10
For the previous example, the third-order equivalent topology is given in Figure 12.9.   ■

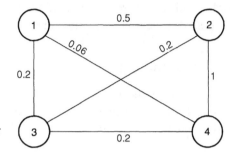

Figure 12.9 Equivalent third-order topology for Example 12.9.

Finally, it can be shown that the maximum reliability matrix for n processors is given by

$$R_{\max} = \bigvee_{i=1}^{n} R^i \qquad (12.3)$$

For example, in the previous example, $R_{\max} = R^1 \vee R^2 \vee R^3$.

To what n do we need to compute to obtain x percent of the theoretical maximum reliability? Is this dependent on the topology? Is this dependent on the reliabilities? In addition, the reliability matrix might not be fixed; that is, it might be some function of time t. Finally, the fact that transmissions over higher-order paths increase signal transit time introduces a penalty that must be balanced against the benefit of increased reliability. There are a number of open problems in this area that are beyond the scope of this text.

12.3 NON-VON NEUMANN ARCHITECTURES

The processing of discrete signals in real-time is of paramount importance to virtually every type of system. Yet the computations needed to detect, extract, mix, or otherwise process signals are computationally intensive. For example, the convolution sum discussed in Chapter 5 is widely used in signal processing.

Because of these computationally intensive operations, real-time designers must look to hardware to improve response times. In response, hardware designers have provided several non-von Neumann, multiprocessing architectures which, though not general purpose, can be used to solve a wide class of problems in realtime. (Recall that von Neumann architectures are stored program, single fetch-execute cycle machines.) These multiprocessors typically feature large quantities of simple processors in VLSI.

Increasingly, real-time systems are distributed processing systems consisting of one or more general processors and one or more of these other style processors. The general, von Neumann-style processors provide control and input/output, whereas the specialized processor is used as an engine for fast execution of complex and specialized computations. In the next sections, we discuss several of these non-von Neumann architectures and illustrate their applications.

12.3.1 Dataflow Architectures

Dataflow architectures use a large number of special processors in a topology in which each of the processors is connected to every other.

In a dataflow architecture, each of the processors has its own local memory and a counter. Special tokens are passed between the processors asynchronously. These tokens, called *activity packets*, contain an opcode, operand count, operands, and list of destination addresses for the result of the computation. An example of a generic activity packet is given in Figure 12.10. Each processor's local memory is used to hold a list of activity packets for that processor, the operands needed for the current activity packet, and a counter used to keep track of the number of operands received. When the number of operands stored in local memory is equivalent to that required for the operation in the current activity packet, the operation is performed and the results are sent to the specified destinations. Once an activity packet has been executed, the processor begins working on the next activity packet in its execution list.

Opcode	n (number of arguments)
Argument 1	
Argument 2	
• • •	
Argument n	
Destination 1	
Destination 2	
• • •	
Destination m	

Figure 12.10 Generic activity template for dataflow machine.

■ EXAMPLE 12.11

We can use the dataflow architecture to perform the discrete convolution of two signals as described in the exercises for Chapter 5. That is, the discrete convolution of two real-valued functions $f(t)$ and $g(t)$, $t = 0,1,2,3,4$.

$$(f * g)(t) = \sum_{i=0}^{4} f(i)g(t-i)$$

The processor topology and activity packet list is described in Figure 12.11. ■

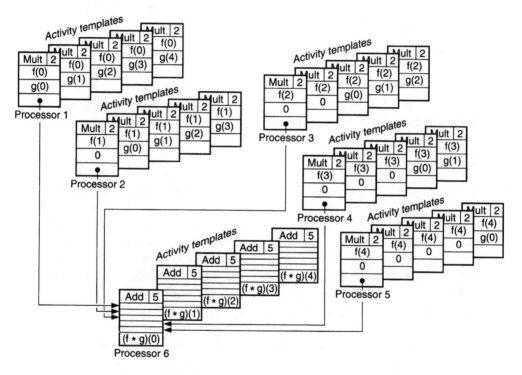

Figure 12.11 Discrete convolution in a dataflow architecture.

Dataflow architectures are an excellent parallel solution for signal processing. The only drawback for dataflow architectures is that currently they cannot be implemented in VLSI. Performance studies for dataflow real-time systems can be found in [148].

12.3.1.1 System Specification for Dataflow Processors Dataflow architectures are ideal because they are direct implementations of dataflow graphs. In fact, programmers draw dataflow diagrams as part of the programming process. The graphs are then translated into a list of activity packets for each processor. An

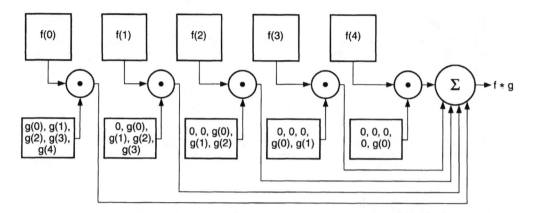

Figure 12.12 Specification of discrete convolution using dataflow diagrams.

example of is given in Figure 12.12. As we have seen in the example, they are well-adapted to parallel signal processing [52], [53].

12.3.2 Systolic Processors

Systolic processors consist of a large number of uniform processors connected in an array topology. Each processor usually performs only one specialized operation and has only enough local memory to perform its designated operation, and to store the inputs and outputs. The individual processors, called *processing elements*, take inputs from the top and left, perform a specified operation, and output the results to the right and bottom. One such processing element is depicted in Figure 12.13. The processors are connected to the four nearest neighboring processors in the nearest neighbor topology depicted in Figure 12.14. Processing or firing at each of the cells occurs simultaneously in synchronization with a central clock. The fact that each cell fires on this heartbeat lends the name *systolic*. Inputs to the system are from memory stores or input devices at the boundary cells

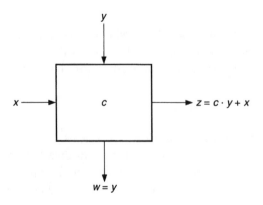

Figure 12.13 Systolic processor element.

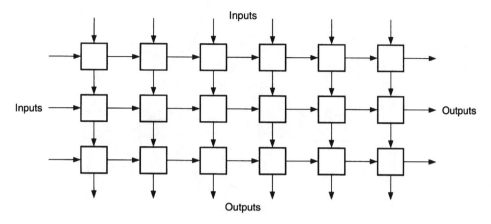

Figure 12.14 Systolic array in nearest neighbor topology.

at the left and top. Outputs to memory or output devices are obtained from boundary cells at the right and bottom.

■ **EXAMPLE 12.12**

Once again consider the discrete convolution of two real-valued functions $f(t)$ and $g(t)$, $t = 0,1,2,3,4$. A systolic array such as the one in Figure 12.15 can be constructed to perform the convolution. A general algorithm can be found in [52]. ■

Systolic processors are fast and can be implemented in VLSI. They are somewhat troublesome, however, in dealing with propagation delays in the connection buses and in the availability of inputs when the clock ticks.

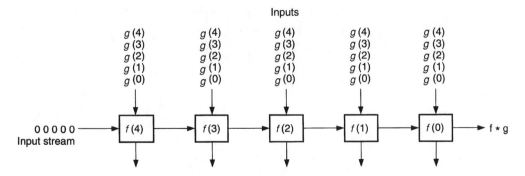

Figure 12.15 Systolic array for convolution.

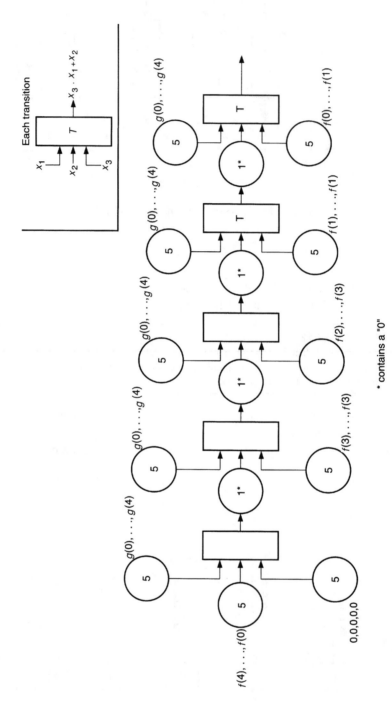

Figure 12.16 Petri net specification of convolution for a systolic array.

12.3.2.1 Specification of Systolic Systems   The similarity of the jargon associated with systolic processors leads us to believe that Petri nets can be used to specify such systems. This is indeed true, and an example of specifying the convolution operation is given in Figure 12.16.

12.3.3 Wavefront Processors

Wavefront processors consist of an array of identical processors, each with its own local memory and connected in a nearest neighbor topology. Each processor usually performs only one specialized operation. Hybrids containing two or more different type cells are possible. The cells fire asynchronously when all required inputs from the left and top are present. Outputs then appear to the right and below. Unlike the systolic processor, the outputs are the unaltered inputs. That is, the top input is transmitted, unaltered, to the bottom output bus, and the left input is transmitted, unaltered, to the right output bus. Also different from the systolic processor, outputs from the wavefront processor are read directly from the local memory of selected cells and not obtained from boundary cells. Inputs are still placed on the top and left input buses of boundary cells. The fact that inputs propagate through the array unaltered like a wave gives this architecture its name. Figure 12.17 depicts a typical wavefront

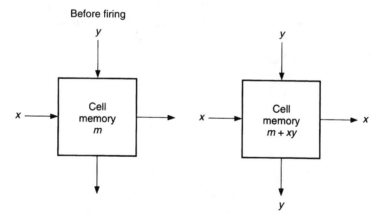

Figure 12.17 Wavefront processor element.

processing element. Wavefront processors are very good for computationally-intensive real-time systems and are used widely in modern real-time signal processing [51], [52]. In addition, a wavefront architecture can cope with timing uncertainties such as local blocking, random delay in communications, and fluctuations in computing times [86].

■ **EXAMPLE 12.13**

Once again consider the discrete convolution of two real-valued functions $f(t)$ and $g(t)$, $t = 0,1,2,3,4$. A wavefront array such as the one in Figure 12.18 can be constructed to perform the convolution.   ■

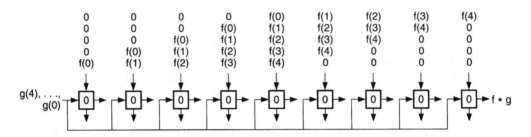

Figure 12.18 Discrete convolution using a wavefront array.

Wavefront processors combine the best of systolic architectures with dataflow architectures. That is, they support an asynchronous dataflow computing structure—timing in the interconnection buses and at input and output devices is not a problem. Furthermore, the structure can be implemented in VLSI.

12.3.3.1 System Specification for Wavefront Processors As is true of the dataflow architecture, dataflow diagrams can be used to specify these systems. For example, the convolution system depicted in the previous example can be specified using Figure 12.12.

Finally, Petri nets and finite state automata or a variation, cellular automata, may have potential use for specifying wavefront systems.

12.3.4 Transputers

Transputers are fully self-sufficient, multiple instruction set, von Neumann processors. The instruction set includes directives to send data or receive data via ports that are connected to other transputers. The transputers, though capable of acting as a uniprocessor, are best utilized when connected in a nearest neighbor configuration. In a sense, the transputer provides a wavefront or systolic processing capability but without the restriction of a single instruction. Indeed, by providing each transputer in a network with an appropriate stream of and synchronization signals, wavefront or systolic computers—which can change configurations—can be implemented.

Transputers have been widely used in embedded real-time applications, and commercial implementations are readily available. Moreover, tool support, such as the multitasking language occam-2, has made it easier to build transputer-based applications.

12.4 EXERCISES

1. For the following reliability matrix draw the associated distributed system graph and compute R^2.

$$R = \begin{pmatrix} 1 & 1 & 1 \\ 1 & 1 & 0 \\ 1 & 0 & 1 \end{pmatrix}$$

2. For the following reliability matrix draw the associated distributed system graph and compute R^2.

$$R = \begin{pmatrix} 1 & 0.2 & 0.7 \\ 0.2 & 1 & 0 \\ 0.7 & 0 & 1 \end{pmatrix}$$

3. For the following reliability matrix compute R^2, R^3, and R_{max} (*Hint*: $R_{max} \neq R^3$).

$$R = \begin{pmatrix} 1 & 0 & 0.6 & 0 \\ 0 & 1 & 0 & 0.8 \\ 0.6 & 0 & 1 & 1 \\ 0 & 0.8 & 1 & 1 \end{pmatrix}$$

4. Show that the $\diamond$ operation is not commutative. For example, if R and S are 3×3 reliability matrices, then in general,

$$R \diamond S \neq S \diamond R$$

In fact, you should be able to show that for any $n \times n$ reliability matrix

$$R \diamond S = (S \diamond R)^{\mathrm{T}}$$

where $()^{\mathrm{T}}$ represents the matrix transpose.

5. Design a dataflow architecture for performing the matrix multiplication of two 5 by 5 arrays. Assume that binary ADD and MULT are part of the instruction set.

6. Design a dataflow architecture for performing the matrix addition of two 5 by 5 arrays. Assume that binary ADD is part of the instruction set.

7. Use dataflow diagrams to describe the systems in exercises 4 and 5.

8. Design a systolic array for performing the matrix multiplication of two 5 by 5 arrays. Use the processing element described in Figure 12.13.

9. Design a systolic array for performing the matrix addition of two 5 by 5 arrays. Use the processing element described in Figure 12.13.

10. Use Petri nets and the processing element described in Figure 12.13 to describe the systolic array to perform the functions described in
    (a) Exercise 7
    (b) Exercise 8

11. Design a wavefront array for performing the matrix multiplication of two 5 by 5 arrays. Use the processing element described in Figure 12.17.

12. Design a wavefront array for performing the matrix addition of two 5 by 5 arrays. Use the processing element described in Figure 12.17.

13. Use dataflow diagrams to describe the systems in
    (a) Exercise 10
    (b) Exercise 11

14. Use Petri nets to specify the wavefront array system shown in Figure 12.18.

13

Hardware/Software
Integration

KEY POINTS OF THE CHAPTER

1. Hardware/software integration is usually more art than science in that it relies on the intuition and experience of the integrators.
2. Special tools such as logic analyzers, oscilloscopes, and so forth are invaluable.
3. The integration phase should be regarded as if you are treating a stomach ailment—add code to the system very slowly so as to avoid the introduction of errors that are hard to trace.

The process of uniting modules from different sources to form the overall system is called *integration*. Integration occurs at the end of the programming phase of the software life cycle. When the system is an embedded one, the process includes hardware/software integration. This process can be complicated when both hardware and software are new. Virtually no text or technical paper on real-time systems discusses perhaps the most difficult phase in the life of the system—hardware/software integration. Although the notion of integrating hardware and software makes sense only in embedded systems, some of the techniques described here still are useful when putting together organic systems.

This chapter includes a collection of notes, observations, and experiences of integrating real-time avionics software. Although the application is relatively narrow, it accurately reflects the way software engineers perform integration—it is based largely on intuition, experience, and yes, even luck.

13.1 GOALS OF REAL-TIME SYSTEM INTEGRATION

The goal of integration in real-time systems is to unite the parts of the system to create the larger whole in a way that conforms to response-time constraints. Each of these parts has potentially been developed by different teams or individuals within the project organization. Although they have been rigorously tested and verified separately, the overall timing behavior of the system cannot be tested until the parts are integrated.

This phase has the most uncertain schedule and is typically the cause of most project cost overruns. Moreover, the stage has been set for failure or success at this phase, by the design and implementation practices used throughout the software project life cycle. Indeed, many modern programming practices were devised to ensure arrival at this stage with the fewest errors in the source code. For example, Ada has built-in tests for consistency of argument lists, and the C programming language uses an associated utility program called "lint" to do the same. Automation can help avoid all of the integration troubles mentioned in this chapter.

To summarize, the goals of real-time system integration are

- System unification
- System verification

13.1.1 System Unification

Fitting the pieces of the system together from its individual components is tricky business, even for non-real-time systems. Parameter mismatching, variable name mistyping, and calling sequence errors are some of the problems usually encountered during system integration. Even the most rigorous unit-level testing cannot eliminate these potential problems completely.

The *system unification* process consists of linking together the tested software modules drawn in an orderly fashion from the source code library. During the linking process, errors are likely to occur that relate to unresolved external symbols, memory assignment violations, page link errors, and the like.

These problems must, of course, be resolved. Once resolved, the loadable code, called a *load module*, can be downloaded from the development environment to the target machine. This is accomplished in a variety of ways depending on the system architecture, but it can include tapes, disks, network connections, modems, or use of an intermediate computer. In any case, once the load module has been created and loaded into the target machine, testing of timing and hardware/software interaction can begin.

13.1.2 System Validation

In Chapter 11 we discussed performing system testing using an appropriate number of system test cases. This test suite is submitted to the overall system. Invariably tests will fail, indicating software or hardware errors whose sources are not always easy to identify.

Formal system validation of real-time systems is a tedious process, often requiring days or weeks. During system validation a careful test log must be kept indicating the test case number, result, and disposition. Figure 13.1 is a sample of such a test log.

Test number	Test name	Pass/fail	Date	Tester
S121	Obstacle avoidance test 1	Pass	5/16/91	P.L.
S122	Obstacle avoidance test 2	Pass	5/16/91	P.L.
S123	Obstacle avoidance test 3	Fail	5/16/91	P.L.
•				
•				
•				

Figure 13.1 Sample test log.

If a system test fails, it is imperative, once the problem has been identified and presumably corrected, that all affected tests be rerun. These include

1. All module-level test cases for any module that has been changed.
2. All system-level test cases.

Even though the module-level test cases and previous system-level test cases have been passed, it is imperative that these be rerun to ensure that no side effects have been introduced during error repair.

13.2 TOOLS

As mentioned before, it is not always easy to identify sources of error during a system test. A number of hardware and software tools are available to assist in the validation of real-time systems. Remember that test tools make the difference between success and failure—especially in deeply embedded real-time systems with limited I/O.

13.2.1 Multimeters

Although the use of voltage or current meters in the debugging of real-time systems may seem odd, they are an important tool in embedded systems where the software controls or reads analog values through hardware. The multimeter facilitates the measurement of voltage, current, or power, and can be used to validate the analog input or output into the system.

13.2.2 Oscilloscope

An oscilloscope, like a multimeter, is not always regarded as a software debugging tool, but it is useful in embedded software environments. Oscilloscopes range from the basic single-trace variety to storage oscilloscopes with multiple traces. Oscilloscopes can be used for validating interrupt integrity, discrete signal issuance, and receipt, and for monitoring clocks. The more sophisticated storage oscilloscopes with multiple inputs can often be used in lieu of logic analyzers, by using the inputs to track the data and address buses in synchronization with an appropriate clock.

13.2.3 Logic Analyzer

The logic analyzer is an important tool for debugging software, especially in embedded real-time systems. The logic analyzer can be used to capture data or events, to measure individual instruction times, or to time sections of code. Moreover, the introduction of programmable logic analyzers with integrated debugging environments has further enhanced the capabilities of the system integrator. For example, more sophisticated logic analyzers include built-in disassemblers and decompilers for source-level debugging and performance analysis. These integrated environments typically are found on more expensive models, but they make the identification of performance bottlenecks particularly easy. Because there are so many types of commercially available logic analyzers, with wide-ranging features, the reader is encouraged to contact vendors (for example, Hewlett-Packard) for specifics. In this chapter, we cover one particular application of the logic analyzer in integrating real-time systems—the timing of code segments.

13.2.3.1 Timing Instructions   The logic analyzer can be used to time an individual macroinstruction, segments of code, or an entire process. To time an individual instruction, find a memory location in the code segment of memory containing the desired instruction. Set the logic analyzer to trigger on this opcode at the desired location, and on the opcode and location of the next instruction, and set the trace for absolute time. The logic analyzer will then display the difference in time between the fetch of the first instruction (the target) and the next instruction. This is the most accurate method for determining the instruction execution time.

13.2.3.2 Timing Code The logic analyzer also provides an accurate method for measuring time-to-complete for any cycle or cycles. To measure the total elapsed time for any cycle in a foreground/background system, set the logic analyzer to trigger on the starting and ending address and opcode for the first instruction of that cycle. (It should be the first instruction of the interrupt handler—usually a disable interrupt instruction.) Disable the interrupts for all higher-priority cycles and set the trace for absolute time. The time displayed is the total time in that cycle.

■ **EXAMPLE 13.1**

A system contains a 10-millisecond cycle whose instructions and data are

Location (HEX)	Op-code (HEX)		Instruction
2356	6300		DPI
2357	2701	1000	LOAD R1, 1000
2359	1401		
.			
.			
.			
264B	6301		EPI

   This module represents part of an interrupt handler in which the first instruction is to disable all interrupts and the last instruction is to enable all interrupts. If we set the logic analyzer to trigger on address = 2357, data = 2701 and capture only address = 2359 and data = 1401, we will find the time to complete the LOAD (2701) instruction (location 2358 contains the data to be loaded by the LOAD instruction). Similarly if we set the logic analyzer to trigger on address = 2357, data = 2701 and capture only address = 264B and data = 6301, we will find the time to complete the entire interrupt routine. If the time measured is 3 milliseconds for a 10-millisecond cycle, then the time-loading will be 33.33%.   ■

   This approach can be used to time one or several modules within a cycle, or even sections of code within a module.

13.2.4 In-Circuit Emulator

During module-level debug and system integration in conjunction with embedded systems, the ability to single-step the computer, set the program counter, and deposit and read from memory is extremely important. Many commercial development environments provide for this capability through the use of an in-circuit emulator. *In-circuit emulation* (ICE) uses special hardware in conjunction with software to emulate the target CPU while providing the aforementioned features. Typically, the in-circuit emulator plugs into the chip carrier

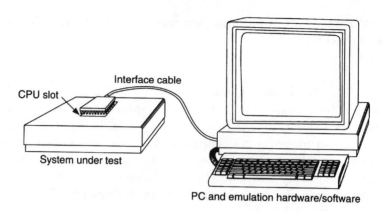

Figure 13.2 Configuration for in-circuit emulator.

or card slot normally occupied by the CPU. External wires connect to an emulation engine composed of hardware and software. Access to the emulator is provided directly or via a secondary computer. Figure 13.2 depicts one configuration.

In-circuit emulators are useful in system patching (see subsequent section), and for single-stepping through critical portions of code. In-circuit emulators are not useful in timing tests, however, because subtle timing changes can be introduced by the emulator.

NOTE 13.1   In certain ICE systems, the symbol table may be too large to load. Privatization of certain global variables can be used to reduce the size of the symbol table. For example, in C, judicious use of the static data type during testing can reduce the number of variables in the global symbol table. This eases the debugging process.

13.2.5 Software Simulators

When integrating and debugging embedded systems, software simulators are often needed to stand in for hardware that does not currently exist or that is not readily available. The author of the simulator code has a task that is by no means easy. The software must be written to mimic exactly the hardware specification, especially in timing characteristics. The simulator must be rigorously tested (sometimes it is not). Many systems have been successfully validated and integrated with software simulators, only to fail when connected to the actual hardware.

13.2.6 Hardware Prototypes/Simulators

In the absence of the actual hardware system under control, simulation hardware may be preferable to software simulators. These devices might be required when the software is ready before the prototype hardware, or when it would be impossible to test the software on the actual hardware, such as in the control of a large nuclear plant.

13.2.7 Debuggers

Source-level debuggers are software or software/hardware tools that provide the ability to step through code at either a macroassembly or high-order language level. They are extremely useful in module-level testing. They are less useful in system-level debugging because the real-time aspect of the system is necessarily disabled or affected.

Debuggers can be obtained as part of compiler support packages or in conjunction with sophisticated logic analyzers.

NOTE 13.2 When removing code during debugging, don't use conditional branching; if `DEBUG`, then use conditional compilation instead. Conditional branching affects timing and can introduce problems akin to the Heisenberg uncertainty principle (probe effect).

13.3 METHODOLOGY

Several well-known strategies for performing system integration can be used in combination to ensure system integrity. These methodologies are not intended to be mutually exclusive, for each provides different coverage of system functionality, and redundant testing is not unwelcome. We discuss these techniques here.

13.3.1 Establishing a Baseline

In any real-time operating system, regardless of the kernel approach chosen, it is important to ensure that all tasks in the system are being scheduled and dispatched properly. Thus, our first goal in integrating the real-time system is to ensure that each task is running at its prescribed rate, and that context is saved and restored. We do this without performing any functions within those tasks; functions are added later.

The process whereby all tasks are being appropriately scheduled (although no actual processing is occurring) is called *cycling*.

As we discussed before, a logic analyzer is quite useful in verifying cycle rates by setting the triggers on the starting location of each of the tasks involved.

Until the system cycles properly, the application code associated with each of the tasks should not be added.

13.3.2 Backoff Method

Once the baseline has been established (i.e., the system is cycling), modules are added to the overall system in as small a batch as possible. This means single modules should be added where appropriate (stubs and drivers may be necessary), while the system is tested to ensure that it still cycles and produces appropriate data if possible. If the system does not cycle after an addition, back off. The module that has been added is somehow responsible for the problem.

The success of the backoff method depends on the fact that one change at a time is made to the system so that when the system becomes fouled, the problem can be isolated.

To summarize, the recommended integration approach involves an independent unit test (performed by a system integrator or tester, not the module designer), followed by a phased integration (the backoff method) with regression testing after each step. This ensures that the system is grown incrementally, with an appropriate baseline at each stage of the integration.

The overall approach is shown in Figure 13.3. The approach involves establishing a baseline of running kernel components (no applications programs). This ensures that interrupts are being handled properly and that all cycles are running at their prescribed rates, without worrying about interference from application code. Once the baseline is established, small sections of applications

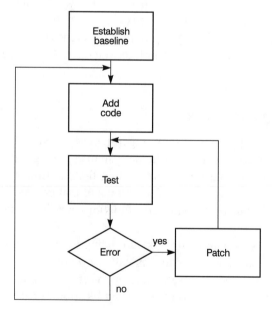

Figure 13.3 Inline patch.

code are added and the cycle rates verified. If an error is detected, it is patched if possible. If the patch succeeds in restoring the cycle rates properly, then more code is added.

Patching is done in embedded systems because generally it would be too time consuming to repair the error in source code, re-compile, re-assemble, re-link, and download to the target machine. Once a number of patches have been implemented (and carefully recorded in a notebook), they can be made to the source code and a new load module built. In nonembedded systems, patching is sometimes convenient when using a symbolic debugger, again because fixing the code at source level and re-compiling may take longer.

13.3.3 Patching

The process of correcting errors in the code directly on the target machine is called *patching*. Patching allows minor errors detected during the integration process to be corrected directly on the target machine, without undergoing the tedious process of correcting the source code and creating a new load module. Patching requires an expert command of the opcodes for the target machine unless a macroassembly-level patching facility is available. It also requires an accurate memory map, which includes the contents of each address in memory, and a method for depositing directly to memory. This capability is provided by many commercial development environments and by in-circuit emulators.

Patching, which is analogous to placing jumper wires on prototype hardware, typically requires only a minor change of memory contents. If the patch needed fits into the memory space accorded to the code to be changed, then it is considered an *in-line patch*. In Figure 13.4, for example, a 1 was supposed to be added to register 1 instead of a 0. This error can easily be changed by altering the memory location containing the LOAD R1,0 instruction to LOAD R1,1. If the patch requires more memory than is currently occupied by the code to be replaced, it is considered an *oversized patch*. In this case a

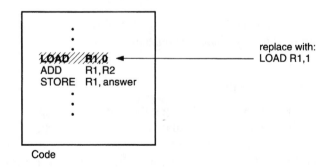

Code

Figure 13.4 Locations and instructions for logic analyzer example.

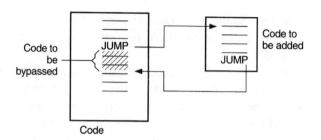

Figure 13.5 Placing an oversized patch.

jump to some unused portion of memory is required, followed by the patched code, followed by a return jump to the next significant location. This technique is illustrated in Figure 13.5.

The loading of patches during system integration can often be automated through the use of batch files. However, a large number of patches, and patches on top of other patches, can become confusing. It is imperative that a careful record be kept of all patches made, that the patches eventually find their way back to the source code, and that a new system be generated before validation testing begins. This is essential from a maintenance standpoint. Final testing should never be performed on a patched system.

13.4 THE SOFTWARE HEISENBERG UNCERTAINTY PRINCIPLE

The uncertainty principle, originally postulated by Werner Heisenberg in 1927, states essentially that one cannot know the exact position of a physical particle and its momentum simultaneously. An analogy to the Heisenberg uncertainty principle applies in software integration and should be kept in mind [91]. Mathematically, we can state the Heisenberg uncertainty as follows [9]:

$$\Delta p\, \Delta x \approx h \qquad (13.1)$$

where Δp represents the uncertainty of position, Δx represents the uncertainty of momentum, and h is Planck's constant.

13.4.1 Real-World Analogies

Consider a lepidopterist observing butterflies in the jungle. From a distance he can watch the butterfly with binoculars and, if he approaches silently, with the naked eye. If he gets too close to the butterfly, he will startle it and it will fly away. This is caused by the fact that photons have been reflected from the observer's body, striking the butterfly and causing the observer to be seen.

The electron microscope can be seen as an example of the principle. In this case, electrons focused by a magnetic field are used to bombard the material under inspection. The electrons, having passed through the specimen, form an image on a fluorescent screen or photographic plate. But some of the bombarding electrons will likely collide with atoms of the specimen under study and not simply pass through, thus affecting the specimen. Increasing the number of bombarding electrons enhances the image, but also increases the likelihood of interaction with the specimen.

It has also been shown that the inverse relationship between time and frequency in periodic signals is related to the uncertainty principle [147]. In this case, consider the fact that periodic signals cannot be both time-limited and band-limited simultaneously. That is, the less band-limited the signal is, the more frequency-limited it is, and so forth.

13.4.2 The Software Heisenberg Uncertainty Principle

With software systems, we are not explicitly dealing with electrons and their momentum, but in a way, the uncertainty principle can be applied. We can restate the uncertainty principle as

$$\Delta r \, \Delta s \approx H \qquad (13.2)$$

where Δr is the uncertainty of the code, Δs is the uncertainty of test specifications, and H is some constant. The best illustration of the principle in this form can be found in the testing of software.

13.4.3 Testing of Software

In this case, the more closely a system is examined, the more likely the examination process will affect the system being tested. This is especially true for real-time systems in which test software affects timing. Software reliability is also affected by the very code that is added to measure the correctness of the system.

For example, recall the interrupt-handling procedure discussed in Example 2.13. The code is repeated here for convenience.

```
LOAD    R1,0
LOAD    R2,1
STORE   R1,intclr        set clear interrupt signal low
STORE   R2,intclr        set clear interrupt signal high
STORE   R1,intclr        set clear interrupt signal low
EPI                      enable interrupt
```

This is a classic example of software Heisenberg uncertainty or the "probe effect."

Recall that the CLEAR, LOAD, and STORE instructions take 0.75 microsecond, but the interrupt pulse is 4 microseconds long. If the CLEAR instruction takes place within a certain time interval, a spurious interrupt will be caused. However, "single-stepping" through the code with a debugger will eliminate the problem, since the time between instructions will be increased, as will the addition of "test probe" code.

13.4.4 Time- and Memory-Loading

One might also view the inverse relationship between time- and memory-loading in a real-time system as a manifestation of the uncertainty principle.

13.4.5 Other Implications

The software Heisenberg uncertainty principle should be taken as a warning that testing methods often affect the systems that they test. When this is the case, nonintrusive testing should be considered. Furthermore, wherever there is an inverse correlation between two variables affecting a system, Heisenberg uncertainty is suggested. And the analogous relationship between the physical and software uncertainty principles may later suggest approaches for developing software metrics, fault-tolerant systems, and testing methodologies. Finally, the physical Heisenberg uncertainty principle can be used to demonstrate that the Halting problem is unsolvable [91], thus closing the circle.

13.5 EXERCISES

A computer system is to control the elevators in a 50-story office building. The building has two banks of elevators with three elevators each. The first bank services floors 1 through 25 only, while the second bank services floors 25 through 50. Passengers bound for floors 26 through 50 use the first set of elevators to ride to the 25th floor, where an elevator is already waiting for them or will be coming. Two control scenarios are

- *Central control* Each elevator has only enough intelligence to protect the occupants (e.g., by not opening doors between floors). All other tasks are controlled by a central computer which keeps track of requests for elevators from different floors, the elevator destination requested, stopping, and starting.
- *Distributed control* The central computer tracks requests for an elevator from all floors. The individual elevators report some information to the central processor upon request (e.g., travel direction or stopped floor). Once dispatched to a floor, the elevators independently do the rest of the job.

1. For the distributed control model, what functions would the computers (one per elevator and the central computer) carry out, and what information would they exchange? Draw dataflow diagrams and statecharts to depict this functionality.

2. For the central control model and for typical building traffic (make assumptions), would a microcomputer be sufficiently fast to control the system? Is the bottleneck somewhere else?

3. Compare the above two control scenarios with respect to
   (a) Response times
   (b) Reliability

4. You are to model a microwave oven system in the language of your choice. The oven consists of a timer, temperature sensor, door position sensor, and a light switch. There is a keyboard to set the timer and temperature and a panel of LEDs to display the status of the oven. The software must model the system and protect against unsafe conditions (e.g., door open and oven on). For this system
   (a) Draw a statechart to model a microwave oven system with which you are familiar.
   (b) Write a set of specifications for the software simulator.
   (c) Write a set of test cases to test the simulator.
   (d) Code and test the simulator.

   You should make assumptions about certain events. For example, the event that the door is opened after some period of time while the oven is on can be considered a Poisson event. Similarly, power surges or failures might be Poisson with different average arrival time.

   Assume now that the software modeling the hardware is to be replaced with actual hardware. Discuss how the techniques described in this chapter can be used to your advantage.

14

Real-Time Applications

KEY POINTS OF THE CHAPTER

1. Real-time systems are complex.
2. The first real-time application may have been Project Whirlwind.
3. Real-time databases are special applications.
4. Real-time imaging is an important but challenging application area.
5. Real-time languages may not be suitable for "real" applications.

It is appropriate to close the text with a discussion of several interesting specialty areas for real-time systems designers and some real-time applications.

14.1 REAL-TIME SYSTEMS AS COMPLEX SYSTEMS

Although tremendous problems are involved in building real-time multiprocessing systems (all the problems of uniprocessing systems plus intercommunication, resource sharing, load balancing, etc.), most real-time systems are usually distributed heterogeneous multiprocessing systems. This is true in most military applications and in industrial applications where standard components such as RISC workstations connected by local area networks (LANs) and wide area networks (WANs) are the implementations of choice. Special-purpose architectures, such as those discussed in Chapter 12, are increasingly found to be noncompetitive over the life of a system when compared to approaches that use off-the-shelf hardware.

It is increasingly being recognized that the construction of large-scale, real-time systems is not just about real-time systems and scheduling. The fact is that most large, modern, practical computer applications embody many properties that are currently being studied largely in isolation. For example, most combat systems are real-time and distributed, seek to be reliable, and are fault-tolerant. Although it is important to study these issues independently, collectively these properties have a complex interrelationship. Globally, there is increasing activity in the area of "complex systems" as a new, multidisciplinary field of study. In a sense, this book is an attempt to discuss some of the areas that the complex systems designer (no longer the "real-time" systems designer) will need to understand. Throughout this text it has been argued that a holistic approach is the only way to build complex, distributed, real-time applications.

14.2 THE FIRST REAL-TIME APPLICATION?

In 1947 MIT, in conjunction with the U.S. Navy, began development of Project Whirlwind (see Figure 14.1). This project was the first high-speed electronic digital computer able to operate in "real-time" and to be put to use as a practical device. The goal of the project was to develop an airplane trainer/analyzer that would simulate aerodynamic forces acting on the pilot's controls. The pilot's reactions would have to take effect as promptly in the simulator as they would in a real airplane. Thus, the equipment had to operate within these "real response times" [132]. Whirlwind was begun by Jay W. Forrester, who sought to develop

Figure 14.1 Photograph of the U.S. Navy's Whirlwind computer. (Courtesy of Jay Forrester and the MIT Museum.)

an airplane trainer/analyzer that would simulate aerodynamic forces acting on the pilot's controls. The pilot's reactions would have to take effect as promptly in the simulator as they would in a real airplane. Thus, the equipment had to operate within these "real response times." We might also argue that Whirlwind was "complex" because in addition to speed, reliability was also of great importance, and it was during this project that the military concept of "command and control" was introduced [132].

Whirlwind's features were made possible through the use of ferrite cores, which were faster than the cathode-ray tube memories of previous systems. Ferrite cores of the same kind were also used for computer memories in the 1950s in the United States such as the 1953 UNIVAC 1003 model, the 1954 IBM 704, and others [75]. Another distinctive feature of Whirlwind was the inclusion of an "algebraic compiler," an early pseudoprogramming language resulting from the work of Laning and Zierler [75].

During the project's final stages, the Whirlwind team became assimilated into the Air Force's Semiautomatic Ground Environment (SAGE) air defense system project [132]. As a result, the basic ideas of Project Whirlwind were incorporated into SAGE. Thus, while it is widely held that SAGE was the first real-time application, Project Whirlwind seems to deserve this credit.

14.3 REAL-TIME DATABASES

An important application area for real-time systems is in databases. A real-time database system is a transaction processing system in which transactions and data have explicit timing constraints (deadlines). Real-time databases are used in a variety of applications, including process control, radar systems, computer-integrated manufacturing, traffic control, virtual reality, and multimedia.

Designing real-time databases involves

1. Analyzing the system requirements to identify data
2. Determining the hardware capabilities
3. Identifying the different data criticalities and integrity constraints

Ordinary database management systems provide concurrency control techniques that seek to preserve data consistency (e.g., read and write locking) and logical consistency (e.g., two-phase locking). Real-time databases must also impose concurrency control that preserves the schedule and data temporal consistency requirements. As with most real-time systems, minimizing average response is less important than guaranteeing the timing constraints of critical transactions. In the case of database systems, serializable execution of concurrent transactions may also be of less interest.

A real-time database system must operate within the context of the host operating system and use existing services. Hence, construction of a real-time database is nearly impossible with non-real-time operating systems, and most real-time databases are constructed on top of special real-time operating systems. Consequently, commercial real-time database systems have yet to emerge. Most of the available "hard" real-time databases use proprietary algorithms and are suitable chiefly for softer real-time applications where transaction deadlines are "negotiable."

As an example of a real-time database, the architecture for the U.S. space station "Freedom" is shown in Figure 14.2. The primary role of this system is to provide integrated data processing and communication services for both the core function and payloads. The system needs to be robust in that it must support 30 years of continually changing data processing and networking needs.

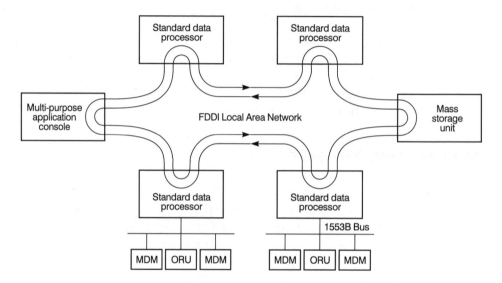

Figure 14.2 Data management system of space freedom.

The system consists of a Fiber Distributed Data Interface (FDDI) ring. Several standard data processors are attached to the core network, along with specialized hardware such as communication and tracking hardware, defined as orbital replaceable units (ORU). These devices are then interfaces to other devices via the Mil-Std-1553B bus architecture or via multiplexer/demultiplexer (MDM) units. The standard data processor is actually a multiprocessing system connected via Multi Bus II and contains a network interface unit (NIU) that runs the network operating system and a bus interface unit (BIU) that interfaces with the MDMs or the ORU hardware through the 1553B bus. The embedded data processor (EDP) runs a version of real-time UNIX (LynxOS), which is POSIX-compatible. This complex, multiprocessing real-time system is mission critical, and simulations have shown that it must handle approximately 5000 database queries in a period of 6 seconds. Various scheduling disciplines, including rate-monotonic are being investigated to optimize performance. A detailed description of the system can be found in [28].

14.4 REAL-TIME IMAGE PROCESSING

Real-time image processing differs from "ordinary" image processing in that the logical validity of the system requires not only correct but also timely outputs. It is often said that image processing in real-time is no more than a minor variation on image processing without regard to time; faster machinery will make any speed problems eventually go away. But real-time imaging is not just about speedy hardware. It involves at least three fundamental tradeoffs: performance versus image resolution, performance versus storage and input/output bandwidth, and number of tasks versus synchronization. Of these problems, only the first and possibly the second might be solved by faster machines. Furthermore, the problems of expressing image algorithms (especially for multiprocessing architectures), of finding appropriate programming languages, of testing and reliability, and of practical software engineering technique are not readily solved simply with faster hardware.

Because of its nature, there are both supports for and obstacles to real-time image processing. On the positive side, many imaging applications are well-suited for parallelization and hence faster, parallel architectures. Furthermore, many imaging applications can be constructed without using language constructs that destroy determinism. Finally, special real-time imaging architectures are available or can theoretically be constructed.

On the down side, many imaging applications are time critical and are computationally intensive or data intensive. And there are no standard programming languages available for real-time image processing. Finally, real-time processing science itself is still struggling to produce usable results, especially for parallel processing machines.

Real-time image processing covers a multidisciplinary range of research areas, including (but not limited to) image compression, target acquisition and tracking, remote control and sensing, image enhancement and filtering, networking for real-time imaging, advanced computer architectures, computer vision, optical measurement and inspection, and simulation. These research areas are critical in such applications as robotics, virtual reality, multimedia, industrial inspection, high-definition television, advanced simulators, computer-integrated manufacturing, and intelligent vehicles.

In summary, real-time systems are unique in that semantic validity entails not only functional correctness but also deadline satisfaction. A generalized real-time image processing system is shown in Figure 14.3. It functions by taking an analog video input from a camera or sensing device and digitizing it. The image is then enhanced or filtered to remove noise. If object or motion detection is

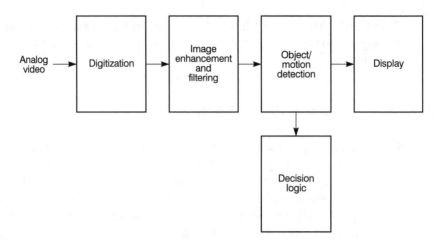

Figure 14.3 A generalized real-time image processing system.

required, that process is applied. If appropriate, an object recognition algorithm or other decision logic is applied to the modified image. In most cases, some sort of image display is also required. For many applications, these steps must be executed in real-time—for example, at the 30 frames per second rate needed for continuous motion perception.

14.4.1 Virtual Reality

To investigate one real-time imaging application briefly, consider virtual reality. Virtual reality (VR) systems are complex computer simulations involving visual, audio, tactile, and other feedback to entice a person's perceptual mechanisms into believing they are actually in an artificial world. Although virtual reality has obvious applications in combat simulation and training, its most promising applications are civilian, including exercise and recreation, physical rehabilitation and therapy, occupational training, and psychological diagnosis training. In these types of systems, high performance and deadline guarantees are essential to ensure that the illusion of reality is maintained.

Virtual reality systems come in at least three paradigms:

■ Telepresence—where a human operator can remotely control robits or other devices as if the operator were physically present. For example, an individual can don a special suit that would permit the repair of an underwater structure via a robot whose movements reflected those of the operator. The operator "thinks" that they are underwater and are working on the real structure.

■ Immersion—where a simulator is implemented that can actually fool the senses of the human subject into believing that the simulated scenario is real. Fans of television science fiction programs, such as "Star Trek: The Next Generation," are familiar with this type of virtual reality.

■ Augmented reality—where a display of live information is supplemented with simulated information. A simulated X-ray view of a patient's body superimposed on a monitor display of the live patient for diagnostic purposes is such an example.

A generalized architecture for each paradigm is shown in Figure 14.4. In case (a), telepresence, a human operator interacts with a helmet-mounted display, hand controls, and foot levers connected to the VR processor. The processor then relays the control information via satellite to a remote ship. The ship is attached to a tethered robot that moves in accordance with the human's movements. The human also receives feedback information from the robot in the form of visual images and possibly force feedback on the hand or foot levers.

In case (b), immersion, a specially designed room provides a human participant with simulated images (criminals and bystanders) through a helmet-mounted display. Motion sensors in the ceiling and light reflectors on the floor help to track the participant's movement in order to aid in generating the correct perspective for the 3-D images in the room.

Finally, in case (c), augmented reality, a diver is equipped with a goggle-mounted display that augments the real-world view of the submarine with computer-generated overlays that give the diver information about the inner workings of the ship for the purpose of repair.

In each case, extensive run-time support is needed for high-resolution graphics, helmet-mounted displays, digital cameras, motion sensors, force and tactile feedback peripherals, and other devices.

Because VR systems represent complex, multitasking, graphics simulations that involve control and tracking problems, they are perhaps the most challenging of all real-time systems; using today's technology, perfect results are not obtainable. Virtual reality also involves concurrent programs and processors, shared peripherals, and the important notion that synchronization is at least as important as timeliness. For example, in virtual-reality-type flight simulators, even a slight skew in the synchronization of a pilot's commands and the resultant display update (e.g., a turn is made) can cause nausea.

14.4.2 Multimedia

Advances in multimedia computers have significantly affected research in multimedia computing. Multimedia systems can be collectively viewed as a combination of voice, images, animation, full-motion video and audio. The primary area of research in multimedia computing deals with multimedia hardware and software systems, as well as tools development for computer-aided learning (e.g., encyclopedias, interactive games). In particular, much research focuses on distributed multimedia systems. Distributed multimedia systems

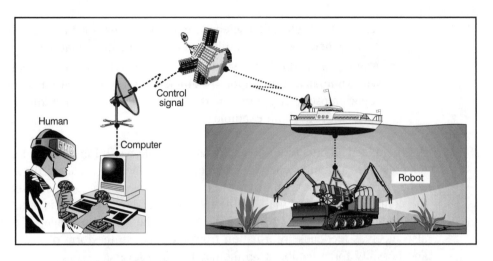

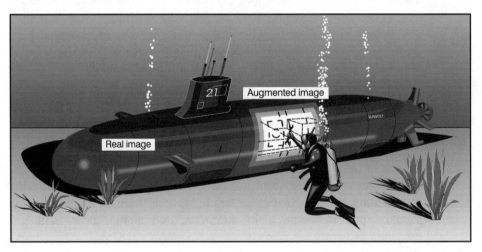

Figure 14.4 Virtual reality paradigms: (a) Telepresence, (b) immersion, (c) augmented reality.

require synchronization, large storage, indexing, and retrieval of data. For example, as with VR, in multimedia applications, it is clear that audio speech output must be in synchrony with the image of a person speaking.

Multimedia systems are complex systems that need to deal with high processing power, high-speed networks, large storage devices, video and audio compression techniques, real-time operating systems, software development, storage and retrieval of data, parallel techniques, and architectures for distributed environments. Large-scale multimedia storage will be an integral part of the emerging distributed multimedia computing infrastructure. Work has been done to provide high bus bandwidth and a high-performance multimedia real-time operating system that supports real-time scheduling. In the software tools development, research has been centered around a new object-oriented language paradigm. A major concern in multimedia system is audio and video compression. An important consideration in constructing deterministic, predictable, and synchronized multimedia systems is whether the compression techniques are deterministic.

A generalized multimedia architecture is given in Figure 14.5. In this design, compressed and uncompressed audio and video (and control inputs such as timing) are input into the system. A local database may be accessed for the purpose of decompression (such as in vector quantization techniques) or to provide local information to supplement the system (e.g., background scenery).

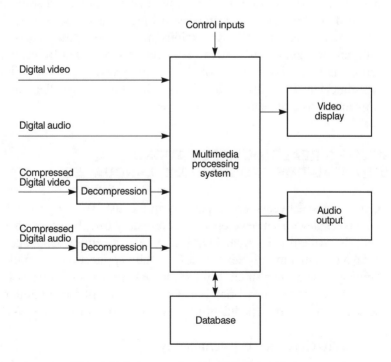

Figure 14.5 A generalized multimedia architecture.

The processing system manipulates the data in a variety of ways (for example, consider the foreign film system shown in Chapter 5), but ultimately the system outputs video and audio.

14.5 REAL-TIME UNIX

An important real-time "application" is not really an application at all but an operating system. However, because of its commercial importance, the UNIX operating system and its real-time relatives are of great interest to applications developers.

Real-time UNIX solutions seek to guarantee response times through considerations in one of the following areas: kernel features, memory management, real-time I/O, and user tools.

The standard UNIX kernel is not considered amenable to real-time because it does not provide for preemptive scheduling and because the kernel services are not re-entrant. Real-time UNIX kernels seek to guarantee response times by providing a re-entrant and interruptible kernel and preemptive priority scheduling. Good interprocess communication and synchronization are also necessary.

Real-time UNIX also provides real-time memory management by providing data integrity for all data structures. Some real-time kernels use over 3000 semaphores to protect as many data structures. (Is there a potential for deadlock here?) Also available are preallocation of files to prevent disk fragmentation (and its insidious problems) and process locking in memory to reduce swap times.

Many real-time UNIX versions also provide user tools in the form of programmer control of system resources (not afforded by ordinary UNIX) and rate-monotonic scheduling tools based on spreadsheets. An architecture for one real-time UNIX is shown in Figure 14.6. For an excellent discussion of this implementation of real-time UNIX, see [48].

14.6 BUILDING REAL-TIME APPLICATIONS WITH REAL-TIME PROGRAMMING LANGUAGES

Over the last 20 years, and especially in the last 10, several specialized real-time languages have been developed. It is probably true, however, that most real-time code is written in C, Ada, FORTRAN, and assembly language, with C++ and Ada95 gaining rapidly. Nevertheless, certain applications are built using specialty languages, and their suitability for the task merits some discussion.

As we mentioned briefly in Chapter 3, real-time programming languages seek to provide for schedulability analysis in one of three ways:

■ To eliminate nondeterminancy
■ To augment the language to provide explicit timing and control

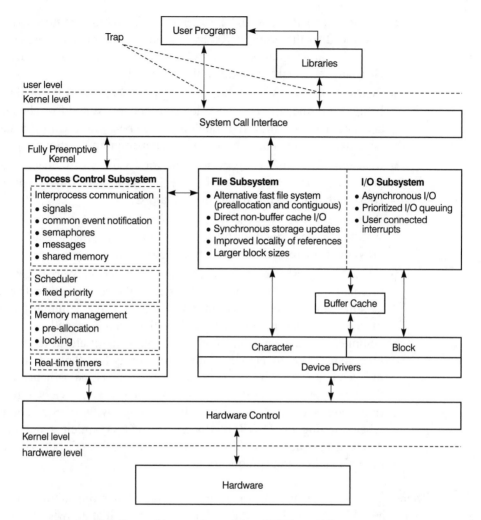

Figure 14.6 One architecture for real-time UNIX see [48].

■ To construct the language jointly with the operating system (e.g., POSIX compliant languages)

Some of the languages that have been developed over the last 20 years to handle real-time applications include

■ Ada95: A language that seeks to address the real-time problem by augmentation (in this case of the standard Ada language). This was discussed in Chapter 3.

■ occam-2: A programming language designed for use on transputers that uses augmentation to provide some explicit timing and control. This language has seen commercial use in the UK.

- PEARL: The Process and Experiment Automation Realtime Language developed in the early 1970s by a group of German researchers. Pearl uses the augmentation strategy and has fairly wide application in Germany, especially in industrial control settings.

- Real-time Euclid: An experimental language that enjoys the distinction of being one of the only languages to be completely suited for schedulability analysis. This is achieved through language restriction. Unfortunately, the language has not found its way into mainstrain application.

- Real-time C: Actually a generic name for a variety of C macroextension packages. These macroextensions typically provide timing and control constructs that are not found in standard C.

- Real-time C++: A generic name for several object class libraries specifically developed for C++. These libraries augment standard C++ to provide an increased level of timing and control.

- Java: A language used frequently in World Wide Web pages. It was originally intended for embedded systems like consumer electronics and is still gaining acceptance in that domain. Java combines a virtual machine (an interpreter) with a C++-like language and an associated compiler that converts the source code into interpreter directives called byte codes. The advantage of this approach is that the code is machine independent (i.e., it is targeted for the virtual machine)—hence its use in the heterogeneous world of the Web. In some ways, Java is a great real-time language. It allows for multithreading (with POSIX compliance when running on UNIX platforms), provides explicit synchronization mechanisms such as spinlocks, and is object-oriented, but without such drawbacks as garbage collection.

There are, of course, many other real-time languages/operating environments with names like MACH, EIFFEL, MARUTI and ESTEREL that are widely referenced in the literature. Many of these languages are used for highly specialized applications or in research only. For a thorough discussion of real-time languages, see [156].

14.7 EXERCISES

1. Research the real-time programming languages discussed in this chapter and write a report comparing and contrasting these languages with respect to the language features discussed in Chapter 3.

2. From the research literature, identify and discuss at least three real-time languages not mentioned in this book.

3. Using any of the languages above, construct a software model for the system described in Section 13.5. Many compilers for these languages are available for free on the Internet.

Glossary

A

Accept operation.   Operation on a mailbox that is similar to the pend operation, except that if no data are available, the task returns immediately from the call with a condition code rather than suspending.

Access time.   The interval between when data are requested from the memory cell and when they are actually available.

Accumulator.   An anonymous register used in certain computer instructions.

Activity packet.   A special token passed between the processors in a dataflow architecture. Each token contains an opcode, operand count, operands, and a list of destination addresses for the result of the computation.

Actual parameter.   The named variable passed to a procedure or subroutine.

Address bus.   The collection of wires needed to access individual memory addresses.

Alpha testing.   A type of validation consisting of internal distribution and exercise of the software.

ALU.   See arithmetic logic unit.

Analog-to-digital conversion.   The process of converting continuous (analog) signals into discrete (digital) ones.

Anonymous variable.   A hidden variable created by the compiler to facilitate call-by-value parameter passing.

Application programs.   Programs users write to solve specific problems.

Arithmetic logic unit.   The CPU internal device that performs arithmetic and logical operations.

Assemblers.   Software that translates assembly language to machine code.

Assembly language.   The set of symbolic equivalents to the macroinstruction set.

Associative memory.   Memory organized so that it can be searched according to its contents.

Asynchronous event.   An event that is not synchronous.

Atomic instruction.   An instruction that cannot be interrupted.

B

Background.   Non-interrupt driven processes in foreground/background systems.

BAM.   See binary angular measurement.

Banker's algorithm.   A technique sometimes used to prevent deadlock situations.

Bathtub curve.   A graph describing the phenomenon that in hardware components most errors occur either very early or very late in the life of the component. Some believe that it is applicable to software.

Belady's Anomaly.   The observation that in the FIFO page replacement rule, increasing the number of pages in memory may not reduce the number of page faults.

Beta testing.   A type of system test where preliminary versions of validated software are distributed to friendly customers who test the software under actual use.

Binary angular measurement.   An n-bit scaled number where the least significant bit is $2^{n-1} \cdot 180$.

Binary semaphore.   A semaphore that can take on one of two values.

Binary tree.   A collection of n nodes, one of which is a special one called the **root**. The remaining $n - 1$ nodes form at most two subtrees.

Black box testing.   A testing methodology where only the inputs and outputs of the unit are considered. How the outputs are generated inside the unit is ignored.

Blocked.   The condition experienced by tasks that are waiting for the occurrence of an event.

Broadcast communication.   In statecharts, a technique that allows for transitions to occur in more than one orthogonal system simultaneously.

Buffer.   A temporary data storage area used to interface between, for example, a fast device and a slower process servicing that device.

Burn-in testing.   Testing that seeks to flush out those failures that appear early in the life of the part and thus improve the reliability of the delivered product.

Burst period.   The time over which data are being passed into a buffer.

Bus arbitration.   The process of ensuring that only one device at a time can place data on the bus.

Bus contention.   Condition in which two or more devices attempt to gain control of the main memory bus simultaneously.

Bus cycle.   Memory fetch.

Bus grant.   A signal provided by the DMA controller to a device indicating that it has exclusive rights to the bus.

Bus time-out.   A condition whereby a device making a DMA request does not receive a bus grant before some specified time.

Busy wait.   In polled loop systems, the process of testing the flag without success.

C

Call-by-address. See call-by-reference.

Call-by-reference. The process in which the address of the parameter is passed by the calling routine to the called procedure so that it can be altered there.

Call-by-value. Parameter passing method in which the value of the actual parameter in the subroutine or function call is copied into the procedure's formal parameter.

Calling trees. See structure chart.

CASE. Computer-aded software engineering.

Catastrophic error. An error that renders the system useless.

CCR See condition code register.

Cellular automata. A computational paradigm for an efficient description of SIMD massively parallel systems.

Chain reaction. In statecharts, a group of sequential events where the nth event is triggered by the $(n - 1)$th event.

Checkpoints. Code that outputs intermediate results to allow an external process to monitor the efficacy of the process in question.

Checksum. A simple binary addition of all program code memory locations used to verify the contents.

Circular queue. See ring buffer.

CISC. See complex instruction set computer.

Class definitions. Object declarations along with the methods associated with them.

Clear box testing. See white box testing.

Code inspection. See group walkthrough.

Collision. Condition in which a device already has control of the bus and another obtains access. Also, simultaneous use of a critical resource.

Compaction. The process of compressing fragmented memory so that it is no longer fragmented. Also called coalescing.

Compiler. Software that translates high-order language programs into assembly code.

Complex instruction set computers. Architectures characterized by a large, micro-coded instruction set with numerous addressing modes.

Composition. An operation applied to a reliability matrix that determines the maximum reliability between processors.

Compute-bound. Computations in which the number of operations is large in comparison to the number of I/O instructions.

Condition code register. Internal CPU register used to implement a conditional transfer.

Conditional transfer. A change of the program counter based on the result of a test.

Content-addressable memory. See associative memory.

Context. The minimum information that is needed in order to save a currently executing task so that it can be resumed.

Context switching. The process of saving and restoring sufficient information for a real-time task so that it can be resumed after being interrupted.

Continguous file allocation. The process of forcing all allocated file sectors to follow one another on the disk.

Continuous random variable. A random variable with a continuous sample space.

Control flow diagram. A real-time extension to dataflow diagrams that shows the flow of control signals through the system.

Control specifications. In dataflow diagrams, a finite state automaton in diagrammatic and tabular representation.

Control unit. CPU internal device that synchronizes the fetch-execute cycle.

Cooperative multitasking system. A scheme in which two or more processes are divided into states or phases, determined by a finite state automaton. Calls to a central dispatcher are made after each phase is complete.

Coprocessor. A second specialized CPU used to extend the macroinstruction set.

Coroutine system. See cooperative multitasking system.

Correlated data. See time-relative data.

Counting semaphore. A semaphore that can take on two or more values.

CPU. Central processing unit.

CRC. See cyclic redundancy code.

Critical region. Code that interacts with a serially reusable resource.

CU. See control unit.

Cycle stealing. A situation in which DMA access precludes the CPU from accessing the bus.

Cyclic redundancy code. A method for checking ROM memory that is superior to checksum. See Chapter 11.

Cycling. The process whereby all tasks are being appropriately scheduled (although no actual processing is occurring).

Cyclomatic complexity. A measure of a system reliability devised by McCabe.

D

Daemon. A device server that does not run explicitly but rather lies dormant waiting for some condition(s) to occur.

Dangerous allocation. Any memory allocation that can preclude system determinism.

Data bus. Bus used to carry data between the various components in the system.

Dataflow architectures. A multiprocessing system that uses a large number of special processors, and computation is performed by passing activity packs between them.

Dataflow diagrams. A structured analysis tool for modeling software systems.

Dead code. See unreachable code.

Deadlock. A catastrophic situation that can arise when tasks are competing for the same set of two or more serially reusable resources.

Deadly embrace. See deadlock.

Death spiral. Stack overflow caused by repeated spurious interrupts.

Decode. The process of isolating the opcode field of a macroinstruction and determining the address in micromemory of the programming corresponding to it.

Defect.   The preferred term for an error in requirement, design, or code. See also fault, failure.

Demand page system.   Technique where program segments are permitted to be loaded in noncontiguous memory as they are requested in fixed-size chunks.

Density.   In computer memory, the number of bits per unit area.

De-referencing.   The process in which the actual locations of the parameters that are passed using call-by-value are determined.

Derivative of f at x.   Represents the slope of the function f at point x.

Deterministic system.   A system where for each possible state, and each set of inputs, a unique set of outputs and next state of the system can be determined.

Digital-to-analog conversion.   The process of converting discrete (digital) signals into continuous (analog) ones.

Direct memory access.   A scheme in which access to the computer's memory is afforded to other devices in the system without the intervention of the CPU.

Direct mode instruction.   Instruction in which the operand is the data contained at the address specified in the address field of the instruction.

Discrete random variable.   A random variable drawn from a discrete sample space.

Discrete signals.   Logic lines used to control devices.

Dispatcher.   The part of the kernel that performs the necessary bookkeeping to start a task.

Distributed real-time systems.   A collection of interconnected self-contained processors.

DMA.   See direct memory access.

DMA controller.   Device that performs bus arbitration.

Dormant state.   In the task-control block model, a state that is best described as a TCB belonging to a task that is unavailable to the operating system.

Double-buffering.   A technique using two buffers where one is filled while the data in the other is being used.

DRAM.   Dynamic random access memory.

Drive line.   In core memory, a wire used to induce a magnetic field in a toroid-shaped magnet. The orientation of the field represents either a 1 or a 0.

Dynamic memory.   Memory that uses a capacitor to store logic 1s and 0s, and that must be refreshed periodically to restore the charge lost due to capacitive discharge.

Dynamic priority system.   A system in which the priorities of tasks can change. Contrast with fixed priority system.

E

Effort.   One of Halstead's metrics (see Chapter 11).

Embedded system.   Software used to control specialized hardware attached to the computer system.

Encapsulation.   A condition that arises when a class of objects and the operations that can be performed on are isolated in both access and implementation.

Event. Any occurrence that results in a change in the state of a system.

Event determinism. When the next states and outputs of the system are known for each set of inputs that trigger events.

Event flag. Synchronization mechanism provided by certain languages.

Exception. Error or other special condition that arises during program execution.

Exception handler. Code used to process exceptions.

Execute. Process of sequencing through the steps in micromemory corresponding to a particular macroinstruction.

Executing state. In the task-control block model, a task that is currently running.

Executive. See kernel.

External fragmentation. When main memory becomes checkered with unused but available partitions, as in Figure 8.5.

F

Failed system. A system that cannot satisfy one or more of the requirements listed in the formal system specification.

Failure. A fault that causes the software system to fail to meet one of its requirements. See also defect.

Failure function. A function describing the probability that a system fails at time t.

Fault. The appearance of a defect during the operation of a software system; synonymous with error or bug. See also failure.

Fault tolerance. The ability of the system to continue to function in the presence of hardware or software failures.

Fetch. The process of retrieving a macroinstruction from main memory and placing it in the instruction register.

Fetch-execute cycle. The process of continuously fetching and executing macroinstructions from main memory.

File fragmentation. Analogous to memory fragmentation but occurring within files, with the same associated problems.

Finite state automaton. A mathematical technique used to represent systems with finite input and output spaces. Also known as a finite state machine.

Firing. In Petri nets or in certain multiprocessor architectures, when a process block or process performs its prescribed function.

Firm real-time system. A system with hard deadlines where some low probability of missing a deadline can be tolerated.

Fixed priority system. A system in which the task priorities cannot be changed. Contrast with dynamic priority system.

Fixed-rate system. A system in which interrupts occur only at fixed rates.

Flip-flop. A bistable logic device.

Flow chart. Graphical algorithm representation.

Flush. In pipelined architectures, the act of emptying the pipeline when branching occurs.

Foreground.   A collection of interrupt driven or real-time processes.

Formal parameter.   The dummy variable used in the description of a procedure or subroutine.

FSA.   See finite state automaton.

FSM.   See finite state automaton.

Function points.   A widely used metric set in nonembedded environments; they form the basis of many commercial software analysis packages. Function points measure the number of interfaces between modules and subsystems in programs or systems.

Functional requirements.   Those system features that can be directly tested by executing the program.

G

Garbage.   Memory that has been allocated but is no longer being used by a task (that is, the task has "lost track of it").

General register.   CPU internal memory that is addressable in the address field of certain macroinstructions.

General semaphore.   See counting semaphore.

General polynomial.   The modulo-2 divisor of the message polynomial in CRC.

Granularity.   See scale factor.

Group walkthrough.   A kind of white box testing in which a number of persons inspect the code line-by-line with the unit author.

H

Hamming code.   A coding technique used to detect and correct errors in computer memory.

Hard error.   Physical damage to memory cell.

Hard real-time system.   Systems where failure to meet response time constraints leads to system failure.

Hybrid system.   A system in which interrupts occur both at fixed frequencies and sporadically.

Hypercube processor.   A processor configuration that is similar to the linear array processor except that each processor element communicates data along a number of other higher dimensional pathways.

I

ICE.   See in-circuit emulation.

Immediate mode instruction.   An instruction in which the operand is an integer.

Implied mode instruction.   An instruction involving one or more specific memory locations or registers that are implicitly defined in the operation performed by instruction.

Incidence matrix.   A realiability matrix in which the entries are either 1 or 0.

In-circuit emulation.   A device that uses special hardware in conjunction with software to emulate the target CPU for debugging purposes.

Indirect mode instruction.   Instruction where the operand field is a memory location containing the address of the address of the operand.

Induction variable.   A variable in a loop that is incremented or decremented by some constant.

Information hiding.   The process of isolating highly changeable sections of code.

Inheritance.   In object-oriented programming, inheritance allows the programmer to define new objects in terms of other objects that inherit their characteristics.

In-line patch.   A patch that fits into the memory space allocated to the code to be changed.

Input space.   The set of all possible input combinations to a system.

Instruction register.   CPU internal register that holds the instruction pointed to by the contents of the program counter.

Integration.   The process of uniting modules from different sources to form the overall system.

Internal fragmentation.   Condition that occurs in fixed-partition schemes when, for example, a process requires 1 kilobyte of memory, while the only 2-kilobyte partitions are available.

Interrupt.   A hardware signal that initiates an event.

Interrupt handler.   Special code used to respond to interrupts. Also called an **interrupt service routine**.

Interrupt-handler location.   Memory location containing the starting address of an interrupt-handler routine. The program counter is automatically loaded with its address when an interrupt occurs.

Interrupt latency.   The delay between when an interrupt occurs and when the CPU begins reacting to it.

Interrupt register.   Register containing a bit map of all pending (latched) interrupts.

Interrupt return location.   Memory location where the contents of the program counter is saved when an interrupt is processed by the CPU.

Interrupt vector.   Register that contains the identity of the highest-priority interrupt request.

Intrinsic function.   A macro where the actual function call is replaced by in-line code.

J

Jackson Chart.   A form of structure chart that provides for conditional branching.

K

Kalman filter.   A mathematical construct used to combine measurements of the same quantity from different sources.

Kernel.   The smallest portion of the operating system that provides for task scheduling, dispatching, and intertask communication.

Kernel preemption. A method used in real-time UNIX that provides preemption points in calls to kernel functions to allow them to be interrupted.

Key. In a mailbox, the data that are passed as a flag used to protect a critical region.

L

Leaf. Any node in a tree with no subtrees.

Least recently used rule. The best nonpredictive page replacement algorithm.

Leveling. In dataflow diagrams, the process of redrawing a diagram at a finer level of detail.

Linear array processor. A processor organized so that multiple instructions of the same type can be executed in parallel.

Linker. Software that prepares relocatable object code for execution.

Little's law. Rule from queuing theory stating that the average number of customers in a queuing system, N_{av}, is equal to the average arrival rate of the customers to that system, r_{av}, times the average time spent in that system, t_{av}.

Live variable. A variable that can be used subsequently in the program.

Livelock. Another term for process starvation.

Load module. Code that can be readily loaded into the machine.

Locality-of-reference. The notion that if you examine a list of recently executed program instructions on a logic analyzer, you will see that most of the instructions are localized to within a small number of instructions.

Lock-up. When a system enters in which it is rendered ineffective.

Look-up table. An integer arithmetic technique that uses tables and relies on mathematical definition of the derivative to compute functions quickly.

Loop invariant optimization. The process of placing computations outside a loop that do not need to be performed within the loop.

Loosely coupled system. A system that can run on other hardware with the rewrite of certain modules.

LRU. See least recently used rule.

M

Machine code. Binary instructions that affect specific computer operations. Also called **machine language**.

Macrocode. See macroinstruction.

Macroinstruction. Binary program code stored in the main memory of the computer. Also called **macrocode**.

Mailbox. An intertask communication device consisting of a memory location and two operations—post and pend—that can be performed on it.

Main memory. Memory that is directly addressable by the CPU.

Major cycle. The largest sequence of repeating processes in cyclic or periodic systems.

MAR. See memory address register.

Mask register. A register that contains a bit map either enabling or disabling specific interrupts.

Master processor. The on-line processor in a master/slave configuration.

MDR. See memory data register.

Memory address register (or MAR). Register that holds the address of the memory location to be acted on.

Memory data register (or MDR). Register that holds the data to be written to or that is read from the memory location held in the MAR.

Memory-loading. The percentage of usable memory that is being used.

Memory locking. In a real-time system, the process of locking all or certain parts of a process into memory to reduce the overhead involved in paging, and thus make the execution times more predictable.

Mesh processor. A processor configuration that is similar to the linear array processor except that each processor element also communicates data north and south.

Message exchange. See mailbox.

Message polynomial. Used in CRC (see Chapter 11).

Methods. In object-oriented systems, functions that can be performed on objects.

MFT. Multiprogramming with a fixed number of tasks.

Microcode. A sequence of binary instructions corresponding to a particular macro-instruction. Also called **microinstructions**.

Microcontroller. A computer system that is programmable via microcode.

Microinstructions. See microcode.

Micro-kernel. A nano-kernel that also provides for task scheduling.

Micromemory. CPU internal memory that holds the binary codes corresponding to macroinstructions.

Microprogram. Sequence of microcode stored in micromemory.

Minor cycle. A sequence of repeating processes in cyclic or periodic systems.

Mixed listing. A printout that combines the high-order language instruction with the equivalent assembly language code.

Mixed system. A system in which interrupts occur both at fixed frequencies and sporadically.

Multimedia computing. Computing that involves computer systems with high-resolution graphics, CD-ROM drives, mice, high-performance sound cards, and multitasking operating systems that support these devices.

Multiplexer. A device used to route multiple lines onto fewer lines.

Multiprocessing operating system. An operating system in which more than one processor is available to provide for simultaneity; contrast with multitasking operating system.

Multitasking operating system. An operating system that provides sufficient functionality to allow multiple programs to run on a single processor so that the illusion of simultaneity is created; contrast with multiprocessing operating system.

Mutex. A common name for a semaphore variable.

MUX. See multiplexer.

MVT. Multiprogramming with a variable number of tasks.

N

Nano-kernel. Code that provides simple thread-of-execution (same as "flow-of-control") management; essentially provides only one of the three services provided by a kernel—that is, it provides for task dispatching.

Nonfunctional requirements. System requirements that cannot be tested easily by program execution.

Nonvolatile memory. Memory whose contents are preserved upon removing power.

Non-von Neumann architecture. An architecture that does not use the stored program, serial fetch-execute cycle.

No-op. A macroinstruction that does not change the state of the computer.

NP-complete problem. A decision problem that is a seemingly intractable problem for which the only known solutions are exponential functions of the problem size; compare with NP-hard.

NP-hard. A decision problem that is similar to an NP-complete problem (except that for the NP-hard problem not even an exponential time solution can be found).

nth Order reliability matrix. The composition of a reliability matrix with itself $(n - 1)$ times.

N-version programming. A technique used to reduce the likelihood of system lock-up by using redundant processors, each running software that has been coded to the same specifications by different teams.

Nucleus. See kernel.

O

Object code. A specific collection of machine instructions.

Object-oriented language. A language that provides constructs that encourage a high degree of information hiding and data abstraction.

Opcode. Starting address of the microcode program stored in micromemory.

Operating system. A unique collection of systems programs.

Organic system. A system that is not embedded.

Orthogonal process. In statecharts, the combined functionality of a set of orthogonal processes.

Orthogonal product. In statecharts, a process that depicts concurrent processes that run in isolation.

Ostrich algorithm. A technique that advises that the problem of deadlock be ignored. This solution is viable only in noncritical systems.

Output space. The set of all possible output combinations for a system.

Overlay. Dependent code and data sections used in overlaying.

Overlaying. A technique that allows a single program to be larger than the allowable user space.

Oversized patch. A patch that requires more memory than is currently occupied by the code to be replaced.

P

Page. Fixed-size chunk used in demand-paged systems.

Page fault. An exception that occurs when a memory reference is made to a location within a page not loaded in main memory.

Page-frame. See page.

Page stealing. When a page is to be loaded into main memory, and no free pages are found, then a page frame must be written out or swapped to disk to make room.

Page table. A collection of pointers to pages used to allow noncontiguous allocation of page frames in demand paging.

Parnas partitioning. See information hiding.

Partial order relation. In process scheduling, an indicator that any process can call itself (reflexivity); if process A calls process B, then the reverse is not possible (antisymmetry), and if process A calls process B and process B calls process C, then process A can call process C (transitivity).

Patching. The process of correcting errors in the code directly on the target machine.

PC. See program counter.

PDL. See program design language.

Peephole optimization. An optimization technique where a small window of assembly langage or machine code is compared against known patterns that yield optimization opportunities.

Pend operation. Operation of removing data from a mailbox. If data are not available, the process performing the pend suspects itself until the data become available.

Petri net. A mathematical/pictorial system description technique.

Phase-driven code. See state-driven code.

Ping-pong buffering. See double-buffering.

Pipeline. An intertask communication mechanism provided in UNIX.

Pipelining. A technique used to speed processor execution that relies on the fact that fetching the instruction is only one part of the fetch-execute cycle, and that it can overlap with different parts of the fetch-execute cycle for other instructions.

Polled loop system. A real-time system in which a single and repetitive test instruction is used to test a flag that indicates that some event has occurred.

Polymorphism. In object-oriented programming, polymorphism allows the programmer to create a single function that operates on different objects depending on the type of object involved.

Post operation. Operation that places data in a mailbox.

Power bus. The collection of wires used to distribute power to the various components of the computer system.

Pragma. In certain programming languages, a pseudo-op that allows assembly code to be placed in-line with the high-order language code.

Preempt. A condition that occurs when a higher-priority task interrupts a lower-priority task.

Preemptive priority system. A system that uses preemption schemes instead of round-robin or first-come/first-serve scheduling.

Primary memory. See main memory.

Priority ceiling protocol. A method used in interrupt driven systems to avoid priority inversion; dictates that a task blocking a higher priority task inherits the higher priority for the duration of that task.

Priority inversion. A condition that occurs because a noncritical task with a high execution rate will have a higher priority than a critical task with a low execution rate.

Process blocks. Subsystems used to calculate the overall system reliability.

Processing elements. The individual processors in a multiprocessing system such as a systolic or wavefront architecture.

Program counter. The CPU internal register that holds the address of the next instruction to be executed.

Program design language. A type of abstract high-order language used in system specification.

Propagation delay. The contribution to interrupt latency due to limitation in switching speeds of digital devices and in the transit time of electrons across wires.

Prototype. A mock-up of a software system often used during the design phase.

Pseudocode. A type of program design language.

R

Raise. Mechanism used to initiate a software interrupt in certain languages such as C.

RAM scrubbing. A technique used in memory configurations that include error detection and correction chips. The technique, which reduces the chance of multiple bit errors occuring, is needed because in some configurations memory errors are corrected on the bus and not in memory itself. The corrected memory data then need to be written back to memory.

Random variable. A function mapping elements of the sample space into a real number.

Rate-monotonic system. A fixed-rate, preemptive, prioritized real-time system where the priorities are assigned so that the higher the execution frequency, the higher the priority.

Reactive system. A system that has some ongoing interaction with its environment.

Read/write line. Logic line that is set to logic 0 during memory write and to logic 1 during memory read.

Ready state. In the task-control block model, the state of those tasks that are ready to run, but not running.

Real-time system. A system that must satisfy explicit (bounded) response time constraints or it will fail.

Recovery block. Section of code that terminates in checkpoints. If the check fails, processing can resume at the beginning of a recovery block.

Recursion. A method whereby a procedure can be self-referential; that is, it can invoke (call) itself.

Reduced instruction set computer. Architecture usually characterized by a small instruction set with limited addressing modes and hard-wired (as opposed to microcoded) instructions.

Reduction in strength. Optimization technique that uses the fastest macroinstruction possible to accomplish a given calculation.

Re-entrant procedure. A procedure that can be used by several concurrently running tasks in a multitasking system.

Register direct mode instruction. Instruction in which the operand field is a register.

Register indirect mode instruction. Instruction in which the operand address is kept in a register named in the operand field of the instruction.

Regression testing. A test methodology used to validate updated software against an old set of test cases that have already been passed.

Reliability matrix. In a multiprocessing system, a matrix that denotes the reliability of the connections between processors.

Response time. The time between the presentation of a set of inputs to a software system and the appearance of all the associated outputs.

Reverse Polish notation. The result of building a binary parse tree with operands at the leaves and operations at the roots, and then traversing it in post-order fashion.

Ring buffer. A first-in/first-out list in which simultaneous input and output to the list is achieved by keeping head and tail pointers. Data are loaded at the tail and read from the head.

RISC. See reduced instruction set computer.

Root. In overlaying memory management, the portion of memory containing the overlay manager and code common to all overlay segments, such as math libraries.

Round-robin system. A system in which several processes are executed sequentially to completion, often in conjunction with a cyclic executive.

Round-robin system with time-slicing. A system in which each executable task is assigned a fixed time quantum called a **time slice** in which to execute. A clock is used to initate an interrupt at a rate corresponding to the time slice.

S

Sample space. The set of outcomes to some experiment.

Sampling rate. The rate at which an analog signal is converted to digital form.

Scale factor. A technique used to simulate floating point operations by assigning an implicit noninteger value to the least significant bit of an integer.

sccs. Source code control system for management of system code; typical for UNIX operating systems.

Schedualability analysis. The compile time prediction of execution time performance.

Scheduler. The part of the kernel that determines which task will run.

Scratch pad memory. CPU internal memory used for intermediate results.

Screen signature. The CRC of a screen memory.

Secondary memory. Memory that is characterized by long-term storage devices such as tapes, disks, and cards.

Self-modifying code. Code that can actually change itself; for example, by taking advantage of the fact that the opcodes of certain instructions may differ by only one bit.

Semaphore. A special variable type used for protecting critical regions.

Semaphore primitives. The two operations that can be performed on a semaphor, namely, wait and signal.

Semidetached system. See loosely coupled system.

Sense line. In core memory a wire that is used to "read" the memory. Depending on the orientation of the magnetic field in the core, a pulse is or is not generated in the sense line.

Serially reusable resource. A resource that can only be used by one task at a time and that must be used to completion.

Server. A process used to manage multiple requests to a serially reusable resource.

SEU. See single event upset.

Signal. Exception-handling mechanism provided by certain languages, such as C.

Signal operation. Operation on a semaphore that essentially releases the resource protected by the semaphore.

Single-event upset. Alteration of memory contents due to charged particles present in space, or in the presence of a nuclear event.

Slave processor. The off-line processor in a master/slave configuration.

Soft error. Repairable alteration of the contents of memory.

Soft real-time system. A system in which performance is degraded by not destroyed by failure to meet response time constraints.

Software. A collection of macroinstructions.

Software reliability. The probability that a software system will not fail before some time t.

Spatial fault tolerance. Methods involving redundant hardware or software.

Speculative execution. In multiprocessing systems, a situation that involves an idle processor optimistically and predictively executing code in the next process block, as long as there is no dependency in that process block on code that could be running on other processors.

Spin lock. Another name for the wait semaphore operation.

Sporadic system. A system with all interrupts occurring sporadically.

Sporadic task. A task driven by an interrupt that occurs aperiodically.

Spurious interrupts. Extraneous and unwanted interrupts that are not due to time-loading.

SRAM. Static random-access memory.

Stack. A first-in/last-out data structure.

Stack machines. Computer architecture in which the instructions are centered on an internal memory store called a stack, and an accumulator.

Starvation. A condition that occurs when a task is not being serviced frequently enough.

State-driven code. Program code based on a finite state automaton.

Static memory. Memory that does not rely on capacitive charge to store binary data.

Statistically based testing. Technique that uses an underlying probability distribution function for each system input to generate random test cases.

Status register. A register involved in interupt processing that contains the value of the lowest interrupt that will presently be honored.

Stress testing. A type of testing wherein the system is subjected to a large disturbance in the inputs (for example, a large burst of interrupts), followed by smaller disturbances spread out over a longer period of time.

Structure chart. Graphical design tool used to partition system functionality.

Suspended state. In the task-control block model, those tasks that are waiting on a particular resource, and thus are not ready. Also called the blocked state.

Swapping. The simplest scheme that allows the operating system to allocate main memory to two processes simultaneously.

Switch bounce. The physical phenomenon that an electrical signal cannot instantaneously change from its logical false condition.

Synchronous data. See time-relative data.

Synchronous event. Event that occurs at predictable times in the flow-of-control.

Syndrome bits. The extra bits needed to implement a Hamming code.

System. An entity that when presented with a set of inputs produces corresponding outputs.

System programs. Software used to manage the resources of the computer.

System unification. A process consisting of linking together the testing software modules in an orderly fashion.

Systolic processors. Multiprocessing architecture that consists of a large number of uniform processors connected in an array topology.

T

Task-control block. A collection of data associated with a task including context, process code (or a pointer to it), and other information.

TCB. See task control block.

Telepresence. A form of virtual reality in which a human operator can remotely control robots or other devices as if the operator were physically present.

Temporal determinism. A condition that occurs when the response time for each set of outputs is known in a deterministic system.

Temporal fault tolerance. Techniques that allow for tolerating missed deadlines.

Test-and-set instruction. A macroinstruction that can atomically test and then set a particular memory address to some value.

Test probe. A checkpoint used only during testing.

Test suite. A collection of test cases.

Thrashing. Very high paging activity.

Throughput. A measure of the number of macroinstructions per second that can be processed based on some predetermined instruction mix.

Time-loading. The percentage of "useful" processing the computer is doing. Also known as the utilization factor.

Time overloaded. A system that is 100% or more time-loaded.

Time-relative data. A collection of data that must be time correlated.

Time-slice. A fixed time quantum used to limit execution time in round-robin systems.

Transceivers. A transmit/receive hybrid device.

Transputer. A fully self-sufficient, multiple instruction set, von Neumann processor, designed to be connected to other transputers.

Trap. Internal interrupt caused by the execution of a certain instruction.

Tri-state. A high-impedance state that, in effect, disconnects a device from the bus.

U

Unit. A software module.

Unreachable code. Code that can never be reached in the normal flow-of-control.

User space. Memory not required by the operating system.

Utilization facator. See time-loading.

V

Vector processor. See linear array processor.

Version control software. A system that manages the access to the various components of the system from the software library.

Volatile memory. Memory in which the contents will be lost if power is removed.

von Neumann bottleneck. A situation in which the serial fetch and execution of instructions limits overall execution speed.

W

Wait and hold condition. The situation in which a task acquires a resource and then does not relinquish it until it can acquire another resource.

Wait operation. Operation on a semaphore that essentially locks the resource protected by the semaphore, or prevents the requesting task from proceeding if the resource is already locked.

Wait state. Clock cycle used to synchronize macroinstruction execution with the access time of memory.

Watchdog timer. A device that must be reset periodically or a discrete signal is issued.

Wavefront processor. A multiprocessing architecture that consists of an array of identical processors, each with its own local memory and connected in a nearest-neighbor topology.

White box testing. Logic-driven testing designed to exercise all paths in the module.

Bibliography

[1] Adrion, W. Richards, Martha A. Branstad, and John C. Cherniavsky. Validation, verification, and testing of computer software. *ACM Computing Survey* (June 1982):159–192.

[2] Aho, Alfred V., Ravi Sethi, and Jeffrey D. Ullman. *Compilers: Principles, Techniques and Tools*. New York: Addison-Wesley, 1986.

[3] Aho, Alfred V., and Jeffrey D. Ullman. *The Theory of Parsing, Translation, and Compiling, Vol. I: Parsing*. Englewood Cliffs, N.J.: Prentice-Hall, 1972.

[4] Allard, James R., and Lowell B. Hawkinson. Real-time programming in common LISP. *Communications of the ACM* 35, 9 (Sept. 1991): 64–69.

[5] Allworth, S. T., and R. N. Zobel. *Introduction to Real-Time Software Design*. 2nd ed. New York: Springer-Verlag, 1987.

[6] American National Standards Institute. *American National Standard Programming Language FORTRAN*. ANSI X3.9–1978. New York: American National Standards Institute, 1978.

[7] American National Standards Institute. *American National Standard Reference Manual for the Ada Programming Language*. ANSI/Mil-Std-1815A-1983. New York: American National Standards Institute, 1983.

[8] Andrews, Warren. RISC-based boards make headway in real-time applications. *Computer Design* (Oct. 1991): 69–80.

[9] Asimov, Isaac. *Understanding Physics Vol. III*. London: George Allen & Unwin Ltd., 1966.

[10] Baker, T. P. A stack-based resource allocation policy for real-time processes. *Proceedings of the 11th Real-Time Systems Symposium*. Lake Buena Vista, Fla. (Dec. 1990): 191–200.

[11] Bartee, Thomas C. *Computer Architecture and Logic Design*. New York: McGraw-Hill, 1991.

[12] Baruah, Sanjoy K., Aloysius K. Mok, and Louis E. Rosier. Preemptively scheduling hard real-time sporadic tasks on one processor. *Proceedings of the 11th Real-Time Systems Symposium.* Lake Buena Vista, Fla. (Dec. 1990): 182–190.

[13] Bernhard, Robert. Super-minicomputers—The hottest game in town. *Systems & Software* 4(1985): 44–58.

[14] Blackman, M., *The Design of Real-Time Applications.* New York: John Wiley & Sons, 1975.

[15] Bodilsen, Svend. Scheduling theory and Ada 9X, *Embedded Systems Programming* (Dec. 1994): 32–52.

[16] Boehm, Barry. *Software Engineering Economics.* Englewood Cliffs, N.J.: Prentice-Hall, 1981.

[17] Boehm, Barry. A spiral model of software development. ACM SIGSOFT. *Software Engineering Notes* 11, 4 (Aug. 1986)

[18] Boussinot, Frédéric, and Robert DeSimmi. The ESTEREL Language. *Proceedings of the IEEE,* 79, 9 (Sept. 1991): 1293–1304.

[19] Brooks, Frederick P. *The Mythical Man Month.* New York: Addison-Wesley, 1982.

[20] Bucci, Giacomo, Maurizio Campanai, and Paolo Nesi. Tools for specifying real-time systems. *Real-Time Systems Journal,* (Jan. 1995).

[21] Burns, Alan, and Andy Wellings. *Real-time Systems and Their Programming Languages.* New York: Addison-Wesley, 1990.

[22] Campbell, Joe. *C Programmer's Guide to Serial Communications.* Indianapolis: Howard Sams & Co., 1988.

[23] Cave, William C., and Alan B. Salisbury. Controlling the software life cycle—The project management task. *IEEE Transactions on Software Engineering* (July 1978): 326–334.

[24] Chirlian, Paul M. *Analysis and Design of Integrated Electronic Circuits.* 2nd ed. New York: Harper & Row, 1987.

[25] Clark, Edmund M. Jr., David E. Long, and Kenneth McMillen. A language for computational specification and verification of finite state hardware controllers. *Proceedings of the IEEE,* 79, 9 (Sept. 1991): 1283–1292.

[26] Cox, Brad. *Object-oriented Paradigms.* New York: Addison-Wesley, 1988.

[27] Cox, Brad. *Object-oriented Programming: An Evolutionary Approach.* New York: Addison-Wesley, 1991.

[28] Daigle, John N. *Queuing Theory for Telecommunications.* New York: Addison-Wesley, 1992.

[29] Davari, Sadegh, Ted F. Jr. Leibfried, Swami Natarajan, David Pruett, Lui Sha and Wei Zhao. Real-time issues in the design of the data management system for the space station Freedom. *Proceedings of the*

First Real-Time Applications Workshop, July 1993, New York, IEEE CS Press: 161–165.

[30] Davis, Martin. *Computability and Unsolvability.* New York: Dover Publishing Co., 1973.

[31] DeMarco, Tom. *Structured Analysis and System Specification.* Englewood Cliffs, N.J.: Prentice-Hall/Yourdon, 1978.

[32] DeMillo, Richard A., Richard J. Lipton, and Alan Perlis. Social processes and proofs of theorems and programs. *Communications of the ACM* 22, 5 (May 1979).

[33] Desmonde, W.H. *Real-time Data Processing Systems: Introductory Concepts.* Englewood Cliffs, N.J.: Prentice-Hall, 1964.

[34] Dijkstra, E. W. Cooperating sequential processes. *Technical Report EWD-123.* Eindhoven, Netherlands: Technological University, 1965.

[35] Dijkstra, E. W. Go to statement considered harmful. *Communications of the ACM* 11, 3 (Mar. 1968).

[36] Dijkstra, E. W. Solution of a problem in concurrent programming control. *Communications of the ACM* 11, 3 (Mar. 1968).

[37] DiMaio, A., C. Cardigno, S. Genolini, S. Crespi-Reghizzi, R. Bayan, C. Destombes, C. V. Atkinson, and S. J. Goldsack. DRAGOON: An Ada-based object-oriented language for concurrent, real-time, distributed systems. *Systems Design with Ada, Proc. Ada-Europe International Conference*, Madrid. Ada Companion Series. Cambridge: Cambridge University Press, June 1989.

[38] DOD-STD-2167A. Military standard defense system software development. Washington, D.C.: U.S. Department of Defense, 1988.

[39] Dorf, Richard C., *The Electrical Engineering Handbook*, Piscataway, N.J.: CRC Press/IEEE Press, 1993.

[40] Dougherty, E. R., and C. R. Giardina. *Mathematical Methods for Artificial Intelligence and Autonomous Systems.* Englewood Cliffs N.J.: Prentice-Hall, 1988.

[41] Ellis, Margaret A., and Bjarne Stroustrup. *The Annotated C++ Reference Manual.* New York: Addison-Wesley, 1990.

[42] Fagan, M. E. Design and code inspections to reduce errors in program development. *IBM Systems Journal* 15, 3 (1976): 211.

[43] Feigenbaum, Armand V. *Total Quality Control.* 3rd ed. New York: McGraw-Hill, 1983.

[44] Ferrintino, A. B., and H. D. Mills. State machines and their semantics in software engineering. *Proc. IEEE COMPSAC*, 1977.

[45] Fetzer, James H. Program verification: The very idea. *Communications of the ACM* 31, 9 (Sept. 1988): 1048–1062.

[46] Forestier, J. P., C. Forarino, and P. Franci-Zannettacci. Ada++ : A class and inheritance extension for Ada. *Proc. Ada-Europe International Conference*, Madrid. Ada Companion Series. Cambridge: Cambridge University Press, June 1989.

[47] Freedman, A. L., and R. A. Lees. *Real-Time Computer Systems*. New York: Crane, Russak & Co., 1977.

[48] Furht, Borko, Dan Grostick, David Gluch, Guy Rabbat, John Parker, and Meg McRoberts. *Real-time Unix Systems Design and Application Guide*. Boston: Kluwer Academic Publishers, 1991.

[49] Garrett, Patrick H. Advanced instrumentation and computer I/O design: real-time system computer interface engineering, Piscataway, N.J.: IEEE Press, 1994.

[50] Garver, Roger. How to implement ISO 9000. *T & D* (Sept. 1994): 36–42.

[51] Ghezzi, Carlo, Jazayeri Mehdi, and Dino Mandrioli. *Fundamentals of Software Engineering*. Englewood Cliffs, N.J.: Prentice-Hall, 1991.

[52] Giardina, Charles R. *Parallel Digital Signal Processing: A Unified Signal Algebra Approach*. Wayne, N.J.: Regency Publishing, 1991.

[53] Giardina, Charles R. *Parallel Multidimensional Digital Signal Processing*. Wayne, NJ: Regency Publishing, 1991.

[54] Goodenough, J. B., and L. Sha. The priority ceiling protocol: A method for minimizing the blocking of high-priority Ada tasks. *Technical Report CMU/SEI-88-SR-4*. Carnegie-Mellon University: Software Engineering Institute, 1988.

[55] Gopinath, Prabha, Thomas Bihri, and Rajiv Gupta. Complier support for object-oriented real-time software. *IEEE Software* (Sept. 1993): 42–49.

[56] Habermann, A. N. Prevention of system deadlocks. *Communications of the ACM* 12, 7 (July 1969): 171–176.

[57] Halang, W. A., and A. Stoyenko. Constructing predictable real-time systems. Boston: Kluwer Academic, 1991.

[58] Halstead, M. H. *Elements of Software Science*. Amsterdam: North-Holland, 1977.

[59] Harbison, Samuel P., and Guy. L. Steele, Jr. *C: A Reference Manual*. Englewood Cliffs, N.J.: Prentice Hall, 1991.

[60] Harel, David. On visual formalisms. *Communications of the ACM* 31, 5 (May 1988): 514–530.

[61] Harel, D., H. Lachover, A. Naamad, A. Pnueli, M. Politi, R. Sherman, and A. Trauring. STATEMATE: A working environment for the development of complex reactive systems. *IEEE Transactions on Software Engineering* 16, 4 (Apr. 1990): 403–414.

[62] Hatley, D., and I. Pribhai. *Strategies for Real-Time System Specification.* New York: Dorset House, 1987.

[63] Hayes, John P. *Computer Architecture and Organization.* 2nd ed. New York: McGraw-Hill, 1988, pp. 210–211.

[64] Henize, John. Understanding real-time UNIX. Concurrent Computer Corporation, One Technology Way, Westford, Mass. 01886.

[65] Hetzel, Bill. *The Complete Guide to Software Testing.* 2nd ed. Wellesley, Mass.: QED Information Sciences, 1988.

[66] Hill, Frederick J., and Gerald R. Peterson. *Digital Systems: Hardware Organization and Design.* 3rd ed. New York: John Wiley & Sons, 1987.

[67] Horowitz, Ellis. *Fundamentals of Programming Languages.* 2nd ed. Rockville, M.: Computer Science Press, 1984.

[68] Howden, William E. Life cycle software validation. *Software Life Cycle Management.* Maidenhead, England: Infotech, 1980, pp. 101–116.

[69] IEEE/ANSI Std. 830–1984. *IEEE Guide to Software Requirements Specification.* New York: IEEE, 1984.

[70] *IEEE Software Magazine*, Special Issue on Real-Time Realities (Sept. 1992).

[71] *IEEE Transactions on Software Engineering, Special Issue on Analysis of Real-Time Systems.* SE 18 (Sept. 1992).

[72] IEEE Std. 1016. *Recommended Practice for Software Design Description.* New York: IEEE, 1987.

[73] Ingalls, Dan. Object-oriented programming. Video tape, Apple Computer, Inc. 1989. Part of the University Video Communications collection, Distinguished Lecture Series, Volume II.

[74] Jain, Raj. *The Art of Computer Systems Performance Analysis.* New York: John Wiley & Sons, Inc. 1991.

[75] Joel, A. E. Communication switching systems as real-time computers. *Proceedings of the Eastern Joint Computer Conference—1957.*

[76] *Joerg, Werner B. A subclass of Petri nets as a design abstraction for parallel architectures. ACM Computer Architecture News 18, 4 (Dec. 1990): 67–75.*

[77] Jones, Gregory W. *Software Engineering.* New York: John Wiley & Sons, 1990.

[78] Jovanovic, Vladan, Stevan Mrdalj. A structured specification technique for hypermedia systems. *Communications of the ACM*, 36, 11 (Nov. 1993): 18–20.

[79] Kernighan, Brian W. Why Pascal is not my favorite language. *Computing Science Technical Report No. 100.* Murray Hill, N.J.: Bell Laboratories (July 18, 1981).

[80] Kernighan, Brian W., and Dennis M. Ritchie. *The C Programming Language.* 2nd ed. Englewood Cliffs, N.J.: Prentice-Hall, 1990.

[81] Kfoury, A. J., Robert N. Moll, and Michael A. Arbib. *A Programming Approach to Computability.* New York: Springer-Verlag, 1982.

[82] Kleinrock, Leonard. *Queuing Systems, Vol. 1: Theory.* New York: John Wiley & Sons, 1975.

[83] Knuth, Donald E. *The Art of Computer Programming, Vol. 3: Searching and Sorting.* New York: Addison-Wesley, 1973.

[84] Koffman, Elliot. *Turbo Pascal.* 2nd ed. New York: Addison-Wesley, 1987.

[85] Krishna, C. M., and Y. H. Lee. Guest editor's introduction: Real-time systems. *Computer* (May 1991): 10–11.

[86] Kung, H. T. Why systolic architectures? *Computer* (Jan. 1982): 37–46.

[87] Kung, Sun-Yuan, K. S. Arun, Ron J. Gal-ezer, D.V. Bhaskar Rao. Wavefront array processor: Language, architecture, and applications. *IEEE Transactions on Computers* C-31, 11: (Nov. 1982): 1054–1066.

[88] Lamb, D. *Software Engineering: Planning for Change*, Englewood Cliffs, N.J.: Prentice-Hall, 1988.

[89] Lamport, L., R. Shostak, and M. Pease. The Byzantine generals' problem. *ACM Transactions on Programming Languages and Systems* 4, 3 (July 1982): 382–401.

[90] Laplante, Phillip A. Fault-tolerant control of real-time systems in the presence of single event upsets. *Control Engineering Practice* 1, 5 (Oct. 1993): 9–16.

[91] Laplante, Phillip A. The Heisenberg uncertainty principle and the Halting problem. *ACM SIGACT Newsletter* 22, 3 (Summer 1991).

[92] Laplante, Phillip A. The Heisenberg uncertainty principle and its application to software engineering. ACM SIGSOFT *Software Engineering Notes* 15, 5 (Oct. 1990).

[93] Laplante, Phillip A. A novel single instruction computer architecture. *ACM Computer Architecture News* 18, 4 (Dec. 1990).

[94] Laplante, Phillip A. A single instruction computer architecture and its application in image processing. *Proceedings of the SPIE Conference on Image Processing.* Boston (Nov. 1991).

[95] Laplante, Phillip A. Software considerations for single event upsets. *Proceedings of the 12th Biennial Guidance Test Symposium.* Alamogordo, N.M. (Oct. 1985).

[96] Laplante, Phillip A. Some thoughts on cleanroom software development and its impact on system test. *Proceedings of the Third AT&T Software Quality Symposium.* Holmdel, N.J. (Dec. 1988).

[97] Laplante, Phillip A., Ajmal H. Arastu, and Michael E. McLane. The software life cycle and its relation to system test. *Proceedings of the Third AT&T Software Quality Symposium*. Holmdel, N.J. (Dec. 1988).

[98] Laplante, Phillip A., Eileen Funck-Rose, and Maria Gracia-Watson. An historical overview of early real-time system developments in the US. *Real-Time Systems Journal* (Jan. 1995).

[99] Laplante, Phillip A., and D. Sinha. Positional logic and its application to database systems. *Proceedings of the International Conference for Young Computer Scientists*. Beijing (July 1991).

[100] Lawson, Harold W. *Parallel Processing in Industrial Real-Time Applications* Englewood Cliffs, N.J.: Prentice-Hall, 1992.

[101] Lehoczky, John, Liu Sha, and Ye Ding. The rate monotonic scheduling algorithm: Exact characterization and average case behavior. *Proceedings of the 10th Real-Time Systems Symposium*. Santa Monica, Calif. (Dec. 1989): 166–171.

[102] Leveson, Nancy G., and Janice L. Stolzy. Safety analysis using Petri nets. *IEEE Transactions on Software Engineering* 13, 3 (Mar. 1987): 386–397.

[103] Levi, Shem-Tov, and Ashok K. Agrawala. *Real-time System Design*. New York: McGraw-Hill, 1990.

[104] Liu, C. L., and J. W. Layland. Scheduling algorithms for multi-programming in a hard real-time environment. *Journal of the ACM* 20, 1 (1973): 46–61.

[105] Locke, C. D., and J. B. Goodenough. A practical application of the ceiling protocol in a real-time system. *Technical Report CMU/SEI-88-SR-3*. Carnegie-Mellon University: Software Engineering Institute, 1988.

[106] Lyu, Michael R., ed. *Software Reliability Engineering*, Piscataway, N.J.: IEEE Press, 1996.

[107] MacWilliams, F. J., and N. J. A. Sloane. *The Theory of Error-Correcting Codes*. Amsterdam: North-Holland, 1977.

[108] Mano, M. Morris. *Computer System Architecture*. Englewood Cliffs, N.J.: Prentice-Hall, 1982.

[109] Mano, M. Morris. *Digital Logic and Computer Design*. Englewood Cliffs, N.J.: Prentice-Hall, 1979.

[110] Markov, John. RISC Chips. *BYTE* (Nov. 1984): 191–206.

[111] Martin, J. *Programming Real-Time Computer Systems*. Englewood Cliffs, N.J.: Prentice-Hall, 1965.

[112] McCabe, T. J. A complexity measure. *IEEE Transactions on Software Engineering* 2, 4 (Dec. 1976): 308–320.

[113] Melliar-Smith, P. M. Interval logic to real-time systems. *Lecture Notes in Computer Science*. G. Voos and J. Hartmanis, eds. New York: Springer-Verlag, 1988, pp. 224–242.

[114] Mellor, Stephen J., and Paul T. Ward. *Structured Development for Real-Time Systems*. Vols. I, II, III. Englewood Cliffs, N.J.: Prentice-Hall/Yourdon, 1986.

[115] Mok, A. Fundamental design problems of distributed systems for the hard real-time environment. Ph.D. thesis, MIT Laboratory for Computer Science, May 1983.

[116] Moore, David L. Object-oriented facilities in Ada 95. *Dr. Dobb's Journal*, (Oct. 1995): 28–35.

[117] Moshos, George J. *Data Communications Principles and Problems*. New York: West Publishing Co., 1989.

[118] MTOS-UX/Ada product profile. Jericho, N.Y.: Industrial Programming Inc., 1989.

[119] Musa, J. D. The measurement and management of software reliability. *Proceedings of the IEEE* 68, 9 (Sept. 1980).

[120] Myers, Glenford J. *Reliable Software Through Composite Design*. New York: Van Nostrand Reinhold, 1975.

[121] Mynatt, Barbee Teasley. *Software Engineering with Student Project Guidance*. Englewood Cliffs, N.J.: Prentice-Hall, 1990.

[122] Orr, Kenneth. *Structured System Development*. Englewood Cliffs, N.J.: Yourdon Press, 1977.

[123] Papoulous, Anathasios. *Probability, Random Variables and Stochastic Processes*. New York: McGraw-Hill, 1965.

[124] Parnas, D. L. A rational design process: How and why to fake it. *Proceedings of TAPSOFT Joint Conference on Theory and Practice of Software Development*. Berlin (Mar. 1985).

[125] Parnas, D. L., and Paul C. Clements. On the criteria to be used in decomposing systems into modules. *Communications of the ACM* 15, 12 (Dec. 1972): 1053–1058.

[126] Patterson, James G. *ISO 9000 Worldwide Quality Standard*. Menlo Park, Calif.: Crisp Publications, 1995.

[127] Paulish, Daniel J., and Karl H. Möller. *Best Practices of Software Metrics*. Piscataway, N.J.: IEEE Press, 1992.

[128] Paulish, Daniel J., and Karl H. Möller. *Software Metrics: A Practitioner's Guide to Improved Product Development*. First published by Chapman & Hall Limited, 1992. Exclusive North American distribution rights assigned to IEEE Press, Piscataway, N.J.

[129] Peterson, James L., and Abraham Silberschatz. *Operating Systems Concepts*. New York: Addison-Wesley, 1985.

[130] Pham, Hoang. *Software Reliability and Testing*, Piscataway, N.J.: IEEE Press, 1995.

[131] *Proceedings of the IEEE*, Special Issue on Real-Time Systems (Jan. 1994).

[132] Redmond, K. C., and T. S. Smith. *Project Whirlwind—The History of a Pioneer Computer* Bedford, Mass.: Digital Press, 1980.

[133] Rich, Charles, and Richard C. Waters. Automatic programming: Myths and Prospects. *IEEE Computer* (Aug. 1988): 40–51.

[134] Ripps, David L. *An Implementation Guide to Real-Time Programming.* Englewood Cliffs, N.J.: Yourdon Press, 1990.

[135] Ross, D. Structured analysis (SA): A language for communicating ideas. *IEEE Transactions on Software Engineering* SE-3, 1 (Jan. 1977).

[136] Rothstein, Michael F. *Guide to the Design of Real-Time Systems.* New York: Wiley Interscience, 1970.

[137] Schoch, D. J., and P. A. Laplante. A real-time systems context for the framework for information systems architecture. *IBM Systems Journal* 34, 1 (1994): 20–38.

[138] Schwartz, Mischa. *Information Transmission, Modulation and Noise.* New York: McGraw-Hill, 1980.

[139] Selby, R. W., V. R. Basili, and F. Terry Baker. Cleanroom software development: An empirical evaluation. *IEEE Transactions on Software Engineering* SE-13, 9 (1987): 1027–1037.

[140] Sha, L., and J. B. Goodenough. Real-time scheduling theory and Ada. *Technical Report CMU/SEI-88-TR-33.* Carnegie-Mellon University: Software Engineering Institute, 1988.

[141] Sha, L., and J. B. Goodenough. Real-time scheduling theory and Ada. *Technical Report CMU/SEI-89-TR-14.* Carnegie-Mellon University: Software Engineering Institute, 1989.

[142] Shaw, A. C. Communicating real-time state machines. *IEEE Transactions on Software Engineering* 18, 9 (1992): 805–816.

[143] Shaw, Alan C. *The Logical Design of Operating Systems.* Englewood Cliffs, N.J.: Prentice-Hall, 1974.

[144] Shen, Chia, Krithi Ramamritham, and John A. Stankovic. Resource reclaiming in real-time. *Proceedings of the 11th Real-Time Systems Symposium*, Lake Buena Vista, Fla. (Dec. 1990): 41–50.

[145] Shiva, Sajjan G. *Computer Design & Architecture.* 2nd ed. New York: HarperCollins, 1991.

[146] Silberschatz, Abraham, James L. Peterson, and P. Glavin. *Operating Systems Concepts.* 3rd ed. New York: Addison-Wesley, 1994.

[147] Slepian, D., H. O. Pollack, and H. T. Landow. Prolate spheroidal wave functions, Fourier analysis, and uncertainty principle I and II. *Bell System Technical Journal* 40, 1 (Jan. 1961): 43–84.

[148] Som, S., R. R. Mielke, and J. W. Stoughton. Strategies for predictability in real-time data-flow architectures. *Proceedings of the 11th Real-Time Systems Symposium*, Lake Buena Vista, Fla. (Dec. 1990): 226–235.

[149] Sommerville, Ian. *Software Engineering*. 4th ed. New York: Addison-Wesley, 1992.

[150] Sperry, Tyler. Real-time operating systems: let the buyer be aware. *Embedded Systems Programming Product News*, (Summer 1995): 12–21.

[151] Spivey, J., *The Z Notation: A Reference Manual*. Series in Computer Science. Englewood Cliffs, N.J.: Prentice-Hall, 1989.

[152] Stankovic, J., and Krithi Ramamritham. *Hard Real-Time Systems—A Tutorial*. Washington, D.C.: Computer Science Press (IEEE), 1988.

[153] Stankovic, John A., Maro Spuri, Marco Di Natale and Giorgio C. Butazzo. Implications of classical scheduling results for real-time systems. *IEEE Computer*, 2, 6 (June 1995): 16–25.

[154] Steininger, A., and H. Schweinzer. Can the advantages of RISC be utilized in real-time systems? *Proceedings of the Euromicro '91 Workshop on Real-Time Systems*. Paris (1991): 30–35.

[155] Stimler, Saul. *Real-Time Data-Processing Systems*. New York: McGraw-Hill, 1969.

[156] Stoyenko, A. D. Evolution and state-of-the-art of real-time languages, *Journal of Systems and Software* 18 (Apr. 1992): 61–84.

[157] Stoyenko, A. D., and E. Kligerman. Real-Time Euclid: A language for reliable real-time systems. *IEEE Transactions on Software Engineering* SE-12 (Sept. 1986): 940–949.

[158] Tripp, Leonard L. *IEEE Standards Collection*, Piscataway, N.J.: IEEE Press, 1994.

[159] *Turbo C User's Guide Version 2.0*. Scotts Valley, Calif.: Borland International, 1988.

[160] Walpole, Ronald E., and Raymond H. Myers. *Probability and Statistics for Engineers and Scientists*. 2nd ed. New York: Macmillan Publishing, 1978.

[161] Warnier, J. D. *Logical Construction of Programs*. New York: Van Nostrand Reinhold, 1974.

[162] Washabaugh, Douglas M., and Dennis Kafura. Incremental garbage collection of concurrent objects for real-time applications. *Proceedings of the 11th Real-Time Systems Symposium*. Lake Buena Vista, Fla. (Dec. 1990): 21–30.

[163] Wheeden, Richard L., and Antoni Zygmund. *Measure and Integral*. New York: Marcel Dekker, 1977.

[164] Wirth, Niklaus. *Programming in Modula-2*. 2nd ed. New York: Springer-Verlag, 1983.

[165] Wulf, W., and Mary Shaw. Global variables considered harmful. SIGPLAN *Notices* 8, 2 (1973): 28–34.

Index

Index

359

About the Author

Phillip A. Laplante is Dean of the Burlington County College/NJIT Technology and Engineering Center. He holds a Ph.D. in Computer Science and Electrical Engineering, and a professional engineering license in the state of New Jersey. He has over 14 years experience in designing real-time systems and was the lead software engineer in the design and implementation of a new generation of inertial measurement systems for the space shuttle. He has taught courses and consulted in real-time design throughout the United States and Canada, and has published widely on real-time systems, image processing, real-time imaging, and software engineering.

He has written seven other books, including three others with IEEE Press–*Great Papers in Computer Science, Introduction to Real-Time Imaging* (with Ed Dougherty), and *Real-Time Imaging: Theory, Techniques and Applications* (with Alex Stoyenko). He is also co-editor (with Alex Stoyenko) of the journal, *Real-Time Imaging*, and the IEEE Press Series on Complex Systems Engineering.